# PEARLS *of the* PARROT *of* INDIA:

## *The Walters Art Museum* Khamsa *of Amīr Khusraw of Delhi*

JOHN SEYLLER



*The* WALTERS ART MUSEUM

BALTIMORE, MARYLAND 2001

EDITOR
Deborah Horowitz

DESIGNER
Leigh Jordan Friedman


600 North Charles Street
Baltimore, Maryland 21201



Distributed by University of Washington Press, Seattle, Washington.

This publication was made possible through the support of the Andrew W. Mellon Foundation Fund for Scholarly Research and Publications. A subvention was also provided by the University of Vermont.

ISBN 0-911886-51-6
ISSN 0083-7156

COVER
Majnūn's father visits him in the wilderness. By Lāla. *Khamsa* of Amīr Khusraw, 1597–98, f. 100b. 23.5 x 15.2 cm. Walters Art Museum, W.624.

Printed by Eichhorn Printing, Cockeysville, Maryland

In October 2000, the Walters Art Gallery became the Walters Art Museum. Accordingly, the *Journal of the Walters Art Gallery* has changed its name to the *Journal of the Walters Art Museum.*

# Contents


ACKNOWLEDGEMENTS ..... 4

INTRODUCTION ..... 5

CHAPTER 1 The Life of Amīr Khusraw ..... 7

CHAPTER 2 The *Khamsa* and Its Literary Tradition ..... 13

CHAPTER 3 The Context of Mughal Painting ..... 25

CHAPTER 4 The Walters Art Museum *Khamsa* of Amīr Khusraw ..... 39

PLATES The Walters Art Museum *Khamsa* ..... 45

CHAPTER 5 Painting Cycles in Islamic Manuscript Illustration ..... 105

CHAPTER 6 The Illumination and Binding of the Walters *Khamsa* ..... 119

CHAPTER 7 Conclusion ..... 141

APPENDIX A Other Copies of the *Khamsa* of Amīr Khusraw ..... 143

APPENDIX B The Tradition of Illustration of the *Khamsa* of Amīr Khusraw ..... 159

BIBLIOGRAPHY ..... 169

GLOSSARY ..... 173

INDEX ..... 174

# Acknowledgements

Like many comparable studies, this book was long in the making. I received financial support for several summers and years of research from the Getty Postdoctoral Program, the University of Vermont, and the Institute for Advanced Study, Princeton. Through its support of the Asian Studies Program at the University of Vermont, the Freeman Foundation provided a publication subvention.

I am grateful to many institutions across the world for allowing me access to their collections and for granting permission to reproduce some images. I am particularly indebted to Adrian Roberts and Doris Nicholson of the Bodleian Library, Henry Ginsburg, Jeremiah P. Losty, and Muhammad Isa Waley of the British Library, and Daniel Walker of The Metropolitan Museum of Art. At the Walters Art Museum, I have benefitted from the generous assistance of past and present staff, including Elizabeth Burin, Donna Strahan, and Roger Wieck. I would like to express my appreciation to Gary Vikan and Marianna Shreve Simpson for agreeing to sponsor this publication. Above all, Hiram Woodward helped make this book a reality, and he and Deborah Horowitz have enhanced it with their judicious editing.

I also wish to thank Oleg Grabar and Karin Rührdanz for many stimulating discussions of manuscript issues at a critical juncture in this project, and my wife, Anna, for her advice and encouragement.

# Introduction

More than any other kingdom in the long and glorious history of South Asia, the Mughal empire still captures the popular imagination of the inhabitants of the Indian subcontinent. It is not difficult to understand why this is so. Other Indian dynasties match the Mughals in the longevity of their reigns, but the Mughals' rule of some two hundred and fifty years (ca. 1526–1857) looms large in the national consciousness because it extended well into the nineteenth century and because it finally gave way to the colonial rule of the British empire, a period which for many represents a lamentable national humiliation. Similarly, the Mughal empire is often heralded as the heyday of Indian unity, when vast areas of the modern-day states of India, Pakistan, and Bangladesh were joined under a single standard. There is also the Mughals' remarkable physical imprint on the land: to this day their soaring tomb complexes and majestic fortresses crown the major cities of northern India and Pakistan, and less ostentatious tombs and smaller structures dot the primary roads traversing the country. No less formidable a legacy is provided by their literature, particularly the histories that record in meticulous detail the seemingly superhuman exploits of the emperors and their legions, as well as the tremendous pomp and ceremony of the court. And, finally, there are the paintings and objects, now mostly consigned to museums the world over, which evoke the sheer splendor of the Mughal court in their stirring imagery and preciousness.

It was admittedly this last aspect of Mughal culture that first attracted me to Indian art and continues to sustain me in my travels and studies. I am hardly alone in this respect, for over the past half century Mughal art has gradually begun to assert a greater presence in the lexicon of world art. There is little doubt that this higher visibility has been the result of a series of exhibitions, primarily in the United States and Britain, beginning with *The Art of Mughal India* (Asia Society, 1963), *Paintings from the Muslim Courts of India* (The British Museum, 1976), *The Grand Mogul: Imperial Painting in India 1600–1660* (Sterling and Francine Clark Art Institute, 1978), and *The Imperial Image: Paintings for the Mughal Court* (Freer Gallery of Art, 1981). The Festival of India in Britain in 1982 and the United States in 1985–86 brought a windfall of major exhibitions, notably *The Art of the Book in India* (British Library, 1982), *The Indian Heritage: Court Life and Arts Under Mughal Rule* (Victoria and Albert Museum, 1982), *Akbar's India: Art from the Mughal City of Victory* (Asia Society, 1985), and *India: Art and Culture 1300–1900* (Metropolitan Museum of Art, 1985). These were followed by exhibitions in Paris, *A la Cour du grand Moghol* (Bibliothèque Nationale and Musée Guimet, 1986) and *Miniatures de l'Inde impériale* (Musée Guimet, 1989). All these exhibitions and their accompanying catalogues contributed enormously both to the popularization of Mughal art and to the advancement of its study.

At the same time, these exhibitions had another, perhaps less intended effect on the presentation of Mughal culture, as they defined a Mughal *Zeitgeist* largely in terms of reigns. The names of Akbar, Jahāngīr, and Shāh Jahān—while never becoming household names—became familiar and convenient human labels for a complex culture whose principles and practices were quite alien to Western audiences. Although this trend helped make foreign fare more palatable to these audiences, it also encouraged scholars themselves to look for and locate the emperor's presence in a host of individual objects. Manuscript and jade cup alike were seen to reflect not just an epoch or ideology, but a unique, often personal vision of the world emanating from one emperor or another. Individual artists garnered the highest praise when they were thought to have grasped and expressed that vision in their work; other competing visions and aspects of Mughal culture were ignored or obscured.

Many fewer studies of Mughal painting began with a different, less Olympian vantage point, seeking not to define an age, but to unravel all the mysteries of an individual creation. Indeed, when I began this study about fifteen years ago, only two Mughal manuscripts had been the subjects of monographs.[1] As can be seen in the bibliography, the situation was only slightly better in Persian painting. Since that time, however, other scholars have also recognized the need for detailed studies of the most important individual manuscripts of various schools of Islamic and Indian art. By virtue of these more comprehensive studies, we are slowly piecing together a more nuanced picture of how paintings and illustrated manuscripts were actually made and used at various individual courts and commercial centers. We are also now in a position to do more careful comparative work, considering the approach to a particular text in a given manuscript within the broader sweep of Islamic and Indian painting. Thus, in the last twenty years alone there have been pioneering studies of the tradition of illustration of some of the major Islamic texts: the *Shāhnāma* of Firdawsī, the *Khamsa* of Niẓāmī, the *Kalīla wa Dimna*, the *Haft Awrang* of Jāmī, and now the *Khamsa* of Amīr Khusraw. These laborious investigations are still in their infancy, and their results have yet to be subjected to critical scrutiny. The problem of putative traditions of illustration is examined at length in Chapter 5.

The focus of this study, a sumptuous copy of the *Khamsa* of Amīr Khusraw in the Walters Art Museum, acquired by Henry Walters, was known primarily from short entries in two of the aforementioned exhibitions, and still briefer references in general books on Islamic or Indian painting.[2] After I had been working in earnest on this project for about three years, I learned that another scholar, Barbara Brend, had undertaken a parallel study for her dissertation.[3] I was satisfied that her background and interests were somewhat different from mine, fuller in some respects and less complete in others, and I continued with my work. Shortly thereafter, Brend published the first article on the paintings of the Walters *Khamsa*, which is a somewhat abbreviated formulation of her discussion of the manuscript in her dissertation.[4] Here, again, readers will see that we have arrived at very different conclusions about a number of matters, ranging from minor problems of attribution to more fundamental ones involving the mechanisms and meaning of manuscript illustration.

NOTES

1. P. Chandra, *The* Ṭūṭī-Nāma *of The Cleveland Museum of Art and the Origins of Mughal Painting* (Graz, 1976); and A. Schimmel and S. C. Welch, *A Pocket Book for Akbar: Anwari's Diwan* (New York, 1983).

2. J. Losty, *The Art of the Book in India* (London, 1982), no. 66; and S. C. Welch, *India: Art and Culture 1300–1900* (New York, 1985), no. 111. References to individual paintings are found in the entries for each in Chapter 4.

3. B. Brend, *Illustrations to the* Khamsah *of Amīr Khusrau Dihlavī in the Tīmūrid Period* (Ph.D. thesis, School of Oriental and African Studies, University of London, 1986).

4. B. Brend, "Akbar's *Khamsah* of Amīr Khusraw Dihlavī—A Reconstruction of the Cycle of Illustration," *Artibus Asiae*, 49, nos. 3/4 (1988/89), 281–315.

CHAPTER 1

# The Life of Amīr Khusraw

Toward the end of his brilliant career, Amīr Khusraw Dihlawī, the most famous Persian-language poet of the Indian subcontinent and the self-styled Parrot of India,[1] mused about his prodigious oeuvre:

> At age thirty-two, when I composed one quatrain, I had to think and ponder before I could produce another. But now when I am sixty-four and the pearls of my teeth are about to fall, my mind tells me that this is the proper time to let pearls of poesy drop from my mouth. The harder I try to seal my mouth, the more profusely these pearls come out.... Often I plunge into seas unfathomed even by the perfect masters, and without any great trouble bring out so many bright pearls that I can hardly gather them. But as the days for decorating and ornamenting verses are now past, I pick up only one or two that are worth picking up and string them together while the rest lie on the surface of my mind, soiled and neglected, for if I were to collect all the fine pearls, there would not have been four *diwans* but four oceans....[2]

Together with contemporary historical sources, such autobiographical remarks provide an unusually detailed account of the poet's life. His father, a Turkish warrior by the name of Amīr Sayf al-Dīn Maḥmūd, was born in the Central Asian city of Kish and escaped the fury of the Mongol invasions by migrating southward to settle in Mominpura, some 180 miles north of Delhi.[3] There he entered the service of the Delhi sultan Shams al-Dīn Iltutmish (reigned 1211–36), thereby acquiring the title Sayf-i Shamsī. His marriage to the daughter of an Indian nobleman produced three sons: ʿIẓẓ al-Dīn ʿAlī Shāh, Ḥusam al-Dīn Qutlugh, and Khusraw, whose full name is sometimes given as Abū al-Ḥasan Yamīn al-Dīn .[4] Born in A.H. 651/A.D. 1253, Khusraw's position as the second of the family's three sons freed him from the obligation of following his father's martial occupation.[5] Although Sayf al-Dīn himself was illiterate, he recognized the value of an education, and his position at court afforded him the means of training his sons.

Khusraw took quick advantage of the educational opportunities at the Delhi court, showing a special proclivity for poetry almost from the moment of his birth. Khusraw promoted his reputation as a prodigy and included accounts of the early blooming of his talent in several of his *dīwāns*. In his earliest collection of poems, *Tuḥfat al-Ṣighar* (The Gift of Youth), written between the ages of sixteen and nineteen, he remarks that he was unable to resist the poetical metaphors of beauty even as a boy:

> My father used to send me to the "maktab" for study, but I repeated only rhymes, and my learned teacher S'aduddin Mohd., the calligraphist, popularly known as the Qadi (God's mercy be upon him), tried to teach me calligraphy, while I composed verses about the silken down on fair faces. In spite of the persistent efforts of my teacher, continuous and long like the tresses descending from head to foot on the back of a beauty, I would not renounce my infatuation for the locks and the mole. As a consequence, at that tender age I began to compose verses and ghazals that roused the admiration and wonder of my elders.[6]

The reputation of the precocious Khusraw soon drew the attention of scholars and teachers, who tested him in recitation and composition. In one case, he was called upon to demonstrate his skill by incorporating four disparate elements into a single quatrain, a feat that he performed with impressive ingenuity.[7] The arbiter of the contest was so taken by this sign of Khusraw's immense talent that he proposed that the young poet be known by the sobriquet Sulṭānī (king), a name that alluded at once to another title of Khusraw's father (*Sulṭān-i Shamsī*) and to the regal position the youth would hold among poets.[8] Indeed, the poet followed this suggestion and used Sulṭānī as his *takhalluṣ*, or nom de plume, in many of his early works before he adopted the name Khusraw.[9]

At the age of eight, Khusraw suffered the loss of his father and was placed in the charge of his maternal grandfather, ʿImād al-Mulk, who held an influential post under Sulṭān Ghiyāṣ al-Dīn Balban.[10] Much as his master Iltutmish had before him, Balban rose from slavehood to become a powerful commander whose successful campaigns against the Mongols led to his accession to the throne in 1265, thereby ending a series of short-lived reigns. The young Khusraw was not yet embroiled in the tumultuous political affairs of the Delhi sultanate. Instead, nurtured by constant exposure to the pleasures of courtly life and the conceits of the powerful members of his grandfather's social circle, Khusraw continued to devote himself to absorbing the complicated metaphors and literary associations that form the heart of Persian poetry. He claims proudly that he realized his poetic talent not through formalized study with an individual master, but through serious application of his innate ability.

> I was only twelve years old when the foundations of the various forms of verse were laid strongly in my mind. When the scholars and savants of the time saw my proficiency in poetry they were amazed and their amazement added to my pride, for on listening to my verses they used to encourage me heartily. But I hardly required any such encouragement, for I was already so enamoured of this fascinating art that from morning till evening my head was bent like that of the pen consuming the lampsoot, and I strained my eyes over "the black and white" day and night in order to achieve a high name for sagacity and enlightened wit. From time to time the contemporary artists used to test my skill and I displayed to them my art with the burning eloquence of my tongue. As no famous master had ever trained me, who could point out the subtleties of verse and could check my wandering pen from the paths of error or help to bring to light the excellence that lay hidden in my faults, for some time I placed before me, like parrots learning to speak, the mirror of imagination, and learnt poetry from the images that were reflected in that mirror.[11]

His grandfather's death in 1272–73 removed the last vestiges of Khusraw's youthful independence. At age twenty, Khusraw began his professional career as a poet and courtier by entering the service of ʿAlāʾ al-Dīn Kishli Khān, nephew of Sulṭān Balban. Kishli Khān, who held the post of Chief Chamberlain to his uncle and ruled the province of Multan in western India, was renowned for his munificent patronage of music and poetry. For two years, Kishli Khān showered rewards on Khusraw for his witty verses and high-flown encomiums and made him a confidant, a quite customary role for favored poets. But Khusraw soon discovered the fickleness of the good fortune brought by intimate access to such powerful men. When Khusraw's recital at a gathering of lords prompted a lavish gift from Prince Naṣīr al-Dīn Bughrā Khān, the younger son of Balban, as a token of admiration, the ire of the poet's own jealous patron forced him to flee to Samana in the Punjab.

There, about 1274, Khusraw found his second major patron, Bughrā Khān. Having established an intimate rapport with his new benefactor, Khusraw was compelled to accompany the prince when he was called to join a royal campaign to quell a rebellion in Laknawtī, an area in the province of Bengal far to the east. The long and arduous expedition culminated in complete victory for the royal forces, and Bughrā Khān was installed as the new governor of the territory. However, Khusraw longed to quit the inhospitable region for his beloved Delhi. Thus he parted company with Bughrā Khān and joined the triumphant return to the capital.

In Delhi, Khusraw was introduced to Bughrā Khān's brother, Prince Muḥammad Khān, a highly refined individual whose appreciation of culture easily surpassed that of both his younger brother and their father, Balban. The fortuitous union of patron and poet fostered in the prince's court in Multan a brilliant literary circle that revolved around Khusraw and his fellow poet, Amīr Najm al-Dīn Ḥasan (1257–1336). So avid was Muḥammad Khān's interest in literature that he twice invited the foremost poet of the age, Shaykh Saʿdī (ca. 1210–92), to come to Multan from distant Shiraz. Although the aged Saʿdī declined the offer, he graciously replied with a book of verses and a message of esteem for Khusraw, demonstrating that Khusraw's fame had spread even to Persia.[12] This happy and productive five-year period of Khusraw's life ended with Muḥammad Khān's fatal encounter with Mongol troops led by Tīmūr in March 1285 near the river Ravi. A distraught Khusraw fell into the hands of the vile Mongols, but quickly escaped to Multan and then made his way back home to Delhi.

Stricken with grief at the death of his heir apparent, Balban resolved the subsequent dynastic turmoil by choosing as his successor not the estranged Bughrā Khān, but his grandson, Muʿizz al-Dīn Kaiqubād (reigned 1287–90), who took advantage of his new power to indulge his every whim. In the meantime, Khusraw joined the entourage of Ḥātim Khān (Amīr ʿAlī Sarjāndār), as much to escape the web of intrigue spun at court by Kaiqubād's minister Niẕām al-Dīn as to partake of Ḥātim Khān's fabled generosity. Despite this prudent tack, Khusraw was soon drawn into the affairs of court when Ḥātim Khān was ordered to accompany the new king in his journey eastward to meet the challenge mounted by his father. The imminent clash was forestalled by cooler heads, and Khusraw witnessed the reconciliation of father and son on the banks of the Saru.

Khusraw proceeded back toward Oudh with Ḥātim Khān, who had been appointed governor of that province. Although he enjoyed his lord's bounty in Oudh and much preferred the province's salubrious climate to that of marshy Lakhnawtī, Khusraw pined for his friends and family in Delhi; indeed, his profound personal attachment to that city emerges as a leitmotif in his work. Granted his wish by Ḥātim Khān, Khusraw finally returned to Delhi, whereupon Kaiqubād summoned him immediately to commission a poem in commemoration of the ruler's reconciliation with his father. Together with the king's lavish enticements, the opportunity for fame that such a historical subject would bring inspired Khusraw to make his first attempt at the epic genre of the *maṣnawī*. Employing the meter of *Makhzan al-Asrār* (Treasury of Secrets) of Niẓāmī, the most famous master of the maṣnawī, he produced *Qirān al-Sa'dayn* (The Conjunction of the Two Auspicious Stars) in just six months, completing it in Ramaẓān 688/September–October 1289.[13] Amid the hyperbole of Khusraw's lengthy description of the inhabitants, climate, and renown of Delhi, which he called the Arch of Islam and the Garden of Eden, are some informative observations about several of the capital's monuments.[14]

The sultan's declining health precipitated a coup that saw an Afghan tribe form the new Khaljī dynasty, headed by Jalāl al-Dīn (reigned 1290–95), who assumed the name Fīrūz Shāh. This development affected Khusraw only slightly, for as the poet's modern biographer Muhammad Wahid Mirza writes,

> He was henceforth a part of the royal paraphernalia that changed hands at the death of each successive monarch and like the black canopy, the crown and the throne, the palaces, the slaves and elephants became the property of the new master.[15]

Indeed, his status as poet laureate was by now so secure that each new claimant to the throne bestowed ever greater honors upon him. Fīrūz Shāh, an elderly man who appreciated poetry and even composed verses himself, honored him with the title of *mushafdar* and an annual stipend of 1,200 *tankas*, an amount equal to the salary of the poet's high-ranking father.[16] Khusraw therefore sang the praises of his new master, chronicling a string of military victories in his second *maṣnawī*, *Miftāḥ al-Futūḥ* (The Key to Success), which he completed on 2 Jumādā II 690/2 June 1291.[17]

The benevolent Fīrūz Shāh suffered the all but inevitable fate of his office, being murdered treacherously at the order of his nephew and son-in-law 'Alā' al-Dīn Khaljī (reigned October 1296–January 1316), who used the vast booty he had acquired in a campaign in the Deccan to secure his accession to the throne. 'Alā' al-Dīn, who assumed the epithet "the second Alexander," proved to be a shrewd warrior and administrator. He repulsed five Mongol invasions, plundered fabulously rich Hindu strongholds, renewed civic structures, and waged a successful domestic campaign to limit the corrupting effects of greed and wine. His prosperous twenty-year reign also saw the zenith of Khusraw's fame, a reputation enhanced greatly by the production of the *Khamsa* (Quintet), a collection of five *maṣnawīs* modeled directly upon the romances of Niẓāmī's *Khamsa*.

Although the new sultan himself was practically illiterate, he adorned his court with an unprecedented number of literary luminaries. The foremost of these was Khusraw, of course, who revelled in the glory of such an accolade. Ever hopeful of still greater favor, Khusraw dedicated many of his works to 'Alā' al-Dīn. Nonetheless, the poet was not altogether satisfied with his relationship with the king, which was quite unlike the intimate companionship he had enjoyed with many of his previous patrons. Objecting to 'Alā' al-Dīn's demand that he should be subject to compulsory attendance in court, Khusraw complains,

> If day and night I attend not the court of your Majesty to perform my humble services, it matters little, for when a hundred crowned heads bow before you daily you can easily forgive the absence of a beggar.... If I stand before you day and night how can my mind produce poetry? Without thought surely my poetry will be but frivolous and shallow.[18]

He reinforced this appeal to the king to understand the unique circumstances necessary for the creation of poetry by asserting its efficacy:

> When the poet wets the point of his pen he performs the service of two hundred years in a moment. Do not think lightly of the poets' work, for each of their sweet words spells a life. Of what value is the pure gold to you when after your death it would no longer be of any service? You should buy an eternal life with gold so that your renown may always live....[19]

Not surprisingly, Khusraw's suggestion that the king dispense his wealth to poets to ensure his place in history was accompanied by constant requests for more money. Although the generous salary and title the poet had received from Fīrūz Shāh were maintained by 'Alā' al-Dīn, and even supplemented occasionally by gifts as expansive as a village, Khusraw was frustrated by the king's newly parsimonious behavior, which he considered wholly inappropriate to his status.

> O King! I know that there never was a wiser king, for you are a thorough connoisseur of skill, a good critic of verses and a friend of poetry. But alas! I have fallen on such unlucky times that I can hardly get a decent living. If I do not prosper in your time, how can I ever do so after you? How sad that there be a king like you and a poet like me stricken with want! The allowance which I get from your Majesty is my right and the reward of my service, for I remain always beside the royal stirrup.... But as I want to praise you, how can I write verses without some reward? You cannot possibly be unaware of the generosity shown to poets by other kings, who often gave away treasures for an ode. Khaqani, in reward for one ode, got a thousand dinars for each verse and the poet Mu'izzi sat on a gold chair in Merv. When Firdausi wrote his Shahnamah, the king gave him an elephant-load of gold, and yet his miserliness has become a tale. 'Unsuri also got endless favours from Sultan Mahmud so that all his furniture was of gold. That patronage which the kings showed to the poets has left behind everlasting panegyrics and an eternal fame to their generosity. We know when they lived and what patronage they received from the kings: but to-morrow when we are dead and gone, what would people tell about us? O King of the World, for this reason, charity to poets is imperative![20]

At the request of Prince Khiẓr Khān, Khusraw told of the prince's great love for the Hindu princess Devaldi in his third historical *maṣnawī, 'Ashīqa,* (Love Story), also known as *Duwal Rānī Khiẓr Khān* (Devaldi (or Duwal) the queen and Khiẓr Khān), which he completed in Ẕī'l-Qa'da 715/January–February 1316. The poem departs from convention not only in casting the affairs of contemporary figures in the genre of a romance, but also by setting the tale of the troubled lovers in an acutely observed Indian environment. Khusraw describes India's wondrous flowers and magical animals, and finds somewhat chauvinistically that Indian women surpass all others of the world in beauty and elegance. The passionate, albeit tragic union of the Persian and Indian worlds is paralleled by Khusraw's enrichment of the vocabulary and metaphors of a well-established poetical form with local Indian words and customs.[21] But Khusraw also described India as a land in which Islam reigned supreme, as a forest stripped of the thorns of idolatry, and as a place where the cawing crows of Hinduism were subdued and even the fish were Sunnis.[22]

Khusraw's most explicit expression of pride in his native land appears in his fourth historical *maṣnawī, Nuh Sipihr* (The Nine Heavens). Completed in 30 Jumādā II, 718/24 August 1318, the poem glorifies the heavenly spheres and the new king, the fourth son of 'Alā' al-Dīn, Mubārak Khān, who assumed the name Quṭb al-Dīn (reigned 1316–20). The famous third *sipihr* or heaven celebrates the many virtues of India, which is likened to Paradise itself.[23] Khusraw extols her warm, lush climate, claiming that the mild discomfort of the summer heat is much preferable to the real hardships brought by bitter winters elsewhere. He praises her learnedness in science and philosophy, and the wisdom of her peoples, who created chess, music, and stories that foreigners have admired and adopted. Even as he credits her people with the knowledge of all languages of the world, he enumerates her many regional languages and pays homage to ancient Sanskrit, which he considers second only to Arabic in grammar, purity, and profundity of meaning. The poet proudly contrasts the purity of Persian spoken in India with the substandard pronunciations found in many regions of Iran itself. Finally, Khusraw boasts that the excellence of Indian poetry is conclusive evidence of her superiority, immodestly citing his own presence in the country as proof!

The venerable Khusraw enjoyed the favor of one final patron, Ghiyāṣ al-Dīn Tughluq Shāh (reigned 1320–25). Continuing the pattern set by his predecessors on the throne, Ghiyāṣ al-Dīn commissioned Khusraw to write a *maṣnawī, Tughluqnāma,* a paean commemorating his defeat of the usurper Khusraw Khān and the founding of the Turkish Tughluq dynasty.

In contrast to this long series of secular masters, Khusraw served a single spiritual one, Niẓām al-Dīn Awliyā. Like Khusraw, Niẓām al-Dīn was of Turkish ancestry but of Indian birth. He became a disciple of the Sufi master Farīd al-Dīn Ganjshakar, leader of a mystical order founded in the late twelfth century by Khwāja Ḥasan Mu'īn al-Dīn Chishtī, who emphasized asceticism and service of the poor as a path to enlightenment. In turn, Niẓām al-Dīn established a monastery near Delhi, where he encountered Khusraw while the poet was still quite young. The personal aura of the saint and the meritorious effect that he had on his numerous adherents must have impressed Khusraw, who adopted the teacher as his spiritual guide in 1272–73, credited him as a source of poetic inspiration, and praised him in every subsequent work. This affection was reciprocated by Niẓām al-Dīn, who claimed he never tired of the one he called "God's Turk."[24] On 27 Jumādā II, 715/28 September 1315, he gave the spiritual novice a special robe and the four-cornered cap as a sign of formal admission to the Chishtī order.[25]

The apparent contradiction of Khusraw's familiarity with the indulgent pleasures of his courtly milieu and the austere existence of his Sufi mentor was dissolved for both master and disciple by political reality as well as by rapturous experience of verse and music. Although the Muslim rulers of India increasingly sought to claim the mantle of religious leadership for themselves, they also realized the political efficacy of forging alliances with spiritual leaders whose blessings and charitable works contributed to the religious and social legitimacy of the regime. Hence, courtiers such as Khusraw, who could function as liaisons between the two realms, were especially valuable to their masters.

Khusraw's two worlds were never closer than they were under 'Alā' al-Dīn, who personally revered Niẓām al-Dīn and encouraged the members of his court to do likewise. This bond was ruptured by the much less devout and secure Mubārak Shāh, who resented Niẓām al-Dīn's influence even to the point of threatening his life. A peaceful, though hardly amiable relationship was restored under Tughluq Shāh, who pressed the saint to return the vast sums of money given to him and others by the usurper Khusraw Khān in a last-ditch attempt to retain their favor. Moreover, the king sternly challenged the religious propriety of festivities during which the saint's followers engaged in ecstatic singing.

Niẓām al-Dīn's death on 18 Rabī' II, 725/16 April 1325 sapped the life from the grieving Khusraw. Just as the saint had presaged, Khusraw quickly followed his master to the grave, departing from this world on 29 Ẕī'l-Qa'da 725/26 November 1325.[26] He lies buried near Niẓām al-Dīn's tomb in Delhi, where preceptor and poet alike have been venerated by generations of admirers ever since.

## NOTES

1. The poet refers to himself several times as the *Ṭūṭī-i Hind* (Parrot of India) in *Ghurrat al-Kamāl* and *Nuh Sipihr*.

2. *Baqīya Naqīya* (The Pure Remnant), cited in M. Mirza, *Life and Works of Amir Khusrau* (Lahore, 1962), 167. In his *Tażkirat al-Shu'arā*, the fifteenth-century author Dawlat Shāh Samarqandī estimates that Amīr Khusraw's oeuvre exceeded 400,000 *abyāt* (distiches, sing. *bayt*). Prince Baysunghur called off his attempt to collect all of Khusraw's writings when the total passed 120,000 *abyāt* and he heard accounts of still more.

3. Kish, now known as Shahr-i Sabz, is located on the border between Tajikistan and Uzbekistan; Mominpura, also called Mominabad, is the modern Patiyali (district Etah) in Uttar Pradesh.

4. Mirza, *Life and Works*, 17, note 1, dismisses this name as speculation.

5. Mirza, *Life and Works*, 17, gives references in Khusraw's writings to his birth. In the commentary to the critical edition of *Maṭla' al-Anwār*, Ghanzafar Yu. Aliev suggests that Khusraw was the family's third son.

6. Preface of *Tuḥfat al-Ṣighar*, cited in Mirza, *Life and Works*, 20. Persian culture considered long locks of hair and small facial moles to be marks of beauty.

7. Preface of *Tuḥfat al-Ṣighar*, cited in Mirza, *Life and Works*, 21.

8. Mirza, *Life and Works*, 21–22. Similarly, his *takhalluṣ* (chosen name) Khusraw means "prince."

9. These names are mentioned in the *ghazals* of *Tuḥfat al-Ṣighar*. See Mirza, *Life and Works*, 22, note 1.

10. See Mirza, *Life and Works*, 29–30, especially note 2, for a discussion of the duties of this position.

11. *Ghurrat al-Kamāl*, cited in Mirza, *Life and Works*, 32.

12. Mirza, *Life and Works*, 53. This event gave rise to the legend that Sa'dī came to Delhi explicitly to visit Khusraw. Sa'dī's estimation of Khusraw is the exception to his otherwise unfavorable opinion of the quality of poetry in India, widely regarded as the backwoods:

To enter the services of the Indian princes thou must have a good dress; a turban of gold cloth and a garment of silk. Thou shouldst have the paunch of an ox and a flowing beard; there is no need, however, for intellect, wisdom, sense, or sagacity!

This passage is cited in R. P. Masani, *Court Poets of Iran* (Bombay, 1938), 82.

13. See Mirza, *Life and Works*, 76, citing *Qirān al-Sa'dayn*, 174, for the duration of the project. The poem itself contains 3,944 verses written in the meter hexametric *sarī'*. See Mirza, *Life and Works*, 174–76, and Sir H. M. Elliott and J. Dowson, *The History of India as Told by Its Own Historians* (London, 1871; reprint New York, 1966), III, 544–57 for a translation of selected passages.

14. S. A. Rahman, "Patriotism in Amīr Khusrau's Works" *Indo-Iranica*, 15 (1962), 5–6, cites Khusraw's observations that the Qutb Minar was topped by a golden canopy and the Jami' Masjid by nine domes as examples of architectural information provided by the poet.

15. Mirza, *Life and Works*, 78.

16. Mirza, *Life and Works*, 179.

17. See Mirza, *Life and Works*, 176–77, for a brief description of the short poem, which is written in hexametric *hajaz*.

18. Mirza, *Life and Works*, 110–11.

19. Mirza, *Life and Works*, 112.

20. Mirza, *Life and Works*, 109.

21. Prince Khiẓr actually included even more Hindi words in his sketch for the story, but some were dropped by Khusraw. In the preface of *Ghurrat al-Kamāl*, he remarks that, "It is not very pleasant to introduce Hindui words into pure Persian, except when unavoidable. I have used them only where absolutely necessary." Cited in Mirza, *Life and Works*, 227. See also Elliott and Dowson, *The History of India*, 556.

22. Elliott and Dowson, *The History of India*, 546.

23. Elliott and Dowson, *The History of India*, 557–66, provide an abstract of this text.

24. Mirza, *Life and Works*, 118, citing the *Haft Iqlīm* of Amīn Raẓī on the authority of *Afẓal al-Fawā'id* (The Best of Observations).

25. Mirza, *Life and Works*, 119.

26. Mirza, *Life and Works*, 137, note 1, points out that the commemorative ceremony held annually on 18 Shawwāl may be taken as a record of Khusraw's death on that date in 725/27 September 1325.

CHAPTER 2

# The *Khamsa* and Its Literary Tradition

Khusraw's constant association with the courts of various princes and sultans was in keeping with the tradition of Persian poetry, which from the tenth century onward germinated and flourished almost exclusively on courtly soil. Despite his assertion that he had not been taught by a master, Khusraw was well acquainted with the works of many famous poets. In a passage of the preface to *Ghurrat al-Kamāl* (Prime of Perfection), he remarks,

> I examined most of the (forms of poetry) that could be produced through imagination, and studied constantly the works of great masters. From these I culled what was sweet and thus acquired a real taste for the pleasures of poetry. My eyes and intellect brightened when I saw the writings of Anwari and Sana'i, and wherever I beheld a poem bright as gold-water I chased it like a running stream. Every diwan I came across, I not only studied but imitated in my compositions.[1]

Such imitation was the usual course of study for budding poets, who, in so doing, learned to manipulate the conventional imagery and rhyme schemes of each genre of poetry. Students determined to acquire proficiency in a given genre thus set themselves the task of emulating the manner of poets considered to be unsurpassed in that genre.

The poet Khāqānī (ca. 1126–99), an acknowledged master of the *qaṣīda*, was the object of many of Khusraw's schoolboy attempts in this vein of panegyrical verse.[2] In the preface to his earliest collection of *qaṣīdas, Tuḥfat al-Ṣighar* (The Gift of Youth), the young poet concedes that he found Khāqānī's esoteric word selection and convoluted style difficult to absorb, a shortcoming that he attributes to his youthful inexperience.[3] It is no surprise, therefore, that Khusraw continued to strive to achieve Khāqānī's elusive style in his second *dīwān, Wasṭ al-Ḥayāt* (The Middle of Life), a collection of fifty-eight *qaṣīdas* compiled at age thirty-two.[4] Khusraw showed similar admiration for the esoteric meanings and complicated verses of Awhada al-Dīn Anwarī (died 1185), another poet who excelled in *qaṣīdas*. Khusraw's early tribute to Anwarī took the form of imitation in *Tuḥfat al-Ṣighar*,[5] while his mature estimation of that master placed him among the few poets with an original style.[6]

All of these homages to the general qualities of a master's work fall well within the traditional boundaries of imitation. With the prestigious *maṡnawī*,[7] however, Khusraw raised the level of imaginary competition to one of personal rivalry, making repeated reference in his works to the unquestioned master of the *maṡnawī*, Niẕāmī Ganjavī (1141–1217).[8] His choice of a model to emulate could not have been better, for Niẕāmī's *Khamsa* (Quintet), five separate poems collected and given this Arabic title sometime in the century after their creation, is widely regarded as the apogee of Persian literature.[9]

Niẕāmī's first poem, *Makhzan al-Asrār* (Treasury of Secrets), follows in the tradition of philosophical discourses established by Sanā'ī of Ghazni (1045–1131) in his *Ḥadīqat al-Ḥaqīqat* (Garden of Truth). *Makhzan al-Asrār* is didactic in nature, with two-thirds of the text assuming the form of twenty discourses, each culminating in a short illustrative anecdote. The date of this text is controversial, but recent research points to 1184–85 as the most likely time of completion.[10] *Khusraw wa Shīrīn* (Khusraw and Shīrīn), the second poem of the *Khamsa*, was finished soon after. It takes as its subject a Sasanian king, Khusraw Parwīz II (590–628), and his troubled love for Shīrīn. The third *maṡnawī*, *Laylā wa Majnūn* (Laylā and Majnūn), turns from royal affairs to a more popular one—the maddeningly intense and forbidden love of a young Arab for a girl of a different tribe. Niẕāmī claims that he wrote this poem, which numbers 4,659 verses, in less than four months, evidently completing the work in September 1188.[11] Given free rein by his patron for the subject of his fourth *maṡnawī*, *Haft Paykar* (Seven Portraits), Niẕāmī uses another Sasanian king, Bahrām, as a means of uniting seven individual stories told to Bahrām by princesses representing the seven regions of the ancient world. Each of these stories is entertaining in its own right, but collectively they assume greater importance, representing different facets of human experience in kaleidoscopic fashion. The poem was finished in July 1197, a few years before Niẓāmī's fifth *maṣnawī, Iskandarnāma* (Story of Alexander). This final poem is devoted to Alexander the Great, revered throughout the Islamic world under the name Iskandar or Sikandar; it is exceptional in its division into two parts, *Sharafnāma* (Book of Honor) and *Iqbālnāma* (Book of Wisdom), which respectively present Alexander as conqueror and sage. At 10,500 verses, it is by far the longest of the five components of the *Khamsa*, which numbers about 30,000 verses in all, written over approximately fifteen years.

Khusraw began his response to Niẓāmī's monumental work with a modest challenge, adopting the meter of *Makhzan al-Asrār* for his first effort at the *maṣnawī, Qirān al-Sa'dayn.*[12] In it, he lauded the eminent Persian poet: "The verse of Nizami is like a pearl in its purity and the whole world is full of pearls scattered by him."[13] Nine years later, in 698/1298–99, Khusraw set out to create a full-scale response to the whole of Niẓāmī's *Khamsa.* Although Khusraw included a dedication to the reigning sultan, 'Alā' al-Dīn, in each of the five works of his own *Khamsa*, it is clear that poetic—not royal—conceit fanned Khusraw's ardor for this grandiose design, which he hoped would assure him a place among the greatest Persian poets of all time.[14]

Khusraw self-consciously remarked upon the difficulty of the task of imitation at some point in each of the five poems, alternately lamenting the futility of his effort before the pinnacles of Niẓāmī's work and proudly proclaiming the success of his own ascent. These statements allow us to trace the downward spiral of Khusraw's aspirations as he gradually realized the shortcomings of his two-year project.

In the heady days of *Maṭla' al-Anwār* (The Rising of the Luminaries), written in no more than a fortnight, Khusraw spoke impudently of outstripping his rival:

> When my ambition first moved its charger towards the sky, fortune granted me all her treasures. Every work I attempted turned out better than I had hoped.... The fame of my eminence rose and reverberated in Nizami's grave.
>
> Maybe the seal of perfection has been impressed upon Nizami's work, but the coins I am manufacturing will break that seal; the poet of Ganja has won immortal fame through his five treasures (masnavis), but I will make five keys to open his five treasures and compete with him for the domain, over which he has held sway so long.... Yes, such shall be the excellence of my masnavis that even the most discerning critic will not be able to distinguish his work from mine.[15]

In the same poem, he stated the more modest goal of being regarded as a meritorious follower of his Persian predecessor:

> With this alphabet, which may amuse children, I have written an imitation of the great master's work. If it is not sweet, there is music in it, if there is no life in it, there is a skeleton.... From his birth-place Ganja he scattered out the five treasures, and with those five I want to match my own strength...so that the wise ones may say of me: "Bravo! thou worthy pupil of Nizami."[16]

The task of surpassing Niẓāmī grew more daunting in *Shīrīn wa Khusraw.* Khusraw complained that Niẓāmī had exhausted all the interesting material:

> Nizami left nothing unsaid; his hands spared no pearl unstrung. O Khusrau, make yourself known for reticence like the eagle; do not prattle much like a domestic sparrow.[17]

In *Majnūn wa Laylā*, Khusraw vacillated in his assessment of his work. On the one hand, he openly conceded that his own work was inferior to Niẓāmī's, but refused to suffer the criticism of others: "My Majnun Laila may not be equal to Nizami's work, but it is not for every silly ass to estimate my worth."[18] He then rationalized that Niẓāmī was able to achieve his superiority by virtue of his single-mindedness:

> Nizami confined himself to a single branch of poetry; instead of frittering away his energy in all directions, he strove in the masnavi alone. He was a man of one art; so in that art he excelled the whole world. Surely, a man of discrimination will apply himself only to the work for which he has an aptitude! And to his one task the poet of Ganja dedicated his whole life. He said 'good-bye' to the world and its attractions, and retreated to a quiet corner. His masnavi was the only demand on his time, a mind unruffled by distracting cares, his livelihood provided by the generosity of princes and great men—how could a combination of such happy elements fail to produce poetry of the highest excellence? But I, unhappy man, boil with my worries like a cauldron. From morn to night and from night to morn I have never a moment of peace; my unbridled worldly ambition compels me to stand with folded hands before a patron no better than myself; and nothing comes into my hands till I have sweated in labour from head to foot. The payment made to me, moreover, is regarded as a gift, not as remuneration for my toil—like the ass which, after having carried its load, has its rationed grass thrown before its face with

> contempt. If, under these circumstances, I can find a week or so of leisure, am I to devote it to praising my kindly patron or to expressing the poetic aspirations of my soul? And what sort of precious stones can one dig out of the rocks in such a short time?[19]

On the other, he became proud once more, declaring:

> No one could imitate Nizami better than this. If he himself had read my poem he would not have recognized it from his own, and I see no difference between them except that one is the product of his mind and the other of my soul.[20]

In *Āʾīnah-i Sikandarī* (Mirror of Alexander), Khusraw again bemoaned the lack of new material.

> But since all the pearls have been carried away by my predecessor, I have no alternative but to string potsherds together; and if you object to my doing so, please blame the person who has put me to this task....[21]

Amīr Khusraw concluded his final book, *Hasht Bihisht* (Eight Paradises), with a wistful comparison of his work to Niẓāmī's *Haft Paykar*:

> This poem is an echo of that old work, and contains all the wealth which that old treasure has got.... Honey, no doubt, is valuable, but vinegar also has its purchasers: the pearl is costly, yet amber also possesses some value...and even if there be no real gold in this poem it has the glitter of gold.[22]

Khusraw's ambivalence about the success of his reply to Niẓāmī outlived him. 'Ubayd-i Zakānī (died 1371) famously ridiculed his efforts as "a stew cooked in Nizami's pot and a foolish self-conceit."[23] Others, including the renowned fifteenth-century poet Jāmī, lauded his work as the best imitation of Niẓāmī,[24] a judgment corroborated by the fact that the two texts were sometimes copied together in a single manuscript, with Khusraw's version inevitably after or around Niẓāmī's.[25] One measure of Khusraw's success in adapting Niẓāmī is the legion of authors who attempted to follow in his footsteps—some four hundred by one count. A more tangible gauge of the popularity of his *Khamsa* text is the sheer number of extant copies, a list of which appears in Appendix A.

### *KHAMSA*

### *MAṬLAʿ AL-ANWĀR*

Khusraw began his reprise of Niẓāmī's *Khamsa* with *Maṭlaʿ al-Anwār*, a work of 3,310 verses completed in a period of just two weeks in 698/1298–99. The model for this *maṣnawī* in his own *Khamsa* is Niẓāmī's *Makhzan al-Asrār*, which determines the number of syllables and the sound of the final syllable in the title, the meter, and the format of twenty discourses.[26] Khusraw also followed Niẓāmī's lead in his use of a series of prefatory invocations and eulogies, beginning with praise of God (*hamd*), prayers for himself (*munājāt*), and one or more homages to the Prophet (*naʿt*). The second of three homages to the Prophet in *Maṭlaʿ al-Anwār* celebrates the *miʿrāj*, or Muḥammad's miraculous journey, and is often the only portion of this prefatory section to be illustrated. Like Niẓāmī, Khusraw acknowledged his spiritual and temporal masters, and so extoled Niẓām al-Dīn Awliyā and 'Alā' al-Dīn Khaljī. Khusraw then described his motives in recasting Niẓāmī's work, and recounted the mystical guidance he received in so doing. Both author and patron are depicted only rarely in later illustrated copies of the text, perhaps because manuscript designers intuitively understood that to pay tribute to them in this way would be to infringe upon the present sovereign's exclusive right to the limelight.

The bulk of *Maṭlaʿ al-Anwār* assumes the form of twenty didactic discourses (*maqālat*) that expound the Muslim view of the principles by which the world operates. The substance of these discourses is summarized by Ghazanfar Aliev in his essay accompanying the critical edition of the *Khamsa*.

> The first chapter is dedicated to the question of the principal destiny of man in the opinion of the Muslim theology and accordingly with its Sufi doctrine. The second chapter is on the benefit of accumulated knowledge of man. In the same chapter Amir Khusrau criticizes laziness of mind and ignorance. The third chapter is logically linked with the preceding two: with the help of the Word the man masters secrets of limitless knowledge, the Word being a great power given to mankind, that is why, as the poet says, man should not waste words. The fourth and fifth conversations are wholly dedicated to Islam and its prescriptions. Further on the poet praises Sufism and Sufis who bring to people the real understanding of God's word (the sixth conversation), and lauds abstinence and asceticism (the seventh conversation) practiced by Sufis. The eighth conversation deals with the doctrine of the supreme feeling, the Sufi Love to God.

The following chapters (9–12) praise man's virtues sanctified by Islam. The thirteenth conversation contains edifications to the crowned ones, the poet considering one of their main tasks that of protection of the poor. In the following conversations (14–15) Amir Khusrau exposes the vices that, in his opinion, are gnawing at the base of society: treason and oppression, the two being very frequently met with in high society. In the sixteenth conversation the poet comes back to the evaluation of man's virtues which he considers innate, exclusively. The contents of the seventeenth conversation is [*sic*] the praise of youth which is compared to a vernal odoriferous garden fatally menaced by autumn. Penitence is discussed in the eighteenth conversation. The contents of the conversation 19 and 20 is [*sic*] connected with the poet's personal experience; he complains of the vicissitudes of life. The last conversation edifies his own daughter Mastura.[27]

Each discourse ends in a short, original anecdote that embodies in colorful terms the principle that Khusraw has set forth; the final line is typically an exhortation that Khusraw directs to himself. The concise, physical nature of these stories makes them the logical place for illustrations; indeed, no discourse is enhanced by an illustration anywhere other than in its anecdote. Some anecdotes, notably those of the seventh, thirteenth, and seventeenth discourses, are illustrated quite frequently, probably because their narratives are variations of well-established literary themes in which kings and sages figure prominently. Many other anecdotes are illustrated rarely, and two (those of the ninth and fifteenth *maqālat*) seem to have been bypassed altogether, almost certainly because their protagonists do not lend themselves easily to depiction.

## SUBJECTS OF THE ANECDOTES OF *MAṬLAʿ AL-ANWĀR*

1. A man questions Moses about what he experienced when he saw God. Moses replies that he realized in the sight of God, all human desire is presumptuous and all knowledge inconsequential.
2. A learned man and a king fall asleep before a lamp, and each has a dream in which he is asked of his troubles in life. The learned man responds that he undergoes travails despite his knowledge; the king offers that while the learned man can suffer lapses in protection and be burned by the royal lamp, he himself takes refuge in the scholar's erudition.
3. An old traveler is asked by a brash youth how he fares so well. The traveler replies that he guards his words carefully and speaks only when it is truly useful.
4. Impressed by the piety of a brahman who is crawling toward his icon, his chest scraping the ground at every advance, a Muslim pilgrim removes his shoes and continues barefoot.
5. Offered a reward by Khiẓr, a legendary saint, for ninety years of unswerving worship of God, a pious hermit asks for only a vision of God.
6. A darvish (or dervish) asks Shiblī, a legendary mystic, to explain abandonment. Shiblī hastens home, and, returning a short time later, recounts the story of the one small coin he kept in his beggar's robe as a reminder of the possessions that had shackled him with desire and pride.
7. Taking pity on an aged hermit who survives on bitter roots, a courtier asks him why he has forsaken the company of men for such a mean existence, and then raises the prospect of a more comfortable position at court. The hermit scoffs at the offer and wonders aloud why anyone who could be satisfied with bitter roots would ever stoop to royal service.
8. A bathhouse worker espies the visiting king and is stricken with a mystical love. The king returns his attentions with a furtive glance that flashes like lightning. With this spark, the bathhouse worker is consumed by the heat of his love.
9. A thorn snags the robe of an ascetic living in the desert. The ascetic takes this occurrence to be a gesture of friendship on the part of the thorn and kneels in reciprocal respect. After a year, the thorn turns to dust, and the ascetic rises to upbraid it for the apparent insincerity of its action.
10. After the death of his father, a man kills his own brother so that he alone will inherit the family fortune. He makes his way to court, where he expects his case to be adjudicated. Instead, he sees two friends sentenced to death, each wanting to die before the other so that he would not have to suffer the sight of his friend's death. This dramatic display of loyalty between men who do not even share a bond of blood awakens the conscience of the fratricide, and he confesses his crime to the king. The king thereupon orders him to be executed and the two friends to be released.
11. In a desert on the way to Mecca, several men grow so weakened by thirst that they fall to the ground. As they struggle to stave off death, a camel rider appears. Seeing their parched condition, he pours water into a cup and brings it to the man closest to him. To his amazement, the man refuses the life-sustaining water, whispering that his friend needs it more urgently. The camel rider abides

this request only to discover that water is declined by the next man and by every one of his companions in turn, each deferring conspicuously to the needs of the others. This gesture of generosity is virtuous but foolhardy, for all the men soon perish from thirst. The camel rider stares at the cup, quaffs its contents, and ponders the nature of generosity.

12. Engaging an infidel in hand-to-hand combat, ʿAlī knocks him to the ground and renders him so vulnerable that his last defense is mere spit. ʿAlī does not dispatch the insolent wretch to hell immediately, but allows him to regain his feet, whereupon he decapitates him and splits him asunder. The Prophet sees all this and asks ʿAlī why he granted the enemy a momentary reprieve. ʿAlī replies that he did not want to kill the man for his personal insult to him, but for his sinful idolatry, and thus waited until his own wrath no longer clouded the righteousness of his action.

13. A king out hunting accidentally shoots a youth who had fallen asleep while guarding the fields. When the king sees the calamity wrought by his arrow and hears the anguished cries of the youth's widowed mother, he dismounts, puts his sword to his own neck, and offers her a choice of two forms of compensation: his own head on a golden basin or a second basin piled high with gold. The bereaved woman is moved by the justness of his action and chooses not to exact revenge with his blood, reasoning wisely that it would do nothing to restore her son to her, and accepts the monetary recompense.

14. One day a dishonest herdsman who habitually watered down the milk that he sent to market has his goats swept away suddenly by a torrent of water pouring down from the mountains. A local wise man offers no sympathy to the distraught shepherd, but pointedly chastises him with the observation that the very water he used to adulterate his milk had become the agent of his ruin.

15. An old crow afflicted by a chronic eye disease complains to another crow. That bird discloses the source of a tree whose leaves—if they are in pristine condition—can remedy the condition. The crow locates the tree only to discover that he has spoiled every leaf by fouling it with his excrement, and that the tree no longer holds the promise of relief.

16. While making the barren desert verdant by his very presence, Jesus encounters an ignorant man who abuses him with vile invective. Jesus responds to the taunts with kindness and explains the man's behavior by saying that all people act as they are accustomed to do; Jesus further says that he can ameliorate ill manners and spirits by speaking with his life-giving breath.

17. One early morning, a tulip-cheeked, sweet-lipped youth strutting about a garden passes an old man, back bent with age and long beard hanging from his wizened cheeks. The sight of such a fair one awakens memories of youthful desires in the old Sufi, and he ventures a lustful overture to the youth, exhorting him to indulge himself in pleasure at every opportunity. The youth, well pleased with his own beauty, casts a disdainful glance at the stooped figure and asks him sardonically what he is looking for on the ground. The chastened old Sufi retorts, "My youth, but I'll never find it." He then admonishes the youth that as surely as all flowers in a garden wither over time, he too will lose his bloom.

18. A saint who has remained awake each night for forty years, his eyes fixed on the sky in anticipation of seeing the Night of Power, succumbs to sleep on the very night that he has awaited for so long.[28] In the early morning he hears a voice emanating from the heavens informing him that he closed his eyes on exactly the wrong occasion, and that his long efforts have been in vain.

19. A hunter and his dog track two foxes, who are ultimately caught in a trap. The hunter, having grown thirsty from the heat of the day and his excessively warm coat, and knowing that his captive prey cannot escape, postpones the slaughter of the two foxes while he goes to a river to refresh himself. The two foxes dread their imminent demise, but rue it all the more for the separation from each other that death will bring. Not so, observes one, for we may be joined after death in other ways.

20. A king gazing out from the heights of his castle catches sight of a beautiful woman. He sends a messenger to press his desirous intentions upon her, but the virtuous woman protests, asking how the king can possibly find her body attractive. The messenger persists and replies that it is in fact her eyes that have made the king restless. Reckoning her virtue to be more precious than her sight, the woman plucks out her eyes and asks the messenger to deliver them to the king. Dumfounded by this dramatic defense of chastity, the king relents at last.

## *SHĪRĪN WA KHUSRAW*

*Shīrīn wa Khusraw*, the second book of the *Khamsa*, was completed at the beginning of Rajab 698/April 1299. It numbers 4,124 couplets and follows the meter of Niẓāmī's prototype.[29] It unfolds in the usual fashion, beginning with a formal praise of God and the Prophet and then continuing with encomia on Niẓām al-Dīn Awliyā and 'Alā' al-Dīn Khaljī. After brief digressions on truth and love and a bit of advice to his children, Khusraw begins his narrative with the death of the Sasanian king Hurmuz and the subsequent accession of Khusraw Parwīz. Khusraw Parwīz is forced into exile from Ctesiphon by a rebellion led by Bahrām Chūbīna, against whom he wages an unsuccessful military campaign. To distract Khusraw's attention from his political travails, his boon companion Shāhpūr shows the king a portrait of Shīrīn, whose beauty causes him to fall in love immediately. His ardor for Shīrīn, niece of the queen of Armenia, is fueled when Khusraw finally lays eyes on her when they meet by chance during a hunt. But political exigencies require Khusraw to leave his beloved and wed Maryam, daughter of the Qaiṣar (Emperor) of Rūm, as a price for the Qaiṣar's support against Bahrām Chūbīna. Fortified by this alliance, Khusraw renews the battle with Bahrām Chūbīna, regains the Persian throne, and begins to expand his realm. Growing wary of Khusraw's increasing power, the Qaiṣar ships his treasures from Asia Minor to Abyssinia, but a breeze blows them off course into the hands of Khusraw, who distributes his windfall. Upon the death of Maryam, who had grown disheartened at the tension between her husband and her father, Khusraw courts Shīrīn again. They preside over the wedding of ten pairs of youths. The spectacle of marriage rites spurs Khusraw to propose, a gesture that causes Shīrīn to reveal her lingering doubts about him. A quarrel ensues and Khusraw returns to Persia, where he marries Shakar, a beauty of Isfahan.

Spurned by Khusraw for a second time, Shīrīn goes riding and meets Farhād, a handsome sculptor who has renounced his status as son of the Emperor of China. She asks the lovestruck Farhād to construct a channel to bring milk from one part of the country to another. He agrees, asking in return only an occasional glance of her. The jealous Khusraw attempts unsuccessfully to dissuade Farhād from this labor of love, but tricks him into committing suicide by disillusioning him with false news of Shīrīn's death. Shīrīn retaliates by sending an old woman to become the attendant of Shakar, whom she poisons. Beset by loneliness, Khusraw rides to Shīrīn's castle. Gazing down upon him from the rooftop, Shīrīn has second thoughts about Khusraw; she invites him inside and orders music played for them. The music softens their estranged hearts, and the two pledge themselves to each other once more. Khusraw and Shīrīn marry at last. Khusraw soon turns from passion to philosophy and engages his counselor Buzurg Umīd in extended discourse. This short-lived period of regal harmony is brought to an abrupt end by a coup by Shīrūya, Khusraw's son, who murders Khusraw and provokes the suicide of Shīrīn.

## *MAJNŪN WA LAYLĀ*

In the third book of the *Khamsa, Majnūn wa Laylā*, Khusraw again takes his title from Niẓāmī's *maṡnawī*, reversing once more the order of the names of the two protagonists. He provides both the number of verses (2,660) and the date of completion (698/1299) near the end of the poem. After the usual sequence of praises of God, the Prophet, Niẓām al-Dīn Awliyā, and 'Alā' al-Dīn Khaljī, Khusraw again measures his effort against the standard of Niẓāmī. Before starting his labors on the narrative proper, Khusraw slyly alludes to the feasibility and motivation of his project by telling two short stories. The first cites the example of two demons who have such prodigious energies that they can be harnessed only by being set to work on absolutely futile tasks. The second recounts the tale of a shepherd who aspires to a much better station in life and puts himself within reach of it by becoming skilled with both pen and sword. Between these complementary lessons about futility and self-advancement, Khusraw offers more personal words of advice to his son Khiẓr, urging him not to choose the way of the pen as he had.

The story begins with the birth of Qays, an Arab boy. The customary prophecy given upon this joyous occasion contains one worrisome note: that the boy's bright future will be darkened by the madness of love. The seeds of this portentous fate take root at school, where among the ranks of pupils the handsome Qays first beholds the beautiful Laylā. So strong is their mutual attraction that it becomes the stuff of scandal, which Laylā's parents try to suppress by removing Laylā from school. Qays remains in school, but only in body, for his mind is given over already to thoughts of Laylā. Soon, the wild-eyed youth begins to wander about, singing ceaselessly of his love for Laylā. His behavior is now so bizarre that children pelt him with stones and adults deride him with the name Majnūn ("insane," literally, "possessed by *jinns*").

Majnūn finds refuge from a hostile world in the solitude of the wilderness. His father eventually discovers him and tries in vain to console him. He begins to take practical steps to allay his son's distress. First he visits Laylā's family in hope of persuading them to give Laylā's hand in marriage, but his efforts come to naught. Then he tells his sorry tale to Nawfal, the chieftain of his tribe; Nawfal responds by demanding under threat of force the marriage of the two lovers. When Laylā's father rejects this offer too, Nawfal attacks Laylā's tribe to compel them to yield Laylā to Majnūn, but breaks off the battle at Majnūn's request. As Majnūn looks upon the carnage of battle, he is so appalled that he allows scavenging crows to peck at his own eyes, which he blames for the love that has brought ruin to him. Laylā learns of Majnūn's actions through a friend and is heartened by them. Nawfal then tries to resolve the situation by giving his own daughter to Majnūn in marriage. A dismayed Majnūn acquiesces to this arrangement out of duty, but the marriage remains unconsummated, for he cannot bring himself even to gaze upon his bride.

Majnūn's behavior shocks all those around him, and his father dies of shame. Meanwhile, news of his marriage reaches Laylā, who is stunned by this apparent breach of love. Her anguished heart is calmed as Majnūn explains matters in a letter, but Majnūn's social disgrace has only increased, and he retreats to the desert once more. Two friends track him down, hoping to rehabilitate him. Their entreaties cause Majnūn to waver momentarily, but the thought of melancholy solitude beckons still more powerfully, and he retreats to a garden. Alone again, Majnūn hears the lovelorn song of a nightingale and answers in kind. Majnūn intuitively realizes, however, that a less hospitable environment is better suited to his fierce passion, and he flees to the wilderness, where beasts lie peaceably near him in recognition of his kindred spirit. One day, the haggard Majnūn wanders back toward Laylā's neighborhood. The streets are deserted in the midday sun, and Majnūn sees only a miserable cur. Majnūn showers the dog with affection, cradling it in his lap and preparing a bed for it with his ragged clothes, actions inspired not so much by pity as by surrogacy, for the doleful lover reasons in his own way that the dog could at least be near Laylā.

Laylā wastes away from her unhappiness until one night she dreams that she is finally reunited with her beloved in the desert. Although Laylā awakens to find that this was a dream, its power rouses her to act, and she rides out into the desert on a camel. She finds Majnūn asleep and holds him in her lap. There the two lovers remain entranced until evening. With their love stoked but not consummated, Laylā reluctantly prepares to return to her family, and a virtually catatonic Majnūn is unable to protest.

This one-day reunion precipitates their undoing, for it intensifies their longing all the more. To test Laylā's love of Majnūn, Majnūn's friend informs her that Majnūn has died. This foolish action has unforeseen consequences: after weeping bitterly in a palm grove over the loss of her one reason to live, Laylā lapses into unconsciousness and expires. Majnūn hears of this calamity and hastens to knock at Laylā's door. He observes the preparations being made for her funeral and sets out for the graveyard. Lingering near Laylā's funeral procession until her corpse is placed in the grave, the bereaved Majnūn leaps into the open grave, fervently embraces her corpse, and dies instantly, never to be separated again from his beloved.[30]

### *Ā'ĪNAH-I SIKANDARĪ*

*Ā'īnah-i Sikandarī* (Mirror of Alexander), composed in 699/1299 and containing 4,450 couplets, begins with the obligatory praises of God, the Prophet, Niẓām al-Dīn Awliyā, and 'Alā' al-Dīn Khaljī.[31] Khusraw then extols the virtues of poetry, gives advice to another of his offspring, his four-year-old son Rukn al-Dīn Ḥājjī, and mourns the passing of his mother. In this introduction and at several points throughout the poem, Khusraw takes up another conceit initiated by Niẓāmī: an address to the cupbearer, he who tenders the wine of eloquence in a revelatory vessel. But Khusraw deliberately does not attempt to imitate Niẓāmī as faithfully as he did earlier. He provides an abstract of the whole of Niẓāmī's story and asserts that it is only a starting point for his own more expansive narrative. He levels specific criticisms against Niẓāmī's assertions that Alexander was a prophet, a religious status far more elevated than his own conception of Alexander, and that Alexander died at a purportedly tender age, a fact seemingly belied by the awesome number of his legendary feats.[32]

This preface sets the stage for Khusraw's own selective account of Alexander's life. Emboldened by his past military successes, Alexander leads his troops toward China and sends a message to its leader, the Khāqān, urging him to submit lest he meet the same ignominious end as Alexander's other opponents. The Khāqān sends an ambassador bearing sword and soil, a gesture that signals the Khāqān's intent to defend his territory. Alexander attacks. As the armies clash, a champion from Alexander's side, Parīkaysh, rides out to engage a brave Chinese champion, Tangū, in single combat and subdues him with a lasso. Alexander participates in the battles, once taking on the Khāqān himself and later confronting a formidable champion named Kanīfū. Alexander triumphs where his champions had failed, and he defeats Kanīfū by wresting him from his horse with a lasso. Having brought the captive to court on a long tether, Alexander removes the youth's armor only to discover that Kanīfū is actually a woman. She explains to the astonished Alexander how she acquired her martial skills and relates the prediction that she would marry the one who defeated her in battle. Smitten by the unlikely combination of valor and beauty, Alexander ponders this possibility and entertains her in courtly style. Now the Khāqān himself proposes individual combat with Alexander, a challenge Alexander gladly accepts. The two rulers wield arrows and swords against each other, but Alexander ultimately unhorses his opponent with a powerful thrust of his arm. The Khāqān surrenders first on the field of battle and later at court, where he declares his total submission. Alexander treats his subjugated foe with every measure of respect and allows him to return home.

In the north, Alexander wages successful campaigns against the Russians and Almanis, and then strays to search for the miraculous Fountain of Life. As he wanders, he passes through the land controlled by the barbarian Yājūj, who are gnome-like in appearance and bestial in behavior.[33] Alexander's men capture some of the curious creatures to examine them closely, but what they see is so hideous that Alexander decides to erect a mammoth bulwark of copper, iron, and lead to keep the repulsive Yājūj at bay.

Alexander returns to his homeland in the spring with Kanīfū in tow. His dalliance with her grows serious; they make love, but do not marry. After a short transitional story about artificers who fabricate imitation rice and sesame seeds, Khusraw begins to describe Alexander's keen interest in marvelous inventions. The most remarkable of these is the wondrous handiwork of Chinese painters, who claim the ability to make paintings that are not only more skillful than those made by Alexander's countrymen, but which are actually indistinguishable from nature itself. Alexander puts their boast to the test and discovers that the Chinese painters have perfected the art of mirror-making. Alexander sees in this technical curiosity some practical applications, and he orders a revolving mirror set atop a tall tower by the seashore; with this device, he keeps close watch on pirate activity in the area. Alexander also brings force to bear on other peoples whose chief transgression is their religious recalcitrance. So it is that he denounces Zoroastrians for their practice of fire worship and marches to Azerbaijan to raze their temples. Likewise, he proceeds to an area near the Nile to mete out a deadly punishment to a group of Greeks who do not share his own belief in God. One Greek who escapes this fate is Plato, whose subsequent reputation for wisdom attracts even a world conqueror to his cave.

Alexander embarks on a long sea voyage toward the Western Isles with Khiẓr, Elias, and Aristotle, pausing once to send his son Iskandarūs a letter bequeathing him the empire. Meanwhile, Alexander presses on with his investigation of the world, at one point descending into the sea in a glass diving bell to examine submarine mysteries. Beneath the waters he meets an angel who reveals the infinite scope of all experience and informs him of the little time remaining to him. Alexander is relieved by this revelation and brings his journey to a close. Soon the aged king dies, but his death is kept secret for a time. Once proper succession occurs, Alexander's casket is carried in an elaborate funeral procession to his burial spot.

### *HASHT BIHISHT*

After composing the first four poems of the *Khamsa* in about a year, Khusraw slackened his pace, completing the final book, *Hasht Bihisht* (Eight Paradises), about two years later, in 701/1302. The delay was evidently due not to the length of the book (3,344 couplets), but to its originality, for it follows only the structure of Niẓāmī's *Haft Paykar* and not the substance of his individual stories.[34] After the usual sequence of encouragement he received from his friend 'Alī as he began the poem. He repeats Niẓāmī's device of having Bahrām Gūr visit a series of seven princesses installed in different pavilions, but reconfigures it slightly. Khusraw then offers some advice for his infant daughter 'Afifa.

The hero of the poem is Bahrām, a king enamored of hunting and the company of women. One day, in the presence of Dilārām, a Chinese maiden who always accompanied Bahrām on his hunting trips, the king demonstrates his prowess with a bow as he transforms a male onager (gūr) into a female and a female onager into a male by striking each with arrows in such a way that the animal appears to lose or gain horns. Offended by Dilārām's remark that his feat would be surpassed sometime like any other skill, Bahrām pulls her from her horse and exiles her to the forest. There Dilārām meets an old man who instructs her in the twelve modes of music, particularly in four that induce listeners to laugh, cry, sleep, or awaken. Intrigued by accounts of a woman whose skill on the barbiton (a kind of lute) is such that she could charm creatures with her music, Bahrām comes to hear her play. The king is duly impressed, but echoes Dilārām's earlier statement that every skill would be surpassed one day. Dilārām concurs, but declares that this rule has a single exception: Bahrām's accomplishment at the hunt! Startled by the irony of the statement, Bahrām recognizes Dilārām and forgives his estranged beloved.

To temper Bahrām's passion for the hunt and thus redirect his energies to the affairs of state, Nu'mān and Bahrām's other counselors order seven magnificent pavilions built and occupied by princesses from the seven climes, and then invite Bahrām to visit a different one on each day of the week. Bahrām is pleasantly diverted by the princesses, who dress entirely in the color of their respective pavilions and entertain him with stories.

Bahrām begins his rounds on Saturday at the Black Pavilion, which Khusraw designates as the second of his paradises, the first one being the encapsulating story of Bahrām's hunting adventures. In this paradise resides an Indian princess, whose musk-colored clothing and surroundings are dark like her skin. She receives Bahrām and spins the following tale. The king of Ceylon tests the loyalty of his three sons by sending them into exile. An Ethiopian traveler who happens upon them on the road inquires about his missing camel and is convinced by the princes' responses that they have stolen the animal. Arrested and brought to trial, the men maintain that their exceedingly detailed descriptions of the missing camel are mere deductions, a protestation proved true and explained when the beast is found the next day. Impressed by their remarkable perspicacity, the king rewards the three men with various honors. One day he overhears them cast aspersions not only on the lowly origin of the food and drink served at a feast held in their honor, but even on his own ancestry, expressing their belief that his blood was not that of a king, but that of a butler. Enraged by these statements, but cautioned by their vindication in the previous case, the king decides not to punish the travelers until he can ascertain the validity of their charges. He is astounded to discover that they are correct about every matter and is amazed by their later explanations of their insightful deductions. Nonetheless, the prospect of having still more disturbing truths revealed by these exceptional powers of deduction is too daunting for the king to imagine, and so, after bestowing more riches upon the young men, he bids them a firm farewell.[35]

On Sunday, Bahrām decamps to the third paradise, where the princess from Nīmrūz dwells in saffron-colored splendor.[36] She recounts to Bahrām a tale that features the most precious element of this color. A goldsmith named Ḥasan embezzles some material from the golden elephant he has made for the king. The wife of a rival goldsmith cajoles Ḥasan's wife into coaxing from him the means by which the precise weight of such a large object could be measured; he explains that one could compare the amount of water displaced by the golden elephant with that displaced by an object of the weight originally prescribed. The dull-witted wife then spills the details of this ingenious test to her devious confidante. That woman in turn relays the information to her husband, who thereupon brings his charge of embezzlement before the king. The king tests the validity of the charge by using the very procedure that Ḥasan had described, determines that the goldsmith is guilty, and imprisons him in a high tower. One day Ḥasan calls down to his wife to bring to the tower a stretch of silk tipped with a bit of sugar. Taking hold of one end of the sweetened cloth, which an ant has transported to the top of the tower, the goldsmith tells his wife to tie herself to a rope fastened to the other end so that she can come up to see him. As the simple-minded woman goes up one side of the tower, the goldsmith rappels down the other, leaving his imprudent wife imprisoned in his place, where she is ridiculed by the townspeople. The embezzler Ḥasan is located, but he earns his freedom by his wits when he shows the king that he has demonstrated his admirable cleverness in each one of his actions throughout the affair.

Bahrām spends Monday in the company of the Sclavonian princess, who is ensconced in an emerald green environment.[37] She transfixes him with this story: A king learns the technique of metamorphosis from a magician, but foolishly demonstrates it for his vizier. The treacherous vizier seizes the opportunity to appropriate the king's body, left temporarily unoccupied while the metamorphosis was under way, and proceeds to pass himself off as the king. This guise is particularly rewarding in the harem, where he is rebuffed by only one queen who suspects the subterfuge. Meanwhile, the king's soul has alighted in the body of a green parrot, an innocuous form that allows him to exercise his innate judiciousness in unlikely circumstances. In one case, the parrot serves on a tribunal for resolving a dispute between a prostitute and a banker. The woman demands of the banker a thousand gold pieces as recompense for her amorous behavior toward him in a dream; the parrot orders the banker to count out the money before a mirror and the woman to take her payment from the money's reflection, so that her compensation has the same substance as her claim. The edifying parrot is purchased for the queen, who puts him in a golden cage in her chambers. When he sees that she has not been deceived by the vizier, the parrot reveals his true identity. Together they trick the vizier into metamorphosing into a bird, enabling the king to exchange the parrot's body for his own and to kill the wicked official.

Tuesday brings Bahrām to the door of the fifth paradise, a lush pomegranate-colored pavilion presided over by a Russian princess. Inspired by the flowery red color of her surroundings, she regales Bahrām with a story in which flowers work the magic of love. It goes as follows: Five friends—a prince, a merchant, a miner, a carpenter, and a gardener—reach a city, where the prince is smitten by a woman's portrait. They learn that the woman is the king's mistress and that she is sequestered in a high tower. The friends agree to employ their respective skills to help the prince satisfy his passion. The gardener makes the acquaintance of an old woman who habitually takes flowers to the woman. He persuades her to substitute his magically enhanced flowers for her regular blooms and to deliver them on behalf of the prince. Thus the friends arouse the interest of the kept woman and eventually breach the walls of her tower, thereby allowing the prince to spend some nights with her. Now they begin to plot her escape. The prince and his friends invite the king to dinner on seven successive nights; on each he is served by an enticing and apparently different cupbearer, who is none other than his mistress disguised in costumes of seven different colors. When they offer the king their possessions as a parting gift, he thinks of the beautiful cupbearers in their service and becomes elated at the prospect of having at his disposal seven maidens every bit as beautiful as his current mistress. Thus the king happily accompanies the five friends to water's edge, unaware that they have already spirited away his mistress from her tower and have stowed her in their ship.

On Wednesday, Bahrām visits the sixth paradise, a wonderland of violet blue inhabited by a princess from Rūm. She tells this story: A young man from Rūm hears a traveler talk of an enchanted place where everyone dresses in violet and only half the residents speak. His curiosity becomes an overnight obsession, and he sets out immediately with several friends for this magical, distant country. When the youth finally reaches the legendary place, his companions halt from fear, leaving him to proceed alone into a garden replete with magical statues but devoid of living beings. This situation changes at nightfall, when a bevy of maidens arrive and perceive the presence of the cowering youth. They escort him before a beautiful queen, who offers him every courtesy, including the favors of one of her attendants. He drifts into sleep. He awakens alone and rubs his eyes in disbelief. For a week, he is similarly enchanted by night and disillusioned by morn, until at last he wakes to find himself in a desert. He quickly becomes smitten with another girl, apparently a mortal, but she too proves to be a phantom. A hermit takes pity on the bewildered youth and offers him shelter, but phantasmagoria sweeps him up again, depositing him in a land where he is pronounced king and is hosted by different beauties on each day of the week. The last of these proffers violets, a flower the youth is unable to resist despite many earlier warnings. Dizzied by their power, he lurches out the very building through which he had entered the magical garden long before, now dressed completely in violet and unable to speak—the very conditions that mark all visitors to this mysterious land.

The Arab princess of the sandalwood-colored pavilion entertains Bahrām on Thursday with this story: A vizier who was having an affair with the second wife of the king of Yemen covers his perfidy by accusing the prince of attempted incest. The queen confirms this lie, and the king is compelled to punish his son, Rāma, with exile. Rāma makes the acquaintance of three men who offer to help him exonerate himself. The first gives him a magic ointment that will make him invisible. The second teaches him a magic spell that causes others to fall immediately into slumber. The third instructs him to stare for a year at a certain statue in Egypt and to apply wax to the image when it begins to move. Rāma follows these orders and is amazed to behold the demonic being he has conjured up, a *dīv*, entirely at his command. Now Rāma returns to court to exact revenge on his nemesis. Disguised as an old woman dressed in sandalwood-colored robes, he ingratiates himself with the vizier by purportedly curing an affliction he had ordered the *dīv* to inflict. Using the cloak of invisibility and the services of the *dīv* again, Rāma gains access to the vizier's house, where he takes advantage of the vizier's harem and makes his way to the vizier's daughter's bed. Once there, he deliberately allows himself to be rendered visible by smoke, thereby revealing his handsome countenance to the girl and luring the guards into hot pursuit. He stymies them by casting the spell of sleep and humiliates them further by shaving off their beards. Soon after, an invisible Rāma returns to the daughter's chamber, abducts the girl, and quickly wins her heart. Finally, disguised again as a woman in sandalwood-colored robes, he reappears at court, to which the *dīv* magically transports the duplicitous vizier and queen as they sleep together. Rāma sheds his disguise to reveal his identity to his father, who restores him to his rightful position as heir and blesses his marriage to the vizier's daughter.

On Friday, Bahrām arrives at the eighth paradise, the pure white abode of the princess of Khwārazm.[38] She dazzles Bahrām with this story: A king, whose enthusiasm for marriage is cooled by the prospect of betrayal, acquires a magical talisman with a keen ear for hypocrisy and deception, laughing raucously whenever it hears a falsehood. He places the statue in his chambers. He selects four marriageable princesses and installs them in separate towers, the first with access to the stables, the second overlooking the camels' quarters, the third with a vista onto the river, and the fourth situated above a wine shop. He summons each in turn for daily and then weekly engagements. The first princess is strikingly charming, but the king is perplexed when she pretends to faint when he taps her lightly on the cheek with a rose. The talisman laughs at the princess's action, an outburst that annoys the woman even as it worries the king. The second woman displays similarly unwarranted physical sensitivities, this time complaining that a luxurious fur hurts her skin, a claim that provokes talismanic mirth again. The third princess displays excessive squeamishness at the sight of girls frolicking in a pool, a pastime that ends in accidental drowning; again the statue's derision raises doubts about her sincerity. The fourth woman, attractive without wiles and responsive without capriciousness, does not set off the talisman, but the king remains strangely indifferent to her. After a time, the king's worst suspicions about women are confirmed when he discovers that the first three princesses have betrayed him with secret trysts. The first is found being beaten by her paramour, a black muleteer. The second is tracked to the camel stables, where she chafes her skin willingly with a camel-driver. The third turns out to be an adept swimmer, who has perfected her skills by paddling nightly across the river with the aid of a clay jar to visit her Hindu lover. Only the fourth princess is innocent of deceit and shows exemplary behavior. The king thus decides to mete out appropriate punishments to the unfaithful women, forcing the first two to live by day the brutish lives they evidently considered appealing by night, and causing the third to drown in the river of her betrayal. He recognizes that the guileless fourth princess intoxicates by her virtue, and makes her his queen.

Bahrām amuses himself in this manner for a time, surrendering to the sensory pleasures of each princess and her pavilion. But these pleasures do not supplant those of the hunt altogether. Thus, one day Bahrām strikes out in pursuit of an onager, chases him into a deep cave, and disappears from sight forever.

NOTES

1. Preface of the *Ghurrat al-Kamāl*, cited in Mirza, *Life and Works*, 32.

2. Derived from Arabic poetry, a *qaṣīda* is a long (usually between 13 and 200 couplets) monorhyme used for panegyrics; it is intended to be recited before the personage it honors.

3. Preface to the *Tuḥfat al-Ṣighar*, cited in Mirza, *Life and Works*, 153.

4. Mirza, *Life and Works*, 155, 157.

5. Mirza, *Life and Works*, 154, and note 3.

6. N. Ahmad, "An Accomplished Critic," in *Amir Khusrau: Memorial Volume* (New Delhi: Ministry of Information and Broadcasting, 1975), 114. The author also indicates that Khusraw took Raẓī al-Dīn Nīshāpūrī, a sixth-century poet, and the more contemporary Kamāl al-Dīn Iṣfahānī (died 1237) as his models in the *qaṣīda*.

7. Unlike the *qaṣīda* and the *ghazal*, the *maṣnawī* (or *masnawī*) rhymes the two hemistiches (*miṣrā'*) of each couplet (*bayt*), but varies the rhyme with virtually every line. The *maṣnawī*'s flexibility makes it particularly useful for lengthy works, in which the repetition of a monorhyme would be exceedingly tedious. Although the *maṣnawī* is employed for epic, romantic, and philosophical subjects alike, L. Elwell-Sutton, *The Persian Metres* (Cambridge, 1976), 244, points out that certain meters have been associated traditionally with each of these genres.

8. Scholarly estimates of the dates of this author's birth and death vary considerably. Here I follow those set forth by E. Berthels, "Niẓāmī Gandjawī," *Encyclopaedia of Islam*, new ed. (Leiden, 1993), VIII, 76.

9. The five poems were linked as a series not long after Niẓāmī's death, initially under title *Panj Ganj* (Five Buried Treasures), and later under the Arabic title for five, *Khamsa*.

10. Berthels, "Niẓāmī," 77.

11. Berthels, "Niẓāmī," 78.

12. The meter is *sarī'*.

13. Mirza, *Life and Works*, 188, citing *Qirān al-Sa'dayn*.

14. In hope of gaining some reward for his accomplishment, the poet apparently presented the *Khamsa* not to the sultan, but to Iftikhar al-Dīn, his prime minister. Khusraw was quite discouraged by the minister's slowness in granting honors and remuneration that he considered his due. See Mirza, *Life and Works*, 190, note 2.

15. M. Habib, *Hazrat Amir Khusrau of Delhi* (Lahore, 1979), 71.

16. Mirza, *Life and Works*, 191–92.

17. Z. Sajjadi, "Khusrau—From Iranian Angle," in *Amır Khusrau Memorial Volume* (New Delhi, 1975), 196.

18. Habib, *Hazrat Amır Khusrau of Delhi*, 73.

19. Habib, *Hazrat Amır Khusrau of Delhi*, 74–75. The Persian verses are found in *Majnūn wa Laylā* (Moscow, 1964), 281–82.

20. Mirza, *Life and Works*, 198, translating *Majnūn wa Laylā*, 276.

21. Habib, *Hazrat Amir Khusrau of Delhi*, 73, translating *Ā'īnah-i Sikandarī*.

22. Mirza, *Life and Works*, 203.

23. Mirza, *Life and Works*, 191.

24. Mirza, *Life and Works*, 192, note 4, citing Jāmī's introduction to his *Tuḥfat al-Aḥrār*: "In its delicate and fine ideas, it is such that the finest writers of the world acknowledge their inability to reply to it...."

25. See, for example, the *Khamsa* manuscript in the Topkapi Saray Museum (H. 1008), listed in Appendix A.

26. The meter is hexametric *sarīʿ*. A. Schimmel, "Persian Poetry in the Indo-Pakistani Subcontinent," in E. Yarshater, ed., *Persian Literature* (Albany, 1988), 408, notes that Khusraw's *Maṯlaʿ al-Anwār* and all subsequent imitations of Niẓāmī's *Makhzan al-Asrār* have titles which end in *ār*.

27. *Maṯlaʿ al-Anwār* (Moscow, 1975), 66–67.

28. The Night of Power (*shab-i qadr*) is the twenty-seventh day of the holy month of Ramaẓān, a date on which the first verses of the Koran were revealed.

29. The meter is *hajaz*.

30. The conclusion of this story is recounted in greater detail in Habib, *Hazrat Amir Khusrau of Delhi*, 86–88.

31. The meter is *mutaqārib*.

32. The first of these points is noted by Mirza, *Life and Works*, 200.

33. Yajūj is often rendered as Gōg and Magōg, as it is in Appendices A and B.

34. It employs the meter of *Haft Paykar*, i.e., *khafīf*.

35. This story is recounted in greater detail in Habib, *Hazrat Amır Khusrau of Delhi*, 77–85.

36. Nīmrūz is part of Sistan, a region in eastern Iran.

37. Sclavonia refers to the land of the Slavs, i.e., modern-day Bosnia, Croatia, and Serbia.

38. Khwārazm is the western part of Transoxiana. The pavilion takes its color from the camphor tree.

CHAPTER 3

# The Context of Mughal Painting

Like Amīr Khusraw, the Mughals straddled two worlds: their ancestral homeland in the high plateaus of Central Asia and northeastern Persia, and the great expanses of northern India, a fertile land that beckoned with the promise of great wealth and political opportunity. In many ways, Mughal culture was a constantly changing blend of these two worlds. The Turkic and Persian elements were strongest at the outset of the sixteenth century, when Bābur, the ruler of a small and impoverished principality with its capital at Kabul, recognized that Uzbek power in the region would thwart his hopes of further conquest there and began a series of military thrusts southward into the neighboring Punjab, initially at the invitation of one faction of the faltering Lodī dynasty. In April 1526, Bābur achieved a decisive victory at Panipat, near Delhi. Soon thereafter, he took possession of Agra, the Lodī capital. Within a few years, he had defeated rival forces in the state of Rajasthan to the west, and in Bihar to the east. Ignoring the wishes of many of his followers, Bābur decided to shift his seat of power from Kabul to Agra, strategically located at the center of his new territorial conquests. Bābur's commitment to maintain rule over a predominantly Indian kingdom broke with the pattern of his Islamic predecessors, who saw incursions into India mainly as an opportunity for plunder, and established him as the founder of the new Mughal dynasty. Nonetheless, Bābur held his new dominion in low regard. In his memoirs, written in Chaghatay Turkish, he offers this scathing assessment of India:

> Hindustan is a place of little charm. There is no beauty in its people, no graceful social intercourse, no poetic talent or understanding, no etiquette, nobility, or manliness. The arts and crafts have no harmony or symmetry. There are no good horses, meat, grapes, melons, or other fruit. There is no ice, cold water, good food or bread in the markets. There are no baths or madrasas. There are no candles, torches, or candlesticks.... The one nice aspect of Hindustan is that it is a large country with lots of gold and money.[1]

Although many of these perceived deficiencies could never be rectified, Bābur did vow to introduce to India one of the amenities of his arid homeland: proper baths and gardens, which provided relief as much by the clarity of their military, harmonious, geometric designs as by their cooling waters and fragrant groves. Dismayed at the lack of sites suitable for such oases, however, Bābur reluctantly settled on a loathsome place near the Jumna River in Agra; in a caustic and telling aside, he relates that the local inhabitants were so impressed by the foreign-inspired transformation of this place that they nicknamed it "Kabul."[2]

Bābur cast an acute eye on the major political and literary figures of his time. His pithy remarks on some of the major Persian poets, artists, and musicians of the day reveal him to be a deeply cultivated individual capable of making discriminating assessments independently. Of Mīr 'Alī Sher Nawā'ī, a minister and poet of considerable renown, Bābur declares that he was unequaled in the number and quality of his Turkish compositions, but that he stumbled badly in a work on metrics, making mistakes in scansion in four of twenty-four quatrain meters.[3] Similarly, Bābur candidly proclaims that his contemporary, Bihzād, a painter who later came to embody the apogee of Persian painting, "painted extremely delicately, but he made the faces of beardless people badly by drawing the double chin too big. He drew the faces of bearded figures quite well."[4] Bābur himself wrote verse late in life,[5] and he followed princely Persian custom in maintaining a small library of books, some of which were acquired as spoils of war.[6]

Although Bābur's extensive descriptions of the marvelous Indian flora and fauna testify that he derived some pleasure from his experience in India, the later years of his memoirs lack the pocket biographical sketches in which he had earlier so obviously delighted. This silence is a sure sign that Bābur found the intellectual life in his new environment wanting in many respects. To the end of his days, Bābur continued to look to Kabul as his cultural touchstone, writing to his sons, "There were such conquests and victories while we were in Kabul that I consider Kabul my lucky piece and have made it royal demesne. Let none of you covet it."[7]

Upon Bābur's death in December 1530, the Mughal empire was divided among his four sons in such a way that it soon became untenable. Within a decade, Humāyūn became emperor in name only, as he lost control of one region of north India after another to resurgent Afghan forces through a disastrous combination of ill-advised military strategy and indolence. In 1544, Humāyūn was compelled to seek refuge at the Safawid court of Shāh Ṭahmāsp (reigned 1524–76). Ṭahmāsp offered assistance with the implicit provision that Humāyūn convert from the Sunnī sect to the Shī'a, and the new allies began to plot the reconquest of the lost empire. Typically, Humāyūn's first step was to challenge his brother Kāmrān for control of Qandahar, and thence Kabul, which he captured conclusively in 1553. With his ancestral base secured, a refortified Humāyūn turned toward the Punjab, gateway to the Indian lands ruled again by an Afghan regime, albeit one enfeebled by its own perils of succession. By July 1555, Humāyūn had overcome the Afghan opposition and assumed the throne at Delhi. He had barely begun to savor the fruits of his victory when, in January 1556, he met a precipitous end, falling headlong down a steep flight of stairs leading from the roof of his library.

Not all of Humāyūn's experience with books and libraries was so calamitous, of course. Like most members of the ruling class, Humāyūn had been educated in Persian literature, but he also saw fit to sponsor authors of scientific, historical, and literary texts, keep a series of librarians in his employ, and even write a bit of poetry himself.[8] And while some of the books he acquired or had produced in India probably contained paintings, Humāyūn's appreciation of this art must have been whetted considerably by his subsequent exposure to the treasures of the Safawid royal library. By good fortune, the Safawid ruler, Shāh Ṭahmāsp, heir and patron of many of these glories, had recently lost interest in painting and agreed to let several members of his atelier accompany Humāyūn home. By November 1549, at least six artists had joined Humāyūn at his temporary court in Kabul, where they produced a modest and little-known body of painting, which has recently become the subject of assiduous scholarship.[9] In 1554, two of these artists, Mīr Sayyid Alī and 'Abd al-Ṣamad, continued with Humāyūn on to India, where within a few years they headed an enormous atelier. Until this point, however, both Humāyūn and his artists remained firmly rooted in Persian culture, which was gradually displacing most aspects of the Central Asian Turkic culture into which Humāyūn had been born. The first tentative grafts of Indian culture had yet to appear either in the one known text he had illustrated, two copies of Niẓāmī's *Khamsa*, or in the subjects and style of the independent paintings; indeed, the only feature that distinguishes most of his paintings from contemporary Persian examples is a detail of costume adopted by Humāyūn, a turban with a tall conical center rising above a squarish base.[10]

It was during the long reign of Akbar (1556–1605), born on Indian soil in November 1542 while his exiled father Humāyūn was traversing Sind (in southern Pakistan), that Indian elements first began to assert themselves in Mughal culture. The throne that Akbar inherited in February 1556 was a precarious one, with real and potential enemies pressing on all sides. But the young Akbar moved expeditiously to rebuff all challenges. The most immediate threat was posed by a Hindu minister named Hemū, who, swelled with success, abandoned his role as proxy for one of the three Muslim princes attempting to restore the Afghan kingdom and sought to rule in his own right under the title of Rāja Vikramāditya. Hemū advanced from the south, seizing Agra and Delhi, and seemed poised to realize his personal ambitions. But Akbar disregarded the advice of many followers, who advocated retreating from the Punjab toward the safety of Kabul, and followed the counsel of his regent, Bayram Khān, to engage Hemū immediately, despite the enemy's vastly larger army. The Mughals' decisive victory occurred on 5 November 1556 on the plains at Panipat, where Bābur had triumphed a generation before.

The Mughals continued to extend their control in India, regaining Delhi and vanquishing in quick succession rival forces at Lahore and Ajmer to the north and west, and Jaunpur and Gwalior to the east and south. In 1560, this relentless expansion was interrupted briefly by a critical change in the Mughal power structure, when long-brewing factional strife between Bayram Khān and influential members of the harem finally came to a boil. Akbar, who at age seventeen was probably eager to rid himself of his guardian, sided with his Turkic and Sunnī relations against Bayram Khān, a Persian by birth and thus a follower of Shī'a Islam. This was Akbar's first brush with the invidious power of religious sectarianism, a lesson that he was not soon to forget. Akbar took the opportunity to break openly with Bayram Khān, compelling him to resign and to undertake the pilgrimage to Mecca, during which he was murdered. With Akbar now firmly in control, the Mughal armies pressed on toward the central Indian kingdom of Malwa, which fell in 1561.

Even as external foes capitulated, internal ones sprung up. Some aggrieved Uzbek nobles in the Mughal administration rebelled, first in Malwa, and then in the eastern Gangetic basin. In 1566, the trouble spread to Kabul, where Akbar's half-brother, Muḥammad Ḥakīm, had been installed as ruler. Cast out of the city by devious plotters, the weak Muḥammad Hakīm became the stalking horse of the Uzbeks, who persuaded him to try to claim the Mughal throne. This threat too was soon quelled, though Muḥammad Ḥakīm retreated to make similar mischief some fifteen years later. Meanwhile, Mughal armies prevailed in one part of Rajasthan after another, usually merely by a display of overwhelming force, but twice by raising devastating sieges of proud Rajput bastions. The breaching of the seemingly impregnable fortress of Chitor and the wanton slaughter of 30,000 of its inhabitants in 1568, and the surrender of Ranthambor in the following year, were effective demonstrations of the reality of Mughal military force. These resounding victories paved the way for an assault on the wealthy region of Gujarat, whose capital, Ahmedabad, came into Akbar's possession in 1572. Gujarat also held the prize of access to the busy ports of western India, which enjoyed a burgeoning commercial trade as well as the constant traffic of pilgrims on their way to Mecca. Akbar's advance into this area in 1573 brought about direct contact with Portuguese merchants based at their Goa colony further down the coast. An imperial mission to Goa returned a few years later with both artisans trained in exotic skills and an assortment of European curiosities, among them a fantastic pipe organ. More substantial contact followed in 1580 with the arrival of the first Jesuit mission to the Mughal capital.

Akbar's initial seat of government was at Delhi, the traditional capital for the Muslim dynasties of India. In 1565, the capital was moved to Agra, where the Mughals began to construct a massive fortified city of local red sandstone, whose 500 buildings were described as having "beautiful designs of Bengal and Gujarat."[11] Similar impressive fortifications were raised over the next eighteen years at Ajmer, Lahore, and Allahabad to anchor Mughal control of north India. In 1569, Akbar stopped at Sikri, thirty-eight kilometers from Agra, on his annual pilgrimage to the tomb of a Chishtī saint at Ajmer, to pay his respects to Shaykh Salīm al-Dīn Chishtī, a master of the same Chishtī order that Amīr Khusraw had joined toward the end of his life. When the emperor's prayers for a male heir were finally answered in August 1569, he was so elated that he honored the saint by ordering the construction of a new capital on the site, which later became known as Fathpur-Sikri. Most functions of the Mughal court were shifted there from Agra in 1571. In August 1585, however, Akbar left Fathpur-Sikri, never to return. Although Akbar's chronicler states that "the pleasant palaces of that city did not engage his heart,"[12] a less disingenuous explanation for Akbar's sudden abandonment of Fathpur-Sikri is that the city's close ties to Muslim institutions at nearby Ajmer became a liability at a time when the emperor was disengaging himself ever more from public forms of Islamic worship.[13]

Political considerations were paramount in the choice of Lahore as the new seat of the court. Akbar's tumultuous relations with his half-brother Muḥammad Ḥakīm, who was permitted to retain a nominal position as governor of Kabul even after another bout with sedition in 1580, finally came to an end with the latter's alcohol-induced demise in July 1585. With Mughal control in the region left open to Uzbek challenge once more, Akbar moved the huge imperial entourage northward through the Punjab to Kabul, his mere presence simultaneously discouraging Uzbek adventurism and facilitating the Mughal subjugation of Swat and Kashmir. In May 1586, Akbar and the court reached Lahore, where they settled for the next twelve years, albeit with frequent prolonged excursions to the surrounding areas for hunting, travel, and conquest. Lahore soon witnessed the pageantry of the marriages of Akbar's three sons and the annual ritual weighing of the emperor against an assortment of precious goods, but was also beset by a serious four-year famine in the mid-1590s. The desperate conditions of the populace were noted by Jesuit priests, whose mission arrived at the Mughal court in April 1595. A disastrous conflagration in the palace led Akbar to leave Lahore for Kashmir from mid-May to mid-November 1597, a period that coincides with the writing of the Walters *Khamsa* in that city.

Although Akbar remained in the Punjab and Kashmir, other conquests continued further afield. In the 1590s, the Mughals easily extended their dominion to Sind and Baluchistan in the south, Qandahar in the west, and Orissa along the remote eastern coast of India. By contrast, the five wealthy independent Islamic kingdoms along the southern frontier of the empire offered firm resistance to Akbar's diplomatic overtures and military expeditions throughout the decade. Akbar dispatched his second and third sons, Murād and Daniyāl, to head military operations in the northern Deccan, but it soon became clear that both princes were overmatched by the task. Upon the death of the Uzbek leader, 'Abdullāh Khan, in February 1598, Akbar recognized that the Uzbeks no longer posed a significant threat. In November, he left Lahore for Agra, which was re-established as the capital. Akbar then proceeded to Khandesh in the Deccan, where he personally took command of the imperial forces. By January 1601, the enemy capitulated and Akbar ended his campaign in the Deccan, a region that by force and strategem was to frustate Mughal territorial designs for the better part of the following century.

For the remaining five years of his life, Akbar had to contend with his openly rebellious son Salīm, who declared himself king and established a court at Allahabad. However irritating Salīm's regal pretensions must have been to Akbar, the prince never presented a real challenge to the throne; indeed, Salīm's personal excesses led many to support his own son, Khusraw, as Akbar's successor. Father and son were finally reconciled in late 1604, less than a year before Akbar died on the night of 25 October 1605.

### AKBAR AND HINDU CULTURE

Early in his reign, Akbar helped consolidate the territorial gains he had earned militarily by making a series of personal and institutional gestures designed to assuage the large Hindu population. One of the most important was his decision to encourage marriage among Mughal and ruling Rajput families. Akbar took the lead in this practice by wedding the daughter of the raja of nearby Amber, the first of many such transformations of potential enemies into intimate allies. But Akbar also issued decrees that affected the populace directly. Some measures, such as the termination of the time-honored practice of forcibly converting captives to Islam on pain of death, were driven by his sense of justice and his conviction that one's beliefs must be chosen freely; others, such as the abolition of a tax levied at pilgrimage sites and the poll-tax (*jizya*) on non-Muslims, were made with the recognition that such onerous and politically roiling taxes were unnecessary in light of the robust fiscal state of the empire. Other acts were more idiosyncratic in nature. Akbar's revulsion at the consumption of flesh led him to ban the slaughter of cows and personally embrace vegetarianism one day each week and for longer stretches periodically throughout the year, practices in keeping with Hindu, Jain, and Sufi customs. He also took up ritual solar worship, common to both Hinduism and Zoroastrianism, and wore markings on his forehead in the Hindu manner. All these gestures contributed to the deliberate fashioning of a synthesis of Muslim and Hindu cultures on an unprecedented scale. Most significant of all, however, was Akbar's practice of admitting Hindus and Indian-born Muslims to even the highest ranks of the Mughal administration, where the prestige and responsibilities of imperial service superseded ethnic loyalty. In this way, he further diluted the influence of Central Asian and Persian nobles and fostered a truly imperial culture.

Akbar's parentage and education inclined him to religious toleration. He was especially attracted by mysticism in its many forms; but in the early 1570s, he began to indulge in theoretical religious speculation of a decidedly ecumenical nature. At first, only Sunnī clerics were permitted to engage in the lively debates at court; within a few years, however, they had to contend with an increasingly varied clamor of religious voices, including those of Shīʿa, Zoroastrians, Jains, Hindus, and Christians. Akbar's personal interest in these debates was a search for a set of universal truths that transcended exclusionary sectarian dogma. He showed a remarkable tolerance of the precepts of all religions, saving his scorn for Muslim clerics who hectored their rivals with petty dogmatism. The abrupt departure from the religious bigotry with which the Muslim ruling class had traditionally viewed their Indian subjects and their ostensibly idolatrous religion was vexing enough to the Sunnī clergy, but when Akbar declared himself to be the ultimate arbiter of Islamic law, thereby explicitly subordinating traditional religious authority to his own, some religious leaders accused Akbar of lapsing into apostasy, a damnable offense used to foment rebellion in Bihar and Bengal. Upon the suppression of this rebellion in 1582, Akbar took another step in the aggrandizement of imperial status by proclaiming the *Dīn-i Ilāhī* (Divine Faith), misconstrued by detractors as a new faith, but described more accurately as a code of discipleship created along the lines of a Sufi order and prescribed for an elite group of nobles.[14] An initiate was called upon to demonstrate the four stages of absolute devotion by vowing to abnegate his life, property, honor, and religion for the emperor if the need arose. A more general and longer-lived reform followed two years later, when Akbar instituted the Ilāhī calendar, which took as its starting point the first New Year's day (*nawrūz*) after the official date of his accession on 11 March 1556, and used Persian solar months rather than the Islamic lunar ones. By designating his reign as the dawn of a new era, Akbar further strengthened the notion that he supplanted Islam as the measure of all things.

### AKBAR'S PATRONAGE AND RECEPTION OF BOOKS AND PAINTING

One of the many sections in the *Āʾīn-i Akbarī* (Annals of Akbar), completed by Abū al-Faẓl in 1596–97, is devoted to the arts of writing and painting. Most art historians have utterly neglected the extensive discussion of the art of writing even as they have lavished attention on the much briefer account of painting. One result of this anachronistic bias is that modern viewers of Mughal art have consistently elevated painting over writing. This understanding of the relative merit of the two arts is the inverse of Abū al-Faẓl's, who explicitly proclaims writing to be greater:

But though it is true that painters, especially those of Europe, succeed in drawing figures expressive of the conceptions which the artist has of any of the mental states, so much so, that people may mistake a picture for a reality: yet pictures are so much inferior to the written letter, inasmuch as the letter may embody the wisdom of bygone ages, and become a means to intellectual progress.[15]

After a formulaic tribute to Akbar's boundless expertise—"His Majesty pays much attention to both [arts], and is an excellent judge of form and thought"—the chronicler continues with a metaphysical discussion of letters—"the lamp of wisdom"—and of the articulate sounds that they represent. He then provides overviews of the eight types of script, calligraphic masters of old, and twelve accomplished calligraphers of the present age.

Turning from the form of writing to its substance, Abū al-Faẓl sketches the breadth of literary knowledge at the emperor's command. At the head of his list of books read out before Akbar is an assortment of Persian literary classics, including "the Bustān, the Shāhnāma, the collected Maṡnawīs [*Khamsa*] of Shaykh Niẓāmī, the works of Khusraw and Mawlānā Jāmī, the Dīwāns of Khāqānī, Anwarī, and several works on History...."[16] This group is followed by a sampling of ancient Indian texts translated from Sanskrit, a task that often fell to Abū al-Faẓl's brother, Fayẓī, or to their archrival, Badā'ūnī. Foremost among these works are two Hindu epics, the *Mahābhārata* and *Rāmāyaṇa*, translated in the 1580s. Other branches of Indian culture were represented by translations from the *Līlāwatī*, a mathematical treatise, a history of Kashmir, and the romance of *Nal wa Daman* (*Nala Damayantī*). Abū al-Faẓl's highlighting of these newly translated Indian texts and his concomitant omission of all works of traditional Islamic learning underscore the encyclopedic nature of knowledge contained in the imperial library, in which Indian culture figured ever more prominently.

Some parts of the library were kept in the harem, a point corroborated by the title used by a later librarian in several inspection notes written on the flyleaves of some manuscripts.[17] Most of the books, however, were apparently housed elsewhere, divided according to the faculty of knowledge that they represented, the language in which they were written, and their monetary value. Only the most valuable manuscripts, which generally bear some indication that they were reserved for the exclusive use of the emperor,[18] seem to have accompanied the imperial entourage as it moved about.[19]

It is paradoxical that the holdings of the imperial Mughal library, which, according to an inventory of 1605 numbered 24,000 volumes, expanded so greatly during the fifty-year reign of Akbar, for the emperor brought an unusual handicap to the throne: an inability to read. In typical fashion, Abū al-Faẓl presents Akbar's unlettered state not as a fault, but as a revelatory virtue:

And his possession of the most excellent sciences together with his disinclination for the learning of letters were a method of showing to mankind, at the time of the manifestation of the lights of hidden abundancies, that the lofty comprehension of the Lord of the Age was not learnt or acquired, but was part of the gift of God in which human effort had no part.[20]

Jahāngīr acknowledged his father's illiteracy more openly, but claimed that "he was so acquainted with the niceties of verse and prose composition that his deficiency was not thought of."[21] The means by which this deficiency was kept from the public eye is implied in Abū al-Faẓl's description of how the emperor actually used the thousands of books at his disposal:

Experienced people bring them daily and read them before His Majesty, who hears every book from the beginning to the end. At whatever page the readers daily stop, His Majesty makes with his own pen a sign, according to the number of pages; and rewards the readers with presents of cash, either in gold or silver, according to the number of leaves read out by them.[22]

One scholar has argued persuasively that Akbar's illiteracy was not the result of a disdain for a lettered education, but a manifestation of dyslexia, a neurological disorder that disrupts the cognitive processing of verbal symbols.[23] Yet the subsequent suggestion that dyslexia, which does not affect the perception of visual information, contributed significantly to Akbar's unparalleled appetite for painting generally, and to the production of heavily illustrated manuscripts specifically, is provocative but ultimately unconvincing.[24] The reasons for this are many. There were many fine illustrated manuscripts made during the course of Akbar's fifty-year reign, but the vast majority of the books in the library were unillustrated. Second, it does not recognize the efficacy of the courtly practice of the oral recitation of books. Despite his handicap, Akbar managed to become educated in all kinds of disciplines, including ones in which texts rarely had images at all. Certainly poetry, the most complicated and highly prized literary genre, does not need visual representation to be understood or appreciated. In texts such as Amīr Khusraw's *Khamsa*, meaning typically resides less in narrative, which lends itself to visual explication, than in verbal plays and rhythms, which do not. Moreover, no matter what the text, paintings remained an essentially superfluous source of information, never obviating the information supplied by verbal description or actual observation. This is apparent in the far greater amount of space allocated to the text in even the most heavily illustrated historical manuscripts, the genre that would benefit most obviously from the addition of illustrations. A careful examination of the scenes depicted in the illustrations finds them to be self-explanatory only rarely. Thus the series of images almost never stands independent of the text, requiring some verbal information to identify the central figures, actions, and intended location. In the end, this line of thought goes astray in assuming that the primary function of paintings in Mughal manuscripts is the explanation or dramatization of a text rather than the ornamentation of an object, a point that will be addressed in detail in Chapter 5.

By what criteria should we measure Akbar's personal interest in painting? Long ago a scholarly consensus emerged that the emperor was deeply preoccupied with painting. The evidence supporting this position is found primarily in a few paragraphs in the *Ā'īn-i Akbarī* (most of which will be quoted here), an annotated list of seventeen painters, and the existence of thousands of paintings of the period.

The centerpiece of the official testimony of Akbar's personal interest in painting is the following:

> Since it is an excellent source, both of study and entertainment, His Majesty, from the time he came to an awareness of things (i.e., his childhood), has taken a deep interest in painting and sought its spread and development. Consequently this magical art has gained in beauty.[25]

Feeling obliged to defend human representation against the charges of idolatry that some already antagonized Muslim clerics must have been inclined to level, Akbar advanced a theological apology for the art:

> I cannot tolerate those who make the slightest criticism of this art. It seems to me that a painter is better than most in gaining a knowledge of God. Each time he draws a living being he must draw each and every limb of it, but seeing that he cannot bring it to life must perforce give thought to the miracle wrought by the Creator and thus obtain knowledge of him.[26]

These two statements declare painting to be an illuminating means of knowing God and the world, thus offering a rationale for the elevation of painting to a uniquely privileged position during the reign of an exceptionally inquisitive emperor. But this rationale is convincing only when the statements are taken in isolation. A broader and more critical reading of the *Ā'īn-i Akbarī*, particularly the fulsome descriptions of Akbar's personal expertise in music, gunmaking, and the production of fine cloth, begins to mitigate the privileged status that painting purportedly enjoyed. Of music, for example, Abū al-Faẓl proclaims, "His Majesty has such a knowledge of the sciences of music as trained musicians do not possess; and he is likewise an excellent hand in performing, especially on the *naqāra*."[27] Of cloth stuffs, the chronicler writes,

> His Majesty himself acquired in a short time a theoretical and practical knowledge of the whole trade; and on account of the care bestowed upon them the intelligent workmen of this country soon improved. All kinds of hair-weaving and silk-spinning were brought to perfection.[28]

Just as Abū al-Faẓl extols the emperor's firsthand knowledge of these other arts, so too does he invoke the divine in defense of practices as controversial as the worship of sun and fire,[29] or as mundane as the display of royal tents.[30] In short, while the chronicler's accounts of institutions and concrete matters can reasonably be considered reliable, the language he uses to describe the emperor's character and accomplishments—and particularly the emperor's hand in innovations and improvements in most matters—is too colored with panegyrical exaggerations to be taken at face value. Without a proper awareness of these literary conventions, one can easily take Abū al-Faẓl's remarks as proof that Akbar's involvement with the visual arts was profound, a conclusion that now appears unsubstantiated, if not altogether erroneous.

The contemporary account of Mughal painters also merits re-examination. In one oft-cited passage in the *Ā'īn-i Akbarī*, Abū al-Faẓl lists seventeen major painters:

> Among the forerunners on this high road of knowledge is Mīr Sayyid 'Alī of Tabriz. He had learnt a little from his father. When he obtained the honour to serve His Majesty and thus gained in knowledge, he became renowned in his profession and bountiful in good fortune. Next there is Khwāja 'Abd al-Ṣamad, the *shīrīn qalam* of Shiraz. Though he knew this art before he joined the royal service, the transmuting glance of the king has raised him to a more sublime level and his images have gained a depth of spirit. Under his tutelage many novices have become masters. Then there was Daswanta, the son of a palanquin-bearer, who was in the service of this workshop and, urged by a natural desire, used to draw images and designs on walls. One day the far-reaching glance of His Majesty fell on those things and, in its penetrating manner, discerned the spirit of a master working in them. Consequently, His Majesty entrusted him to the Khwāja. In just a short time he became matchless in his time and most excellent, but the darkness of

insanity enshrouded the brilliance of his mind and he died, a suicide. He has left several masterpieces. In designing, painting faces, colouring, portrait painting, and other aspects of this art, Basāwan has come to be uniquely excellent. Many perspicacious connoisseurs give him preference over Daswanta. The other famous and excellent painters are Kīsū, Lāl, Mukund, Miskīn, Farrukh the Qalmāq, Mādho, Jagan, Mahes, Khemkaran, Tāra, Sānwlā, Harbans, and Rām. My discourses would get too long if I were to discuss each of them, so I have chosen just one flower from each garden and just one ear from every sheaf.[31]

Despite its brevity, this paragraph is invaluable. It provides biographical sketches of the long-departed Mīr Sayyid 'Alī and the aged 'Abd al-Ṣamad, whose careers are described more fully in earlier Mughal sources, and indicates that the latter supervised the training of other artists.[32] It also explicitly casts Akbar as the galvanizing agent of change in 'Abd al-Ṣamad's style, a claim made again for the third painter listed, Dasavanta.[33] Dasavanta is described as the son of a palanquin-bearer, though the Persian word used to indicate this humble occupation probably actually designates a special caste of wall-painters, an activity mentioned immediately thereafter.[34] While other artists are lauded in Mughal chronicles as producing "matchless" works, Dasavanta stands alone among Indian-born artists in drawing comment on his personality, almost certainly because of his tragic demise. Still more interesting is the ensuing comparison of Dasavanta's work to Basāvana's by "perspicacious connoisseurs," a phrase that implies the regular practice of qualitative evaluations of painters' works.

Abū al-Faẓl then lists thirteen more artists of renown, but conditions his selection by noting that they represent only a sample of the masters at hand. In spite of this disclaimer, the list has widely been construed as hierarchic, sometimes absolutely so, because it conforms reasonably closely to ones modern scholars might make for the period.[35] Indeed, most of the artists named by Abū al-Faẓl were assigned illustrations in the finest manuscripts of the 1580s and 1590s—including seven of the thirteen painters whose work is found in the Walters *Khamsa.* Nonetheless, there are some rather anomalous inclusions and omissions in Abū al-Faẓl's list. Neither Tārā nor Haribans, for example, would figure as major artists by any modern reckoning; the former is known from eleven paintings in five manuscripts from the 1580s and a few portrait faces in a single painting of the 1590s, and the latter is practically unknown.[36] Conversely, Abū al-Faẓl passes over altogether six major artists who contributed to most of the premier manuscripts of the 1950s: Dharmadāsa, Narasimha, Sūrādāsa Gujārātī, Farrukh Cela, Bhīma Gujarātī, and Manōhara. Thus it seems safe to conclude that while the chronicler's roster of master painters was shaped by such factors as productivity, current activity, and contemporary assessments of skill, it was also somewhat haphazard in nature, as Abū al-Faẓl himself conceded. Aside from the fact that it demonstrates that some painters were known by name in the innermost court circles, it signifies no more than the comparable list of contemporary calligraphers.

We are on surer ground when we turn to the institution of the painting workshop, which is documented in detail in two complementary sources. Both the *Ā'īn-i Akbarī* and ascriptions on Mughal paintings agree that the atelier was comprised of slightly more than a hundred artists. Nearly all were Indian-born, hailing from places as far-flung as Gujarat, Gwalior, Lahore, and Kashmir. In addition to Mīr Sayyid 'Alī and 'Abd al-Ṣamad, there were also two other Persian-trained painters: Farrukh Beg, who came from Kabul in late 1585; and Āqā Riẓā, who arrived from Mashhad only slightly later. In both Indian and Persian cultures the acquisition of skill in painting and calligraphy was a hereditary affair, as is indicated in the brief biographical notices available for a few Persian-born artists, the inclusion in the caste name of wall-painters (*gohār*), and the explicit expression of a familial relationship (e.g., Sūradāsa, son of Isar) in many ascriptions.[37] The frequent use of the epithet *khānazāda* (houseborn) in ascriptions on paintings also indicates that many sons followed their fathers into service in the imperial workshop.

The unparalleled scale of production of illustrated manuscripts during Akbar's reign promoted the development of specialized functions in all phases of bookmaking, from the preparation of paper to the fabrication of the binding. A system of formalized collaboration was introduced, with one artist normally charged with the design of an illustration and another with the actual execution of all but the most important faces or figures. A few manuscripts preserve fragmentary ascriptions scrawled in black along the very lower edge of the painted folio; these seem to be work orders intended for use within the atelier itself.[38] By contrast, the larger and more neatly written ascriptions on most manuscripts, added by clerks after the paintings were completed, apparently documented actual achievement for purposes of compensation:

> A very large number of painters has been set to work. Each week the several *dāroghas* [supervisors] and *bitikchīs* [clerks] submit before the king the work done by each artist, and His Majesty gives a reward and increases the monthly salaries according to the excellence displayed.[39]

A terse remark at the end of Abū al-Fażl's discussion of the painting workshop provides a critical clue to the average wage of painters during Akbar's reign:

> By serving in this workshop a great many *manṣabdārs*, *aḥadīs*, and other troopers have gained in distinction. The pay of a foot-soldier is not more than 1200 *dāms* and not less than 600 *dāms*.[40]

The importance of these two sentences has been overlooked. Their placement can only mean that most artists held a nominal military rank, be it the lofty title of *manṣabdār* or *aḥadī* or the humbler one of an ordinary foot-soldier, much like members of military bands in modern times.[41] Moreover, the precise rate of compensation allows us to compare the remuneration of artists to both the value of the paintings they made and to the pay of workmen employed in other departments. With a copper *dām* worth one-fortieth of a rupee in 1595–96, we can therefore calculate that low-ranking imperial artists earned between fifteen and thirty rupees per month, and ones of higher status commensurately more. Such wages accord with what we can now estimate the cost of individual paintings to have been at the Mughal court. Two manuscripts illustrated in the 1580s with large and abundant paintings bear revealing inventories of the costs involved in their production. The cost of the 176 paintings in the Jaipur *Rāmāyaṇa* was recorded as 860 rupees—an average of only five rupees per painting; the total expense of the 168 paintings of the *Razmnāma* was given as 3,602 rupees—an average of twenty-one and a half rupees per painting.[42] Allowing an average production time of forty days for a painting of the size and complexity of those in these two manuscripts, and positing an average painter's salary of twenty rupees, we can determine that the cost of each painting would have been approximately twenty-seven rupees, however, the sum might have been divided among the team of two or three artists.[43]

Painters were better compensated than workmen in many other imperial departments. Musicians who played in the imperial band, for example, earned between 74 and 340 *dāms* per month; gunmakers, 100 to 400 *dāms* per month; and mahouts on the highest breed of elephants, 200 *dāms*.[44] By contrast, servants employed in the harem drew salaries of 20 to 51 rupees per month, that is, nearly twice those of artists and ten times those of the aforementioned workmen, while engravers of the coin dies commanded between 500 and 700 rupees per month.[45] The considerably higher salaries of these last two occupations indicate that two considerations factored heavily in the determination of monthly compensation: the proximity of the activity to the innermost circles of the court and the degree of involvement with the highly revered art of fine writing. Thus painters benefited in part from their many opportunities to stand in the shadow of the court, where untold riches circulated freely. Moreover, their base level of compensation was enhanced by the indeterminate rewards artists received, whether routinely or on truly special occasions alone.[46] Yet painters must have remained quite apart from their social betters, whose income from land grants and administrative positions was measured in the thousands of rupees. Abū al-Fażl's aforementioned remark that supervisors presented the books and paintings to the emperor also underscores the almost total lack of unmediated interaction between the emperor and his artists.[47] Such a distance between patron and painter is corroborated by contemporary visual evidence. In all of imperial Mughal painting there are only two images of an artist personally presenting a painting to the emperor, one of whom is the young Abū al-Ḥasan, who, by all estimations, was Jahāngīr's favorite painter.[48]

Nonetheless, a few artists did assume more prominent roles at Akbar's court. 'Abd al-Ṣamad enjoyed a particularly long and illustrious career, attaining the prestigious positions of master of the mint at Fathpur-Sikri in 1577–78, an official role in the management of the royal household in 1582–83, and the title of *dīwān* of Multan in 1586–87.[49] Another measure of his special relationship at court was Jahāngīr's statement that the artist had received from Humāyūn the

> title of *S̲h̲irin-qalam* (Sweet pen), and in his council had attained a great dignity and was on intimate terms with him (the king). He was one of the chief men of S̲h̲īrāz. My honoured father, on account of his former services, paid him great honour and reverence.[50]

Both Akbar and Jahāngīr extended this special intimacy to 'Abd al-Ṣamad's son, Muḥammad Sharīf. The artist professed his adherence to Akbar's *Dīn-i Ilāhī* in the prefatory phrase added to his signature in the Keir *Khamsa* of Niẓāmī: "the work of the disciple of the beginning of the practice of the four stages of sincerity, with foot in place, Sharīf."[51] The use of this phrase must have carried a significance at the time, for no other artist presumed to express his personal allegiance in this manner. Indeed, it even appears on Muḥammad Sharīf's personal seal, whose impression on the reverse of a painting in the imperial library is evidence that the artist also functioned as a librarian.[52] Muḥammad Sharīf's relationship with the imperial family deepened under Jahāngīr, so much so that the emperor wrote:

> ...his connection with me is such that I look upon him as a brother, a son, a friend, and a companion. As I had perfect confidence in his friendship, intelligence, learning, and acquaintance with affairs, having made

him Grand Vizier, I promoted him to the rank of 5,000 with 5,000 horse and the lofty title of *Amīru-l-umarā*, to which no title of my servants is superior.[53]

It is worth noting, however, that both painters' steady rise in status coincided with a marked decline in their own artistic production; indeed, Muḥammad Sharīf's oeuvre is limited to a mere nine paintings, the last two of which are dated 1591 and 1619.[54]

Not surprisingly, Akbar's religious and cultural pluralism had an effect on his library and painting atelier. Although the workshop produced fine copies of the standard fare of classical Persian literature—the *Khamsas* of Niẓāmī and Amīr Khusraw, the *Gulistān* of Sa'dī, and the *Shāhnāma* of Firdawsī—the library staff was also directed to translate a number of Indian texts from Sanskrit so that Mughal courtiers might learn something of Hindu beliefs. The most comprehensive expositions of Hindu classical literature, the *Rāmāyaṇa* and *Mahābhārata*, were illustrated immediately after their translation in the 1580s. These texts spurred the introduction of entirely new imagery into Mughal painting. Dhoti-clad Hindu kings wear crowns topped with flowers; Hindu gods are rendered consistently with textually prescribed features, including skin color, facial features, and hand-held attributes. But a deep sympathy toward Indian culture permeated the imagery of even classic Persian romances. The first painting of the Walters *Khamsa*, for example, depicts a rarely illustrated anecdote in which a Muslim pilgrim looks upon a brahman's devotion with some admiration (fig. 4). Likewise, two illustrations of the *Hasht Bihisht* portion of the same manuscript represent a magical statue in Egypt and a truth-telling talisman as specimens of distinctly Indian statuary, albeit with only a lotus as an indigenous attribute and in only a generic temple setting (figs. 32 and 33). Yet traces of the native traditions in which at least some of the many Hindu artists in the imperial atelier presumably were trained are largely absent from the Mughal style, especially after 1575.

Christianity had nearly the inverse effect on Mughal culture and art. The coterie of missionaries sent from Goa were greatly encouraged by the reverence that the imperial family showed for Christian images, particularly those of the Virgin, but to their dismay their proselytizing efforts never culminated in the conversion of large numbers of Indians or any member of the imperial family. Copies of Christian texts in translation promoted understanding, but the Mughals responded more enthusiastically to the images used to illustrate these texts. A manuscript of the well-known Plantin Bible, presented at court in 1580, inspired several versions of the allegorical figure of royal piety featured in its frontispiece.[55] A number of faithful copies after Flemish prints of the Virgin and saints began to appear in the 1580s, their Indian origin betrayed largely by minor iconographic aberrations and occasional odd coloring. In 1595, a Portuguese painter was summoned to the Jesuit mission at the Mughal court and remained there for most of the year; although the unnamed painter was kept mercilessly busy during his sojourn, he is known by only two works, both of which are oil copies after Flemish engravings.[56]

Mughal artists quickly demonstrated that their copies of European images were not merely technical displays of their formidable mimetic abilities, for they extrapolated the wondrous formal means used to render exotic European motifs, and soon applied the former to a whole range of paintings. This process seems to have commenced as early as the mid-1560s, when the supply of such foreign images must have been no more than a trickle; thereafter the adaptation of European art blossomed in tentative spurts in the hands of a few painters who were especially receptive to these new visual ideas. The effect of these images on Mughal art was catalytic. Three-dimensional modeling applied to individual forms was surely the most important formal device gleaned from these prints; with it, Mughal painters began to modify the insistently brilliant colors and pronounced contours of Persian art and the concomitant flattened pictorial space. The initial results are somewhat discordant. As individual forms gain unprecedented pictorial weight, they seem to jostle against one another in settings that retain their traditional spatial compression. By the early 1580s, a number of artists were using diagonals systematically to open up the underlying compositional grid, so that the swelling forms of figures could be accommodated more easily in newly spacious courtyards. By the late 1580s, some Mughal artists began to experiment with another European device, atmospheric perspective, and filled the uppermost register of their compositions with minute and bluish cityscapes, trees, and mountains. For the most part this distance-evoking register remains a discrete entity within the picture, unconnected with the space occupied by the main characters of the scene. By the time the Walters *Khamsa* was illustrated in the late 1590s, however, a few Mughal artists had managed to integrate the two spatial zones (see, for example, figs. 4 and 31). In most cases they achieved this new spatial coherence by replacing the familiar high screen of rocks behind the central figures with more gently sloping landscape forms, and by marking out intermediate distances with inward-turned figures rendered in a scale that diminished systematically.

Although the vast majority of paintings of this period were made as manuscript illustrations, the atelier also produced small individual paintings. In some cases, the paintings are full-fledged scenes inspired by familiar literary themes, such as Noah's Ark or the emaciated figure of the lovesick Majnūn, and require no written explanation of their imagery. In other cases, the paintings consist of only a figure or two against a nondescript background. The subjects of these paintings are usually generic types inherited from Persian art—a master and pupil, a mounted prince, a handsome youth—and have no obvious reference in literature or history. These kinds of paintings may have been acquired individually by members of court, but they were also assembled with various specimens of calligraphy into albums, which have survived intact only rarely.

The most interesting type of independent painting was the portrait, a genre virtually unknown in Persian and Indian painting before this time. The earliest expressions of portraiture in Mughal painting seem to date from the late 1570s, and typically are small, full-length views of individuals in profile on a plain green ground. A high-minded impetus behind the sudden development of this genre is suggested by Abū al-Fazl, who writes, "At His Majesty's command portraits have been painted of all of His Majesty's servants and a huge album has been made. Thus the dead have gained a new life, and the living an eternity."[57]

Contrary to our expectations, low-ranking or even unidentified courtiers are the first figures recorded in this manner. Curiously, the emperor and his immediate family did not often avail themselves of this means of assuring their own immortality. Despite accounts that adherents of the *Dīn-i Ilāhī* were presented with miniature portraits of their worldly and spiritual master to be worn in their turbans, no such medallion-sized portraits of Akbar survive from his reign. Indeed, to our knowledge, only a handful of independent portraits of Akbar were made during his lifetime. One of these, an equestrian portrait by Muḥammad Sharīf, shows Akbar as a powerfully built, dark-skinned figure with narrow eyes and a thin mustache (fig. 1). This accords reasonably well with a description of the emperor's physical appearance provided by a Jesuit missionary:

> [He is] of good stature, sturdy body, legs and arms, broad-shouldered. The configuration of his face is ordinary, and does not reflect the grandeur and dignity of the person because, besides being Chinese-like as the Mughals usually are, it is lean, sparse of beard, wrinkled and not very fair. The eyes are small but extremely vivid and when he looks at you it seems as if they hurt you with their brightness, and thus nothing escapes his notice, be it a person or something trivial, and they also reflect sharpness of mind and keenness of intellect. And so he is much feared by his subjects. To his people he displays a certain amount of cheerfulness which in no way detracts from his imperial bearing. He dresses plainly.[58]

Fig. 1. Equestrian portrait of Akbar. By Muḥammad Sharīf. ca. 1585. 16.0 x 12.4 cm. British Museum 1948 10-9-066 (By permission of the British Library).

Yet even in this ostensibly naturalistic painting, observation is clearly tempered by artistic convention and habit. Thus, while the configuration of the emperor's brow and nose differs from that of the swordbearer behind him, the coincidence of smooth features and taut, ageless skin in both figures suggests that Muḥammad Sharīf never attempted to produce a faithful record of every feature of his two subjects. Instead, like other Mughal artists of this period, he concentrated on Akbar's dusky complexion and thin, downturned mustache and grafted them on to a relatively standard figure type.

Such portraits were rarely incorporated into contemporary manuscript illustrations. Mughal painters occasionally indulged in a form of visual flattery employed elsewhere in the Islamic world, that is, endowing the figures of rulers in illustrations of literary texts with the reigning king's features.[59] The practice now appears to have begun as early as the reign of Humāyūn, whose own distinctive facial shape and pointed beard grace the figure of Nawfal in one illustration of the Bibliothèque Nationale *Khamsa* of Niẓāmī, while a youthful face presumed to be that of Prince Akbar stands in for the traditionally bearded one of the mature king Bahrām Gūr in another.[60] Despite the vastly greater number of

Fig. 2. Akbar receives ambassadors from Badakhshān and the Deccan. Designed by Miskīn, painted by Śravaṇa, eight special faces painted by Mādhava. *Akbarnāma*, ca. 1586–87. 33.1 x 20.0 cm. Victoria and Albert Museum I.S. 2-1986 114/117.

manuscripts illustrated during Akbar's reign, the sovereign's image is known to have been inserted into only three manuscripts: twice in the British Library *Gulistān* of Sa'dī, where in one instance it is complemented by a dedicatory inscription praising Akbar,[61] and once each in the Cleveland *Ṭūṭī-nāma* of ca. 1570 and the Keir *Khamsa* of Niẓāmī of ca. 1586–90.[62] Thus, Akbar's surreptitious appearance in a scene on the lacquer covers of the British Library *Khamsa* of Niẓāmī is quite exceptional.[63]

The emperor, of course, figures prominently in the many stories commissioned and illustrated in the 1580s and 1590s to celebrate the lives of Bābur, Humāyūn, Akbar, and their glorious Timurid ancestors. Nowhere is this more evident than in the three illustrated copies of the *Akbarnāma* produced between 1585 and 1597. The earliest manuscript, now preserved in the Victoria and Albert Museum (V&A), originally illustrated a still unidentified Akbari history; ten years later, in 1595–96, when Abū al-Faẓl had just finished composing his new history of Akbar, the *Akbarnāma*, members of the library staff substituted the text of the revised history, even covering over passages of the earlier text on the painted folios of the second volume with snippets of the revised text.[64] In this refurbished manuscript, the emperor is depicted as engaged in a host of royal activities—directing the troops in battle, receiving homage from defeated foes, watching dance performances, and the like. Akbar can be picked out readily in most of these scenes by virtue of his position, which usually is slightly isolated from the surrounding mass of attendants or courtiers. In other examples, royal attributes, such as a plumed turban, serve to distinguish the emperor. Nonetheless, apart from the few illustrated historical events in which Akbar was of such a tender age that he had to be depicted as a boy or youth, Mughal artists regularly portrayed the emperor in *Akbarnāma* illustrations merely by invoking the same visual features that Muḥammad Sharīf accentuates in his equestrian portrait, namely the combination of a dark complexion and thin mustache. Hence, we find that despite a wide range of personal styles, which could endow the emperor on occasion with an idiosyncratically wide face or long nose, Mughal artists began to introduce a very rudimentary kind of portraiture to manuscript illustration.

In the V&A *Akbarnāma*, however, they generally reserved the application of a portrait-like face to the figure of Akbar himself. This is surprising not only because the manuscript was illustrated during the lifetimes of many of the personages depicted therein, when firsthand observation was still possible, but also because a number of paintings bear ascriptions which indicate that a separate artist was assigned to do portraits or "special faces."[65] By careful visual analysis, we can determine that in many cases this special treatment was limited to the emperor, but in others it was extended to several ancillary figures. These figures—who are not necessarily the highest-ranking nobles in the scene—often elude precise identification, for they lack the identifying labels written on the turbans or collars of their counterparts in later Jahāngīrī court scenes, and can rarely be matched with contemporary inscribed portraits of nobles and courtiers.

One notable exception to this rule is a scene that shows Akbar receiving ambassadors from Badakhshan and the Deccan in 1577 (fig. 2). The formal ascription written in red below the illustration names Miskīn as the designer and Śravaṇa as the painter. But this customary information is supplemented by a phrase which specifies that the artist Mādhava executed eight portraits in the painting. Still more extraordinary is the list of the names of four nobles in the outer margin: Rāja Bhagavanta Dāsa (of Amber), Rāja Ṭodaramāla, Ṣādiq Khān, and Khidmat Rāī. One of these, Ṣādiq Khān, a governor old enough to have served under Humāyūn, can be identified as the white-bearded figure turning toward his companion in the center of the painting.[66] Likewise, a wealth of independent portraits of Rāja Man Singh of Amber allows us to identify him as the portly, dark-skinned figure standing before Ṣādiq Khān. Yet in both these instances, the figure's identity is still determined more by virtue of relatively standard features such as complexion, corpulence, or age than by specific facial details.

These examples suggest that by the 1580s the tradition of rendering the likeness of specific individuals was already sufficiently established in Mughal painting to make inroads into an entirely different kind of painting. This trend continued modestly in the 1590s, culminating in the many identifiable historical figures in the 1596–97 Beatty *Akbarnāma*. By the early seventeenth century, however, when independent portraits had become a much more important genre and manuscript illustration had fallen from favor, this tradition had completely penetrated the two genres of painting, and the iconography of imperial images was influenced profoundly by European symbolism.

## THE *DE LUXE* ILLUSTRATED MANUSCRIPT

Among the many Mughal illuminated manuscripts, a handful stand out by virtue of the conspicuous luxury with which every part of the book was made. In these books, the text paper is almost always burnished to an exquisite finish and sprinkled with gold; the paper of the surrounding margins, supple and often varied in color, is sometimes further adorned with delicate golden floral and animal motifs. The text itself is written in a manner whose elegance is obvious even to the unpracticed eye, the result of painstaking craftsmanship by a preeminent calligrapher. Likewise, the illuminations announcing the major textual divisions are more elaborate than usual, a treatment extended often even to the space between the text columns or around the rubrics. Paintings are sparse but extremely fine, each apparently the handiwork of a single artist. When all these features come together to create a truly superb work, we may advisedly use the term *de luxe* manuscript.

No manuscript produced early in Akbar's reign rivals the level of quality achieved in the *de luxe* manuscripts of the 1580s and 1590s, but a few represent clear steps in that direction. The *'Ashīqa* of Amīr Khusraw in the National Museum, completed by highly esteemed Sulṭān Bāyazīd (known as Dawrī) in Muḥarram 976/June–July 1568, exhibits many of the features that come to characterize the *de luxe* type, including fine writing, colored borders with decorations, and at least two large, highly accomplished illustrations.[67] Despite these qualities, the manuscript was never regarded as an extraordinary work, as is indicated by the second-class qualitative category and valuation of 500 rupees assigned to it by later court librarians.[68] Another early manuscript, the 1570 School of Oriental and African Studies *Anwār-i Suhaylī*, takes a different path toward the *de luxe* idea.[69] The calligraphy is undistinguished and the margins are left plain, but the paintings achieve a new physical and aesthetic prominence in the manuscript, moving well beyond simple narrative requirements, no small task in a book of didactic fables.

In the last two decades of the sixteenth century, the imperial atelier produced simultaneously at least three different kinds of illustrated manuscripts: profusely illustrated translations of Hindu texts, equally large historical texts, and a series of Persian literary classics. The last of these types of literature included prose collections of witty, didactic tales, such as the *Gulistān* (Rose-Garden) of Sa'dī and the *Bahāristān* (Garden of Spring) of Jāmī, as well as the poetical masterpieces of the foremost authors of medieval Persia: the *Dīwān* of Anwarī, the *Dīwān* of Shāhī, the *Khamsa* of Niẓāmī, and the *Ḥadīqat al-Ḥaqīqat* of Sanā'ī. Amīr Khusraw was the lone Indian-born poet in this select group.

The production of so many belletristic texts in a span of twenty years was a major impetus behind the flowering of the *de luxe* manuscript, for only they were deemed worthy of the effort involved in the production of a *de luxe* manuscript. Some books, notably the 1588 Sackler Museum *Dīwān* of Anwarī and the ca. 1595 *Dīwān* of Shāhī, are pocket-sized marvels, their minuteness reinforcing their overall daintiness. Others, such as the dispersed 1596 *Gulistān*[70] and the *Ḥadīqat al-Ḥaqīqat* of 1008/1599–1600, are more ambitious in both size and illustration.[71] Grandest of all are the British Library *Khamsa* of Niẓāmī and the Walters *Khamsa* of Amīr Khusraw, to which we now turn.

## NOTES

1. Bābur, Ẓahīr al-Dīn Muḥammad, *The Baburnama. Memoirs of Babur, Prince and Emperor.* Edited and annotated by W. Thackston (New York and Oxford, 1996), 350–51.

2. *The Baburnama*, 360.

3. *The Baburnama*, 214.

4. *The Baburnama*, 26. It is most curious that this critique of a painter's style is more specific than any written during the reigns of Akbar or Jahāngīr.

5. Bābur's descendant Jahāngīr attests that a short manuscript entitled *Qalam-i Turkī* in the Rampur Raza Library is written in Bābur's hand.

6. A lavishly illustrated *Shāhnāma* of ca. 1440 in the Royal Asiatic Society is the only known manuscript impressed with Bābur's personal seal. In *The Baburnama*, 319, Bābur relates that he "entered the fortress and went into Ghazi Khan's library, which held a few valuable books. I

gave some of them to Humayun and sent others to Kamran. Although there were many learned books, there were not so many as I expected."

7. *The Baburnama*, 414.

8. See F. Richard, "An Unpublished Manuscript from the Atelier of the Emperor Humāyūn, the Khamsa Smith-Lesouëf 216 of the Bibliothèque Nationale," in *Confluence of Cultures. French Contributions to Indo-Persian Studies*, ed. F. Delvoye (New Delhi, 1994), 38–39.

9. See Richard, "An Unpublished Manuscript," and Chahryar Adle, "New Data on the Dawn of Mughal Painting and Calligraphy," in *The Making of Indo-Persian Culture*, eds. Muzaffar Alam, F. Delvoye, and M. Gaborieau (New Delhi, 2000), 167–222.

10. For this type of turban, see Richard, "An Unpublished Manuscript," pl. VIII.

11. Abū al-Faẓl, *Ā'īn-i Akbarī* II, 191. C. Asher, *Architecture of Mughal India* (Cambridge, 1992), 51, suggests that this phrase connoted architectural perfection in a style that stretched from one end of the empire to another.

12. Abū al-Faẓl, *The Akbar Nama of Abu-l-Fazl* (New Delhi, rep. 1977), III, 748.

13. See J. Richards, *The Mughal Empire* (Cambridge, 1993), 52.

14. See S. A. A. Rizvi, *Religious and Intellectual History of the Muslims During Akbar's Reign* (New Delhi, 1975), especially 373–417. The estimate of the number of adherents ranges from eighteen to a few thousand.

15. Abū al-Faẓl, *Ā'īn-i Akbarī* (rep. New Delhi, 1977), I, 103.

16. Abū al-Faẓl, *Ā'īn-i Akbarī* I, 110.

17. Dawlat is designated as the custodian of the harem library (*taḥwīldār-i maḥall*) in three manuscripts. See J. Seyller, "The Inspection and Valuation of Manuscripts in the Imperial Mughal Library," *Artibus Asiae*, 57, nos. 3/4 (1997), 248, note 15.

18. They are marked with the term *khāṣṣa*, a term defined immediately as signifying appointed for the exclusive use of His Majesty.

19. A number of books, for example, bear inspection notes that supply the name of either Lahore and Srinagar and a date in the mid-1590s. See Seyller, "The Inspection and Valuation of Manuscripts," 249, notes 19 and 20.

20. Abū al-Faẓl, *Akbarnāma* I, 589.

21. Jahāngīr, *Tūzuk-i Jahāngīrī* I, 33.

22. Abū al-Faẓl, *Ā'īn-i Akbarī* I, 110. I have never seen any evidence of such marks on any manuscript known to have been in the imperial library. Other physical evidence of Akbar's handling of individual manuscripts, such as impressions of his personal seal and inscriptions in his hand, is exceedingly rare.

23. See E. Smart, "Akbar, Illiterate Genius," in *Kalādarśana*, ed. J. Williams (New Delhi, 1981), 99–107. If Akbar suffered from this affliction to the degree that he could barely write, his alleged connoisseurship of writing would be inconceivable.

24. This view is advanced in Smart, "Akbar, Illiterate Genius," 103.

25. Abū al-Faẓl, *Ā'īn-i Akbarī*, as translated by C. M. Naim in Chandra, *The Ṭūṭī-Nāma*, 182.

26. Abū al-Faẓl, *Ā'īn-i Akbarī*, as translated by C. M. Naim in Chandra, *The Ṭūṭī-Nāma*, 184.

27. Abū al-Faẓl, *Ā'īn-i Akbarī* I, 54.

28. Abū al-Faẓl, *Ā'īn-i Akbarī* I, 94.

29. Abū al-Faẓl, *Ā'īn-i Akbarī* I, 50: "...there can be nothing improper in the veneration of that exalted element which is the source of man's existence, and of the duration of his life."

30. Abū al-Faẓl, *Ā'īn-i Akbarī* I, 55.

31. Abū al-Faẓl, *Ā'īn-i Akbarī*, as translated by C. M. Naim in Chandra, *The Ṭūṭī-Nāma*, 183–84.

32. See Chandra, *The Ṭūṭī-Nāma*, 18–26; M. Dickson and S. C. Welch, *The Houghton Shahnameh* (Cambridge, Massachusetts, 1981), 178–200.

33. See M. Beach, "Jahāngīr's *Jahāngīr-Nāma*," in *The Powers of Art*, ed. B. S. Miller (Delhi, 1992), 224–25; and Seyller, *Workshop and Patron in Mughal India*, 313–21.

34. Here I accept the idea first advanced by Moti Chandra that the commonly found *kahhār* is nothing more than an ambiguous Persian transliteration for *gohār*, the name of a caste engaged in painting on walls. The idea is published in Chandra, *The Ṭūṭī-Nāma*, 183, note 14.

35. Beach, *Mughal and Rajput Painting*, 39; A. Okada, *Indian Miniatures of the Mughal Court* (New York, 1992), 77, 95, 118, 128; S. P. Verma, "La'l: The Forgotten Master," in *Mughal Masters. Further Studies*, ed. A. Das (Mumbai, 1998), 69.

36. Tārā added portraits to a painting in the 1596 *Jāmi' al-Tawārīkh* and painted two illustrations in the 1588–91 Jaipur *Rāmāyaṇa*. Haribans is documented by a single ascribed work (f. 58b) in the Chester Beatty Library *Yōga Vaṣiṣṭha*, but Leach has attributed eleven other paintings in the manuscript to him. Since the text of the manuscript was completed in December 1602—some five years after the *Ā'īn-i Akbarī* was completed—the artist must have been active in the 1590s as well.

37. For the meaning of the term *gohār*, see note 34. Many examples of familial relationships among artists appear in the 1598–1600 *Razmnāma*, which is reconstructed in J. Seyller, "Model and Copy: The Illustration of Three *Razmnāma* Manuscripts," *Archives of Asian Art*, 38 (1985), 56–62.

38. See Seyller, "Scribal Notes," 250.

39. Abū al-Faẓl, *Ā'īn-i Akbarī*, as translated by C. M. Naim in Chandra, *The Ṭūṭī-Nāma*, 182.

40. Abū al-Faẓl, *Ā'īn-i Akbarī*, as translated by C. M. Naim in Chandra, *The Ṭūṭī-Nāma*, 184.

41. Richards, *The Mughal Empire*, 298, 301, defines a *manṣabdār* as an officer holding a specified numerical rank and title awarded by the emperor, and *aḥadīs* as a cadre of high-status cavalrymen employed directly by the emperor.

42. For a discussion of this issue and a full transcription of the inventories of expense, see Seyller, "The Inspection and Valuation of Manuscripts." I cannot explain the dramatic difference in the cost of the two manuscripts, which are very similar in size and quality.

43. For the amount of time allocated to different types of Mughal illustrations, see Seyller, "Scribal Notes," 256–61.

44. Abū al-Faẓl, *Āʾīn-i Akbarī* I, 54; I, 119; and I, 132. There are 100 *dāms* to the rupee.

45. Abū al-Faẓl, *Āʾīn-i Akbarī* I, 46; I, 22.

46. For the wages of a skilled workman, as recorded in 1626, see I. Habib, "A System of Trimetallism in the Age of the 'Price Revolution': Effects of the Silver Influx on the Mughal Monetary System," in *The Imperial Monetary System of Mughal India*, ed. J. F. Richards (New York and Delhi, 1987), 154. We have little evidence of the size of the bonuses granted as special measures of appreciation, but as gifts, they probably entered into the courtly realm in which grandiose sums were regularly bandied about. The painter Farrukh Beg, for example, received a gift of 2,000 rupees from Jahāngīr when he returned to court in December 1609, and Bishndāsa was awarded an elephant upon his return in 1620 from an embassy to the court of Shāh ʿAbbās.

47. This point is often obscured in many modern accounts of the creative process in Mughal painting, in which patron and painter purportedly discuss both minute aspects of style and profound visions of reality. See, for example, M. Brand and G. Lowry, *Akbar's India: Art from the Mughal City of Victory* (New York, 1985), 126–27, and Welch, *India: Art and Culture*, 158. One interesting exception to this is an anecdote of Jahāngīr directing an artist to make corrections to portraits of two deceased Uzbek rulers so that they would match the personal recollections of those figures by a noble who had known them. The anecdote is published in "Mutribi" al-Asamm Samarqandi, *Conversations with Jahangir* (Costa Mesa, California, 1998), 128–29.

48. Abū al-Ḥasan is depicted in Bibliothèque Nationale, Estampes, Od 49 4, no. 40, reproduced in A. Okada and F. Richard, *A la Cour du grand Moghol* (Paris, 1986), no. 8. In the *Tūzuk-i Jahāngīrī* (II, 20), the emperor also mentions the occasion upon which the artist brought before him a painting intended to be the frontispiece of the *Jahāngīrnāma*. The second image is in the India Office Collection of the British Library (Johnson Album 27, 10), and is published in Skelton et al., *The Indian Heritage*, no. 37.

49. A full account of the artist's career is found in Chandra, *The Ṭūṭī-Nāma*, 22–26. His last known painting is in the 1595 British Library *Khamsa* of Niẓāmī.

50. Jahāngīr, *Tūzuk-i Jahāngīrī* I, 15.

51. R. Skelton, "Indian Painting of the Mughal Period," in *Islamic Painting and the Arts of the Book*, ed. B. W. Robinson (London, 1976), 240.

52. The seal, which is dated 1003/1594–95, appears on the reverse of a painting of an emaciated ram in the Khalili collection. The painting is discussed in L. Leach, *Paintings from India* (London, 1998), no. 8; the inscribed reverse is reproduced on 138. The presence of the seal does not imply that Muḥammad Sharīf executed the painting.

53. Jahāngīr, *Tūzuk-i Jahāngīrī* I, 14.

54. For a list of paintings by Muḥammad Sharīf, see S. P. Verma, *Mughal Painters and Their Work* (Delhi, 1994), 300–1. The partially undeciphered date on the painting in the Los Angeles County Museum of Art (M.78.9.11) can now be read as the eleventh of the Ilāhī month Farwardīn, year 36, corresponding to 999 Hijrī/31 March 1591. A work in a private collection depicting a camel and his driver bears the date of 1028/1618–19; the painting is reproduced in E. Bahari, *Bihzad. Master of Persian Painting* (London, 1996), fig. 129.

55. See M. Beach, *Early Mughal Painting* (Cambridge, Massachusetts, 1987), figs. 58–59.

56. See G. Bailey, *The Jesuits and the Grand Mogul: Renaissance Art at the Imperial Court of India*, 1580–1630 (Washington, D.C., 1998), 27, and figs. 19 and 21.

57. Abū al-Faẓl, *Āʾīn-i Akbarī* I, 115; Chandra, *The Ṭūṭī-Nāma*, 184.

58. Brand and Lowry, *Akbar's India*, 13, citing J. Correia-Afonso, ed., *Letters from the Mughal Court: The First Jesuit Mission to Akbar* (1580–83) (Bombay, 1980) [no page given].

59. See, for example, the well-known British Library *Khamsa* of Niẓāmī (Or. 6810), folios 214a, 225b, and 273a, in which the countenance of Ḥusayn Bāyqarā is used for the figure of Alexander. The last of these paintings is reproduced in Lentz and Lowry, *Timur and the Princely Vision*, 250.

60. See Richard, "An Unpublished Manuscript," 47, and pls. VII–VIII.

61. British Library Or. 5302, folio 30a, published in Losty, *The Art of the Book in India*, pl. XIX.

62. Akbar's portrait on folio 232b of the *Ṭūṭīnāma* was first pointed out by Beach, *Early Mughal Painting*, 56. On folio 182b of the Keir *Khamsa*, the artist Tārā not only uses Akbar's features for the figure of Bahrām Gūr, but also substitutes a Humāyūn-style turban for the Persian crown that the hero seizes upon slaying two lions. The painting is reproduced in Skelton, "Indian Painting of the Mughal Period," pl. 114.

63. This scene is discussed in Chapter 6.

64. See J. Seyller, "Codicological Aspects of the Victoria and Albert Museum *Akbarnāma* and Their Historical Implications," *Art Journal*, 49, no. 4 (Winter 1990), especially 380–82.

65. This phrase occurs on nos. 23/117, 32/117, 33/117, 53/117, and 91/117.

66. A nearly identical figure inscribed as Ṣādiq Khān is published in T. Falk and M. Archer, *Indian Miniatures in the India Office Library* (London, 1981), no. 12i.

67. See Losty, *The Art of the Book in India*, no. 56, for a discussion of the manuscript.

68. See Seyller, "The Inspection and Valuation of Manuscripts," 309.

69. See J. Seyller, "The School of Oriental and African Studies *Anvār-i Suhaylī*: The Illustration of a De Luxe Mughal Manuscript," *Ars Orientalis*, 16 (1986), 119–51.

70. The text of this copy of the *Gulistān* is preserved in the National Museum, New Delhi (48.6/1). Its colophon indicates that it was completed at Lahore by ʿAbd al-Raḥīm al-Haravī in the last ten days of Bahman Ilāhī of regnal year 40, which corresponds to mid-February 1596. The folio size (29 x 16.5 cm.), 11 lines of fine nastaʿlīq per page, and the size of the text area (21.2 x 11.2 cm.) connect this manuscript to a number of dispersed paintings of the *Gulistān*. The majority of these are in the Cincinnati Art Museum, and are published in E. Smart and D. Walker, *Pride of the Princes: Indian Art of the Mughal Era in the Cincinnati Art Museum* (Cincinnati, 1985), nos. 3a–h.

71. The *Ḥādīqat al-Ḥāqīqat* was written by ʿAbd al-Raḥīm and illustrated with five paintings. Its 301 folios measure 26 x 14.5 cm. The manuscript was offered for sale at Bonhams, London, 26 April 1995. The copious inspection notes on its flyleaves and other details of the manuscript are presented in Seyller, "The Inspection and Valuation of Manuscripts," 305, and figs. 13 and 14.

CHAPTER 4

# The Walters Art Museum *Khamsa* of Amīr Khusraw

The Walters *Khamsa* marks the culmination of the development of the *de luxe* Mughal manuscript in the 1590s. While the celebrated ʿAbd al-Raḥīm had been chosen to pen its companion volume, the British Library *Khamsa* of Niẓāmī, the honor of writing the text of the Walters *Khamsa* fell to the most highly esteemed calligrapher of the day, Muḥammad Ḥusayn al-Kashmīrī, then at the zenith of his long career. The calligrapher's renown can be gauged by the praise lavished upon him by Abū al-Faẓl:

> The artist who, in the shadow of the throne of his Majesty, has become a great master of calligraphy, is Muḥammad Ḥusayn of Kashmīr. He has been honoured with the title of *Zarrīnqalam*, the gold pen. He surpassed his master Mawlānā ʿAbdu'l-ʿAzīz; his *maddāt* [extensions] and *dawāʾir* [curvatures] show everywhere a proper proportion to each other, and art critics consider him equal to Mullā Mīr ʿAlī.[1]

An inscription by Jahāngīr on a copy of the *Gulistān* dated 992/1584 provides a more concrete measure of the calligrapher's high esteem. Noting twice that the manuscript was written by Muḥammad Ḥusayn, Jahāngīr also specified that the late emperor Akbar bestowed 1,000 Akbarī *muhrs* upon the calligrapher at the time the unillustrated book was officially received on 9 Jumādā II 993/8 June 1585.[2] His mention of the calligrapher, which usually appears only on manuscripts written by Mīr ʿAlī or Sulṭān ʿAlī, is a clear indication that greatness was not an attribute reserved exclusively for the past, and that Muḥammad Ḥusayn's status rivaled that of his exalted predecessors.

Born in Kashmir, Muḥammad Ḥusayn was probably little more than a youth when he signed his first work in 1560, for a portrait of the calligrapher appended by the young artist Manōhara to the colophon of Muḥammad Ḥusayn's next dated work, a beautiful *Gulistān* of Saʿdī of 990/1582–83, shows him well into middle-age (fig. 3).[3] The calligrapher remained at the center of the imperial library's production through the 1580s and 1590s, writing the aforementioned *Gulistān* in 992/1584,[4] the *Bahāristān* in February 1595, the Beatty *Akbarnāma* ca. 1596,[5] and, finally, the Walters *Khamsa* itself, completed at Lahore in the forty-second year of Akbar's reign, i.e., March 1597 to March 1598.[6] Muḥammad Ḥusayn's name also appears on a copy of the *Dīwān* of Amīr Ḥasan written for a Mughal noble, Shaykh Farīd Bukhārī, in 1010/1601–2.[7] Individual examples of his handwriting are included in a number of Mughal albums, sometimes in juxtaposition to those of the revered Mīr ʿAlī.[8] An unillustrated copy of Jaʿfar's *Khusraw wa Shīrīn* and a short inscription below a painting of Ibrāhīm ʿĀdil Shāh are dated 1019/1610–11, only a year before his death.[9]

The text of the Walters *Khamsa* is laid out in a format typical of many poetical manuscripts, with four columns of twenty-one lines of elegant nastaʿlīq script on a highly polished biscuit-colored paper. The broad text area, measuring 17.2 x 10.2 cm., subtly accentuates the visual rhythm of the linked couplets of Amīr Khusraw's text and anchors a generous folio size (now 28.4 x 19.0 cm.). The folio, in turn, accommodates both a series of decorative medallions and scenes in the borders and a relatively expansive painting field for the illustrations. The rubrics, or headings for each section of the text, are written in red and blue, often in an alternating pattern.

The writing of such an exquisite manuscript was a painstaking endeavor. The colophons of four of the five poems of the British Library *Khamsa* of Niẓāmī, a text half again as long as Khusraw's work, provide completion dates for various sections of the text ranging from October 1593 to November 1595.[10] From these dates and an amazing sequence of tiny numbers on many intervening folios that mark off the calligrapher's daily output, we can surmise that the calligrapher, ʿAbd al-Raḥīm, labored on the manuscript for exactly thirty-six months, working meticulously at the methodical pace of just sixteen and a half lines of text—less than one side of a folio—each day.[11] Assuming that a similar rate of work was maintained in the

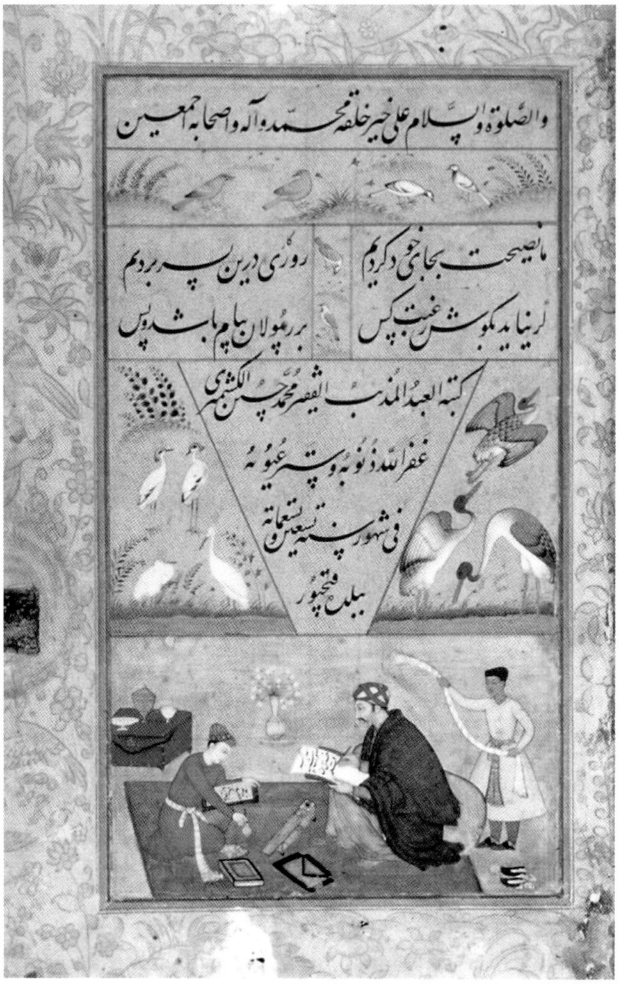


Fig. 3. Colophon portrait of the scribe Muḥammad Ḥusayn *Zarrīn Qalam* and self-portrait of the painter Manōhara. *Gulistān* of Sa'dī, f. 128b. 1582–83. Painting 14.0 x 12.2 cm.; folio 31.3 x 19.5 cm. Royal Asiatic Society Ms. Pers. 258.

production of manuscripts of comparable quality, we can estimate that Muḥammad Ḥusayn copied out the text of the Walters *Khamsa* in approximately twenty-four months. This would place the inception of the project sometime between March 1595 and March 1596. In all likelihood, Muḥammad Ḥusayn took up his pen in early 1596, shortly after completing the text of the Beatty *Akbarnāma*.[12] The commissioning of a copy of Amīr Khusraw's *Khamsa* immediately upon the heels of Niẓāmī's masterpiece would have been a natural choice by the emperor and his librarians.

Although most of the Walters *Khamsa* remains in excellent condition, the manuscript has been altered slightly from its original form. The book now consists of 211 folios of text and illuminations. The beginning and end of the manuscript are intact, but twenty-two folios have been excised, making an original total of 233 folios. The lacunae can be discerned through various means. The surest indication is an interruption in the text, which is normally indicated by a discrepancy between the catchword at the bottom of a verso side of one folio and the first words of the following folio. At three places in the *Khamsa*, however, someone has tried to conceal these losses by rubbing out the original catchword and writing in one that matches the following verses.[13] Thus, to verify a lacuna conclusively, it is necessary to check the text of the Walters *Khamsa* against a critical tradition of Amīr Khusraw's text. Moreover, since the *Khamsa* text was generally copied very faithfully, with infrequent variations being limited to an alternative word or two within an individual couplet, the writing of the text follows a very predictable pattern of forty-two couplets per page. Hence, with allowances of space for the occasional rubric, it is possible to determine the precise number of verses missing between any two folios, and thus to ascertain whether the lacuna included an illustration.

Complementing this evidence is a system of folio numbers written discreetly in gold leaves or rocks in the lower left of most folios amid the rocks and foliage of the borders. Even in the best of circumstances these tiny numerals can be seen only when light strikes the gold from certain angles, but most numerals have been effaced deliberately so that only the barest of indentations in the paper remains. A second set of folio numbers written in black ink in a modern hand appears in the lower right corner of the folios. This series was written after one folio had been removed, but before the paintings were excised.[14] A supplementary system of foliation within an individual section of the *Khamsa*, a feature found in several other copies of the *Khamsa* of Niẓāmī and its later imitations, appears intermittently in the lower left corner of the folios of *Shīrīn wa Khusraw*. Together these series of numbers establish lacunae at the following junctures: folios 11/12, 15/16, 21/22, 28/29, 58/59 (four missing folios), 119/120 (six missing folios), 149/150, 157/158, 164/165, 181/182 (two missing folios), 184/185 (two missing folios), and 198/199. Except for the gaps at 11/12 and 119/120, with the latter including the *shamsa* (a starburst decorative feature) and the *'unwān* (decorative headpiece) of *Ā'īnah-i Sikandarī*, each lacuna was occasioned by the removal of at least one illustrated folio.

A fourth set of numbers, written in red, enumerates the paintings. This feature, which is standard in illustrated Mughal manuscripts, probably served originally as a kind of inventory of paintings in the manuscript, but today it confirms the number of paintings in a given manuscript and facilitates the identification of dispersed pages. Ten of the original thirty-one illustrations have been separated from the Walters *Khamsa*. Eight of these paintings made their way to The Metropolitan Museum of Art in the early twentieth century (13.228.26–33), but the remaining two have yet to be located. By isolating their precise spots in *Hasht Bihisht* (181/182 and 184/185), however, we can identify their subjects as Bahrām Gūr hunting with Dilārām and the king meeting the three brothers who possessed disturbing powers of deduction, an episode from the story of the princess of the Black Pavilion.[15]

Perhaps the most subtle alteration made to the Walters *Khamsa* is the remargining of the folios. The borders still bear magnificent decorations, but the cropping of several figures, the abbreviated form of some medallions, and the disappearance of the gold ruling near the edge of the borders are evidence that at least 1.5 cm. of the upper and lower borders and .5 cm. of the outer border were trimmed from the area delineated by the original gold ruling of the border. The borders probably extended another centimeter or so beyond this frame, so that they would have approximated the dimensions of the modern borders. In some places, the cropping of the lower borders of the folios has caused the original ascriptions of the paintings to be cut off. On two folios, however, this was remedied by reaffixing to the modern border the small tab of paper on which the name of the artist was written originally.[16] A potentially greater loss is the preliminary rubric notes on text pages and informal ascriptions for the border designs, such as those preserved on the *Bahāristān*. Some of this information can be restored by comparison to ascribed borders in the earlier manuscript.

Although the Walters *Khamsa* furnishes ample documentation of its initial manufacture, it is relatively silent about its subsequent history. Unlike most Mughal manuscripts of this period, it contains no additional flyleaves with seals or inscriptions to chart its fate as an imperial possession. Two seals impressed on folios 1a and 211a date from the nineteenth century.[17] A long inspection note over the full-page animal illuminations on folio 90a has been thoroughly effaced, as are the teardrop-shaped seal in the center of the *shamsa* of folio 1a and the seal and inscription on folio 174a.[18]

*Maṭla' al-Anwār*, traditionally the first poem of the *Khamsa*, receives six illustrations—approximately a fifth of the total number of paintings, which is an unusually high proportion in *Khamsa* manuscripts. None of the illustrations is devoted to the long introductory sections of the poem; instead, they fall near the end of the short anecdotes at the conclusion of the fourth, eighth, tenth, thirteenth, seventeenth, and twentieth *maqālat*. Thus the paintings are distributed relatively evenly among the twenty discourses, though well short of anything as mechanical as a regular folio count between paintings.

Once the choice of stories to be illustrated was made, the calligrapher collaborated with the designer of the manuscript to ensure the proper correspondence of the illustration to the relevant text passage. On folio 21b, for example, Muḥammad Ḥusayn manipulated the spacing of the text by writing the sixth and twelfth lines obliquely, thereby reducing the number of lines of text on the page from the usual twenty-one to seventeen. Accordingly, the extended story of the eighth *maqāla* concludes at the very bottom of the page, where it is followed immediately by a full-page illustration of that anecdote. This same device is used before illustrations seven more times in the Walters *Khamsa*.[19] It is clear that the layout of the written page was subordinated to a pre-conceived overall design of the manuscript, which had large paintings positioned at specific points.

In contrast to the multiple and highly structured discourses and anecdotes of *Maṭla' al-Anwār*, the next two poems in the manuscript, the courtly *Shīrīn wa Khusraw* and the passionate *Majnūn wa Laylā*, present romantic themes as sustained narratives. The leisurely pace of these narratives affords more latitude in the choice of subjects to be illustrated. Only the two illustrations involving Farhād (ff. 59a and 66b, figs. 13 and 14) are truly crucial to the central story of *Shīrīn wa Khusraw.* The other three paintings are dedicated to secondary ceremonial subjects, showing the entertainment of Khusraw and Shīrīn (f. 51a, fig. 11) rather than their more commonly represented initial encounter on the hunting ground, their witnessing of the marriage vows of young couples (f. 58a, fig. 12) instead of their own nuptials, and Khusraw's presentation of a ring (f. 80a, fig. 15) in lieu of the favored scene of the consummation of the long-awaited marriage.

With little more than thirty folios, *Majnūn wa Laylā* is easily the shortest of the five poems of the *Khamsa,* yet it too is allotted five paintings. The first (f. 94b, fig. 16) is given over to a minor story that precedes the tale of star-crossed Majnūn. The remaining four illustrations are clustered tightly together, with only one folio separating scenes of Laylā and Majnūn at school (f. 98a, fig. 17) and the visit of Majnūn's father in the wilderness (f. 100b, fig. 18). Although these two subjects are depicted in other manuscripts, they rarely occur in the same manuscript, probably for reasons of their proximity in the text. The designer of the Walters *Khamsa* must not have regarded this as a problem, for again a single folio is all that passes between Majnūn's embrace of a forsaken dog (f. 113a, fig. 20) and the reunion of Laylā and Majnūn (f. 115a, fig. 21).

The position of the final two poems is practically interchangeable in many illustrated copies of Amīr Khusraw's *Khamsa,* but in the Walters manuscript the fourth slot is occupied by the longest poem, *Ā'īnah-i Sikandarī,* which celebrates the exploits of Alexander the Great. Although martial scenes are often included in illustrated copies of *Shīrīn wa Khusraw* and *Majnūn wa Laylā,* primarily as depictions of Khusraw's struggle with Bahrām Chūbīna and Majnūn's participation in the battle of the clans, the designer of the Walters manuscript invoked this familiar genre only twice, once for a peculiarly placed equestrian combat between Alexander and a Chinese opponent (f. 128a, fig. 22), and again in an unprecedented scene of a sea battle against pirates located by Alexander's marvelous mirror (fig. 25).[20] In another unique scene, Alexander resourcefully enlists a torrent of water to smite an unrepentant enemy (f. 153b, fig. 26). This active aspect of Alexander's nature is balanced by a more obviously benign, contemplative side, highlighted in rare depictions of his gracious reception of defeated foes (ff. 135a, 139a, figs. 23 and 24) and in his reflections upon his own fate (figs. 27 and 28).

If *Ā'īnah-i Sikandarī* presents several unusual individual subjects, the illustrations of *Hasht Bihisht* form the most unexpected overall pattern. Most copies of the *Khamsa* have repetitive illustrations of Bahrām Gūr visiting each of the seven pavilions in turn. A few choose instead the stories told by each princess, again for a total of seven for this portion of the *Khamsa.* But the Walters manuscript devotes two illustrations to Bahrām Gūr's slighted pride during the hunt and his later reconciliation with Dilārām (ff. 181/182), and another to the appearance of the seven princesses together before Bahrām (f. 182b, fig. 30), all on three consecutive folios. These are followed by paintings embedded in the stories recounted by the princesses of five of the seven pavilions, falling between four and ten folios apart. The sheer length of the stories of *Hasht Bihisht* and their infrequent illustration make the exact subjects chosen by the Mughal designer seem quite idiosyncratic.

Formal ascriptions written in the lower border of the painted folios establish that thirteen painters were called upon to produce the twenty-nine known illustrations of the Walters *Khamsa.* Most were senior artists in the atelier, and all but one, the relatively unknown 'Alī Qulī, had contributed to the companion volumes of the *Bahāristān* and the British Library *Khamsa* of Niẓāmī. Two artists, Dharmadāsa and Sānvala, executed four paintings each, while eight other painters rendered two or three illustrations each. With the exception of Sānvala's work, which is concentrated in two pairs of consecutive illustrations (ff. 58a–59a, 135a–139a), artists' assignments were scattered throughout the manuscript. Mughal painters apparently worked alone on this type of project, for only Farrukh Cela's painting on folio 182b is ascribed as being a collaborative effort. Since Farrukh was involved in a similar arrangement in two of his three illustrations in the British Library *Khamsa* of Niẓāmī, his collaboration with Miskīn in the Walters manuscript must have reflected a continuing awareness in the atelier of Farrukh's shortcomings in figural drawing.[21]

## NOTES

1. Abū al-Faẓl, *Ā'īn-i Akbarī*, I, 109.

2. The flyleaf is published in Seyller, "The Inspection and Valuation of Manuscripts," fig. 15.

3. Of the many individual specimens of his work, one in an album in the Topkapi Saray Museum (H. 2137, folio 37a) is signed Muḥammad al-Ḥusaynī and is dated 968/1560–61.

4. Royal Library RCIN 1005022.

5. The manuscript lacks a colophon, but the name of the calligrapher is suggested in an inscription written by Jahāngīr on the first folio, which is now covered over by a thin sheet of paper and is fully legible only under infrared radiation. The inscription includes the words *Kashmīrī ke dar 'ilm-i khaṭṭ* (Kashmiri, who in the art of writing...). As noted by the authors of *Paintings from the Muslim Courts of India* (London, 1976), no. 49, this phrase must refer to Muḥammad Ḥusayn Kashmīrī. A complete translation of the imperial inscription appears in Seyller, "The Inspection and Valuation of Manuscripts," 335–36.

6. The colophon of the Walters manuscript reads "It reached completion by the poor, the miserable, sinning slave Muḥammad Ḥusayn *Zarrīn Qalam* on the date of the year 42." The tiny vertical stroke that precedes the numbers 42 gives the appearance of making the date 142, a historical impossibility, but should probably be regarded as an extended dot over the *nūn* in the word *sana* (year).

7. Khudabakhsh Library, Patna HL no. 329.

8. Individual calligraphic specimens written by Muḥammad Ḥusayn are listed below:

Album. Folios 1a (dated 999/1590–91), 4a (done at Lahore), 6a, 7b, 9b, 10a, 10b, 11a, 11b, 13a, 14a (signed "Kashmīrī"), 15a (dated 1002/1593–94), 15b, 16a, 16b, 17a, 18a, 18b, 19b (dated 1002/1593–94), 21a, 22b, 23a, 24a, 25a, 25b, 26a, 26b. Royal Library, Windsor RCIN 1005039.

Album of calligraphy. 56 examples of calligraphy signed alternately as Muḥammad Ḥusayn or "Kashmīrī." Two borders dated 999/1590–91 and 1000/1591. 73 pages, 37.2 x 23.9 cm. Published: Sotheby's, London, 18 October 1995, lot 68.

Dārā Shikūh Album, folios 17a, 29a, 40b, 51a, 53a, 54b, 64b, 65a, 68b, 69a. British Library, Oriental and India Office Collections, no. 3129. Published: Falk and Archer, *Indian Miniatures in the India Office Library*, no. 68.

Two specimens of calligraphy, one signed Muḥammad Ḥusayn, the other, Muḥammad Ḥusayn *Zarrīn Qalam*, attached to the reverse of two paintings of Muslim clerics. British Library, Oriental and India Office Collections, Johnson Album 7, nos. 10–11. Published: Falk and Archer, *Indian Miniatures in the India Office Library*, no. 96i–ii.

Specimen dated 1011/1602–3, signed Muḥammad Kashmīrī. 17.5 x 10.8 cm. Bibliothèque Nationale, Mss. Or., Supplément persan 392, folio 120. Published: Richard and Okada, *A la cour du grand moghol*, no. 144.

Single leaf attached to the reverse of Flight of a Simurgh. Collection Prince Sadruddin Aga Khan. Published: Fischer and Goswamy, *Wonders of a Golden Age*, no. 21.

Four lines of calligraphy attached to the back of a *Jahāngīrnāma* page. Collection Prince Sadruddin Aga Khan. Published: Fischer and Goswamy, *Wonders of a Golden Age*, no. 37, p. 86.

Four lines of calligraphy on the back of an unidentified portrait. Private collection. Published: Fischer and Goswamy, *Wonders of a Golden Age*, no. 64.

Nine lines of calligraphy. 13.5 x 9.0 cm. Museum Rietberg RVI 870.

Four lines of calligraphy. Museum of Art, Rhode Island School of Design 17.498. Published: Brand, "The City as an Artistic Center," fig. 7.3, in *Fatehpur-Sikri*, 1987.

Unidentified quatrain. 16.5 x 10.3 cm. Pierpont Morgan Library M.458.4b. Published: B. Schmitz, *Islamic and Indian Manuscripts and Paintings in the Pierpont Morgan Library* (New York, 1997), fig. 210.

Six lines of calligraphy attached to a painting of ca. 1600. Dated 983/1575. 18.7 x 10.4 cm. Free Library of Philadelphia M52.

Four lines of calligraphy. Free Library of Philadelphia M70.

Four lines of calligraphy. Chester Beatty Library Ms. 31. Published: Brand and Lowry, *Akbar's India*, no. 20.

Six lines of calligraphy. 20.6 x 10.1 cm. Navin Kumar collection.

Album page signed by Muḥammad Ḥusayn *al-Kātib* (al-Kashmīrī). Published: Christie's, 16 October 1980, lot 60.

Rhyming couplet signed Muḥammad Ḥusayn *al-Kātib*. Text area 20.6 x 9.9 cm., page 36.2 x 25.4 cm. Published: Christie's, 11 October 1988, lot 86.

Eight lines of calligraphy embellished with five small birds. Folio 39.3 x 26.5 cm.; text area 20.7 x 9.8 cm. Published: Sotheby's, 18 October 1995, lot 71.

Two pairs of two couplets signed by Muḥammad Ḥusayn beside a painting of three biblical women ascribed to Śankara; four couplets signed by Muḥammad Ḥusayn on the reverse. Published: Sotheby's, 18 October 1995, lot 90.

Two couplets signed Muḥammad Ḥusayn on the reverse of a painting of the nativity of St. John the Baptist ascribed to Kesava. Published: Sotheby's, 18 October 1995, lot 91.

Specimen signed Muḥammad Ḥusayn Kashmīrī. Gulshan Album, Teheran, no. 104.

Specimen dated 1019/1610–11, signed Muḥammad Ḥusayn *Zarrīn Qalam* Jahāngīr Shāhī. Gulshan Album, Teheran, no. 259.

9. The manuscript of *Khusraw wa Shīrīn* is preserved in the Khudabakhsh Library, Patna, and is discussed in its *Catalogue of the Arabic and Persian Manuscripts in the Oriental Public Library at Bankipore* (rep. Delhi, 1977), III, no. 274, 14–16. The dated inscription appears beneath a well-known painting of Ibrāhīm 'Ādil Shāh of Bijapur in the Náprstek Museum, Prague (A. 12181). M. Bayani, *Khwushnawisan* (Teheran, 1969), III, no. 1001, supplies the year of Muḥammad Ḥusayn's death as 1020/1611–12. The author of the *Mir'āt al-'Ālam* also gives the date of his death as 1020/1611. By contrast, R. P. Srivastava, "Mohammad Hussain Kashmiri *Zarin Qalam*," *Lahore Museum Bulletin*, 3, no. 2 (July–December 1990), 71, asserts that Muḥammad Ḥusayn died in 1620. He also states that the Khudabakhsh Library possesses a manuscript of *Dīwān* of Ḥāfiẓ completed in Hyderabad by Muḥammad Ḥusayn in 1023/1614. A *Būstān* of Sa'dī in a private collection with one painting dated 1025/1616 bears a flyleaf note which indicates that it was written by Muḥammad Ḥusayn *Zarrīn Qalam*, but that most of the folios were penned by Mīrzā Muḥammad 'Alī Beg. This suggests that the latter calligrapher completed a project left unfinished by Muḥammad Ḥusayn's death.

10. The colophon on folio 109b is dated 20 Mihr regnal year 38/5 October 1593. The poem ending on folio 168a was completed 10 Isfandārmuẕ regnal year 38/2 March 1594. On folio 284b, the calligrapher writes that *Sharafnāma* was realized in Shahrīwar regnal year 40/August–September 1595. The final colophon of the manuscript is dated 24 Āẕar regnal year 40/24 November 1595. The manuscript, which now has 325 folios, was originally 370 folios in length.

11. Minute numbers appear at the edge of the text area or the central intercolumnar space sixty-two times on folios concentrated in the first third of the manuscript. In every case, these numbers are consecutive, run up to 30 or 31, as if marking the end of each day's work within a month. This can be verified by the sequence of ten numbers on the seven folios leading up to the colophon of *Khusraw wa Shīrīn* on folio 109b. Number 3 appears at line 4 of folio 102b, number 4 is noted in the middle of line 20 of folio 103a, and so on. The scribe records the number 14 on both line 21 of folio 107a and the middle of line 16 of folio 107b, but writes a number 16 over the erroneous number 15 on folio 108a, and after 7 lines on folio 109b signs that he completed his work on day 20 of the month of Mihr. After folio 120, the calligrapher generally replaces these numbers with a system of tiny red dots that appear regularly at identical intervals and have the same function.

12. One painting in the *Akbarnāma* manuscript is dated 22 February 1596, and another is dated 30 April 1597. These dates, however, refer to the execution of paintings, which normally followed the writing of the text by months or even a few years. For example, the *'unwān* on folio 169b of the British Library *Khamsa* of Niẓāmī is dated A.H. 1004 (6 September 1595–28 August 1596), a minimum of eighteen months after the date mentioned in the colophon on the preceding folio (2 March 1594), but conceivably contemporary with the completion of the writing of its own poem (August–September 1595).

13. Folios 58b, 119b, 184b.

14. This is clear from folio 17b, which is numbered 18 in black, i.e., only one more than the original total despite the fact that another illustrated folio was removed at folios 15/16. This series was obliterated systematically after folio 35b, perhaps because it made the lacunae obvious to most readers.

15. The last line of text of folio 181b, which is original folio number 198, concludes with the verse of page 65:5 of the critical edition. This leaves a gap of 53 hemistiches before The Metropolitan Museum of Art painting (13.228.28, fig. 29), which is original folio 200, and whose verso is filled with text corresponding to pages 71:3–75:2 of the critical edition. Thus, the missing folio had a painting with 9 hemistiches (or 5 1/2 lines of text) on one side and 42 hemistiches on the other. The subject of Bahrām Gūr hunting gazelles appears in 18 other copies of the *Khamsa*, albeit customarily at a slightly earlier point in the text.

The second missing illustration is less predictable, for the episode of the king encountering the three princes of Ceylon is illustrated in only three manuscripts. Several lines of text on the verso of folio 184, which is original folio 203, are written obliquely, a device commonly found before an illustration. The text ends abruptly on page 95: mid-7 of the critical edition, and folio 185a resumes 109:8. Therefore, 145 1/2 hemistiches are missing along with a short segment of the title on page 109. At 42 hemistiches per manuscript page, this is slightly more than three full pages of text. Folio 185b bears an original folio number of 206. Therefore, two folios are lacking here, one with 13 hemistiches on the painted side. Together this evidence suggests that the painting fell on the recto side of the first missing folio, which was original folio 204.

16. Folios 128a (Jagannātha) and Metropolitan Museum 13.228.32 (Dharmadāsa).

17. The rectangular seal impressed a total of five times is that of one 'Abd al-Rajī Muḥammad Shafī', dated 1247/1831–32. The smaller oval seal, impressed thrice, belongs to Muḥammad Zakī and is dated 1241/1825–26. The larger oval seal on folio 211a bears the name of Muḥammad 'Alī without a date.

18. The teardrop-shaped seal is almost certainly that of the Mughal emperor Shāh Jahān (reigned 1627–58). The words *īn kitābkhāna* (this library) are still legible in the effaced inscription on folio 174a.

19. Folios 66a, 79b, 112b, 114b, 164/165 (Metropolitan Museum 13.228.27, in which the text precedes the painting) (fig. 28), 184b, and 187b.

20. For an example of the battle of the clans, see Figure 46 from a contemporary *Khamsa* of Niẓāmī.

21. Farrukh Cela collaborated with Dhanrāja on folio 123a and Bulāqī on folio 273a. Of the 42 other paintings in the Niẓāmī manuscript, only one by Khema Karana (f. 117a) resorts to this type of collaboration, again with Bulāqī. The suggestion by G. Minissale, "Three New Inscriptions in the Emperor Akbar's *Khamsa* of Niẓāmī, Or. 12,208," *Oriental Art*, 44, no. 1 (1998), 61–64, that these faces were added by Bulāqī much later than the original paintings should be dismissed.

PLATES

# The Walters Art Museum *Khamsa*

Detail of f. 113a.

*MAṬLAʿ AL-ANWĀR*

# I A Muslim pilgrim learns a lesson in piety from a brahman who is crawling toward his icon

Ascribed *ʿamal-i* Basāvana
21.6 x 13.5 cm
Removed from the manuscript between folios 15 and 16
The Metropolitan Museum of Art, gift of Alexander Smith Cochran, 1913 (13.228.29)
Published: M. Dimand, *A Handbook of Muhammadan Art* (New York, 1944), fig. 33; S. C. Welch, "The Paintings of Basawan," *Lalit Kalā*, 10 (1961), fig. 4; S. C. Welch, *The Art of Mughal India* (New York, 1963), pl. 8a; A. Papadopoulo, *Islam and Muslim Art* (Paris, 1976), no. 557; Okada, *Indian Miniatures of the Mughal Court*, fig. 96; S. Blair and J. Bloom, *The Art and Architecture of Islam* 1250–1800 (New Haven and London, 1994), fig. 367

The fourth *maqāla* extols the merit of selfless devotion as a means of worship in Islam and concludes with a lesson of piety that transcends religions. A devout Muslim on the pilgrimage to Mecca meets a Hindu brahman on the road to the temple at Somnath in Gujarat, which was renowned for its wealth of idols. Seeing the brahman grovel on the ground, the perplexed pilgrim asks the Hindu why he does not make his way on his feet. The brahman replies that he has proceeded in this manner for years, ever since he gave his heart to his idol. Khusraw then compares the Hindu's absolute, albeit misguided devotion to his god to the resolute flight of an arrow fired at the wrong target and exhorts his fellow Muslims, who know the correct object of faith, to advance with the same single-minded purpose.

The two pilgrims travel convergent paths toward God in Basāvana's illustration of this tale. Dressed in the traditional Hindu dhoti and *dupatta* and adorned with a proper *tilāk* mark of Śiva's devotees, the brahman crawls forward, hands splayed and heels raised in a position whose apparent thrust belies his painstaking pace. He glances back at his upright Muslim counterpart, who carries prayer beads, a book (presumably the Koran), a pair of shoes, and a pilgrim's staff. Neither pauses for conversation, creating an impression of urgency quickened by the peripatetic figures and animals around them.

Basāvana imbues every element in the painting with a physicality unequalled by any contemporary Mughal artist. He achieves this effect by forgoing precise linear patterns in favor of roughly outlined forms and richly textured surfaces and by subduing the customary brilliant palette with a range of subtle tones. Through these techniques, he imparts a palpably dusty, swelling musculature to the brahman, a heavy coarseness to the Muslim's robe and cloak, and a rare organic quality to the tangled roots of the banyan tree beside the road. Even genre characters such as the snarling dog and fowler carrying his net and camoflauge screen are enlivened to an unprecedented degree. Together with the minuscule figures working the distant fields, these innovative and uniquely Indian expressions testify to the thoroughness of Basāvana's assimilation from European art the principles of modeling, recession, and atmospheric perspective.



FIGURE 4

پا برهنش نیز ز دل ساختم
گفت چو دل در رهت باختم
عمل بساون

# II A bathhouse keeper is consumed by the heat of his passion for his beloved

Ascribed *ʿamal-i* Narasimha
18.2 x 12.0 cm
Removed from the manuscript between folios 21 and 22
The Metropolitan Museum of Art, gift of Alexander Smith Cochran, 1913 (13.228.31)
Published: E. Wellesz, *Akbar's Religious Thought as Reflected in Mogul Painting* (London, 1952), fig. 29

Khusraw's remarks on the joys and travails of love, the subject of the eighth *maqāla*, are epitomized in the parable of a lowly bathhouse keeper whose passion is kindled by a glimpse of a fair king. The king initially disregards the fire that he stoked so casually, but soon returns to the bathhouse when he himself is stirred by the heat of love. His passion sparked anew, the bathhouse keeper bursts into flames before his beloved.

Although the metaphor of burning passion is common to many cultures, it seldom assumes literal form in the phenomenal world, as it does in this rarely illustrated story. This full-page scene centers on the mounted king, who bites his finger in astonishment at the spectacle of the bathhouse keeper engulfed by flames. The domed bathhouse establishes the occupation of the tormented man even as it anchors the sloping yellow arena of the fatal encounter. The king's large entourage plays a similar role, lending him the pageantry of elephants and attendants bearing a flywhisk and other royal symbols while providing a measure of balance to the dark cityscape in the upper left. Only the two figures appropriately quenching their thirst at a well enjoy a respite from the consternation rippling through the crowd of retainers.

This painting highlights the strengths of Narasimha, a portrait specialist who executed only the principal faces in many of his works of the 1590s. Narasimha used a distinctive system of contour shading to create a kind of dark corona around the faces of the most prominent figures. In some cases, such as that of the king, he strengthened the contrast between figure and ground by extending this corona—often rendered as dark tufts—around much of the figure. Combined with dark, multiple outlines and unusually subtle modeling of both drapery and faces, this technique greatly enhanced the luminosity of his densely colored, minute figures.

Narasimha employs a remarkably similar composition in a painting from a contemporary *Gulistān* of Saʿdī in the Cincinnati Art Museum.[1] The landscape is comprised of two flat areas for the central drama, a lightly colored, organic outcrop swelling up behind onlookers in wave-like fashion, and a foreground ridge set at an opposite angle. A virtually identical dark tree with light-tipped leaves and bright birds again serves as the primary vertical accent.

1. The painting is reproduced in color in Smart and Walker, *Pride of the Princes*, no. 3b.

# III The fratricide who sees two friends sentenced to death, each wanting to die before the other, confesses his crime to the king

Attributed here to Mukunda
23.3 x 15.4 cm
Folio 24b
Walters Art Museum (W.624)

This illustration depicts the story of the tenth *maqāla* with a spectacle of the two friends condemned to death, but selects a slightly earlier moment in the narrative than do the illustrations of five previous manuscripts. The two dedicated men are bound only by their friendship, their imminent execution suggested merely by the presence of two guards with drawn swords. Several retainers in the foreground gesture toward the two friends, who address the sovereign in a final appeal for clemency. As in the earlier examples, the repentant fratricide is not distinguished from among the crowd of impassive onlookers.

The painting bears many of the hallmarks of Mukunda, a senior artist in the imperial atelier. The disturbing discordance between the angle of the base of the light purple coffered pavilion and its platform is entirely in keeping with Mukunda's awkward, boxy rendering of architectural form. A similar disregard for spatial logic occurs in the freestanding position of the large canopy, which is turned parallel to the courtyard walls to provide a unifying backdrop to the four figures below.

The hand of Mukunda may also be identified in a minor detail in the pattern of the carpet beneath the enthroned king. Articulated by a strong color, the borders of the carpet medallions emerge from the darker field as a series of distinctive undulating forms, a feature seen in many of Mukunda's contemporary works, notably folios 29a of the *Bahāristān* and 184b of the British Library *Khamsa* of Niẓāmī.[1]

Together with the ascribed work on folio 203b of this manuscript (fig. 33), these projects provide a clear idea of Mukunda's personal figure style. He employs a relatively limited range of facial types, characteristically endowing a figure with a spade-shaped head, heavy-lidded eyes, and a puckered mouth, a countenance exemplified here by the attendant opposite the king. His figures are cloaked in stiff, opaquely colored jamas so mechanically modeled that, in some instances, they seem almost metallic.

1. The former painting is published in J. Strzygowski, ed., *Asiatische Miniaturenmalerei im Anschluss an Wesen und Werden der Mogulmalerei* (Klagenfurt, 1933), Abb. 137; the latter painting is reproduced in Brend, *The Emperor Akbar's* Khamsa *of Niẓāmī*, fig. 23.



FIGURE 6

# IV Having accidentally killed a youth, a king offers to make amends to the aggrieved mother by giving her a choice of a basin bearing his own head or one heaped with gold

Attributed to Miskīn
23.5 x 14.9 cm
Removed from the manuscript between folios 28 and 29
The Metropolitan Museum of Art, gift of Alexander Smith Cochran, 1913 (13.228.26)
Published: M. Dimand, "Mughal Painting Under Akbar the Great," *Bulletin of The Metropolitan Museum of Art*, 12 (1953), 49; Welch, "The Paintings of Basawan," fig. 16; Ettinghausen, *Paintings for the Emperors and Sultans of India in American Collections*, pl. 7; Grube, *The Classical Style*, no. 92; P. Vaughan, "Miskin," *Master Artists of the Imperial Mughal Court* (Bombay, 1991), fig. 15

Khusraw's thirteenth *maqāla* takes up a constant theme of Islamic courtly literature and exhorts sovereigns to heed their duty to rule with wisdom and unwavering justice. The poet exemplifies this dictum with the tragic story of a king who mistakes a sleeping youth for a bird and slays his innocent victim with an arrow. The wails of the boy's bereaved mother soon reach the king, who discovers the calamity of his inadvertent crime. Placing two golden basins and his sword before the woman, the dismayed king offers the widow her choice of compensation: his head on one salver or a great mound of riches on the other. Mindful of the pointlessness of further bloodshed, the woman accepts the gold and urges the king to continue his just ways.

Miskīn places the traditional elements of the story—the king, the slain youth and his grieving mother, the sword and basins—at the center of this scene. Both figures conceal their anguish behind impassive expressions, a reaction emulated by the king's elegant hunting companions on the right. Sprawled over the brushwood fence that encloses the field he once guarded is the youth himself; although his contorted position is surely intended to convey the agony of his death throes, it shares its impression of weightlessness with living figures by Miskīn's hand.

Miskīn borrows both technique and motif from European prints that circulated throughout the imperial atelier. The richly modeled robes of mother and child are cut from different cloth than the taut jamas of the king's entourage. The wide faces and wavy brown hair of the fallen boy and his three brawling peers betray an obvious debt to European prototypes, as does the crucifix carried by the figure on the right. Likewise, the Mughal fascination with the world beyond takes shape in both the gleaming spires of the miniature town and the ghostly boats plying distant seas.

This emphasis on recession is reinforced by the bright stream and charming animals meandering across the upturned landscape. Miskīn habitually includes animals for this reason, but repeats the three frolicking horses in the upper right so often that the motif originally coined by the Persian master Bihzād becomes his own.

ماند زبان بسته دران داوری
با دل بدخو ز زبان آوری
یافت خبر مادر پسینه خراب
خون شدش از سوز جگر گوشه آب
آنچنان کرد که صحرا بسوخت
هر که دلش داد دلش را بسوخت
طشت طلب کرد و یکی تیغ تیز
طشت دگر کرده برو گنج ریز
گفت بکش ماتم خود سور کن
وام خود از گردن من دور کن
که تبا پیش لب خندان گزید
که پیر انگشت بدندان گزید
بر سر آن خاک کی خونین نهاد
خاک بسر کرده درآمد چو باد
شاه چو دید آن شغب دردناک
گرم فرو جست ز توسن بخاک
تیغ سیاست بسپر خویش برد
در نظر بیوه درویش برد

# V An old Sufi laments his lost youth when a male beauty in a garden rebuffs his amorous advances

Ascribed *ʿamal-i* Lāla
22.4 x 14.3 cm
Folio 35a
Walters Art Museum (W.624)
Published: Brend, "Akbar's *Khamsah* of Amīr Khusrau," pl. 1

The seventeenth *maqāla* admonishes young and old alike to recognize the ephemerality of youth and to behave with suitable decorum. This illustration of its popular anecdote takes on the deprecatory tone of the text, presenting the Sufi as a pitiable character, bent and wizened by age. The Sufi's crooked back and long beard—stock attributes of age in both Persian poetry and painting—are specifically mentioned in the story, and are contrasted to the graceful gait and downy cheeks of the fair youth, who is sometimes depicted as a female.

The Sufi, who has a string of prayer beads tucked under his belt, lifts his hand in a rhetorical gesture to make a futile amorous overture to the handsome youth looming over him. The contrast between the brilliant orange jama of the haughty youth and the pale blue dress of his decrepit suitor further underscores their respective stages of life. Lāla positions the vigorous figure at the dominant part of the composition: the intersection of channels in the formal garden, which is seen from directly above. The arrangement of the garden, a symbol of fragile beauty invoked in the poem, is determined wholly by compositional requirements. The zigzag garden path in the foreground leads the youth and his debonair companions to encounter the one whose bloom has faded; a channel connects the pool on the right to the large text panel above, but abruptly terminates its logical course in the foreground lest it compete with the two figures in the lower right. Even the scalloped outline of the pool to the left complements the curve of the Sufi's hunched back.

Lāla sets two rocks at the bifurcated roots of the slender tree beside the youth in order to balance the placement of his feet just to the left of the central channel. He also includes two men oblivious to the moral truths to be discovered amid the luxuriant blue-green vegetation and burgeoning flowers of the garden: the ubiquitous figure of a man digging, and a keenly observed gardener washing his feet in the swirling water of an octagonal fountain.

# VI A virtuous woman plucks out her eyes and sends them to the king to silence his persistent entreaties

Attributed here to Mādhava
20.6 x 14.3 cm
Folio 40a
Walters Art Museum (W.624)
Published: Brend, "Akbar's *Khamsah* of Amīr Khusrau," pl. 2

Khusraw uses the twentieth and final *maqāla* to offer his thoughts on the moral necessity of the virtue of women, a code disregarded elsewhere in the *Khamsa* by many a female, usually to ruinous ends. He personalizes this social view with advice to his seven-year-old daughter, urging her to tend to her domestic duties, to remain chaste, to use her husband's face as her mirror, and to maintain proper seclusion from other men.

The danger of public exposure is underscored in the corresponding anecdote, which recounts the drastic action forced on a virtuous woman by the lustful attentions of a king who catches sight of her. The woman resists the king's entreaties to come to him, but he persists, claiming that her beautiful eyes have made him restless. Considering her virtue to be a greater treasure than her sight, the woman expunges the source of temptation and sends her eyes to the king, who finally relents in the face of this ultimate display of virtue.

Fig.10. A youth falls under the spell of a singer on a balcony performing for her owner. By Mādhava. *Bahāristān* of Jāmī, 1595, f. 35b. 21.4 x 12.1 cm. Bodleian Library, University of Oxford, Ms. Elliott 254.

On the right, two grieving maids tend to the woman, who swoons from the pain of her self-mutilation. Seated in a covered balcony opposite, the shocked king receives a platter bearing the eyes that he claimed had so disquieted him. The artist accentuates the gulf between the two protagonists with a composition whose disturbingly stark center is occupied only by two attendants standing before a blank wall. Their upward gaze directs attention to the king, a function counterbalanced by the glance of the four figures in the lower left toward the woman in the upper right. Anchoring the other side of the octagonal courtyard are a plantain tree and a rose bush entwined about two cypresses, the latter a traditional Persian symbol of love.

This painting may be attributed to Mādhava, whose painting on folio 35b of the contemporary *Bahāristān* shares many of the features seen here (fig. 10). These include the small figure scale as well as a facial type endowed characteristically with full-blown cheeks, a rotund chin, and a flaring mustache or soft beard. Both compositions are divided into tidy compartments by precisely rendered architectural elements, the most distinctive of which is the thinly painted, elongated brickwork. Mādhava creates spatial recession with trees and buildings lightened by the atmosphere, a device also employed in folio 99b of the British Library *Khamsa* of Niẓāmī.[1] The overlapping bands of clouds and sky, seen also in the *Bahāristān* painting and folio 298a of the British Library *Khamsa*, are further evidence of Mādhava's adoption of the most obvious of European pictorial conventions.[2]

1. The painting is published in Brend, *The Emperor Akbar's* Khamsa *of Niẓāmī*, fig. 13.

2. The latter painting is reproduced in color in Brend, *The Emperor Akbar's* Khamsa *of Niẓāmī*, fig. 39.



FIGURE 9

دید بتی در پس دیوار قصر
شاه چو آن دید قرارش نماند
گرم فرستاد پیامی برو
رفت پس پرده بسی گفت و گوی
تا فکند دست بکامی درو
موی کشانش ز شبستان شاه
کرد بت از پاکی دامان خویش
کرد ملک دیده حیرت پر آب
زهره شکاف همه خوبان عصر
قاعده صبر بکارش نماند
پرده برانداخت ز بیم هلاک

# VII Khusraw and Shīrīn are entertained by musicians

Ascribed *'amal-i* Manōhara
22.4 x 13.2 cm
Folio 51a
Walters Art Museum (W.624)
Published: Titley, "Miniature Paintings," cover

After meeting Shīrīn by chance during a hunt, Khusraw returns with her to her palace in Armenia, where they are greeted in royal fashion by her aunt Mahīn Bānū and entertained by musicians. Shīrīn invites her guest to join her on the throne and tenders a tiny wine cup with one hand. As their intoxication for each other is fueled by wine and song, Khusraw and Shīrīn declare their love.

The artist follows the text immediately above the painting field in representing the first of the lovers' many trysts in a palatial setting rather than on the hunting ground, a locale depicted in the majority of illustrated copies of the text. There are, of course, abundant Mughal models for such a scene of royal entertainment, from which this composition draws the traditional hexagonal pavilion installed at the center of a concentric courtyard. Taking up the three-dimensional conception of form fostered by his father Basāvana, Manōhara manipulates these traditional architectural elements to create an illusion of space. He perforates the surfaces of the pavilion walls, provides a perspectival view of its ceiling, pulls back the curtain screening the voluminous staircase to the right, and places a waterwheel—a favorite element—in a cavernous tank. The intrusive text panel foils a spatial rendering of the pavilion's superstructure, forcing the small, mandatory dome to be set incongruously high above the pavilion.

Rising from its low, carpeted dais, the pavilion appears as a bright island amid the courtyard's deep green grass, which forms still darker eddies around the comely attendants. Manōhara particularizes the traditional slender, high-waisted Persian female type with an unusually small head, pronounced facial features, and very dark hair, which is occasionally gathered in a long, thin braid. His characteristic division of the face into distinct angular facets is especially clear in the figure of Khusraw, whose pointed chin and arched brows are accentuated by modeling.

Manōhara's palette is consistently much hotter than his father's; the brilliant patches of red scattered about the composition are the most obvious example of this, but the orange garments of Khusraw, a lute-player, and the bow-carrier outside the courtyard walls are also untempered by tonal effects used to suggest volume. Only in the purple walls of the pavilion does color yield significantly to form.



FIGURE 11

# VIII Khusraw and Shīrīn preside over the wedding of ten youths and ten maidens

Ascribed *'amal-i* Sānvala
23.5 x 15.0 cm
Folio 58a
Walters Art Museum (W.624)
Published: Titley, "Miniature Paintings," fig. 53; B. Wade, *Imaging Sound* (Chicago, 1998), fig. 106

Seated beside Shīrīn, Khusraw summons priests and orders them to preside over the wedding of ten youths and ten maidens. Khusraw impulsively invites Shīrīn to act on their youthful love and join him in the communal marital rite. Shīrīn demurs, responding that though she does not doubt the ardor of the king's love, she worries about its steadfastness. This insightful remark proves to be prophetic, for Shīrīn's rejection of Khusraw's proposal sparks a quarrelsome separation of the two lovers, who soon find consolation in the amorous attentions of others.

Sānvala minimizes the unique and central feature of this rarely illustrated episode—the marriage of the ten pairs of youths and maidens—by restricting the ceremony to a single couple dressed in marriage raiment. Khusraw and Shīrīn bask contentedly in each other's love, and seem oblivious to their youthful counterparts kneeling unobtrusively to the left of the central dais. Indeed, the compositional prominence of the spectacle of musicians and dancers bursting into song and dance is a measure of the extent to which the illustration of this marriage ceremony has been transformed into a scene of entertainment suited to any festive occasion. This reduction of a textually specific event to one of a limited number of generic situations is quite typical of the imperial atelier, which was attuned as much to pictorially efficient methods of illustration as to the common themes of human experience.

Sānvala's works generally resemble those of Mukunda, another senior artist, but display a broader range of faces and colors and a greater facility with landscape. The large, roundish faces depicted in this painting constitute a relatively narrow segment of that range, perhaps because nearly all the figures are shown in three-quarter view. Despite the joyous occasion, a number of figures acquire a chronically worried expression as a result of the artist's penchant for upturned eyebrows and puckered mouths.



FIGURE 12

کسی کش عشق باشد در خیالش
همی کردند یکیک را فراهم
شود همسر بکابین حلالش
بفرمان دو صاحب چاره سازان
همی جستند راه عشقبازان
ببوی وصل دلها گشت خرسند

# IX Saddened by the news of Khusraw's marriage to Shakar, Shīrīn takes a ride with her maids and meets the sculptor Farhād

Ascribed *'amal-i* Sānvala
22.6 x 14.7 cm
Folio 59a
Walters Art Museum (W.624)
Published: E. Grube, *The Classical Style in Islamic Painting* (New York, 1968), no. 91.1; Marshall, "The Poet and the Prince," fig. 9; W. Wiebke, *Die Frau im Islam* (Leipzig, 1980), 92

Two paintings in the manuscript are dedicated to the most critical episodes in the fatal affair of Shīrīn and Farhād: the initial contact of the Armenian queen with the sculptor on Mt. Bīsitūn and Farhād's demoralizing visit from the jealous Khusraw. The illustrative tradition of the former accommodates a quite fluid iconography. Farhād ranges in age from textually prescribed youthfulness to grey-bearded middle age; Shīrīn occasionally dismounts to draw close to Farhād in a setting that varies from the proper rocky landscape to a sumptuous palace interior. Common to nearly all outdoor scenes is some attribute of Farhād's occupation, such as the rock-cut equestrian figures that attract Shīrīn's attention, or Farhād wielding a pick.

This illustration falls at the point in the story when the love-smitten Farhād agrees to Shīrīn's request to cut a channel through the mountain to bring milk from his flocks to her court. Sānvala underscores the social disparity between the prospective lovers by wrapping the crowned Shīrīn in a resplendent golden cloak even as he garbs the sculptor, whom Amīr Khusraw has ennobled as a scion of the Chinese imperial family, in a humble brown jama, its edges upturned as an indication of his lowly occupation. Endowed with a wispy beard and a drowsy expression, the corpulent Farhād stands with his hands crossed in respect, hardly seeming to be the embodiment of ardent passion.

Behind the figures rise three clusters of pastel-colored outcrops, in whose lobes appear a number of half-formed animal grotesques. Punctuated by similar outcrops, Sānvala's landscape on folio 150b of the British Library *Khamsa* of Niẓāmī shows the same compositional and coloristic progression from a low, lime-green foreground to miniaturized European figures in a boat and on the opposite shore of a river leading to a city in the distance.[1] This and other comparisons to works ascribed to Sānvala corroborate the tiny ascription, which, like the one on folio 58a, probably replaces an original ascription lost when the manuscript was remargined.

1. This painting is reproduced in color in Brend, *The Emperor Akbar's* Khamsa *of Niẓāmī*, fig. 20.



FIGURE 13

# X Seeing the milk channel nearly completed, Khusraw visits Farhād and tricks him into believing that Shīrīn is dead

Attributed here to Dharmadāsa
24.1 x 15.5 cm
Folio 66b
Walters Art Museum (W.624)
Published: Grube, *The Classical Style*, no. 91.2; Brend, "Akbar's *Khamsah* of Amīr Khusrau," pl. 3

When Khusraw learns of Farhād's devotion to Shīrīn, he becomes disquieted and dreams of a woman who presents vessels of milk and nectar, respectively, to him and to a youth. The youth falters and allows his vessel to slip, a sign that Khusraw's soothsayer interprets to mean that Khusraw will triumph over his rival for the love of Shīrīn. Assuming the guise of a shepherd, Khusraw engages Farhād in a conversation that begins as a mere expression of curiosity but soon turns to its true purpose: to deprive the exhausted Farhād of the salve of love. So distressed is Farhād by the false news of Shīrīn's death that he loses all will to live and dies of a broken heart.

Although the illustration coincides with the textual account of Farhād's demise, the artist follows the stronger pictorial tradition of the story in depicting two figures before the disconsolate Farhād, whose discarded pick seems to float ominously above him. Khusraw's disguise is uncharacteristically complete here; that Khusraw could feign the age and religious status of the elderly mulla seems only slightly less likely than his willingness to assume the subordinate role of the bare-chested shepherd.

The three figures occupy a barren space ringed by outcrops that are much less Persianate in structure and color than those of the preceding illustration. Indeed, their elongated lobes, subdued colors, and tonal modeling recall Dharmadāsa's treatment of rocks on folio 26b of the Walters Art Museum section of the British Library *Khamsa* of Niẓāmī and folios 73a–b of the ca. 1584 *Tārīkh-i Khāndān-i Tīmūriyya*, a large, profusely illustrated historical manuscript.[1]

This attribution to Dharmadāsa is confirmed by many other features. The artist's penchant for strongly modeled figures with focused eyes creating explicit expressions is exemplified by the deep blue garment and tight profile of the astonished shepherd, who closely resembles the figure in the lower left of Dharmadāsa's painting on folio 98a (fig. 17). Likewise, the dress and countenance of the shepherd's elderly companion reappear in the teacher and the door guardian of the same painting. Dharmadāsa uses his favored lost-profile view for the figure of a mendicant striding near the goats grazing in the distance. His habit of including touches of genre in nearly every scene is evidenced in the energetic goats in the foreground.

1. The first of these paintings is reproduced in color in Brend, *The Emperor Akbar's* Khamsa *of Niẓāmī*, fig. 29.

همی گفت این که روزش شب آمد
بشیرین کندنش از دیده خون رفت
بتلخی جان شیرین بر لب آمد
که تا شیرین کنان جان بیرون رفت
دهانش تلخ و شیرین بر زبان بود
همین خو دارد این چرخ جفا کوش

# XI Khusraw sends Shīrīn a ring as a pledge of marriage

Ascribed *ʿamal-i* Farrukh Cela
21.8 x 13.1 cm
Folio 80a
Walters Art Museum (W.624)
Published: A. Krishna, "A Study of the Akbari Artist: Farrukh Chela," in *Chhavi* (Banaras, 1971), fig. 533; Losty, *The Art of the Book in India*, 91

Reconciled at last after a concert in which Khusraw and Shīrīn command the most renowned musicians of the day, Bārbud and Nigīsā, to sing *ghazals* in the language of the other, the two lovers are sequestered in adjacent courtyards, where they prepare for their long-awaited nuptials. Likened to the splendor of the paradisaical house opposite the temple in Mecca, both courtyards bustle with activity. Some servants converse with Khusraw over the din of the celebrations, while others pass platters heaped with goods from one pavilion to the other. In the distance, Shīrīn grows weak at the sight of Khusraw's luminous ring, which, the poet declares, carries the tribute of the seven climes.

Farrukh Cela accommodates this profuse activity in a complicated architectural compound. He encourages the ritual separation of the betrothed by isolating Khusraw and Shīrīn in individual hexagonal pavilions placed at opposite ends of the composition. He then uses a strongly angled courtyard, porch, and monumental gate to provide an avenue between the elegant pavilions for the lovers' imminent union. Although this dramatic diagonal arrangement departs radically from Mughal convention, it is a rather sober development of Farrukh's earlier experiments with the construction of pictorial space in which architecture dominates the landscape or encloses figures. As in folio 65a of the British Library *Khamsa* of Niẓāmī, here Farrukh's penchant for diagonals is combined with a surfeit of sharply delineated architectural features, which range from coffers seen arbitrarily from below to slender, split colonnettes.

Only the stabilizing horizontal of the central porch, the muted colors of the architecture, and the oasis of the distant turquoise courtyard save this painting from the visual cacophony to which its precursor succumbs.

Farrukh's fastidious detail is not limited to architecture but marks nearly all of his very distinctive figures. Often relieved of the task of drawing portraits in collaborative efforts, Farrukh consistently employs a figure type graced with a heavily modeled oval head, beady eyes, a hooked nose, and a pointed chin. He reserves for servants a more vulgar type: a squat figure with a heavy-set jaw, long, pointed nose, and a thoroughly loutish expression. He does not apply this physiognomic distinction to the female attendants, who are uniformly tall, slender, and crowned with high headdresses.



FIGURE 15

# XII Solomon orders one idle demon to fill the sea with sand and another to fill the desert with water

Ascribed *'amal-i* 'Alī Qulī
22.4 x 14.6 cm
Folio 94b
Walters Art Museum (W.624)
Published: Brend, "Akbar's *Khamsah* of Amīr Khusrau," pl. 5

Khusraw interjects this amusing story following his remarks on his reasons for composing the poem and before his words of advice addressed to his son Khiẓr. Considered the ideal ruler in both Muslim and Christian lore, the wise Solomon holds sway over all creatures, who are often depicted gathered around his throne. Although birds are his most prominent subjects, supernatural *dīvs*, or demons, also do Solomon's bidding. The two demons shown here are so industrious that they finish a month's work in only a day and begin to wreak havoc out of boredom. Recognizing the danger of their idleness, the king orders one demon to fill the sea with sand and the other to fill the desert with water, a futile task at which they labor until death. From this anecdote of futility Khusraw draws the moral of the ruinous consequences of disinterested thought, and then wonders how his own accomplishments will be judged.

The rubric in the center of the first line of the text panel marks the beginning of this rarely illustrated story, which breaks for the illustration at the point of the demons' contrary actions. 'Alī Qulī's straightforward rendering of this passage depicts the two demons dutifully—albeit somewhat quizzically—bailing earth and water on the order of Solomon, who is not represented. Behind these brightly colored, fantastic creatures, whose spots, flaring eyes, horns, fangs, short garments, and belled ornaments are all drawn from a long Persian tradition, graze an assortment of tiny deer.

Shrilly colored, round-lobed outcrops establish the tight spatial limits of the landscape, which shows no trace of the European conventions appropriated by many of the other artists who contributed paintings to this manuscript. Unlike his better-known colleagues, 'Alī Qulī is not represented in most earlier or contemporary projects. Indeed, his meager oeuvre numbers a single work in the 1596 *Jāmi' al-Tawārīkh*,[1] two in the 1597–99 National Museum *Bāburnāma*,[2] a pair of paintings of a rooster and a hen and her chicks in the Gulshan Album,[3] two copies after European prints in the same album,[4] and a pair of paintings dated 1616 in the Chester Beatty Library.[5]

1. This painting, now in a private collection, is published in Brand and Lowry, *Akbar's India*, no. 36.

2. Folios 283a–b are ascribed to Allāh Qulī; they are reproduced in M. S. Randhawa, *Paintings of the* Bābur Nāmā (New Delhi, 1983), 131–32.

3. Gulshan Album, Gulistan Library, Teheran, nos. 34 and 35.

4. Gulshan Album, nos. 50 and 51.

5. These are published in L. Leach, *Mughal and Other Indian Paintings from the Chester Beatty Library* (London, 1995), II, nos. 5.316–17.



FIGURE 16

گویند دو دیو با سلیمان
بردند بر اوج بارگاهی
فرمان ده کاردان بود
فرمود که هر دو تن مهیا
روزی کردند کار ماهی
بر مردم و دیو کامران بود
چون در عمل دگر رسیدند
این ریگ برون در آب ریزد
کردند همان که شنیده راست

*MAJNŪN WA LAYLĀ*

# XIII Laylā and Majnūn fall in love at school

Ascribed *ʿamal-i* Dharmadāsa
24.2 x 15.4 cm
Folio 98a
Walters Art Museum (W.624)
Published: R. Godden, *Gulbadan: Portrait of a Princess* (London, 1980), 36; Brend, "Akbar's *Khamsah* of Amīr Khusrau," pl. 6; Beach, *Mughal and Rajput Painting*, fig. 39

Dharmadāsa departs from the conventions of this scene, one of the most frequently illustrated episodes of the two versions of Laylā and Majnūn, by highlighting the personal drama of the two children doomed to love. Laylā, the nearest of the three girls to the master, gazes down at a book, but Majnūn, face furrowed in an intense stare at his beloved, reveals the depth to which his heart has been afflicted by love. The artist enlivens the usual iconography of repetitive rows of small, seated pupils by allowing a boisterous brawl to erupt in the foreground. Outside the walls of the school, whose half-open door is guarded by a familiar doorkeeper, stroll other stock characters of the Mughal world: a bony mendicant, a tender mother and child, and an earnest supplicant.

Dharmadāsa surmounts the large text panel with high, tiled domes, thereby minimizing the obtrusiveness of the large, flat surface in the scene, whose space is enhanced by parallel angles of the central dais and surrounding arcade. A similar concern with illusionistic space is manifest in two contemporary courtyard scenes by the artist, folio 102a of the British Library *Khamsa* of Niẓāmī and folio 73b of the British Library *Akbarnāma*.[1] Here, however, this aspect is undermined by advancing areas of strong color, such as the fuchsia dado, purple carpet, and purple and yellow arcade details.

Together with these architectural elements and the bright green landscape, the deep hues of the children's clothing complete the painting's rich coloristic harmony. Only a few of the figures show Dharmadāsa's characteristic contour modeling, which makes clothing cling to their bodies and imparts a sense of compressed energy to the restless children. The delicately rendered eyes, chins, and napes are also typical of this artist's work.

1. The former is published in Brend, *The Emperor Akbar's* Khamsa *of Niẓāmī*, fig. 14; the latter is reproduced in Wade, *Imaging Sound*, fig. 89.



FIGURE 17

از وسوسه چشم دیو بسته
تسبیح فرشتگان گسسته
زنی بت که چراغ بت پرستان
طاووس بهشت و کبک بستان
فرموده کلاله را سپاری
داده به نثره پلاح داری
افکنده بدوش زلف چون شست
او سحر و نظارگی مست
معجون لبش بر رفشانی
پرورده به آب زندگانی
همخوابه لاله گیسوانش
همشیره انگبین دهانش
قندش نمک طبرزد آلود
خوشخوار تر از گوارش عود
اندر صف آن بتان شیرین
چون زهره و شعار و مه بر دون
زانو زده قیس در دگر سو
هم چرب زبان و هم سخنگو
نازک چو نهال نودمیده
خوش طبع و لطیف و آرمیده
شیرین سخنی که هوش می برد
رونق ز شکرفروش می برد
بودی به سخن چو شکر و شیر
پست سخنش معلم پیر
از رخ بدو شاه بر دمی گرد
صندل به وخورد و خود مکرد
نالنده تیجه در دبستان
چون بلبل مست در گلستان

عمل دهرم داس

# XIV Majnūn's father visits him in the wilderness

Ascribed *'amal-i* Lāla
23.5 x 15.2 cm
Folio 100b
Walters Art Museum (W.624)
Published: Grube, *The Classical Style*, no. 91.3; Titley, "Miniature Paintings," fig. 54; Marshall, "The Poet and Prince," fig. 10; Brend, "Akbar's *Khamsah* of Amīr Khusrau," pl. 7; Beach, *Mughal and Rajput Painting*, fig. 38; Bloom and Blair, *Islamic Arts* (London, 1997), fig. 187

Taking refuge in the wilderness, the abject Majnūn finds solace in mortification and ceaseless hymns of love. His father ventures out to console him, but instead is overwhelmed by the appalling deprivation that his son has endured. Majnūn, however, is heartened at the sight of his father, and rushes to anoint his foot with anguished tears.

The precise correspondence of this gesture of prostration to the action prescribed in the final line of text above the painting exemplifies an unusually direct response of the artist to the text. As in most poetical illustrations, this responsiveness is limited to an easily visualized action, one probably brought to the attention of the artist by the project supervisor or another authority familiar with the text. No heed is shown to the abundant metaphors of this same passage, in which Khusraw likens Majnūn to an extinguished lamp, and describes his lair in the wilderness as the skirt of a mountain and the seam of a grotto.

Fig. 19. A king asks the darvish why he no longer comes in attendance. By Lāla. *Bahāristān*, 1595, f. 17b. 20.6 x 13.2 cm. Bodleian Library, University of Oxford, Ms. Elliott 254.

Indeed, the desolation of the scene is belied by Lāla's brilliantly colored, magical landscape, which strongly recalls his works on folio 17b of the *Bahāristān* (fig. 19) and folio 171a of the 1596–97 Bharat Kala Bhavan *Anwār-i Suhaylī*.[1] Flat, pastel rock formations heave in the middleground, their fan-like crests emphasized by a wiry outline. The background is filled with faint European figures preparing to enter a town set cheerfully between turquoise trees and beneath a radiant golden sky.

An array of lacquered animals, each poised beside his mate, witnesses the tearful meeting between father and son. Lāla displays his facility with modeling in Majnūn's individualized, gaunt face, exposed ribs, and thick, short skirt. He is less successful with Majnūn's crossed, bony limbs, whose ungainly arrangement is typical of the artist's strained efforts at complicated poses. For Majnūn's elderly father, Lāla summons one of his standard countenances: a large, bearded face seen in three-quarter view, with eyes fixed in a blank gaze beneath narrowed eyebrows.

1. The latter painting is reproduced in color in S. P. Verma, "La'l: The Forgotten Master," in *Mughal Masters: Further Studies*, ed. A. Das (Mumbai, 1998), fig. 7.

اندر پی آن ترانه زد کام
وافکند ز اشک باده در جام
دریافت حریف را چو مستان
بازمزه هزار دستان
می گفت دران فراق خونریز
باخود غزل جراحت انگیز
درکرده پری پیاله خاری
دردامن کوه و دز غاری
دل رابتیزه سنگ میداد
رخ را ز طپانچه رنگ میداد
جون چشم پدر فتاد بروی
شد سپت ز سختی غمش پی
جون پچه خستگان بدید سویش
بشتافت بگریه پیش رویش
دیدش جو چراغ مرده بی نور
دور از من و تو ز خویشتن دور
جون روی پدر بدید فرزند
نخجی دل پاره یافت پیوند
خم کرد تن بچشم رسیده
مالید بپای پیر دیده
عمل لعل

# XV Majnūn caresses a dog that lives in Laylā's neighborhood

Attributed here to Dharmadāsa
24.5 x 15.2 cm
Folio 113a
Walters Art Museum (W.624)

While wandering the streets near Laylā's house, Majnūn encounters a stray dog. His heart goes out to the unwanted animal, whose condition is so like his own. He strips off his clothes to prepare a bed for it and puts his arm around its neck. The motivation behind Majnūn's gestures is not simple compassion, however, but his desire to express his love vicariously to a creature that could at least be near his beloved Laylā. Such behavior spurs the community elders to rebuke the youth again.

This image of a finely attired Majnūn embracing the dog in a courtyard breaks dramatically with the pictorial tradition of a half-naked Majnūn caressing a dog in the wilderness.[1] This iconographic deviation is not determined explicitly by the text passages immediately preceding the painting, which appears later in Majnūn's long lament than do the corresponding illustrations in earlier manuscripts, but still illustrates the commiserating pair of creatures. Instead, it seems that the resplendent, but completely uncharacteristic, robes in which Majnūn is dressed were borrowed from a painting executed by Dharmadāsa a few years earlier in the British Library *Khamsa* of Niẓāmī (fig. 40). The artist must have been so pleased with the unusual golden robes he had fashioned for the depiction of the princely Khusraw that he decided to reuse them again, despite the fact that they were entirely inappropriate to Majnūn, a social outcast. The elaborate courtyard in which Majnūn's respectable tribunal is held is another manifestation of Dharmadāsa's unrestrained flight into elegance.

Isolated in the thinly painted grassy area before the open-porched pavilion, Majnūn is all but overlooked by the elders, who consult a book for guidance. Many of the long-faced, bearded figures bear a strong familial resemblance not only to one another, but also to Dharmadāsa's school-master on folio 98a (fig. 17). The domed gateway, corner turret, covered porch, and even the striking fuchsia dado are entirely consistent with Dharmadāsa's precise architecture in that painting but do not strain the usual Mughal arrangement of architectural elements in strict parallel registers.

1. Indeed, Brend, "Akbar's *Khamsah* of Amīr Khusrau," 290, suggests that this is not Majnūn at all, but a young prince fondling a favorite hunting dog.



FIGURE 20

# XVI Laylā and Majnūn are reunited in the wilderness

Ascribed *'amal-i* Narasimha
21.8 x 13.5 cm
Folio 115a
Walters Art Museum (W.624)
Published: Beach, *Early Mughal Painting*, fig. 73; Brend, "Akbar's *Khamsah* of Amīr Khusrau," pl. 8

The painting traditions of the two versions of the story of Laylā and Majnūn draw close to one other at the poignant moment of the lovers' fleeting encounter. Artists illustrating Niẓāmī's text generally depict the star-crossed lovers together in the prescribed palm grove or area beside Laylā's tent and reserve the tableau of wild beasts arrayed peaceably around Majnūn for other situations. By contrast, Amīr Khusraw's text describes the reunion of Laylā and Majnūn as taking place in the wilderness; accordingly, artists charged with the illustration of this scene habitually enlist a throng of paired beasts to establish the setting and to amplify the climax of the lovers' yearning. Occasionally, however, they also use the motif as a generic attribute of Majnūn's own savage state, as in the scene on folio 100b (fig. 18).

Narasimha emphasizes the physical isolation of the two small figures in the wilderness by setting them at the very center of a spacious composition. He reinforces this effect with a favorite device, a vista whose depth is established by rows of bluish trees lightened systematically in accordance with the newly learned convention of European atmospheric perspective. Laylā and Majnūn become the central focus of the landscape relieved from barrenness only by two cypresses, symbols of steadfast love, rising in tandem beside them. The stream passing directly beneath the rock platform upon which the seated figures converse chastely is the most obvious and powerful of the formal means employed here, but Laylā's central position and bright orange *shalwar* also contribute to this end.

Described in the two lines of text above the painting as rejoicing in dance at the sight of the love-intoxicated couple, an assortment of wild and tame animals looks on from a respectful distance. Narasimha's characteristic dark corona appears around many of these sleek, lively creatures, who are neither as strictly paired nor as formal in arrangement as their counterparts in Lāla's painting on folio 100b (fig. 18). In a manner reminiscent of Miskīn, Narasimha endows some beasts, notably the lions and the ibexes, with quite human expressions.



FIGURE 21

*Ā'ĪNAH-I SIKANDARĪ*

# XVII Alexander lassoes an opponent

Ascribed Jagannātha
23.7 x 14.8 cm
Folio 128a
Walters Art Museum (W.624)
Published: Brend, "Akbar's *Khamsah* of Amīr Khusrau," pl. 9

Khusraw uses a summary of Niẓāmī's account of Alexander to begin his own version of the meteoric career of the world-conqueror, whose legendary power and just behavior had elevated him in Islamic literature to the status of archetypal ruler. Khusraw briefly extols Alexander's birth and accession to the throne, his affair with Nushaba, his visit to Mecca, and his demand of treasure and fealty from the raja of India—all episodes that do not appear in the poet's own story.

This illustration of Alexander lassoing an enemy warrior falls at this point in the text, an odd and unprecedented position for an otherwise unexceptional scene of battle. It relates neither to the surrender of the Indian crown, the event described in the text preceding the painting, nor to Alexander's march to China to press his next claim of suzerainty, the event begun and resolved peaceably immediately after the illustration. The lasso itself provides no clue as to the identity of Alexander's opponent; other illustrated copies of the text occasionally employ the noose of humiliation in each of the three individual combats between Alexander's forces and the Chinese, but more often give precedence to the sword. Although Mughal illustrations are rarely detached completely from a specific textual reference, this battle scene unquestionably draws its iconography and structure more from the abundant visual models of this traditional genre than from actual textual prescription. It may well represent the numerous engagements initiated by Alexander in his quest for domination of the seven climes.

The composition follows the customary formula for a display of individual military prowess: the two antagonists are isolated in the center of a field framed by auxiliary figures and a vertically inclined landscape. The outcome of the contest is made clear both by their own unequivocal action and by Alexander's soldiers' pursuit of enemy warriors fleeing to the right.

Jagannātha, whose name is written in red on a small tab of paper cut from the lower margin and later pasted onto the painting, uses strong directional glances to enhance the connections between the peripheral soldiers. Although his figures are not widely varied in type, Jagannātha adds bulging cheeks and particularly sumptuous mustaches to the standard three-quarter face and a measure of subtlety to the profile view. Outcrops marked by saw-toothed contours and parallel hatching are overlaid with a series of rectangular stones; together these produce an extremely flat landscape, whose pale tonality makes it one of Jagannātha's more successful backdrops. The linear cityscape in the distance is equally flat in conception and delicate in execution.



FIGURE 22

# XVIII To the surprise of Alexander, the Chinese warrior-maiden Kanīfū sheds her armor and tells him of her destiny to marry the man who defeated her in battle

Attributed here to Sānvala
24.8 x 15.2 cm
Folio 135a
Walters Art Museum (W.624)
Published: Brend, "Akbar's *Khamsah* of Amīr Khusrau," pl. 10

When Alexander's officers strip the captive warrior of his armor, they are astonished to discover that their valiant Chinese opponent is a woman. The scene of this revelation, an episode selected for illustration in seven earlier manuscripts, occurs in a palatial setting whose unusual expansiveness affords a view of not only the ubiquitous exclusionary wall, carpeted dais, and open-porched pavilion, but also of a natural world that moves imperceptibly from the controlled elements of the garden to the more vigorous ones of a lush landscape.

The formula of a grassy enclosure opening onto a deep landscape that culminates in a city before a bluff appears in a number of Sānvala's works, but never more successfully than here. In folio 294a of the British Library *Khamsa* of Niẓāmī, for example, the European-inspired recession is arrested temporarily by a wall and slowed by a genre scene of a man driving a team of bullocks to draw water from a well.[1] Likewise, Sānvala's painting on folio 98a of the British Library *Akbarnāma* resorts to an archway cut into the thick back wall to provide a middleground view, which is seen from a different perspective than is the riverine cityscape. The presence of a low palm, screen of dark trees, and hemispherical mounds in Sānvala's work on folio 220a of the British Library *Khamsa* of Niẓāmī testifies to the artist's inclination to reuse the same vegetal and topographical forms whenever possible.[2]

This scene and Sānvala's painting on folio 58a (fig. 12) display virtually identical court trappings, including the pinkish stone, dense floral carpet designs, and a spoke-patterned red canopy extending from the front of the pavilion. Sānvala adds to the usual palette of flat orange, light blue, and malachite green, a distinctive velvety red, a light violet, and a chestnut brown. These colors appear frequently in contrasting combinations, as in the red and violet garb of the aged retainer on the dais. Even their location is consistent: nearly all Sānvala's court scenes feature a brown dado and pale blue and black carpets.

Sānvala employs a relatively small scale for his numerous figures, with only the enthroned Alexander swelling to outsized proportions. The variety of views and expressions of the figures lends a sense of coherence and animation to the group, who hold the customary insignia, gifts, and musical instruments.

1. This painting is reproduced in color in Brend, *The Emperor Akbar's* Khamsa *of Niẓāmī*, fig. 38.

2. This painting is published in Brend, *The Emperor Akbar's* Khamsa *of Niẓāmī*, fig. 26.



FIGURE 23

همه روز تا شب در آن رستخیز
یکی خسته را مرهم ریش کرد
یکی نوحه بر مرده خویش کرد
زره از تن و خود از سر کشند

# XIX The prostrate Khāqān of China pays homage to Alexander, who presents the defeated commander with tokens of respect

Attributed here to Sānvala
24.5 x 15.0 cm
Folio 139a
Walters Art Museum (W.624)
Published: Brend, "Akbar's *Khamsah* of Amīr Khusrau," pl. 11

Admitted to Alexander's presence by the emphatic two-armed gesture of the sovereign's adjutant, the Khāqān of China leads his nobles in the requisite display of submission. Following a long-standing Mughal convention employed most prominently in the 1596 *Jāmi' al-Tawārīkh*, the artist identifies the subjugated foes as Chinese Mongols not by racial features but by their distinctive full-sleeved costumes and ceremonial plumed headdresses. Here, the latter are grafted curiously onto a type of black tall, brimmed hat used more commonly to depict exotic European headware. In the foreground, Mughal courtiers hasten to offer gift-laden coffers and platters as well as a golden crown and throne, with which the Khāqān is permitted to rule as Alexander's vassal.

The setting for this second, almost unprecedented scene of submission to Alexander shifts to a circular compound enclosed by a brown textile wall. At the center of this stippled grassy area is a high golden tent ornamented with dense interlace and preceded by a carpeted hexagonal dais. Sānvala copies Alexander's position, gesture, and countenance from his image on folio 135a (fig. 23), and makes only minor changes in the color of the royal robes, the closed front of the throne, and the spidery spread of the throne legs.

The profusion of long-robed figures draws attention to Sānvala's system of modeling cloth, which suffers no disruption of its series of parallel shadows and highlights by irregular folds of cloth shaped by the body. This system imparts a static quality to many of the figures, particularly those wearing knee-length, bulbous jamas.



FIGURE 24

خزانی زمینوع آن خروکست

بزرگان چین رازیابانفرق

بفرسو وسیس نمایدابراس غماز

جهان گشت شرمندز بخش

زمین کل هزاران او ریشاسشه

بصدلید شرمیاری نخلی

که دحیرت آن خرو کیست

زغلنت میان کک بر دخرق

ر ودمهار جانب خانه

کران سنک کی خوبی فلص

ولش سک گشت رنی راد د

نعلطید دنظم اسکندری

همهش فرمان وچس کشید

جدکانبرسرکرامنایه

سپهد چین زایفوازگی

غواوان دران اقشوخ

رنگ نمایش فش ش ش بی شثا

سرش ازرفعت بهاون

کرم کدربرقت دربرا

زبرپایفت سرعایرکی

چوازربارست چواربای

ازبانش نبوش بکیدکا

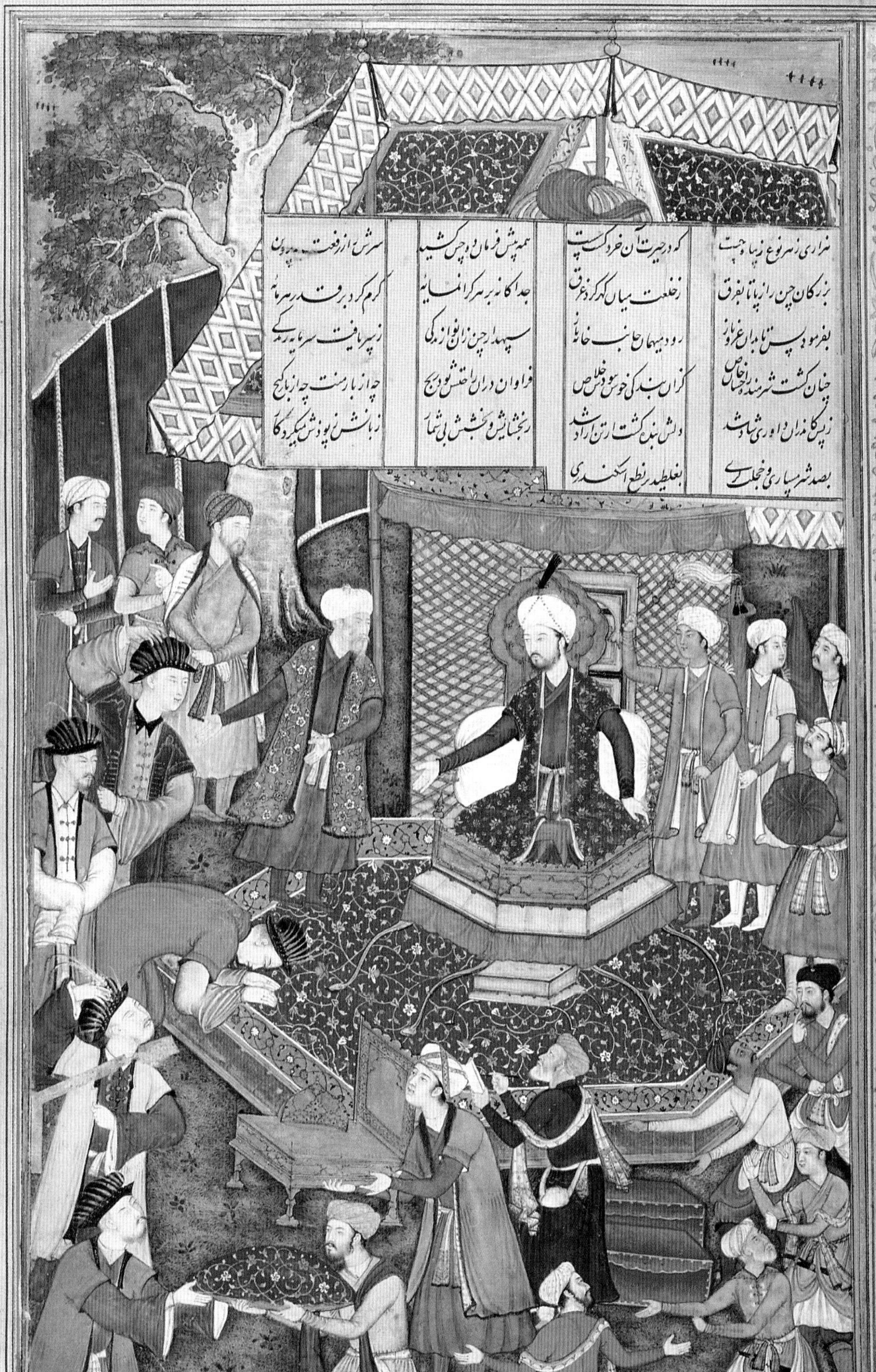

# XX Alexander erects an enchanted mirror that allows him to monitor activity on the high seas

Ascribed *'amal-i* Dharmadāsa
24.4 x 15.7 cm
Removed from the manuscript between folios 149 and 150
The Metropolitan Museum of Art, gift of Alexander Smith Cochran, 1913 (13.228.32)
Published: T. Bowie et al., *East-West in Art, Patterns of Aesthetic and Cultural Relationships* (Bloomington, Indiana, 1966), fig. 307; Brend, "Akbar's *Khamsah* of Amīr Khusrau," pl. 12

Niẓāmī's account of Alexander's mirror, a technically masterful object used for personal contemplation, is recast by Khusraw to accommodate a further-reaching function: the magical reflection of all activity within a radius of sixty leagues. This difference in nature is manifested in the two contemporary Mughal illustrations of the respective subjects. A double-page composition on folios 16b and 17a of the Walters section of the 1595 *Khamsa* of Niẓāmī (fig. 67) shows the process of working the bellows, forging the red-hot metal into round mirrors, and burnishing a nearly finished product.[1] In contrast, this full-page illustration from the *Khamsa* of Amīr Khusraw draws its imagery from the text passages that precede it. These describe Alexander's order to construct at the edge of the Sea of Rūm (the Mediterranean Sea) a tall tower, which is surmounted by a revolving mirror cast under a magical spell. Alexander then orders a hundred ships readied to sail against pirates whose location and activities the surface of this powerful beacon reveals, a detail that Dharmadāsa carefully includes.

The outcome of the great naval battle has not yet been determined. Alexander's troops set out from beneath the shadow of their guiding beacon to pursue a more numerous and more heavily armed enemy, their surge reinforced by a series of jutting banks. Dharmadāsa uses the dynamic zigzag arrangement of land, stern, and prow to create a compositional clarity absent from most land encounters, thereby encouraging the viewer to perceive each vessel's gamut of grim combatants as a unit. This effect is enhanced by the typically taut features and directed glances of Dharmadāsa's figures.

The artist employs a similarly elevated viewpoint and active landscape in folio 76a of the British Library *Akbarnāma* and folio 195a of the British Library *Khamsa* of Niẓāmī.[2] The latter painting is particularly close to this scene, featuring not only a tall tower, but also a genre scene of herdsmen and a muted palette. Such comparisons leave no doubt about the validity of this painting's ascription, which is written on a bit of paper cut from the original border and later applied to the lower right corner of the work.

1. The paintings are reproduced in color in Brend, *The Emperor Akbar's* Khamsa *of Niẓāmī*, figs. 27 and 28.

2. The former painting is published in R. Pinder-Wilson, "History and Romance in Mughal India," *Oriental Art*, 13 (1967), 63; the latter painting is reproduced in color in Brend, *The Emperor Akbar's* Khamsa *of Niẓāmī*, fig. 24.

# XXI When the Greeks refuse Alexander's prophecy and deny God, Alexander orders his men to cut a channel through the mountains to drown them

Attributed here to Sūradāsa Gujarātī
24.6 x 15.2 cm
Folio 153b
Walters Art Museum (W.624)

Alexander's conquest of the world allows him to offer the fruits of civilization—especially faith in God—to the peoples he encounters. Alexander proselytizes his faith by force of example and sword. Feeling secure from the threat of Alexander's power by virtue of the seemingly impenetrable mountains of their country, the Greeks rebuff his envoy and incur the king's wrath.

Alexander commands his men to punish this act of defiance. When the army becomes stalled in the impassable mountainous terrain of Greece, Alexander takes up a stratagem proposed by Khiẓr: to cut a channel from the sea to the Greeks' stronghold, thereby unleashing the fury of the sea upon the fires of sedition. He orders his men to cut through three leagues of rock, a task that Khusraw likens to that of the sculptor Farhād. The soldiers complete the channel in three months and build a fire against the final obstacle. As the stone crumbles, the waters surge forward and engulf the Greeks in a great wave of death. Among the few men to escape this deluge is Plato, who devotes himself to God and soon becomes Alexander's spiritual adviser.

This illustration of the Greeks' demise, found in no other copy of the *Khamsa*, follows the text only in depicting the moment of the flood, but does not convey its spirit of righteous chastisement. Like other scenes representing drownings in Mughal histories and a biblical story, it shows victims struggling to avoid a watery grave; the inclusion of women, infants, and even a stranded goat here adds a poignant tone to the cataclysm. The three men pulling survivors to shore belie the deliberateness of this devastation, whose means are suggested only by the pick and maces held by a second, leaderless cluster of men.

This painting may be attributed to Sūradāsa Gujarātī, a prolific artist who assumed a major role in the 1596–97 *Akbarnāma*. The small-eyed, thin-nosed figures seen here in great numbers are represented less prominently in Sūradāsa's works on folio 106a of the British Library *Akbarnāma* and folio 4a of the 1597–99 National Museum *Bāburnāma*.[1] The heavy round arch and generally blocky architecture of the distant cityscape are highly reminiscent of Sūradāsa's painting on folio 262b of the 1595 *Khamsa* of Niẓāmī, as is the juxtaposition of flat striations and tall outcrops in the mountainous terrain.[2]

1. The former is published in Wade, *Imaging Sound*, fig. 48; the latter is reproduced in color in Randhawa, *Paintings of the* Bābur Nāmā, pl. I.

2. The painting is reproduced in color in Brend, *The Emperor Akbar's* Khamsa *of Niẓāmī*, fig. 33.



FIGURE 26

پہ ورینگ باشد پطرلیگ
کہ یونانیان اپت درویگ
سنودر رپه کرکو کشتی موان
رچشم سیت وردانیود
پول و پنہجو وخاركنی
پسنگ انذراین کباراند
نہت یش جوهی جوفرباند
کهچوشگنا ناوشودارست
زدنداآتش شدوبکر جمند
رویپنگ شیشه چهورپانخی
اجل نداندرا نع دیو كفان

پہ ورپنگ مکهبیطط سنگ
پسنگی کرکو وریزتوان
پسنگ رکهحضر سشش و
کربت برعم کوه زایکنے
تعلیم ودانش لکارآمذ
بهکوکشرپیل خوفرجند
رویپنگ کرزندز انکوست
درآن پردوهنیزم وورنخسیند
زنیروی دریا دران سبک لاخ
جهان درجہان موعیطط فارکر

کریزآ اہنسجار تتوان پت
اکرحضر رسعمرو شیخ پش
بغموو ناسدپه پگام
سجاہی کش خضرشاش سعا
پستونی ارستین ینیخ ی ما
بقندرپه پہ قلب داركن
حوزردیک دریا زکوشہیگ
گرفت آتش وورا ه درخار
دراقثا وپسیلاب دریابكو
نا نذا نذران عزریعطط قاتان

سنود آتش خضم درایپت
بطوفان نوح گلکند درت خویس
مدنالہ خضر خضم احنرام
کش ذندز بازوی ونی وراے
سکایفت ستونی زووہ پستونی
درآن تنسکخنا بودخارکس
شگ شیشه یاسبگ پطط
بداما نکر پرده رباپارکرد
خوشند وشدموح دریاكو
نشائے نہ زیومان یونایان

# XXII Alexander visits the sage Plato in his mountain cave and is told of his imminent death

Attributed to Basāvana
24.7 x 15.2 cm
Removed from the manuscript between folios 156 and 157
The Metropolitan Museum of Art, gift of Alexander Smith Cochran, 1913 (13.228.30)
Published: Welch, "The Paintings of Basawan," fig. 8; Bowie et al., *East-West in Art*, fig. 309; Welch, *The Art of Mughal India*, pl. 8b; S. C. Welch, "A Matter of Empathy: Comical Indian Pictures," *Asian Art and Culture*, 7, no. 3 (1994), figs. 7–7a

Alexander complements his military exploits on behalf of his realm and religion with personal explorations of the unfathomed depths of the mind and the sea. Continuing the long Islamic tradition of such conferences between temporal and spiritual authorities, he seeks out the sage Plato, who offers words of advice on rulership and warnings of Alexander's impending death. Khusraw grants Plato a more prominent role in Alexander's story than does Niẓāmī, who singles out the philosopher only for his ability to charm animals with music.

Dressed in a robe so heavily textured that it suggests fur, Plato gestures in exposition to Alexander, who listens amenably with his hands folded. The shadowy confines of Plato's cave lend an air of intimacy to the quiet exchange of ideas between the two figures. Not daring to intrude, Alexander's retainers, on the right, turn in among themselves, while the grooms and huntsmen in the foreground are preoccupied with their chores. Indeed, the only distraction comes from the nearby figure of a cook hunkered over a simmering stewpot. By his conspicuous placement and carefully observed position and expression, a common genre figure is transformed into a remarkable character study.

In this, his last dated painting, Basāvana works similiar wonders on the animals scattered around the scene. Whether it be the dog dozing contentedly before the fire, a hound slavering from the hunt, or two jackals observing the proceedings with vigilant golden eyes, Basāvana consistently animates—some would even say personifies—his creatures with highly individualized actions and expressions.

Basāvana's landscapes also move away from predictable forms and schematic compositions. The rocks billowing above Alexander and Plato acquire unusual mass and volume from their subtle coloring and division into facets. Figures pass through the traditionally impenetrable screen of rocks in the foreground, which opens onto an area broken up by uncontrived rocks and gullies. Even the walls and domes of the ubiquitous cityscape are well-integrated with the high outcrops and text panel that they abut.



FIGURE 27

نه شاهیست کز ماه تا ماهیست
در بندگی زن که آن شاهی است
به هر کار از آن کس طلب یاوری
که دارد نهان با خدا داوری
با پشمینه پوشان که اندر جهان
جهانیست در زیر هر مو نهان
مدد زان گدا جوی در نیک و بد
که از پادشاهان نجوید مدد
کسی کو بهی جهد شاهان کند
نه اندیشه نیک خواهان کند
ز رنگ خدا داده دل شاد کن
ولی بوی او از دگر گلشن است
بهشتی بود شاه درویش خواه
که تو می خوری او کند نوش باد

# XXIII Alexander is lowered into the sea in a diving bell to seek truth and to demonstrate his faith in God

Attributed here to Mukunda
23.8 x 15.5 cm
Removed from the manuscript between folios 164 and 165
The Metropolitan Museum of Art, gift of Alexander Smith Cochran, 1913 (13.228.27)
Published: *The Arts of Islam: Masterpieces from The Metropolitan Museum of Art, New York* (Berlin and New York, 1981), no. 122; R. Craven, *A Concise History of Indian Art* (London, 1997), fig. 164; E. Koch, "Netherlandish Naturalism in Imperial Mughal Painting," *Apollo*, 152 (2000), fig. 1

Alexander sets sail for the western seas with an entourage that includes the philosopher Aristotle and the prophets Khiẓr and Elias. At one point, he orders his crew to steady the boat with anchors and to prepare a glass diving bell in which he will descend into the depths of the sea for a hundred days. He avows his complete acceptance of divine fate, swearing that "If I should emerge from this terrifying experience, my understanding of the truth of man will be the true understanding. And if there should be a calamity during these days, then before God I will be like a single grain in a hundred thousand."

Depictions of Alexander's consultations before his sea voyage and during the long journey itself far outnumber those of the king's actual descent into the unconquered submarine realm, which teems with wondrous creatures and unknown dangers summoned by his celestial guide. As expected, this minor pictorial tradition is occasioned by the position of the illustration in the text, which concludes above the painting with a description of the crew fastening ropes to the pearly glass vessel and setting it onto the water like a bubble.

Mukunda highlights the personal bravery of Alexander and the wonderment and physical strain of his crew to the virtual exclusion of the more profound and abstract religious dimension of the dramatic action. The text assigns the task of holding the ropes of the diving bell to Khiẓr and Elias, who are customarily distinguished by flaming aureoles. Here, however, those sacred figures are absent altogether, and their duty falls to a boatload of European figures and others dressed in various degrees of European garb. The reason for the substitution of the European figures is the prominence of the boats, which in Mughal painting are almost inevitably manned by European-inspired figures such as the oarsman and the man perched on the mast.

Because Mukunda rarely allows his figures—particularly those in three-quarter view—to shed their characteristic impassiveness, he is compelled to use formulaic gestures to convey the excitement that his figures' drowsy, unfocused eyes and somewhat bloated countenances cannot. His hand is apparent, too, in the deep landscape beyond the churning waters, which compares closely to the more miniaturized setting of folio 19a of the British Library *Khamsa*, especially in the distinctive perpendicular elements of the outcrops.[1]

1. The painting is reproduced in color in Brend, *The Emperor Akbar's* Khamsa *of Niẓāmī*, fig. 2.



FIGURE 28

# XXIV Bahrām Gūr sees a herd of deer mesmerized by the music played by Dilārām

Attributed to Miskīn
24.3 x 14.9 cm
Removed from the manuscript between folios 181 and 182
The Metropolitan Museum of Art, gift of Alexander Smith Cochran, 1913 (13.228.28)
Published: M. Dimand, *Indian Miniatures* (New York, 1959), pl. 3; Grube, *The Classical Style*, no. 93; C. Glynn, "An Early Mughal Landscape Painting and Related Works," *Los Angeles County Museum of Art Bulletin*, 20, no. 2 (1974), fig. 7; Brend, "Akbar's *Khamsah* of Amīr Khusrau," pl. 13; Vaughn, "Miskin," fig. 13; S. Kossak, *Indian Court Painting* (New York, 1997), no. 12

Khusraw retains the essence of Niẓāmī's story of Bahrām Gūr's hunting feat and the banishment of his beautiful female slave, Fitna, in a moment of proud anger. He alters the incident that ultimately reconciles Bahrām with his lover, however, replacing Fitna's display of extraordinary physical strength with Dilārām's performance of spell-binding music, a skill more attuned to Khusraw's own interest in that art. Bahrām marvels at Dilārām's ability to make animals sleep or awaken at the sound of her barbiton, realizes its obvious relevance to their prior argument over innate and learned skills, and apologizes for his sinful arrogance.

Gaps in the text and the manuscript's original foliation indicate that this full-page scene was originally preceded by a painting of Bahrām Gūr hunting with Dilārām, a much more frequently illustrated subject. That both episodes are depicted in only one other copy of the *Khamsa* attests to the originality of this manuscript's painting cycle.

Miskīn's hand is easily recognizable in the typically svelte figures and refined countenances of Bahrām and Dilārām. More distinctive still are the organic outcrops, which are identical to those of Miskīn's painting on folio 69b of the British Library *Akbarnāma*; although the basic model of high, lobed rocks comes from the Persian tradition, the form of these precarious piles of heavily modeled, uniform boulders shows an awareness of Northern European landscape forms.[1]

The scene affords Miskīn an opportunity to indulge his passion for the animal world. Happily extending the range of Dilārām's animal audience beyond the former prey of Bahrām Gūr, Miskīn strews across the patchy landscape a black buck, pairs of partridges and foxes, and even a hyena. He adds to his lively renditions of conventional poses, such as the deer scratching his ear with his hoof, some innovative ones: the sprawling ram and goat, and the impossibly curled, spotted deer above them. These creatures assume uncanny human expressions; while many on the left close their eyes in music-induced drowsiness, the white goat and the fox in a riverside den raise their eyes mischievously.

1. The painting is published in Vaughn, "Miskin," fig. 19.



FIGURE 29

# XXV The princesses of the seven pavilions bow in homage to Bahrām Gūr

Ascribed Miskīnā and Farrukh
23.0 x 14.5 cm
Folio 182b
Walters Art Museum (W.624)
Published: R. Morris, "Some Additions to the Known Corpus of Paintings by the Mughal Artist Farrukh Chela," *Ars Orientalis*, 13 (1982), fig. 4

Annoyed with Bahrām Gūr's neglect of the affairs of state in favor of those of the hunt, the king's courtiers implore his counselor, Nuʿmān, to devise some means of keeping Bahrām Gūr in the capital. Accordingly, Nuʿmān orders the construction of seven palaces, each named after a star and containing a beautiful princess from a different region. The long text panel above the painting concludes with Bahrām Gūr beholding the seven assembled princesses, who, as Khusraw describes the scene, lower their lovely faces to the ground like the setting sun and moon.

This illustration of the prelude to Bahrām Gūr's visit to the seven princesses in turn is almost unprecedented; it neither represents the domes of the seven monochromatic pavilions nor differentiates the prostrate princesses by color, dress, or facial type. The composition even weakens the numerical cohesiveness of the seven maidens—their sole distinguishing attribute as a unit—by arbitrarily placing one princess on the other side of the central fountain. As in folio 100b (fig. 18), the literal illustration of an action specified immediately above the painting indicates both the absence of traditional models for the scene and the artist's inclination to limit the iconographic cues taken directly from the text.

The ascription to Miskīn and Farrukh provides no indication of the role of each artist in their collaborative effort, which apparently is rare in this type of manuscript. Farrukh's contribution seems restricted primarily to the architecture, while the more senior and versatile Miskīn is responsible for most of the figures as well as the landscape and sky. Although the round, three-storied pavilion is more restrained than many of Farrukh's architectural follies, the upturned view of its circular elements, the attenuated columns, and the diagonal tilt of the fountain all stem from his work on folio 65a of the British Library *Khamsa* of Niẓāmī.[1] Bahrām Gūr is clearly of the same issue as Miskīn's figure of Humāyūn on folio 69b of the British Library *Akbarnāma*, and his consorts show a refinement and variety consistent with Miskīn's female types.[2] In particular, the squarish heads and black tresses of five of the seven princesses are derived from indigenous pre-Mughal painting, a tradition that remains alien to Farrukh. However, the three women at the upper right end of the line of princesses display a long-faced and small-eyed countenance modeled in Farrukh's distinctive manner.

1. The painting is reproduced in color in Brend, *The Emperor Akbar's* Khamsa *of Niẓāmī*, fig. 9.

2. The painting is published in Vaughn, "Miskin," fig. 19.



FIGURE 30

# XXVI The story of the princess of the Yellow Pavilion: The foolish wife of the dishonest goldsmith Ḥasan is tricked into changing places with her imprisoned husband

Attributed here to Manōhara
23.4 x 14.3 cm
Folio 188a
Walters Art Museum (W.624)

A foolish woman inadvertently discloses that her husband has embezzled gold from a golden elephant he had sculpted for the king. A rival goldsmith relates this crime to the king, who, after ascertaining the truthfulness of the charge, orders the dishonest craftsman imprisoned in a tall tower. Angry at his dull-witted spouse for bringing ruin upon him, the goldsmith entices her to take hold of a rope that he asked her to pass up to him and pulls the hapless woman into his place as he lowers himself from the tower.

Because most manuscripts of the *Khamsa* illustrate *Hasht Bihisht* with repetitive scenes of Bahrām Gūr visiting the princesses in pavilions varied only by color, the pictorial tradition for the stories told by the individual princesses is quite weak. Even when the story has an obvious dramatic climax, as is the case here, the subject of the illustration depends directly upon the narrative moment at which the text breaks for the painting. The comparative works listed in Appendix B, for example, depict the goldsmith beseeching his wife to grasp the rope, the woman scaling the tower, and the woman languishing in the tower to the derision of the townsmen. The relationship between text and image is complicated on occasion when the scribe manipulates the configuration of the lines of text preceding the illustration to include a number of verses written diagonally. At times, this arrangement is purely ornamental, but more often it is used to coordinate the development of the written narrative with the predetermined subject of its illustration. Hence, it is not surprising that this full-page illustration, which falls at the point of the imprisoned woman bemoaning the injustice done to her, is preceded by a page of text written in diagonals. The artist ignores this moment, perhaps because the text is not carried over to the side of the folio to be illustrated, and depicts the more dramatic action of the ill-fated couple scaling the tower.

Manōhara struggles to adapt the vertical subject to the expansive painting field. He fills the left half of the composition with the brightly dressed pair climbing up and down the lofty purple tower, secured both structurally and visually by a luminous white base ringed by dark grass. Beyond the remarkably voluminous outcrop in the lower right lies an open plain inhabited only by two figures at a well and a man driving a bullock team. Abetted by the illusionistic possibilities inherent in the full-page format, this type of barren vista dotted with fully modeled elements signals the direction that the Mughal landscape will take in the next three decades, as artists extend their interest in three-dimensional form ever deeper into pictorial space.

Although this pervasive interest in volume and space points unmistakably to Manōhara, other features support this attribution as well. Foremost among these are the profile view and intense glare of the goldsmith's wife, which are virtually identical to those of three attendants in Manōhara's work on folio 51a (fig. 11).



FIGURE 31

# XXVII The story of the princess of the Blue Pavilion: The youth of Rūm is entertained in a garden by a fairy and her maidens

Ascribed *'amal-i* Manōhara
23.1 x 13.8 cm
Removed from the manuscript between folios 198 and 199
The Metropolitan Museum of Art, gift of Alexander Smith Cochran, 1913 (13.228.33)
Published: L. Ashton, ed., *The Art of India and Pakistan* (London, 1950), no. 652; *Bulletin of The Metropolitan Museum of Art*, 33, no. 1 (1975), 33; Brend, "Akbar's *Khamsah* of Amīr Khusrau," pl. 15

Among the many tales recounted by travelers at his father's caravanserai, a story about a place inhabited by a mute populace dressed in violet so arouses the curiosity of a youth of Rūm that he sets out immediately for the distant city with the narrator. When they reach the hot spring that marks the entrance of a house and grounds said to be filled with statues, the youth enters and wanders alone in a beautiful garden. At nightfall, the garden comes alive with a number of maidens, who detect the stranger and bring him before the queen. The youth is plied with wine and coquetry, and he quickly becomes ensnared in the tresses of love. The favors of the queen's attendants only whet the youth's ardent desire for her, but after a week of such diversion and seemingly on the verge of consummating his passion, he awakens from a wine-induced stupor to find himself alone in a desert, far from the enchanted garden.

Manōhara's scene is considerably more chaste than the one described by the text. The queen of the fairies and the youth are properly sequestered in a pavilion, but the two lovers forgo the ubiquitous wine cup, which traditionally stirs one's passion and reflects the face of the beloved, in favor of a book. Two fairy musicians serenade the couple, while three of their winged comrades stand at a respectful distance and another hovers above in the night sky. Like the queen herself, these fairies represent a rare variety of their species, for, in addition to the customary pair of colorful wings, they sport a layer of tiny feathers over their bright, tight-fitting garments. Although such creatures appear regularly in Islamic art and lore, several of these fairies assume a somewhat European countenance, a characteristic they share with many mortals by Manōhara's hand.

The three figures stationed before the garden wall display the same angular, heavily modeled faces seen in Manōhara's painting on folio 51a (fig. 11), and perform a similar space-establishing function. The composition is divided abruptly into a light green tiled courtyard and a much darker garden; these two equal registers are joined both by minor repetitions of the opposite color in each register and by the subtle diagonals formed by the pavilion and pool and the gateway and waterwheel. Manōhara enhances the thematic and compositional focus of the painting with color, lavishing bright orange accents and rich goldwork on the pavilion's occupants and trappings. Curiously, he does not employ the violet color that both pervades the fifth pavilion visited by Bahrām and forms a leitmotif of the princess's story.



FIGURE 32

رفت رضوان بمهمانی حور
مجلسی چون بهشت عالم نور
روی در روی یار جانی بود

# XXVIII The story of the princess of the Sandalwood Pavilion: A prince falsely accused of incest exonerates himself with the aid of magic spells taught to him by friends

Ascribed *'amal-i* Mukunda
22.7 x 14.3 cm
Folio 203b
Walters Art Museum (W.624)
Published: Brend, "Akbar's *Khamsah* of Amīr Khusrau," pl. 16

The Arab princess of the Sandalwood Pavilion takes up the popular theme of the untrustworthiness of the king's closest associates as the subject of her story, but she resolves the ensuing predicament with peculiarly Indian magical devices. A vizier, whose illicit liaison with the licentious queen is discovered by the prince, covers up his perfidy by accusing the youth of incest with his mother. Forced into exile, prince Rāma makes three friends, who one night are moved by his plight to share their secret skills with him. The first gives him a magic ointment, which, when applied to the eyes, allows him to see everything and yet remain invisible. The second teaches him a spell that casts the veil of sleep over others. The third instructs Rāma to stare for a year at a certain statue in Egypt and to apply wax to the image when it begins to move. Assiduously obeying these orders, Rāma suddenly beholds the demonic being he has conjured up, a *dīv* utterly devoted to his service. Employing all three of these aids, Rāma bewilders the vizier and his accomplices with a series of tricks before he magically reveals the duplicitous couple to the court and regains his rightful position as heir.

All but two other manuscripts forswear the illustration of this story in favor of Bahrām Gūr's routine visit to the Sandalwood Pavilion itself. This unique illustration, which appears as Rāma thanks the second man for his incantation, anticipates the narrative development of the text on two counts, for it shows Rāma gazing at the idol in an otherwise empty temple courtyard and renders the demonic manifestation of his action standing outside the temple walls.

Rāma directs his unwavering gaze at a large statue placed in the central niche of a tall temple ringed with bulbous finials. Seated in the classic Indian pose of meditation, the garlanded, four-armed figure holds a lotus bud in each of his upraised hands. Two more grisaille statues of dancing attendant figures occupy niches flanking the courtyard gate, which culminates in an equally elaborate superstructure. Although none of these detailed votive images matches the iconography of any specific Indian deity, they all are infused with a distinctly Indian character. In light of Akbar's tolerance of and interest in the beliefs of the indigenous Indian population, it is hardly surprising that even the objects of idolatrous worship are not made unnecessarily hideous in this illustration. Indeed, Mukunda, an artist whose name indicates his Hindu heritage, consistently presents a sympathetic view of such images, which appear prominently in similar settings in folios 266b and 318a of the British Library *Khamsa* of Niẓāmī.[1]

1. The paintings are reproduced in Brend, *The Emperor Akbar's* Khamsa *of Niẓāmī*, figs. 35 and 42.



FIGURE 33

# XXIX The story of the princess of the White Pavilion: A talisman that laughs whenever it observes insincerity laughs when a woman feigns a fainting spell as the king taps her with a flower

Ascribed *'amal-i* Sūradāsa Gujarātī
23.3 x 14.2 cm
Folio 208b
Walters Art Museum (W.624)
Published: Ettinghausen, *Paintings for the Sultans and Emperors of India in American Collections*, pl. 6

A king who has not married for dread of being cuckolded is given a magical talisman that will aid him in distinguishing deceit from sincerity by laughing whenever it witnesses a falsehood. His fears of infidelity temporarily allayed, the sovereign selects four prospective queens and installs them in separate towers, from which he summons them to court for daily and then weekly engagements. The first woman flirts with the king, but soon contrives to escape his attention by feigning a fainting spell, an action that, much to her annoyance, provokes the laughter of the talisman. The next two candidates behave with similar mendaciousness and incur the derision of the statue. The fourth woman refrains from such coquettish deceit, but her devout and dutiful manner paradoxically cools the king's enthusiasm for her. Alarmed by the warnings of the laughing talisman, the king's worst suspicions about women are confirmed when he discovers that the three flirtatious women have betrayed him with secret trysts with a black muleteer, a camel-driver, and a Hindu. He metes out appropriate punishment to each of these and finally weds the fourth woman, a paragon of purity and sincerity.

This illustration depicts the consternation of the guileless king as the first prospective queen pretends to faint when he strikes her lightly with a flower. The hypocrisy of this exaggerated reaction to the king's playful dalliance is heightened by the woman's later submission to an earnest thrashing by her menial paramour, who is not shown. The golden talisman, a statue whose form recalls that of the idol of the previous illustration, witnesses the display of insincerity at close range and bursts into laughter.

Sūradāsa Gujarātī places this romantic tiff in perspective by relegating the three figures to a small, niche-filled pavilion insulated from the unusually varied and active affairs of the court, which include a lively exchange of guards before the central gate, a drinking party in the lower left, and the stabling of horses and camels. These genre digressions are encouraged by the complicated division of the architectural compound into a series of interlocking trapezoidal units and are given visual weight by their bright colors and discrete shapes.

Sūradāsa employs a distinctive set of facial types, most of which are characterized by spade-shaped heads, very dark beards and mustaches, and highly arched brows. The earrings, tassels, and sloping foreheads of the three female servants are echoes of the conventional rendering of females in indigenous Indian painting, a style Sūradāsa probably learned in his native Gujarat.



FIGURE 34

نازنین شد ز نازکی بیهوش
شاه کان دید بر کشید خروش
خنده زد و صورت طلسم زدود

Fig. 35. Shamsa, f. 173v. Walters Art Museum, W.624.

CHAPTER 5

# Painting Cycles in Islamic Manuscript Illustration

The text of Amīr Khusraw's *Khamsa* had been illustrated many times before Mughal artists were given this task in the 1590s. In most cases, the episodes depicted by Mughal painters correspond to the narrative choices made in earlier manuscripts. Is this a coincidence? To answer this deceptively simple question, which compels us to try to define the fundamental principles of Islamic manuscript illustration, I have compiled documentation on all known illustrated manuscripts of the *Khamsa*. Appendix A lists in chronological order each illustrated copy of the *Khamsa* or any of its constituent books; Appendix B presents a subject index of each episode chosen for illustration, with an indication of the exact point at which the text is interrupted for the painting. Do enough patterns emerge in the tradition of illustration for Amīr Khusraw's *Khamsa* that we can really speak of a cycle of paintings—a discrete set of images connected with this particular text? If such a cycle *did* exist for the *Khamsa*, how might the members of the Mughal atelier have known about and responded to it?

Several scholars of Islamic painting have taken up the method pioneered by Kurt Weitzmann for the study of classical and medieval European manuscripts to consider the development of stemmas, or family trees, in the pictorial tradition of individual texts of Islamic literature.[1] Ernst Grube, who has worked extensively on the *Kalīla wa Dimna*, a collection of didactic animal fables illustrated from the thirteenth century onwards, acknowledges the lack of standard iconography in various illustrated versions of this prose text but holds out the promise of the identification of distinct "family groups."[2] In a study of a group of fourteenth-century manuscripts of the *Shāhnāma* (Book of Kings), which are among the earliest illustrated copies of this frequently illustrated Persian text, Marianna Shreve Simpson concludes the opposite, arguing that each manuscript possessed an individual series of illustrations whose iconography was determined primarily by the content of the text around each painting.[3] She dismisses the notion of a single comprehensive model even for three manuscripts produced within a decade or so of one another but paradoxically admits the possibility of a common pictorial source for two of them.[4] Having gathered together a number of copies of the *Maqāmāt* of al-Harīrī, Oleg Grabar draws attention to the unexpected absence of a stemma among them and poses some provocative explanations for their varied imagery.[5]

By far the most relevant case study is Barbara Brend's work on Amīr Khusraw's *Khamsa* itself.[6] Brend compiles data similar to Appendix A and provides a historical overview of each manuscript. Her investigation is limited to manuscripts from the Timurid period, broadly the fifteenth century, which is stretched to include Mughal copies of the *Khamsa* in the belief that the Mughals held the books of their ancestors in particularly high esteem. Yet the arbitrary omission of great numbers of illustrated sixteenth-century copies of the *Khamsa* skews her assessment of the Walters *Khamsa*, most notably in the importance accorded illustrations of subjects she considers unique to the manuscript, but which in fact have precedents in works outside the parameters of her study.[7] Brend assumes the existence of several illustrative traditions. Using Weitzmann's model, she sees the core tradition beginning with long cycles and considers shorter cycles to be selective excerpts; moreover, she links the relative length of the painting cycle to the level of patronage, classifying copiously illustrated cycles as non-princely and shorter ones as princely.[8] She also argues for distinct Persian and Indian variants, with the Walters manuscript showing some tendencies of the latter.[9] All these traditions and sub-traditions are woven together in a brief but tangled conclusion.[10]

These studies mark an initial attempt to understand the reasons behind the choice of particular subjects to be illustrated in a given text. None of them, however, addresses two troubling assumptions implicit in this approach to illustrated manuscripts. One concerns the transmission of visual information. By what means do we suppose that various groups of artists scattered across the Persian-speaking world knew what had transpired at other painting centers in times and places well removed from their own? The other is a tendency to assume that artists would repeat mechanically earlier models whenever they were available. So we may ask, what working methods and set of cultural expectations might have led artists to imitate portions of earlier images or to produce entirely new pictures in Islamic manuscripts?

These are difficult questions, of course, and any one set of answers may well prove to be inadequate for Islamic painting as a whole. Yet we can begin to address these questions by demonstrating that a canonical illustrative tradition did not exist for the *Khamsa* during the fifteenth and sixteenth centuries—a period in which book illustration grew dramatically in both numbers and complexity. To this end, let us examine three different elements—the degree of congruence between the painting cycle of one manuscript and another, the iconographic consistency among illustrations and their fidelity to the textual narrative, and the adaptation of conventional motifs and compositions developed by various workshops.

My reconstruction of the Walters *Khamsa* establishes that the manuscript originally had thirty-one illustrations—an average number of paintings for this text, but a relatively plentiful amount for a manuscript of such high quality. The truest indication of a connection between one manuscript and another is surely the presence of painting cycles of similar length and composition, that is, with same subjects represented in the same number of images. A quick check of the manuscripts listed in Appendix A reveals that the painting cycle of the Walters *Khamsa* does not exhibit this kind of twinned relationship to any previous example. But are enough of the Walters illustrations common to a single manuscript or group of manuscripts to allow us to place the Walters cycle within a certain pictorial tradition or family, such as one defined by provenance or level of patronage?

The task now grows subjective: How many subjects must two manuscripts share for us to assign them to the same family tree? The Walters *Khamsa* shares no more than thirteen subjects with any earlier copy, accounting for approximately two-fifths of its thirty-one illustrations.[11] Two other manuscripts hold slightly fewer subjects in common with the Walters manuscript, one with eleven of its forty-eight illustrations, and the other with five of its thirteen.[12] Yet these areas of overlap can deceive one into positing connections that soon prove untenable, such as Brend's contention that the Walters *Khamsa* relates simultaneously to manuscripts with a Persian, non-princely cycle, an allegedly indigenous Indian cycle, and a princely cycle from Herat.[13] A more fundamental problem is this: If we hold the overlap of two-fifths of the painting cycle to be

Fig. 36. Two friends are condemned to death. *Khamsa* of Amīr Khusraw, f. 28a. Iran, Shiraz, ca. 1560. 23.5 x 19.8 cm. National Library of Russia, St. Petersburg PNS 67.

significant, what should we make of the three-fifths that do not coincide? How can we explain why a workshop would choose to repeat some subjects within the tradition and not others?

Although the Walters *Khamsa* naturally remains our benchmark of comparison, a modest degree of congruence between painting cycles also characterizes the relationships among most other illustrated copies of the text. Hence, the notion of a stemma for the illustrations of this *Khamsa* text seems problematic even at the outset. For the sake of argument, however, let us assume that a discrete pictorial tradition *did* exist for the *Khamsa*. If this were the case, there should be some empirical evidence of it in these overlapping subjects—either in the form of specific visual quotations from one manuscript to another or in the recurrence of unusual and detailed iconography that cannot be explained by an artist's direct reference to the text. Let us examine a few examples in which a given episode is illustrated in several manuscripts to see what the visual evidence suggests.

Each of the twenty discourses of the first poem of the *Khamsa, Maṭla' al-Anwār*, concludes with a short original anecdote that epitomizes Khusraw's musings. A few of these anecdotes are illustrated in most manuscripts of the

Fig. 37. A scholar prostrates himself before ʿAbdullāh ibn Jaʿfar, who presented the smitten man with his beloved singing girl. By Mukunda. *Bahāristān*, 1595, f. 29a. 23.1 x 13.3 cm. Bodleian Library, University of Oxford, Ms. Elliott 254.

*Khamsa.* One of the most popular is the anecdote of the seventeenth discourse, in which an old Sufi happens upon a handsome young man in a garden and begins to make amorous entreaties. Once rebuffed, the old man waxes philosophical, exclaiming that he is looking for his lost youth, and he urges the young man to realize that youth is fleeting; the young man, for his part, chides the stooped old man to learn to act his age.

The Mughal scene includes all the key elements of the story: an old man with a stooped posture and white beard, a vigorous youth, and a garden (fig. 8). But the artist also supplies some extraneous features, permitting the youth to be joined by two companions and summoning two gardeners to tend the formal garden. Other versions of this scene, all of which fall at virtually the same point in the text, present variations of the basic imagery. In the earliest, dated 1485, the Sufi and youth appear alone, separated by a tall central tree.[14] A stream meanders through the foreground and flowers sprout in the landscape, in typical Persian fashion, but there is no hint of a formal garden. A painting from a manuscript dated 1491 provides slightly more elaborate imagery, with the old man and the youth—now crowned—standing on either side of a pair of cypress trees.[15] Three youthful companions cluster together on one side, and a stream flows again in the foreground. A third example returns to a one-on-one encounter, with a slender tree separating the two protagonists, and installs a garden wall beyond the ubiquitous stream and flowers.[16] Two further examples from ca. 1500 transform the youth into a woman, once with a companion[17] and once alone.[18] This female identity continues in a Safawid example of ca. 1560, which is packed to an unprecedented degree with ancillary figures and activities.[19]

Common to all these images are only two figures: the stock figure of an aged man and the object of his youthful obsession. Their relative positions, personal attributes (such as the youth's crown and even his gender), and settings are clearly optional elements. This much variety in imagery for such a short story all but rules out the possibility that artists sought illustrative guidelines either in a common model or in subsequent derivative versions, a process that lies at the heart of a putative illustrative tradition. Are there other means of generating these paintings that might explain the meager degree of visual and iconographic consistency among them?

A series of paintings illustrating the anecdote of the tenth discourse of *Maṯlaʿ al-Anwār* demonstrates one part of the process. A man kills his brother so that he alone will inherit the fortune left by their late father. When he arrives at court to claim his inheritance, he beholds two friends condemned to death, each wanting to die first so that he will not be forced to witness the death of the other. This poignant display of loyalty between men who do not even share the same blood arouses such remorse in the fratricide that he confesses his crime to the king. Thereupon the sovereign orders the two friends released and the fratricide executed.

The Mughal artist obscures the drama of this situation by introducing a host of figures unrelated to the central action (fig. 6). The enthroned king is obvious, and the two condemned friends are readily identifiable since they stand close together before two men with swords. But which figure is isolated enough to be the repentant fratricide?

This confusion does not exist in the earliest illustration of this anecdote, which falls at exactly the same point in the text.[20] The king watches the execution of a single figure, the fratricide, while the pardoned pair of friends stand to the side and give thanks for the king's clemency. An illustration from a manuscript produced in Yazd in 1494 reduces the scene to the pithy imagery of the two bound

Fig. 38. Shīrīn meets Farhād at Mt. Bīsitūn. *Khamsa* of Amīr Khusraw, f. 61a. Iran, 1478. 8.5 x 12.8 cm. Topkapi Palace Museum, Istanbul H. 795.

friends, a single executioner, and a standing onlooker, presumably the fratricide.[21] The king is nowhere to be seen. A contemporary Turkish painting illustrates another moment of the story: an executioner leading the two bound friends before two standing figures.[22] A late sixteenth-century example shows one executioner bearing down on the two friends and another man with a sword standing at some distance.[23] Because the figure in the doorway is identified as a guardian by the staff he holds, the fratricide and the king are left absent once again. A final example from a mid sixteenth-century Shīrāzī manuscript resembles the crowded ambiguity of the Mughal scene (fig. 36). The enthroned king presides over the court, and a single executioner brandishes his sword over the two friends, but if the fratricide is present, the artist has not elected to single him out.

Once again, the various illustrations of this short story display strikingly little common iconography. The two devoted friends sometimes stand and sometimes kneel, but they never fail to make an appearance in this series of images. Yet the king and the fratricide—the other key figures in the story—are only occasional participants. The setting too seems to be arbitrary, for it is alternately a courtyard or a generic landscape. There is an overall similarity between the two latest versions of this scene, the sixteenth-century Shīrāzī and Mughal paintings, which are separated by only a generation or so, but a much stronger comparison to the Mughal scene of the fratricide can be made with a Mughal illustration from the *Bahāristān*, produced by the same artist, Mukunda, only three years before the Walters manuscript (fig. 37). As one might expect, the figure and facial types are similar. More important is the utter interchangeability of the figures in this standard courtyard composition, which is simply reversed and adapted. In one case, the two friends stand just beyond the dais; in the other, the central figure prostrates himself before the king, and two women take the place of some innocuous retainers. This suggests that the artist did *not* develop his illustration of the story of the fratricide and the two loyal friends around a specific and derivative iconographic core. Rather, he apparently conceived the painting as a certain type of scene into which he could insert a few identifying figures—in this case merely a pair of bound figures and an executioner—anywhere within an acceptable composition of his choosing. This conception of how specific manuscript illustrations were constructed is completely antithetical to the belief that the key element of Islamic manuscript illustration was a discrete unit of textually specific visual information that was habitually passed along from one manuscript to another.

Another aspect of Islamic manuscript illustration is highlighted by a series of paintings from the second book of the *Khamsa, Shīrīn wa Khusraw*. At a low point during her tempestuous relationship with Khusraw, Shīrīn goes out riding to gather her thoughts and happens upon a marvelous sculpture cut into the side of a mountain. She soon catches sight of its maker, a handsome young rock-carver by the name of Farhād, who is immediately smitten by her melodious voice and her veiled beauty. Shīrīn takes advantage of the sculptor's lovesickness and asks him to cut a channel through the mountain so that milk from flocks in her homeland can flow directly to her palace. Farhād agrees and asks in return only the occasional glimpse of his newly beloved. Shīrīn invites Farhād back to her palace, where she coaxes him into admitting that he is no commoner but the estranged son of the Chinese emperor. He then sets to work on his Herculean undertaking and swoons upon her occasional visits.

This section of the poem is usually illustrated by two scenes: One depicts Shīrīn watching Farhād at work, and the other shows their brief time together at the palace. The

Fig. 39. Majnūn caresses a dog that lived in Laylā's neighborhood. Detached folio from a *Khamsa* of Amīr Khusraw written at Balkh 1503–4, paintings added in Herat ca. 1525. 15.2 x 12.2 cm. The Metropolitan Museum of Art, Rogers Fund, 1913 (13.160.3).

representation of two dissimilar subjects is probably the result of some indecision about the best spot to interrupt the text for the illustration, an ambivalence more likely and understandable in a long narrative section of this story than in the brief anecdotes of *Maṭla' al-Anwār*. A painting from a manuscript written at Balkh in 1503, for example, follows a rubric announcing Farhād's appearance at the palace and his receipt of a fine robe of honor; accordingly, Farhād is divested of his sculptor's clothing and tools.[24] Conversely, illustrations of the rendezvous in the mountains appear throughout this section, both at the point of Shīrīn and Farhād's initial encounter and at that of her later visits, which are described several folios apart.

The Walters illustration shows a mounted Shīrīn escorted by several court ladies arriving before Farhād (fig. 13). Sānvala's Farhād is hardly the picture of an energetic sculptor, his occupation indicated neither by any ongoing activity nor by the customary niche sculpture but by a mere pile of tools beside him. Nor does the artist heed the situation described in the text, for he greatly anticipates the completion of the proposed channel as he depicts a channel emptying from the mountain behind Farhād into the rectangular pool at his feet. The presence of several goats leaves little doubt that their milk already courses through this labor of love.

An illustration of this same scene in a Persian manuscript dated 1478 dispenses with such embellishments and presents in straightforward fashion all the important elements of the episode: a mounted figure of Shīrīn, a bearded Farhād wielding a pick, an assortment of other tools, the marvelous niche sculpture, and the milk channel (fig. 38). In a painting made in 1494 at Yazd, another artist fashions a somewhat less comprehensive illustration, preferring a dismounted Shīrīn addressing a clean-shaven Farhād, who once again is actively occupied with stone-cutting, with both the niche sculpture and the milk channel to show for his effort.[25] A Turkish example of ca. 1500 reduces the image still further to only a mounted Shīrīn and her friends addressing a beardless Farhād; the niche sculpture has disappeared, as has the milk channel.[26] A single tool hanging from Farhād's belt is all that suggests his livelihood. A mid-sixteenth-century Safawid example diverges from even this minimal iconography and shows a seated and crowned Shīrīn conversing with an old, bearded Farhād with not a sculpture, channel, or tool in sight.[27] Because these images depict the same basic event, they appear as a group in Appendix B and could easily be construed as evidence of some common painting cycle. But when we examine the illustrations carefully, we are hard-pressed to describe a connection among them that is anything more than a mere coincidence of subject. Is this all there is to the notion of an illustrative tradition?

Two successive illustrations from the third book of Amīr Khusraw's *Khamsa, Majnūn wa Laylā*, relate episodes from Majnūn's self-imposed exile to the wilderness. In the first, an emaciated Majnūn wanders in from the desert and sees a mangy dog that lives in the neighborhood where Laylā's house stands. Majnūn commiserates with the wretched animal and makes the dog the surrogate object of his unrelenting ardor for Laylā, placing his arm around the neck of a creature that could at least pass by his beloved's house. This behavior, considered outlandish by the scandalized community, causes the community elders to summon the youth for questioning.

The touching moment of Majnūn befriending the dog was illustrated many a time in *Khamsa* manuscripts. Three examples from the 1490s are fairly typical. One shows Majnūn, naked from the waist up, holding the dog across his lap, with an assortment of animals as the only witnesses.[28] Another depicts Majnūn as semi-cloaked, holding the creature so that their two heads are close together; a tent and a well establish the proximity of the town, and several humans join two animals in beholding the spectacle.[29] A Turkish example presents Majnūn kneeling before the dog—not holding him in his lap—and introduces Majnūn's father, who explains his son's behavior to five men.[30] Two sixteenth-century examples repeat the entwined figures of Majnūn and the dog. One retains the outraged elders, but deviates from the tradition by putting Majnūn tantalizingly close to Laylā's tent (fig. 39). And a late sixteenth-century example from Qazwin shows Majnūn's father addressing him directly as two deer look on.[31]

The Mughal example seems very odd in the context of this tradition, for the artist has managed to rehabilitate Majnūn socially where his family and friends have failed; instead of appearing in his customary savage state—his defining attribute—Majnūn now sits dressed in fine courtly attire, complete with turban (fig. 20). This iconographic anomaly is not occasioned by reference to the text, which, despite being manipulated by the use of obliquely written verses on the folio immediately preceding this full-page painting, merely continues to express Majnūn's distress. Rather, the source of this iconographic deviation lies in another painting by this same artist, Dharmadāsa, from a *Khamsa* of Niẓāmī produced two years earlier. In a scene of the princely Khusraw carelessly allowing his horse to wander loose among crops, there is a very similar figure dressed in an identically patterned, golden robe, which is virtually unknown in Mughal painting of this period (fig. 40). This figure was evidently so pleasing to the artist that he reused it in four other manuscripts of the late 1590s—once for the unexpectedly youthful figure of a king Dābishlīm in an illustration to a manuscript of the 1596–97 *Anwār-i Suhaylī* (fig. 41), again for a princely calligrapher in a well-known scene of a Mughal atelier in the *Akhlāq-i Nāṣirī*,[32] and yet again for the figure of Alexander in an illustration from a dispersed *Khamsa* of Niẓāmī of ca. 1595.[33] Most remarkably, Dharmadāsa returned to this same finely dressed, youthful figure in the Walters *Khamsa* even when the figure's regal clothing diverged radically from both the traditional iconography (Majnūn as half-naked and emaciated) and the written text. Such a free movement of certain figural motifs within an artist's own work and within his workshop generally parallels the kind of formal adaptation seen earlier in the composition of the fratricide and the two friends (fig. 6). This working method, which is both logical and efficient, regularly overwhelms whatever awareness artists had of specific iconographic and formal features of earlier models.

Another instructive example is the illustration of a long-awaited reunion of Laylā and Majnūn in the wilderness,

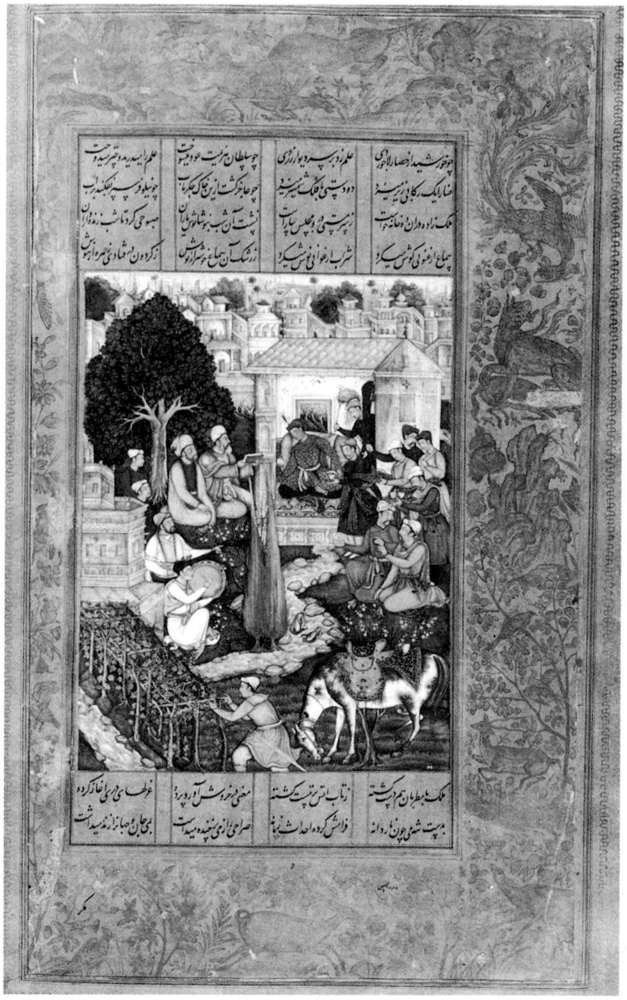

Fig. 40. Khusraw is enthroned when as a young man he became drunk and allowed his horse to wander off and damage crops and vines. By Dharmadāsa. *Khamsa* of Niẓāmī, 1595, f. 40b. 13.7 x 10.7 cm. British Library Or. 12208 (By permission of the British Library).

an episode not found in Niẓāmī's version of the story. One day, after a particularly vivid dream of being with her beloved, Laylā decides to take action and rides out into the desert on a camel. When she finally finds Majnūn, he is surrounded by beasts and appears stiff as a board, as if dead. As she cradles his head in her lap, he awakens for a moment, and then they both faint with joy. They remain in this position for the entire day before Laylā finally rises to leave, whereupon Majnūn is powerless to protest.

In the earliest of the many visual precursors of the Walters illustration, Laylā and Majnūn huddle together in an upright position, while assorted animals surround them and Laylā's camel waits by a stream.[34] A decade later, in a manuscript dated 1495, the lovers are seated in a similar position, although they have switched sides; the number of animals is reduced, but the camel remains.[35] A 1497 illustration finally hits upon the textually prescribed position of

Fig. 41. Dābishlīm, the king of India, approaches the sage Bīdpā'ī. By Dharmadāsa. *Anwār-i Suhaylī*, 1005/1596–97, f. 32. Bharat Kala Bhavan, Varanasi Ms. 9069.

Fig. 42. Laylā visits Majnūn in the desert. *Khamsa* of Amīr Khusraw, f. 172a. Iran, Yazd, 1497. 14.9 x 8.0 cm. Topkapi Palace Museum H. 801.

a prostrate Majnūn lying in Laylā's lap, even as it continues to represent the wild animals and the camel (fig. 42). This same conjunction of motifs appears in two more illustrations produced in 1498 and 1503.[36] Thus, apart from the change in the position of the lovers, these five examples produced within seventeen years are quite consistent in iconography and seem to constitute a relatively strong case for a coherent illustrative tradition for this particular story.

The tradition breaks down in the Walters *Khamsa*, which falls outside this tight time frame by nearly a hundred years (fig. 21). Laylā and Majnūn are together, to be sure, but they are seated quite apart, unlike the two positions seen thus far. Likewise, the lovers are surrounded by pairs of peaceful wild animals rejoicing at the sight of the love-intoxicated couple, but Laylā's means of transportation, the camel, which had figured in every other version of this scene, has disappeared. Two images offer some explanation for this unexpected divergence. One is a very similar scene executed by another Mughal artist for the British Library *Khamsa* of Niẓāmī, illustrated just two years earlier (fig. 43). As noted before, Niẓāmī's account does not have Laylā meet Majnūn in the desert; the woman who joins Majnūn here is his mother, rendered only a bit older, and her male companion is Majnūn's friend Salīm. Otherwise, the paintings are practically identical. Hence, the unprecedented

Fig. 43. Majnūn is visited in the desert by his mother and his friend Salīm. By Sānvala. *Khamsa* of Niẓāmī, 1595, f. 150b. 17.4 x 13.0 cm. British Library Or. 12208 (By permission of the British Library).

Fig. 44. Laylā visits Majnūn in the desert. *Khamsa* of Amīr Khusraw, f. 191b. Turkey, October–November 1500. Painting 13.8 x 11.5 cm., f. 24.8 x 17.4 cm. Topkapi Palace Museum H. 798.

detachment that Laylā and Majnūn display here and the absence of the camel are almost certainly the result of one Mughal artist imitating what his colleague had done a few years before rather than drawing upon distant models more closely linked to the text.

Looking back over these five examples, we can make the following observations: 1) even when illustrations in various copies of the text appear at virtually the same point in the text, they bear no more than an elementary visual resemblance to one another; and 2) many images fail to heed the iconography specified by the text. In short, we are disabused of the likelihood of a pattern of either faithful visual copies or literal illustrations. What we do have is a series of relatively free interpretations of a particular encounter reduced to its most essential elements, such as an old man and a youth in a garden, Shīrīn and the sculptor Farhād, or Majnūn and the dog. As the preceding sentence demonstrates, this basic information can be conveyed easily in just a few words. To my mind, this is exactly how artists knew what to depict in any given manuscript illustration.

Concrete evidence of the verbal transmission of subject matter appears in another illustration of Laylā visiting Majnūn in the desert, with the familiar iconography of Majnūn resting his head in Laylā's lap, from a manuscript dated 1500 (figs. 44 and 45). But along the very edge of the folio is an informal inscription, now partially cut. The inscription is difficult to decipher, but it clearly begins with *taṣwīr* (picture) and also includes the words "Laylā...the head of Majnūn...with him in conversation."[37] This phrase is not missing verse of text, examples of which are always written in the margin close to the text column

Fig. 45. Detail of the inscription on f. 191b (fig. 44).

itself, nor is it the scribe's reminder to himself about the wording of the rubric since there is no rubric on this page. Instead, it is nothing less than a programmatic instruction to the artist. This inscription can be recognized as this kind of note not only because it begins with the word *taṣwīr*, but also by analogy to abundant examples in Western manuscripts and to the more than 115 examples in Mughal painting discovered over the last two decades.[38]

Sometimes these directions appear along the very edge of the folios, where they were placed so that they could be trimmed easily when the manuscript was completed, as in a painting from the natural history section of the *Bāburnāma*, a Mughal dynastic history illustrated about 1590 (fig. 46). Other times they are written at the bottom of the painting field, with the intention that the painter would cover them up in the process of painting (fig. 47). Most often these inscriptions were obscured, but sometimes painters were remiss in obliterating their supervisors' directions, either painting too lightly over them or leaving them plainly visible, perhaps mistaking them for text proper. These prescriptive notes range from the terse: "a picture of many monkeys should be drawn," (fig. 46) to the relatively complete: "The battle of Nawfal with Laylā's army on behalf of Majnūn, and Majnūn throws stones at Nawfal's army" (fig. 47). Such a succinct synopsis of the text simplified the artist's task of knowing what to paint, a convenient practice for painters who might not be able to pick out the relevant narrative details from the subtleties of Persian poetry or who might even be unable to read Persian at all.

The survival of abundant examples of such prescriptive inscriptions in imperial Mughal painting leaves no doubt that the Mughal atelier conveyed information to its artists in this manner. But it is also reasonable to extrapolate from these notes some lessons for smaller painting workshops elsewhere in the Islamic world that may have relied primarily or even exclusively on direct oral communication between supervisor and painter.[39] Indeed, these programmatic notations offer an answer to the apparent dilemma of the formal and iconographic inconsistencies in illustrations of the same scene in various copies of a text. Most of these notes were probably generated by each workshop and used only internally, but it is also possible that written lists of potential subjects for popular texts were passed from one workshop to another, where successive patrons or manuscript designers could make their own selections.[40] In any case, these written instructions and their oral equivalents are *just specific enough* to ensure that the subject is basically the same—Majnūn and the dog, Laylā and Majnūn in the desert—but do not begin to provide the iconographic inventory that would compel artists everywhere to make the sculptor Farhād a handsome, beardless youth who toted his tools around with him and always stood before his handiwork. Nor do these instructions offer the slightest suggestion about *how* to cast the scene formally, so that Majnūn can embrace the dog in any number of positions and can do so alone or before a host of disapproving strangers. This conciseness seems prudent, for it is likely that painters would understand even the most detailed verbal description of new imagery largely in terms of formulae already in their visual repertoire. Most of all, these notations completely obviate detailed reference by the artist to any sort of illustrative tradition or to the text itself.

This simple and eminently repeatable means of generating series of images overshadows other means of disseminating images: the migration of artists, the transfer of individual manuscripts from one collection to another, and the use of working sketches, pattern books, and pounces. Despite a dearth of signatures or ascriptions before the mid-sixteenth century, there is stylistic evidence that some artists brought knowledge of particular scenes with them as they moved from one painting center to another. It is no accident that manuscripts that are closest together in time and place generally display the strongest formal and iconographic continuity in illustrations of the same story. Here again, though, artists would be essentially modifying what they themselves had done rather than responding to a set of images inherited from the remote past.

Artists occasionally foraged visual ideas from older manuscripts in court libraries, perhaps, as has been suggested, copying some as demonstrations of their mastery of tradition.[41] But they simply did not have consistent recourse to visual models formulated elsewhere. Images such as the paintings reproduced here circulated throughout the Islamic world almost exclusively in the form of illustrated manuscripts, small objects intended for private use. A very few summary images associated with the text of the *Shāhnāma* have appeared on ceramics, but generally speaking, unlike Western art, the pictorial tradition was never bolstered by mosaics and frescoes—truly public art—whereby particular treatments of individual scenes could be disseminated widely.[42] Thus, there was only a slight possibility of fostering the canonicity of a particular set of images that one comes to expect from Western art, especially Western religious art, which has an additional layer of authority to promote direct copying.

In some rare instances, it is clear that various ateliers in Islamic lands intended to produce multiple copies of the same text illustrated in the same manner.[43] On the whole, however, Persian and Mughal artists ignored the models provided by previous copies. For example, an inspection note on one *Khamsa* manuscript illustrated in Herat about 1525 indicates that the manuscript was in the imperial Mughal library before the Walters *Khamsa* was made.[44] Nonetheless, the Walters manuscript repeats only two of the thirteen subjects illustrated in the earlier manuscript, to which the atelier presumably could have had access. Yet even when Mughal artists took up the same subject, as in the now-familiar example of Majnūn and the dog, they did not hasten to copy any part of the earlier illustration (fig. 39). Similarly, entirely different sets of illustrations were chosen for the four Mughal manuscripts of the *Anwār-i Suhaylī*,[45] three copies of the *Khamsa* of Niẓāmī,[46] and two imperial versions of the *Rāmāyaṇa*.[47] Gestures to the past, including Amīr Khusraw's own imitation of Niẓāmī's *Khamsa* text, undoubtedly were appreciated in cultivated circles, but these never went so far as to encourage the wholesale repetition of an entire cycle of paintings in an illustrated manuscript. Rather, the gestures were more occasional and subtle, generally taking the form of variations on a familiar language of themes and forms.[48]

Fig. 46. Monkeys. Designed by Mahesa, painted by Śyāma. *Bāburnāma*, f. 382b. ca. 1590. 20.4 x 14.5 cm. British Library Or. 3714 (By permission of the British Library).

Sketches and pounces must have played only a minor role in this process. Although few examples of working ephemera have survived, sketches in albums in Istanbul and Berlin are predominantly isolated decorative motifs, such as clouds or trees or rock clusters, rather than figural ones; even then, these figural sketches rarely contain more than a single figure.[49] Occasionally, these individual figures are the kernel of the illustration, but more often they are appealing motifs that could be plugged into other kinds of scenes. There are very few examples in which an entire scene is pounced, which would be necessary for a whole composition to be transmitted from one center to another.[50]

If we now understand that verbal cues rather than visual models were foremost in determining the subject and basic imagery of Mughal manuscript illustrations, we must struggle a while longer before we fully understand

Fig. 47. Majnūn enters the battle of the clans. By Bhagavāna. *Laylā wa Majnūn*, ca. 1595, f. 21b. 8.7 x 11.4 cm. Bodleian Library, University of Oxford, Ms. Pers., d. 102.

the factors that normally shaped the initial selection of the scenes to be illustrated. Most scholars have realized that the miniatures in Islamic manuscripts cannot be studied in isolation. But as our scope of enquiry has expanded, we have precipitately assumed that the truly meaningful unit of a manuscript was the complete run of images within it, in other words, its painting cycle. This assumption has led us to posit all too readily a connection between one illustrated copy of a text and another and to seek to identify a specific overarching rationale—usually political—that governed the choice of each member of that series. It is no accident that iconological readings of manuscript illustrations are proposed only when the patron is known; in such cases, one is sorely tempted to look to external matters, such as the state of a prince's political fortunes, for the key to explain an otherwise disparate group of images.[51] On the whole, however, such politicized interpretations have been unconvincing.

Let us propose a different scenario. Once the text was chosen, a patron and his librarians, or even the marketplace and commercial workshops, would decide what kind of book was to be produced—altogether unillustrated, lightly illustrated, or heavily illustrated. Then, probably together, they chose the particular stories to be depicted. It is unlikely that we will ever untangle the many factors that affected the selection of scenes for any one manuscript, but generally this decision seems to have been improvisational in nature, sometimes inspired by episodes that lent themselves to visualization, sometimes spurred by memories of images someone had seen in other copies of the text and other times prompted by a purely aesthetic interest in distributing images throughout the manuscript. Once the subjects were determined, artists set about depicting them in familiar schemes. What distinguished one manuscript from another, and one class of patrons from another, was not specific imagery—that is, iconography—but the level of sophistication of the artists employed to produce the paintings and the quality of the materials with which they worked. As Oleg Grabar has aptly expressed it, the primary purpose of paintings in manuscripts was "to transform books, not to illustrate a text."[52]

But I will go further and suggest that the notions of canonical illustrative traditions and thematically coherent painting cycles are inappropriate to Islamic painting. Even a modest acquaintance with the complicated structure and allusive, metaphorical nature of Persian poetry suggests that narrative efficiency was never a paramount concern in Persian literature; the situation cannot have been much different with Persian painting itself. Likewise, it is very doubtful that any of the iconographic idiosyncrasies mentioned here (such as Majnūn being dressed in fine clothes rather than rags) would have ever altered a reader's understanding of the substance of the text, which, after all, physically surrounds the painting. In the final estimation, images in Persian manuscripts are essentially ornamental devices upon which readers could linger with pleasure and project sentiments aroused by the text.[53] To ensure that viewers would be stimulated in this manner, the Persian or Mughal artist would fabricate a scene composed of a series of beautiful and often irrelevant visual passages. This tendency, though present to some extent even in the fourteenth century, when most illustrations were little more than iconographic signs, became a dominant trend in the fifteenth and sixteenth centuries as ever higher levels of luxury were commanded at court. Elaborate, consistent, and directed iconography, the very essence of the notion of a painting cycle, had a minimal role in such an art.

## NOTES

1. K. Weitzmann, *Illustrations in Roll and Codex* (Princeton, 1947). See J. Lowden, *The Octateuchs* (University Park, Pennsylvania, 1992), especially 79–104, for a stimulating critique of aspects of this approach.

2. E. Grube, "Prolegomena for a Corpus Publication of Illustrated *Kalīlah wa Dimnah* Manuscripts," *Islamic Art*, 4 (1990–91), 405–25.

3. M. S. Simpson, *The Illustration of an Epic: The Earliest* Shahnama *Manuscripts* (New York and London, 1979), 251–54.

4. Simpson, *The Illustration of an Epic*, 208–18.

5. O. Grabar, *The Illustrations of the Maqamat* (Chicago and London, 1984), 155–57.

6. Brend, *Illustrations to the* Khamsah.

7. Brend, *Illustrations to the* Khamsah, 448–50, claims that the uniqueness of four subjects (MMA.32, folios 153b, 203b, and 208b) points to a particular religious or political relevance of the scenes for the Mughals. Only one (folio 153b) is actually unprecedented. She makes a similar suggestion for three allegedly rare scenes (folios 135a, 139a, and MMA.27). Only Alexander receiving the homage of the Khāqān (folio 139a) is truly rare; the other two subjects are illustrated seven and four times respectively.

8. Brend, *Illustrations to the* Khamsah, 475.

9. Brend, *Illustrations to the* Khamsah, 475, specifically relates the Mughal copy to Chester Beatty Library P. 124.

10. Brend, *Illustrations to the* Khamsah, 475–76. Her conclusion is worth citing in full:

The earliest extant work of princely quality, the Anthology H. 796 probably started for Iskandar Sulṭān, has a small cycle. This possibly follows a Jalāyrid type, but may mark the inception of a tradition. This line would have been taken to Herat by Iskandar's painters; in Herat it would almost certainly have been exemplified in the workshop of Bāysunghur; and it would have proceeded through the later fifteenth century manuscripts of Herat, to the Mughals. Another branch of this classical line of descent would have been brought back westward to Baghdad, where it is found in [TSM] R. 1021; it would then have been carried to the lands of Shirvāshāh to appear in the manuscript at Baku, a movement which may have brought it back to meet an old Jalāyrid tradition; from this point it would be transmitted to the royal Āq Qūyunlū; and from them to the Safavids.

A lower level of tradition in West Persia probably at first imitates the manuscripts produced for provincial governors, and then, perhaps as the result of the availability of painters from Herat in the mid-fifteenth century, fixes its own tradition conditioned by its own milieu.

11. Azerbaijan (Baku), folios 23a, 26b, 31b, 61b, 70a, 110b, 126b, 163b, 189a, 208a, 227b. The painting on folio 204b depicts the same scene as one presently missing from the Walters manuscript, i.e., Bahrām Gūr hunting with Dilārām.

12. Chester Beatty Library P. 124: folios 49b, 60b, 71b, 89b, 101a, 102b, 118a, 119a, 120b, 162b, 179b. Chester Beatty Library P. 163: folios 23a, 28a, 38a, 120b, 215a.

13. Brend, *Illustrations to the* Khamsah, 446–48.

14. *Khamsa*, Chester Beatty Library, P. 163, folio 38a. The painting is reproduced in color in Bahari, *Bihzad*, fig. 24.

15. Topkapi Saray Museum H. 1008, folio 356a.

16. Topkapi Saray Museum H. 800, folio 36a.

17. *Khamsa*, Staatsbibliothek, Berlin Or. fol. 187, folio 32a.

18. Topkapi Saray Museum H. 799, folio 34a.

19. National Library of Russia, St. Petersburg PNS 67, folio 40b. The painting is reproduced in H. Suleiman and F. Suleimanova, *Miniatures Illuminations of Amir Hosroe Dehlevi's Works* (Tashkent, 1983), pl. 62.

20. *Khamsa*, Chester Beatty Library P. 163, folio 28a. The painting is reproduced in color in Bahari, *Bihzad*, fig. 23.

21. *Khamsa*, Baku M287-27109, folio 26b. The painting is reproduced in Suleiman and Suleimanova, *Miniatures Illuminations*, pl. 26.

22. Topkapi Saray Museum H. 798, folio 32b.

23. British Library Add. 7751, folio 28b.

24. *Khamsa*, Bibliothèque Nationale Supp. persan 1954 (1)(legs Marteau, 1916), detached page in Louvre AO 7104. The painting is reproduced in G. Marteau and H. Vever, *Miniatures persanes exposée au Musée des Arts Décoratifs* (Paris, 1913), fig. 84.

25. *Khamsa*, Baku M287-27109, folio 71a. The painting is reproduced in Suleiman and Suleimanova, *Miniatures Illuminations*, pl. 30.

26. Topkapi Saray Museum H. 798, folio 126a.

27. National Library of Russia, St. Petersburg PNS 67, folio 69b. The painting is reproduced in Suleiman and Suleimanova, *Miniatures Illuminations*, pl. 64.

28. Chester Beatty Library P. 124, folio 101a.

29. *Khamsa*, Staatsbibliothek, Berlin Ms. Or. fol. 187, folio 81b. The painting is reproduced in P. Schulz, *Die persisch-islamische Miniaturmalerei* (Leipzig, 1914), pl. 61a.

30. Topkapi Saray Museum H. 799, folio 104b.

31. British Library Or. 11326, folio 11b.

32. The most recent publication of the painting is in S. Canby, *Princes, Poets & Paladins* (London, 1998), no. 93. The original ascription of the painting has been obliterated and replaced inexplicably with a badly written name often read as Sajnū. Sajnū appears nowhere among the well-documented ranks of artists active during Akbar's reign. Nor can this artist be identified with one of a similar name, Sāhū, whose name is spelled differently. Instead, the painting should be attributed to Dharmadāsa, who characteristically lends his figures tightly drawn features and an intense expression, and who often shows some experimentation with modeling and recession in his architectural interiors.

33. The painting (no. 1976/14), now on loan from the Victoria Gallery, Bath, to the Bristol Museum and Art Gallery, is one of nine paintings from the *Iskandarnāma* portion of a dispersed *Khamsa* manuscript. Three other paintings from the same poem of the manuscript, whose colophon is dated 880/1475, are published in G. Minissale, "Piecing Together The Emperor Akbar's Lost Sharaf-nāme," *Oriental Art*, 44, no. 3 (Autumn 1998), 67–71. Four paintings from the book of *Khusraw wa Shīrīn* were sold at Sotheby's, London, 19 December 1988, lot 270, and are now in the Museum Rietberg (RVI 919); the Bodleian Library owns the following book, *Laylā wa Majnūn* (Ms. 102), which has nine paintings (see fig. 47). Dharmadāsa's painting in the *Iskandarnāma* is numbered 42, which establishes that for a poetical text, the manuscript was quite heavily illustrated, albeit with paintings of only fair quality.

34. Chester Beatty Library P. 163, folio 120b. The painting is reproduced in color in Bahari, *Bihzad*, fig. 27.

35. Berlin Ms. Or. fol. 187, folio 83a.

36. Topkapi Saray Museum H. 799, folio 106a, and Topkapi Saray Museum H. 800, folio 120a.

37. The Persian words may be deciphered as follows: "*...taṣwīr Laylā (?) dar....sar-i Majnūn...bā ū dar sukhun.*"

38. A more fragmentary example appears in the manuscript on folio 187a. For a comprehensive discussion of European examples, see J. J. G. Alexander, *Medieval Illuminators and Their Methods of Work* (New Haven, 1992), 52–71. For Mughal examples, see J. Seyller, "Scribal Notes on Mughal Manuscript Illustrations," *Artibus Asiae*, 48, nos. 3/4 (1987), 252–55. Beyond the examples mentioned therein are a single example in the *Hamzanāma* (Museum für angewandte Kunst, Vienna, 8770/39), fifty-seven in the ca. 1575 *Talisman*, recently identified as *Sirr al-Maktūb* (Rampur Raza Library), and seven on pages from a copy of the *Khamsa* of Niẓāmī discussed in note 34.

39. For example, the discovery of a number of similar programmatic notations beneath the illustrations of a copy of the *Anwār-i Suhaylī* in the Victoria and Albert Museum (I.S. 13-1962) establishes that this working method was also used in the workshop at Golkonda in the Deccan in the late sixteenth century. These examples are discussed in J. Seyller, "Painter's Directions in Early Indian Painting," *Artibus Asiae*, 59, nos. 3/4 (2000), 303–18.

40. Alexander, *Medieval Illuminators*, 114–15, discusses several copies of the Arthurian Romance that seem to have been illustrated from such a checklist of subjects.

41. A. Adamova, "Repetition of Compositions in Manuscripts: The *Khamsa* of Nizami in Leningrad," in *Timurid Art and Culture*, eds., L. Golombek and M. Subtelny (Leiden, 1992), 67–75, demonstrates that a *Khamsa* of Niẓāmī dated 1435 in the State Hermitage, St. Petersburg, repeats to various degrees compositions found in the British Library *Anthology* of 1410 (Add. 27261). This examples leads her to propose that by doing so, artists asserted their place within the Persian pictorial tradition.

42. See B. Schmitz, "A Fragmentary Mīnā'ī Bowl with Scenes from the Shāhnāma," in *Art of the Saljuqs in Iran and Anatolia*, ed., R. Hillenbrand (Costa Mesa, California, 1994), 156–62, for new evidence on this issue and references to earlier literature on the topic.

43. Several copies of the *Jāmi' al-Tawārīkh* were produced in the early fourteenth century. At least six, and possibly seven copies of the *Bāburnāma* were made in the Mughal workshop between 1589 and 1599. The most recent treatment of the former is S. Blair, *The Earliest Illustrated Manuscript of Jāmi' al-Tawārīkh* (London, 1995); the fullest discussion of the latter is E. Smart, *Paintings from the* Baburnama*: a study of sixteenth century Mughal manuscript illustration* (Ph.D. dissertation, University of London, 1977). Additional information appears in the same author's "Yet another illustrated Akbari Baburnama manuscript," in *Facets of Indian Art*, eds., R. Skelton et al. (London, 1986), 105–15.

44. The earliest of the many inspection notes records that the manuscript was deposited with Khwāja 'Ināyatullāh on the date of Farwardīn 19 Khūrdād regnal year 39, which is the equivalent of Ramaẓān 1002/September–October 1594. For a complete list of the inspection notes on this manuscript, see Seyller, "The Inspection and Valuation of Manuscripts," 298.

45. See Seyller, "The School of Oriental and African Studies *Anvār-i Suhaylī*, 119–51. A fifth manuscript of the *Anwār-i Suhaylī* of ca. 1605 was published at Christie's, London, 11 October 1979, lot 31, and is now preserved in the British Library (Or. 13942).

46. The *Khamsa* of Niẓāmī in the Keir Collection was written at Yazd between 1502 and 1506, but the spaces reserved for illustrations were left empty. Between 1585 and 1590, Mughal artists added 41 paintings, which are described by Skelton in *Islamic Painting and the Arts of the Book*, 238–48. These may be compared with the 43 illustrations in a copy divided between the British Library (Or. 12208) and the Walters Art Museum (W.613), which are discussed in Brend, *The Emperor Akbar's* Khamsa *of Niẓāmī*. A third copy of the *Khamsa*, a dispersed manuscript of ca. 1595, is discussed in note 34.

47. The presentation copy of the *Rāmāyaṇa*, now in the Maharaja Sawai Man Singh II Museum in Jaipur, and dated 1588–91, is introduced in A. Das, "Akbar's Imperial *Ramayana*: A Mughal Persian Manuscript," in *The Legend of Rama: Artistic Visions*, ed., V. Dehejia (Bombay, 1994), 73–84; a list of the subjects of its 176 illustrations appears in Seyller, *Workshop and Patron in Mughal India*, Appendix A. The choice of episodes is not followed in the 56 illustrations of a dispersed *Rāmāyaṇa* dated 1594, whose paintings have appeared on the London art market since 1992. For this manuscript, see *Islamic Manuscripts* (London: Sam Fogg Rare Books and Manuscripts, 2000), no. 44.

48. See Lentz and Lowry, *Timur and the Princely Vision*, 376–79, for a series of examples in which a scene is repeated in composition and detail from one manuscript and text to another.

49. A number of examples are discussed and reproduced in Lentz and Lowry, *Timur and the Princely Vision*, 171–77.

50. The only contemporary Mughal example I know is an exceedingly detailed drawing of a darvish praying in a landscape. Every element of the scene has been pricked for pouncing, but the surface shows no sign of having been discolored by actual pouncing. Although the drawing was previously attributed to 'Abd al-Ṣamad, it compares so closely in style to a page by Narasimha from the 1596 *Gulistān* of Sa'dī (Cincinnati Art Museum 1950.286) that it must be by Narasimha's hand. The drawing, which is now in a private collection, is reproduced in *Indian Miniatures, Asian Textiles 1998* (London: Francesca Galloway), no. 4.

51. See, for example, O. Grabar and S. Blair, *Epic Images and Contemporary History. The Illustrations of the Great Mongol* Shahnama (Chicago and London, 1980), 13–27; and E. Sims, "Illustrated Manuscripts of Firdausī's *Shāhnāma* Commissioned by Princes of the House of Tīmūr," *Ars Orientalis*, 22 (1992), especially 55–57.

52. Grabar, *The Illustrations of the Maqamat*, 153.

53. Here I am indebted to the line of thinking presented by Grabar in *The Illustrations of the Maqamat*, especially 153–57. These issues are explored in a still further-reaching manner in O. Grabar, "Toward an Aesthetic of Persian Painting," in *The Art of Interpreting: Papers in Art History*, ed., Susan C. Scott (Pennsylvania State University, 1995), 129–39.

CHAPTER 6

# The Illumination and Binding of the Walters *Khamsa*

Nearly all of the paintings in the Walters *Khamsa* were executed by the same group of master artists who participated in the creation of the Bodleian *Bahāristān* and the British Library *Khamsa* of Niẓāmī. Other teams of artists assigned to produce the exquisite abstract illuminations marking the various headings of the text and the inventive medallions, animal motifs, and figural scenes adorning the borders of every folio also worked on all three manuscripts in succession.

## ILLUMINATIONS

Like the British Library *Khamsa*, the Walters *Khamsa* has an elaborate program of decoration opening the manuscript and separating the poems from one another. The latter manuscript commences in a traditional manner, placing a rather geometric *shamsa* on the otherwise empty recto side of the initial folio and an *'unwān*, or decorative headpiece, immediately above the actual beginning of the text on the verso of the same folio. This arrangement is repeated between the end of *Maṭla' al-Anwār* (f. 41b) and the first page of *Shīrīn wa Khusraw* (f. 42b; fig. 48). Yet when the second poem in the manuscript draws to an end again on the verso of another folio (f. 89b), the illuminators inexplicably elected to substitute for the customary *shamsa* a full-page version of the animal decorations found on many borders. Thereupon, the manuscript continues in predictable fashion with an obligatory *'unwān* above the first verses of *Majnūn wa Laylā* (f. 90b; fig. 49).

The final folios of *Majnūn wa Laylā* and the opening ones of *Ā'īnah-i Sikandarī* were excised from the manuscript, but the number of folios missing makes it likely that a *shamsa* preceded the *'unwān*. However, with the conclusion of *Ā'īnah-i Sikandarī* on a recto side (f. 173a), the illuminators were compelled to improvise decoration for the space before the beginning of the following poem, *Hasht Bihisht*, which the calligrapher had automatically placed on the verso side of the next folio (f. 174b) so as to allow a suitable separation between the two poems. In this case, the illuminators resorted to a combination of their two previous decorative solutions, filling folio 173b with a *shamsa* and folio 174a with another full page of animal decorations. This solution was probably considered an improvement over the peculiar one arrived at in two similar situations in the British Library *Khamsa*, which forced *shamsas* to appear on both sides of an opening.[1] The Walters manuscript concludes unusually with a *shamsa* on the final folio (f. 211b).

The most remarkable aspect of the illuminations of the Walters *Khamsa* of Amīr Khusraw is that five of them are signed by four individual artists, only one less than the total number of signed illuminations in all other sixteenth-century Mughal manuscripts, and double the number of artists.[2] This rare documentation enables us to identify some distinguishing features of individual illuminators within this exceedingly conservative art.

The first *'unwān* of the manuscript is inscribed "gilded by Manṣūr Naqqāsh" on two gold squares at the top of the intercolumnar spaces just below the illumination (fig. 50). In the *Bahāristān* and one of his two illuminations in the British Library *Akbarnāma*, Manṣūr had invoked the traditional decorative formula of most *'unwāns*, which sets a framed rectangular field containing a long cartouche and pendants below the high, springing form of a half-medallion.[3] Here, however, he abandons the architectonic structure of his earlier creations in favor of a unified decorative field organized primarily by a series of interlocking bands. The overall effect is quite different, being broad and even rather than channeled and rising, but the actual decorative components remain essentially the same. For example, he repeats from the *Bahāristān* and the second *Akbarnāma* illumination the double outline of the scalloped contour separating the pale golden bands from more delicate floral decoration above.[4] Likewise, in each of Manṣūr's three signed works, the outermost colored band is juxtaposed with a strong gold band with a running geometric design. The modest density of the floral filler and the Timurid-style

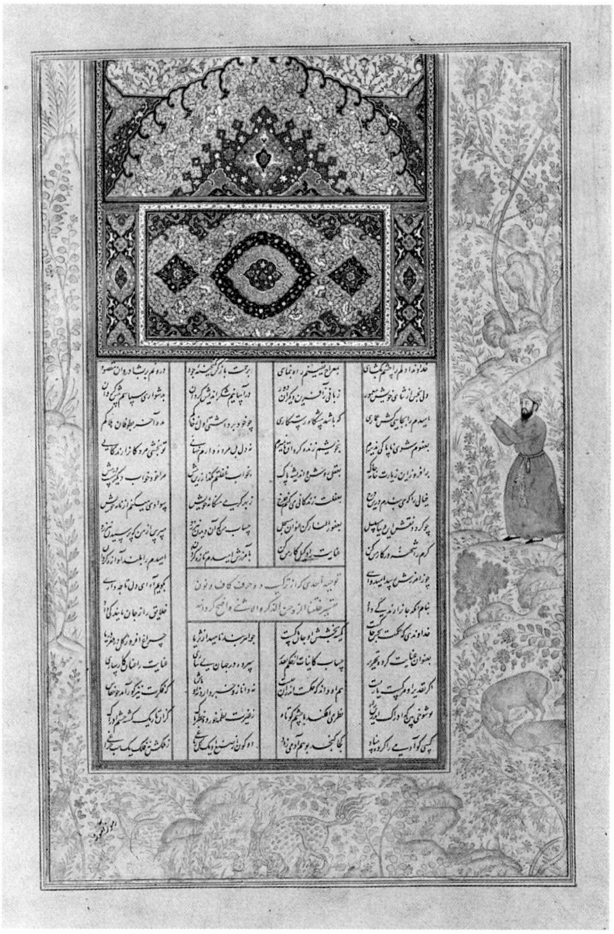

Fig. 48. *'Unwān* of *Shīrīn wa Khusraw.* Illumination signed by Khwāja Jān Shīrāzī, borders attributed to Sulaymān Kalān. *Khamsa* of Amīr Khusraw, f. 42b. Walters Art Museum, W.624.

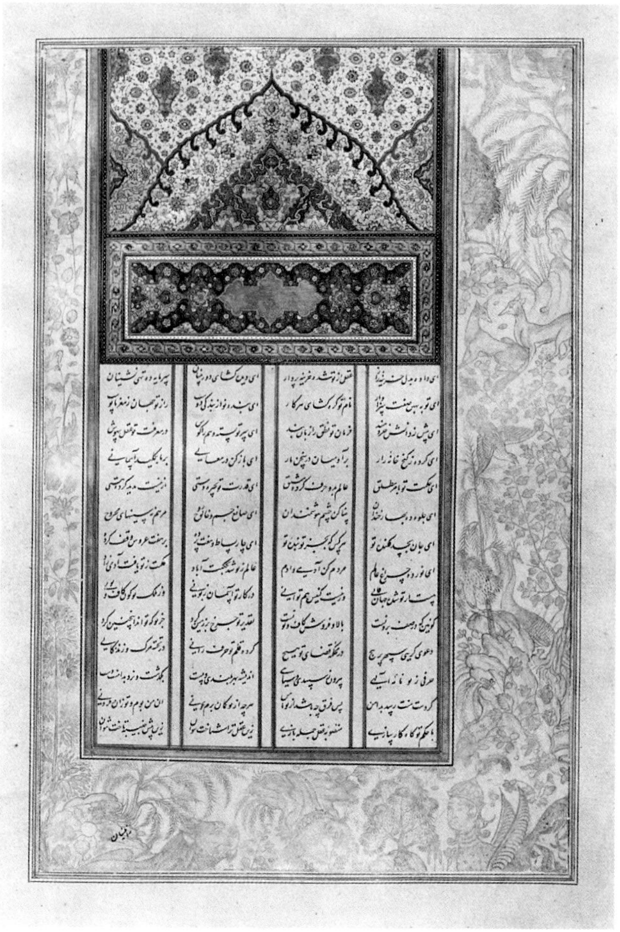

Fig. 49. *'Unwān* of *Majnūn wa Laylā.* Illumination signed by Luṭfullāh Muẕahhib, borders attributed to Ḥusayn. *Khamsa* of Amīr Khusraw, f. 90b. Walters Art Museum, W.624.

strapwork around the major forms of the latter *Akbarnāma sarlawḥ* are also consistent enough with these elements on *shamsas* in the Walters *Khamsa* (f. 1a) and the British Library *Khamsa* (f. 110a) to support an attribution of these illuminations to Manṣūr.[5]

The second artist to conceal his name among the dazzling illuminations of the Walters *Khamsa* is Khwāja Jān Shīrāzī, who signs his name, for the first time with his place of birth (Shiraz), on two small gold cartouches flanking the white band bifurcating the *'unwān* at the head of *Shīrīn wa Khusraw* (fig. 48). Khwāja Jān's designs tend to be more organic than Manṣūr's, as exemplified in the orange-outlined curving hooks that pierce the solidity of the arching element and impart a flickering quality to its edge. The artist also shows a predilection for animated, knotted arabesques, such as the golden ones writhing outside the central medallion or the white ones bracketing the side pendants. Although Khwāja Jān apparently produced a single illumination in the Walters *Khamsa*, the presence of the dense patterns, intricate hooked scrollwork, and penchant for green characteristic of his work on several illuminations in the British Library *Khamsa* and the Chester Beatty Library volume of the *Akbarnāma* suggest that he played a more central role in these two manuscripts.[6]

A third illuminator, Luṭfullāh Muẕahhib, inscribed his name discreetly in the center of the maroon band at the lower edge of the third *'unwān* in the Walters *Khamsa* (fig. 49). Luṭfullāh signed several illuminations in the Gulshan Album and is even portrayed once in the border of one of its folios.[7] His work bears some resemblance to Khwāja Jān's, especially in the hooks that articulate the swelling half-medallion, but lacks some of the nuances that bring excitement to the preceding *'unwān.* The hooks, for example, show less variety in length and lack the brilliant orange detailing. Similarly, the regularity of the space around the cartouche and pendants in the lower rectangle and the uniform size of the brightly colored surrounding flowers create a more static effect.

Fig. 50. *'Unwān* of *Maṯla' al-Anwār*. Illumination signed by Manṣūr. Borders attributed to Manṣūr. *Khamsa* of Amīr Khusraw, f. 1b. Walters Art Museum, W.624.

Fig. 51. *'Unwān* of *Hasht Bihisht.* Illumination signed by Ḥusayn, borders attributed to Ḥusayn. *Khamsa* of Amīr Khusraw, f. 174b. Walters Art Museum, W.624.

Fig. 52. Malkat Agla Khanam, the wife of Prince Shāh Rukh Mīrzā, grants an interview to Tukul Khanam, the daughter of Khiẓr Khwāja Ughlan. Designed by Kesava Kalān, painted by Ḥusayn Naqqāsh. Detail of *Tārīkh-i Khāndān-i Tīmūriyya*, ca. 1584, f. 72a. Whole image 34.3 x 22.2 cm. Khudabakhsh Library, Patna, HL 107.

The final illuminator named in the *Khamsa* is Ḥusayn Naqqāsh, who signed his name prominently in red below one *shamsa* (f. 42a) and between the centermost columns of the final *'unwān* (fig. 51). Ḥusayn's description of himself on the former as a *naqqāsh* (painter) rather than as a *muzahhib* (gilder), a term included by Luṭfullāh and Khwāja Jān in their signatures, seems to have been a deliberate reference to the centrality of painting in the range of his professional activities.[8] Indeed, Ḥusayn is credited with no fewer than eleven paintings.[9] The technical artistic vocabulary employed in the *'unwān* might appear to be quite different from that involved in painting, but a detail from one of the few paintings ascribed to Ḥusayn shows how the artist's facility with abstract patterns could easily be used to good effect in both contexts (fig. 52).[10] Moreover, as I will demonstrate below, since this Ḥusayn is identical to the artist whose name appears below the border designs of one *Bahāristān* folio (fig. 65), we can conclude that his works encompassed the full complement of decorative duties.

Ḥusayn was not unique in this regard. Manṣūr, best known for his magnificent animal paintings made during Jahāngīr's reign, produced the illuminations for the *Bahāristān*, the British Library *Akbarnāma*, and Walters *Khamsa* after he had been painting for at least five years. In the British Library *Akbarnāma*, his assignments of illuminations and paintings were exactly concurrent, with his spectacular opening illumination followed later in the manuscript by four paintings.[11] And, as we will see, Manṣūr extended his work on the illuminated folios to the animal designs on the borders as well. These signed illuminations are important, therefore, in two respects. First, they introduce us to individual artistic habits in aspects of manuscript illumination other than painting. And, second, they alert us to the unexpected degree of versatility exercised within the Mughal atelier.

## BORDER DECORATION

Mughal artists inherited many concepts and forms of border decoration from their Safawid counterparts, but did not apply them systematically to their own manuscripts until the 1590s. The earliest type of Mughal border decoration appears in a copy of another text by Amīr Khusraw, the National Museum *'Ashīqa* of 1568, on which paper stained blue, green, or tan is graced by floral scrollwork in gold. This simple, unobtrusive pattern is virtually indistinguishable from one used occasionally in the Freer Gallery *Haft Awrang*, a great Safawid manuscript dated 1556–65.[12] In the next manuscript with significant border decoration, the unillustrated Royal Asiatic Society *Gulistān* dated 990/1582–83, Mughal artists made extensive use of several more staples of Persian border decoration, such as flying cranes, birds perched in trees, and real and mythical beasts chasing or confronting one another.[13] By contrast, the poetical manuscript of the 1580s with the most exquisite paintings, the Sackler Museum *Dīwān* of Anwarī of 1588, has only a few modest floral or animal designs on its borders, with most left plain, lightly sprinkled with gold, or decorated with marbled paper.[14]

Rapid changes occurred in the late sixteenth century as borders became consistently embellished in illustrated Mughal manuscripts. On the whole, Mughal artists continued the Persian tradition in their choice of motifs and general border arrangements. They shed some of the contrived sinuousness of Persian landscape elements and reduced the prominence of such mythical creatures as the *qilin* (griffin) and *simurgh* (phoenix). At the same time, they began to add a number of indigenous Indian creatures such as bullocks and elephants. They also introduced figures, who appear rarely in Persian borders. Mughal artists set figural motifs into border medallions several times in the 1595 *Bahāristān*, but used this innovation only once in the British Library *Khamsa* later the same year (fig. 53).[15] They then dropped the new combination of figures and medallions altogether in the Walters *Khamsa* and the Chester Beatty Library *Dīwān* of Ḥāfiẓ, but after a nearly ten-year hiatus applied it frequently to the borders of the British Library *Dīwān* of Ḥāfiẓ and the Berlin Album.[16]

Most figural borders in the Walters *Khamsa* are concentrated toward the beginning of *Maṭla‘ al-Anwār* and in the first part of *Shīrīn wa Khusraw*, as though the workshop's interest in elaborate designs waned when the production schedule became more pressing or when the sheer novelty of such designs simply wore off.[17] In the *Khamsa* borders, as in those of the other poetical manuscripts of the 1590s, individual figures emerged from their isolated vignettes to become ever more involved with animals and other figures. For the most part, Mughal artists depicted figures engaged in traditional activities such as praying, reading, and hunting, often excerpting them from contemporary paintings (fig. 54). As the yogis on one folio exemplify, however, sometimes they went beyond the standard Persian repertoire of grooms and fair youths to represent some uniquely Indian types (fig. 55). Mughal artists would not begin to cast figures in specific courtly activities for another decade or so, when they occasionally included informative scenes such as bookmaking or swordmaking.[18] Whatever the activity, the figures were increasingly set apart from other elements in the border by light color, thereby gaining both visual weight and heightened status in the border decoration.

The distinction between figures and setting is reflected in the technique used in the execution of the borders. The nearly total absence of any overlap between the figures and the surrounding rocks and vegetation suggests that an artist began figural border designs by sketching the scattered figures in either faint ink or gold and then constructing a landscape setting around them. This stage can be seen in two of several incomplete figures in the Walters *Khamsa* (fig. 56). Both figures are rendered in gold wash, but their faces remain blank and their contours lack outlines. A slightly later stage is exemplified by Figure 55, in which the holy man in the lower margin has a delicately drawn but uncolored face, while his counterparts in the outer margin have fully realized features and clothes. Occasionally, an artist would take the process one step further and apply full color to the figures' hands and faces, and red or silver to other details (fig. 57). Such painted figures blur further the formal distinction between border decoration and illustration.

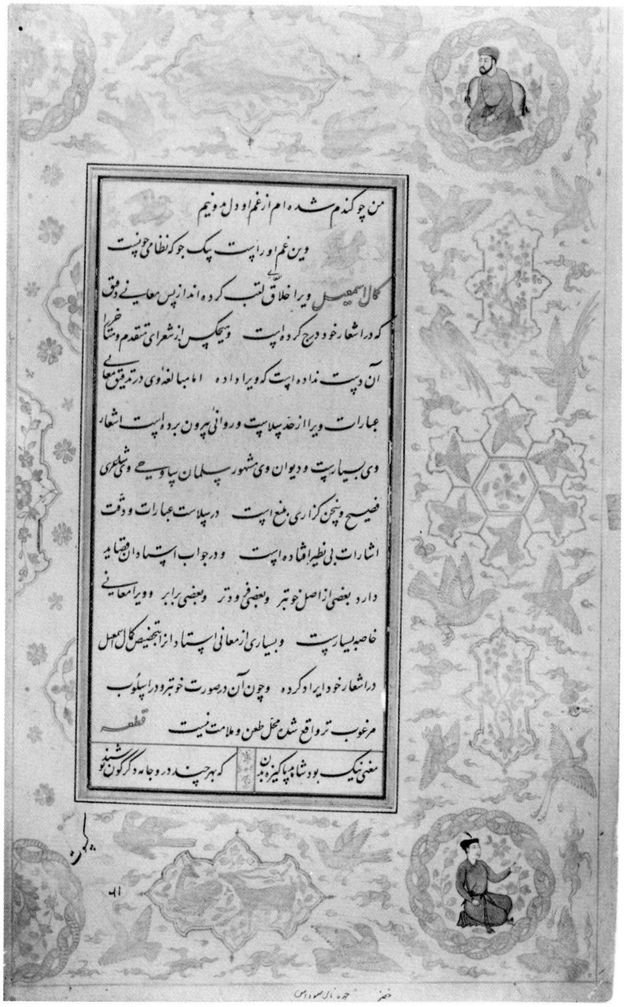

Fig. 53. Borders ascribed to Khiẓr, special faces ascribed to Śivadāsa. *Bahāristān* of Jāmī, 1595, f. 61b. 28.5 x 17.5 cm. Bodleian Library, University of Oxford, Ms. Elliott 254.

The artists assigned to execute the borders were clearly affected by the physical presence of paintings and illuminations. When paintings extended beyond the limits of the text area, leaving little space for extensive border decoration, artists commenced the design of animal scenes or medallions from the point of the paintings' ruling rather than superimposing predetermined patterns on the remaining constricted space. On one painted folio of the British Library *Khamsa*, for example, the peacock and rock in the border decoration show no sign of being cut by the extension of the painting field to the right of the text, which would occur if the border decoration preceded the painting (fig. 43).On another folio from the same manuscript, the artist clearly reduced the scale of the animals to one more suited to a narrow margin.[19] Lightly colored figures are never used

Fig. 54. Borders attributed to Mādhava. *Khamsa* of Amīr Khusraw, f. 12a. Walters Art Museum, W.624.

Fig. 55. Borders attributed to Mādhava, figures attributed to Basāvana. *Khamsa* of Amīr Khusraw, f. 11a. Walters Art Museum, W.624.

Fig. 56. Borders attributed to Sulaymān Kalān. *Khamsa* of Amīr Khusraw, f. 5b. Walters Art Museum, W.624.

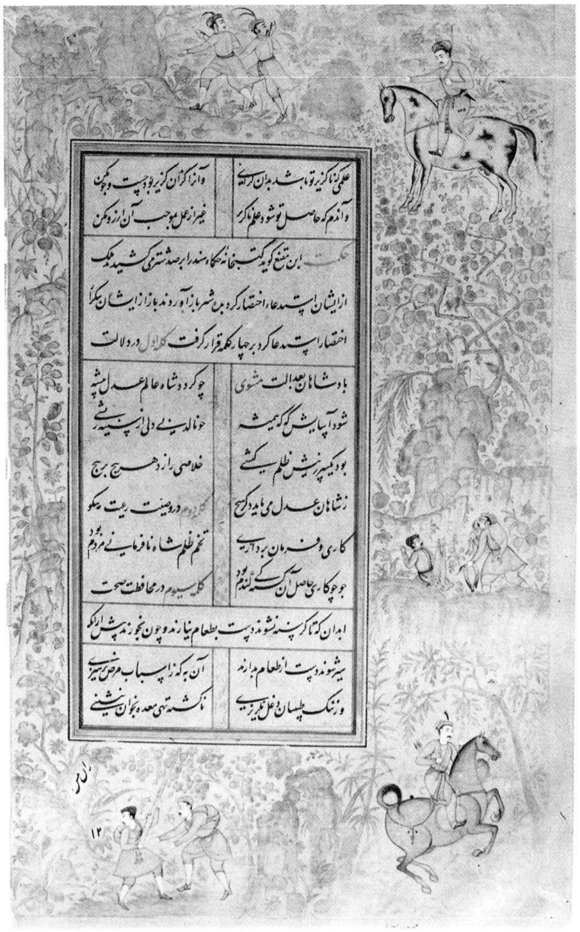

Fig. 57. Borders attributed to Mādhava, figures ascribed to Śivadāsa. *Bahāristān* of Jāmī, f. 12b. 28.5 x 17.5 cm. Bodleian Library, University of Oxford, Ms. Elliott 254.

in borders surrounding paintings, and even animal borders seem more restrained on those folios. This was almost certainly done to limit the visual competition on the page.

Despite this carefully developed system of decoration, some aberrations occur in various manuscripts. In one case, a flowering vase is inverted in relation to the text; in another, a pair of rodents ensconced in a medallion are similarly disoriented.[20] But by far the most striking example occurs on a folio in the Chester Beatty Library *Dīwān* of Ḥāfiẓ, in which the entire menagerie of the border is flipped upside down (fig. 58). This blatant disorientation may have been a matter of simple carelessness, but it also suggests that at least some Mughal artists were illiterate in Persian.[21]

Rather than the absolutely fixed pattern of complementary borders found on opposing pages in later albums (that is, one medallion and one animal border), each opening in these manuscripts is usually decorated with matched pairs of either medallions or animal designs, which differ slightly in the choice of motifs and occasionally in style. The *Khamsa*'s borders are nearly evenly divided between these two types.[22] Although the lively animal borders may hold a greater appeal, all three manuscripts have many different elegant medallions (fig. 59), and some show flashes of such inventive detail as tendrils sprouting animal heads (fig. 60).

Certain medallions, both simple and complex, appear with remarkable consistency in all three manuscripts. This is no accident, for the Mughal workshop used stencils to fix the basic structure of individual medallions. The use of stencils is established by the identical dimensions of every example of a given medallion in the Walters *Khamsa* as well as in its two companion manuscripts. It is also evident from the presence of red or black underdrawings that served as guidelines for the final brushwork in gold, a process visible on many examples of flowers or medallions. Internal details, such as the birds, animals, and floral designs that normally fill the medallions, were rendered freehand, without the aid of a stencil.

Fig. 58. Folio with inverted border designs. *Dīwān* of Ḥāfiẓ, ca. 1598, f. 29a. 28.5 x 18.4 cm. Chester Beatty Library, Dublin P. 150 (By kind permission of the Trustees of the Chester Beatty Library, Dublin).

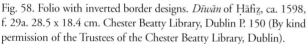

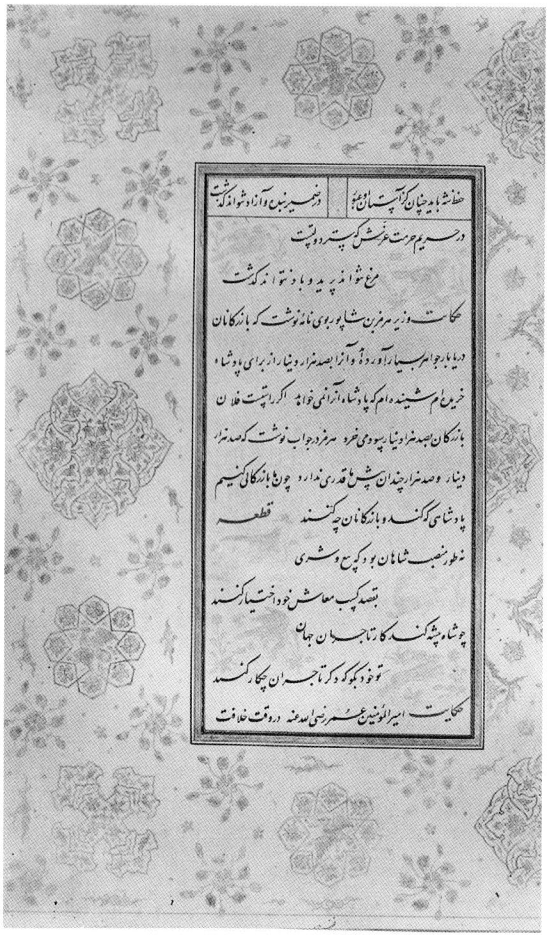

Fig. 59. Borders ascribed to Nanda Cela. *Bahāristān* of Jāmī, f. 23a. 28.5 x 17.5 cm. Bodleian Library, University of Oxford, Ms. Elliott 254.

Animal borders are filled with familiar adversaries, such as a cheetah pursuing a deer or a lion attacking a stag, but slight differences in the motifs themselves, as well as discrepancies in their size, preclude the use of a stencil. Signs of underdrawing are rarely found in animals, suggesting that Mughal artists were sufficiently confident to execute these motifs directly in gold, without preliminary drawings. Nonetheless, the relatively constant vocabulary of animal motifs in the borders of all three manuscripts underscores the inclination of the Mughal workshop to use established formulae whenever possible, balancing desire for variety with concern for efficiency.

The small size of the stencils and the absence of fixed combinations of motifs in most medallion and animal borders in the Walters *Khamsa* suggest that like most contemporary illustrations, these borders were composed by a process of accretion; the artist considered the unit of composition to be the discrete medallion or animal group rather than the border as a whole. Within a decade or so, however, the units replicated through stencilling would develop into relatively complex combinations, such as a large fish grasped in the jaws of two predatory creatures and flanked by a deer and cheetah, and that cluster of motifs might be repeated as many as four times on the same folio (fig. 61). Nonetheless, borders composed by the application of modular stencilled motifs clearly differ from those composed in a comprehensive fashion, as are found on several folios in the Safawid manuscript of the *Haft Awrang* and throughout a copy of the *Panj Ganj* of Jāmī decorated for ʿAbd al-Raḥīm between 1603 and 1607.[23] Both manuscripts make use of large sheet or strip stencils to mass-produce complete designs. By rejecting this readily available technique in favor of one that required more time and thought, the imperial Mughal workshop was able to produce exceptionally dense and varied border designs. In short, in the late sixteenth century, the Mughal atelier seems to have elevated border decoration to an unprecedented status in the art of the book.

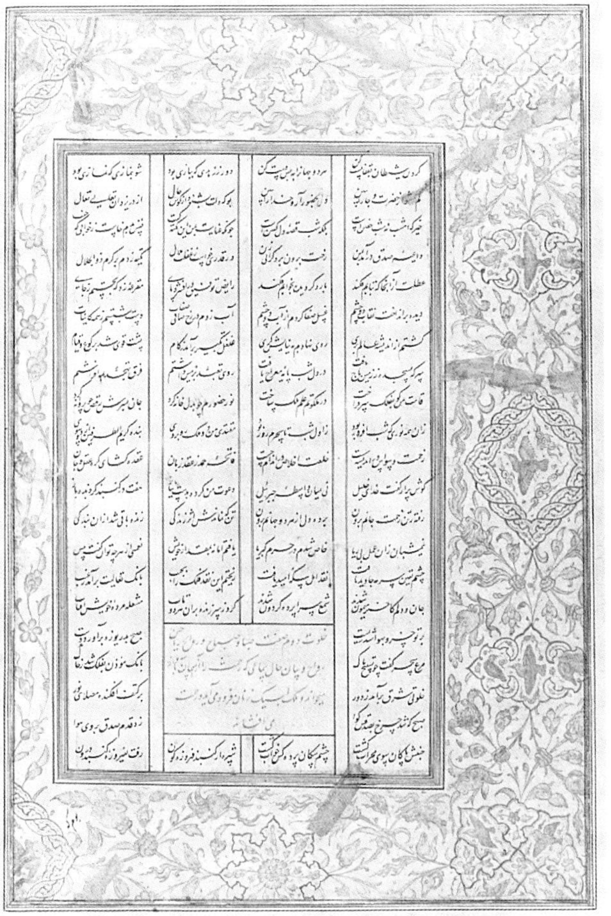

Fig. 60. Borders attributed to Khiẓr. *Khamsa* of Amīr Khusraw, f. 8b. Walters Art Museum, W.624.

Fig. 61. The Berlin Album, f. 2b. ca. 1610. Berlin, Staatsbibliothek zu Berlin - Preussischer Kulturbesitz, Orientabteilung, Libri picturati A 117.

This impression is substantiated by the first known inscriptions recording the artists responsible for the elaborate border designs, a measure of Mughal workshop documentation hitherto provided only for painters and the occasional illuminator. The border ascriptions are preserved in the Bodleian *Bahāristān*, a rare example of a completely untrimmed Mughal manuscript. The *Bahāristān*'s folios were ruled first by scoring the edge of the folio or by drawing lines in light ink; soon thereafter, these were overlaid with a straight gold line. With few exceptions, the informally written ascriptions on the manuscript's borders lie outside this ruling, along the very lower edge of the folios, and were probably intended to be cut off when the completed manuscript was ready for binding. Similar ascriptions almost certainly existed on the British Library *Khamsa* and Walters *Khamsa* as well, but were lost when the two manuscripts were remargined. Another contemporary manuscript, the Chester Beatty Library *Dīwān* of Ḥāfiẓ, retains a single example of an ascribed border.[24] Not every border of the *Bahāristān* is ascribed, of course, but meticulous study of the manuscript has increased the number of known ascriptions from the few published in passing to a total of twenty-seven ascriptions to ten artists.[25] The relative comprehensiveness of the ascribed borders in the manuscript, especially the existence of multiple examples credited to the same artist, allows us to attribute to individual artists most of the unascribed borders of these poetical Mughal manuscripts.

Most medallion borders resist the identification of individual hands precisely because their forms are mass-produced through stencilling. Nonetheless, some distinctions can be made in the choice of motifs and the care with which they are executed. The dominant medallion painter, Nanda Cela, shows a proclivity for open forms with a clear internal structure, which he supplements with a few scattered petals (fig. 59). By contrast, Mukhliṣ often inserts birds or animals into medallions of simpler shape. He also differs in technique, generally leaving the underdrawing visible

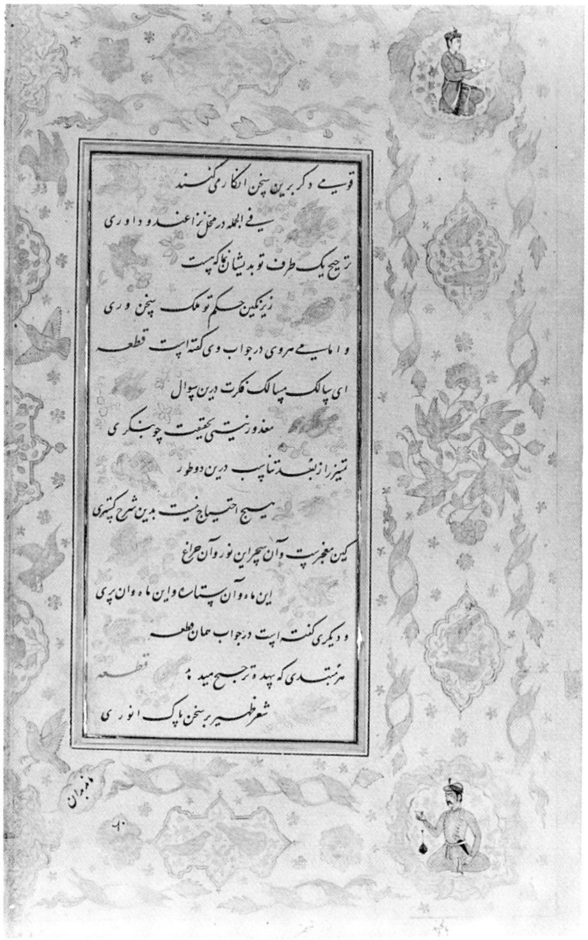

Fig. 62. Borders ascribed to Khiẓr, figures ascribed to Bālacanda. *Bahāristān* of Jāmī, 1595, f. 60b. Bodleian Library, University of Oxford, Ms. Elliott 254.

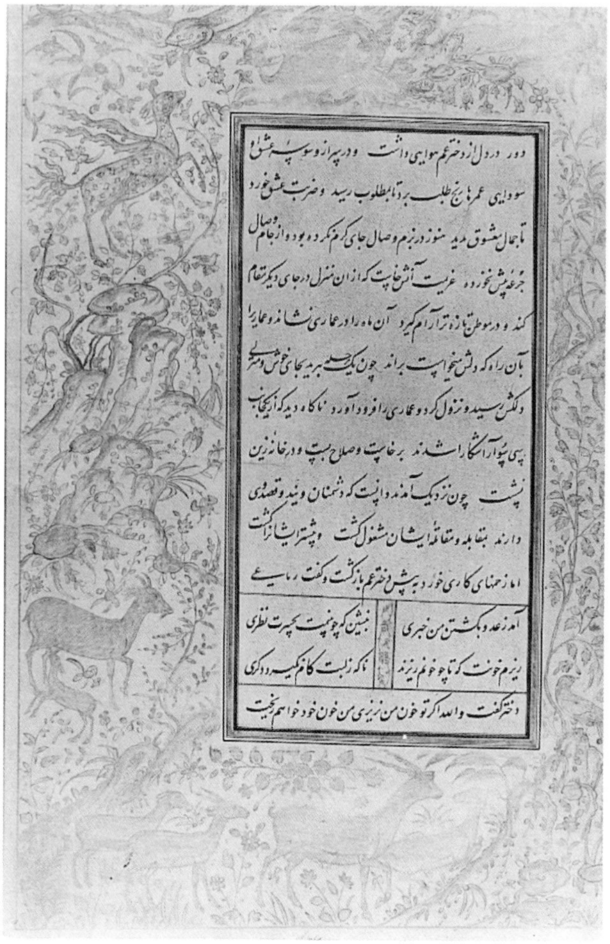

Fig. 63. Borders ascribed to Sulaymān Kalān. *Bahāristān* of Jāmī, 1595, f. 39a. Bodleian Library, University of Oxford, Ms. Elliott 254.

below or beside the summarily drawn gold lines. A third artist known exclusively from medallion borders is Khiẓr, whose works include such flamboyant motifs as a vegetal interlace ending in animal heads (fig. 60), a series of birds in pinwheel configuration (fig. 62), and a medallion frame comprised of entwined snakes (see fig. 53).

Two artists are named in ascriptions on both medallion and animal borders. Sulaymān Kalān, who is otherwise unknown in Mughal painting, produces some unique motifs, such as pairs of opposed rodents in medallions, a mare and suckling colt, fighting elephants, and bullocks. He is also easily identified by technique and style. Sulaymān was not a particularly accomplished draftsman, a deficiency he mitigated by using vigorous—at times even smeary—washes of gold to model his animals and landscape elements. The latter often take the form of lumpy outcrops with club-headed lobes and stepped mounds whose contours are marked by minute perpendicular hatching and heavy shading (fig. 63, see also figs. 48 and 56). He completes the rudimentary landscape with a ubiquitous infill of foliage and flowers, thereby emphasizing the purely ornamental aspect of border decoration.

Ikhlāṣ achieves a relatively similar effect (fig. 65). His rounded outcrops are less idiosyncratic in shape than Sulaymān's, but their discordant shifts in scale and their scattered positions around the border defy to an even greater extent a credible spatial relationship to the creatures nearby. To fill in the areas between forms, Ikhlāṣ usually conjurs up slender trees with angular trunks and limbs, large ferns, and bent bamboo. His most distinctive trait is the strongly outlined contours of his animals.

Three other border painters stand apart from the others by virtue of their skillful draftsmanship and the pictorial quality of their border compositions. Mādhava, one of the most prolific border painters, does this by rendering both figure and ground in more even tone and detail and by minimizing unconnected vegetal decoration (see figs. 54, 55, and 57). Mādhava establishes a credible setting for his

Fig. 64. Detail of f. 1b, Walters Art Museum, W.624.

human and animal encounters by linking long ridges to low, squarish outcrops. He also works in a distinctive technique, giving texture to his carefully drawn animals by means of stippling and dense parallel hatching rather than the washes preferred by Sulaymān. Like Sulaymān, however, Mādhava uses thick contour shading for most of his landscape forms. And although all of these artists work with two tones of gold, Mādhava makes particularly effective use of their subtle contrast in color in trees and fronds.

A much more refined version of this style is found on a few unascribed borders of the three *de luxe* manuscripts, including those of the sole *'unwān* in the *Bahāristān*, the *sarlawḥ* of the British Library *Akbarnāma*, and the first *'unwān* of the Walters *Khamsa* (figs. 50 and 64). In each case, the animals are markedly smaller and considerably more detailed than usual. The artist gives the creatures solidity by means of exceedingly delicate washes; rather than defining shapes by distinct contour lines, he effects a clear edge by subtly pooling the washes along the animals' contours. The outcrops never assume the squarish profiles of Mādhava's but rise in more organic combinations of interlocking lobes, all of which are executed with a lighter touch. A final difference is visible in one standard tree type, which appears before the horseman in the upper border of Figure 57. Whereas Mādhava uses several broad, wet strokes to produce a dark, two-dimensional shape, his counterpart habitually indicates foliage projecting from the tree by staggering tinges of dark gold across the form. The artist's identity is suggested by the appearance of his work on three folios whose illuminations are ascribed to Manṣūr. The existence of firm documentation that Manṣūr worked as both a painter and an illuminator makes it very plausible that the artist was asked occasionally to contribute border designs as well, an assignment made and fulfilled easily on folios already in Manṣūr's temporary charge. This prospect is supported by a similar treatment of rocks in Manṣūr's borders and manuscript illustrations,[26] and it is established conclusively by the recent discovery of two borders signed by Manṣūr Naqqāsh in the Gulshan Album.[27]

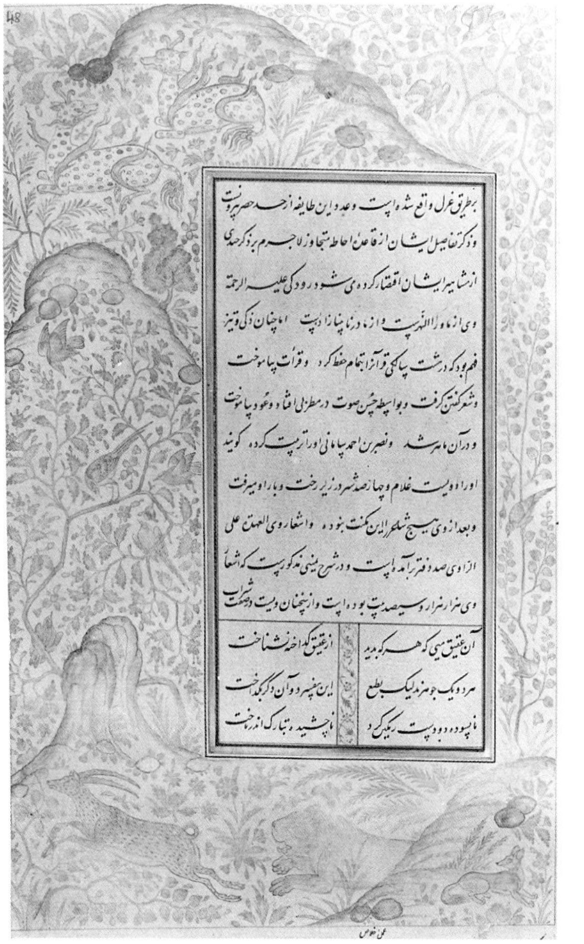

Fig. 65. Borders ascribed to Ikhlāṣ. *Bahāristān* of Jāmī, 1595, f. 48a. Bodleian Library, University of Oxford, Ms. Elliott 254.

Fig. 66. Border ascribed to Ḥusayn. *Bahāristān* of Jāmī, 1595, detail of f. 21b. Bodleian Library, University of Oxford, Ms. Elliott 254.

The most accomplished and most prolific border painter in the Walters *Khamsa* is Ḥusayn Naqqāsh, who also contributed several illuminations to the manuscript (see fig. 51). Ḥusayn's style in the marginal animal paintings is identified on the basis of a single ascribed folio in the *Bahāristān* (fig. 66), but its full range becomes clear from many similar borders in all three manuscripts, most notably those around his signed *'unwān* in the Walters *Khamsa* (fig. 51). The huge cranes and *sīmurghs* in the upper border are among this artist's favorite motifs, with the latter often set in mortal combat with equally imposing dragons. Other unique motifs include peacocks, elephants, animals with their heads twisted back across their bodies, and a lion drinking at a stream. Ḥusayn's outcrops are similar in shape to Manṣūr's, but are consistently larger and almost always have long fronds hanging down from their sides. His technique is very distinct. He displays his skill as a draftsman in his meticulous outlining of all major forms, including outcrops. Ḥusayn forgoes the sporadic accents of heavy washes favored by Sulaymān and Mādhava and the pointillist effect of Manṣūr; instead, he maintains a remarkably even tonality across his unusually dense designs.

Three borders in the *Bahāristān* have two ascriptions—one designating the artist responsible for the medallions or landscape and animals, and the other indicating the artist assigned to do the figures ensconced within them.[28] This kind of collaboration is consistent with practices known from the illustrations themselves, in which specialized portraits were occasionally assigned to different painters, even in these *de luxe* manuscripts. Although one would expect the more specialized role—the painting of the figures' faces—to be granted to artists of greater skill or status, the identities of the painters who are named in this role suggest that it was assigned to novices and well-established painters alike. For example, Bālacanda, an artist who became prominent during the reigns of Jahāngīr and Shāh Jahān, actually began his career by doing figures in the borders of three *Bahāristān* folios. The miniaturistic treatment of figures in his two earliest independent paintings, a double-page composition in the 1596–97 *Akbarnāma*, reveals habits better suited to border decoration and betrays the artist's inexperience with larger compositions.[29] Śivadāsa, a senior artist active from about 1580, was selected to add figures to three *Bahāristān* borders (see figs. 53 and 57). Yet he

Fig. 67. Ironsmiths cast and polish round mirrors in the presence of Alexander. Half of a double-page composition. By Śivadāsa. Detached portion of the BL *Khamsa* of Niẓāmī, 1595, f. 17a. Painting 15.9 x 10.5 cm. Walters Art Museum, W.613.

Fig. 68. Detail of the border of the *Khamsa* of Amīr Khusraw, f. 11a. Attributed to Basāvana. Walters Art Museum, W. 624.

also contributed one painting to the 1595 British Library *Khamsa*, thus functioning as both border figure specialist and primary illustrator in this small group of manuscripts (fig. 67). Mādhava, whose animal borders appear in Figures 54 and 55, also served in multiple capacities. While he was responsible for many animal and medallion borders in all three manuscripts, he also executed one of the six paintings in the *Bahāristān* (fig. 10), three paintings in the British Library *Khamsa*, and one work in the Walters *Khamsa*.[30]

No simple pattern for the distribution of borders to particular artists emerges from these attributions. Many times a particular artist dominates the animal borders of a gathering of four bifolios, as Ḥusayn does in *Maṭla' al-Anwār* (ff. 31–38) and *Shīrīn wa Khusraw* of the Walters *Khamsa* (ff. 51–59), but different hands can often be identified even in a single bifolio, thereby belying what we might assume to be a logical correspondence between the artist and physically indivisible units of the manuscript.

These border painting ascriptions and their ensuing attributions allow us to consider individual artists in this hitherto anonymous aspect of manuscript illumination. Curiously, the idiosyncratic formal features of border paintings that support their attributions to particular artists are normally quite difficult to locate in manuscript illustrations ascribed to the same painter. To my mind, this is because these border paintings lack the two features by which artists are usually distinguished: coherent, developed landscapes and a number of fully articulated figures. In short, the formal constraints of border painting of the 1590s remove these marginal works from the more explicit and familiar manifestations of an individual artist's personal style.

Fig. 69. In the aftermath of a tiger hunt, a prince visits a reclusive sage. Front cover, *Khamsa* of Amīr Khusraw. 28.6 x 19.7 cm. Walters Art Museum, W.624.

Fig. 70. A group of fairies battles *dīvs*. Back cover, *Khamsa* of Amīr Khusraw. 28.6 x 19.7 cm. Walters Art Museum, W.624.

The large number of artists in the imperial workshop, the many facets of these manuscript projects, and the evidence of rigorous production schedules provided both a means and a motivation for work to be divided into a series of specialized tasks. Contrary to our expectations, however, these specialized tasks—joint or individual illustrations, illuminations, and border paintings, as well as designs made for other types of objects—were executed practically interchangeably by many different artists.[31] Nearly all of the border painters—Mukhliṣ, Khiẓr, Ikhlāṣ—were minor painters in their own right.[32] Moreover, no one was automatically exempt from what we might consider decorative work. Basāvana, for example, contributed the borders to one folio from an album compiled during the early years of Jahāngīr's reign.[33] But careful examination of one of the aforementioned yogis demonstrates that Basāvana also painted the borders on a folio close to his first painting in the Walters *Khamsa* (fig. 68). In this border, the ascetic is endowed with a stubbly jaw, muscular brow, and piercing gaze, and the rough texture of his broad-weave cloak is made palpable. These visual interests are practically unique to Basāvana's work, and they are particularly evident in his Muslim pilgrim in Figure 4 and in a much-published painting of a holy man in the *Bahāristān*.[34]

The documentation of the multiple roles performed concurrently in three contemporary luxury manuscripts by artists such as Manṣūr, Śivadāsa, and Mādhava testifies to the versatility of Mughal artists and undermines the conception of a rigid artistic hierarchy. The belief that the prestigious role of painting solo works was inevitably given to artists held in the highest esteem, and the less demanding task of border decoration relegated to more modest talents, is clearly determined by our modern bias in favor of painting. Thus, it seems misguided to try to calculate the prestige enjoyed by an artist at any given time from the sequence and nature of the capacities in which he served.

## BINDING

The last element to be added to the Walters *Khamsa* was its sumptuous lacquer binding (figs. 69 and 70). Seen from a distance of about arm's length, the manuscript's highly polished, slightly bowed binding takes on the appearance of a kind of ornate shell protecting a precious object. Most of each cover is filled by a large rectangular pictorial composition. Under normal conditions, the figures and landscape are barely discernible against the deep red lacquer background, and the lightly colored areas are muted by layers of discolored shellac. Raking light restores something of the binding's original effect. Newly revealed golden outlines of rocks, trees, and foliage glimmer magically, and the scenes fairly sparkle with tiny flecks of gold strewn about the image. Even under ideal conditions, however, the subtlety of this surface brilliance ends as rapidly as it begins, with the rich tonality of the scene yielding abruptly to the garishness of three golden bands extending to the edge of the cover.[35]

If the binding is necessarily a manuscript's most conspicuous element, it is also its most vulnerable. A careful technical analysis of the Walters *Khamsa* reveals that the binding has been altered in one significant respect.[36] The pictorial scene of each cover now appears on a pasteboard panel set into the central recess of a later board of similar composition. The join of these two boards is barely visible, but its precise location can be detected from the abrupt change in color and the pattern of cracking in this area. The substitution of a new outer framing panel is corroborated by its decoration, whose composition and density are unlike any sixteenth-century Mughal pattern.[37] The doublures, or inside covers, are decorated with a uniform field of a very similar floral pattern, and its outermost band even includes grape clusters. The inclusion of this foreign motif points to the binding's restoration in Europe, probably at the end of the nineteenth century. The *Khamsa* lacks the protective leather flap found on most Islamic manuscripts, a feature precluded by the very structure of lacquered pasteboard panels. Its spine is an undistinguished modern black leather strip, which extends slightly beneath the decorative bands of the front and rear covers.

The *Khamsa*'s lacquer covers are among the most spectacular results of the conjoining of two distinct traditions in Islamic bookbinding. Lacquer first appeared on Persian manuscripts in the early fifteenth century, almost certainly in response to examples brought from China. By the 1520s, Persian bookbinding saw another element added to its decorative repertoire. Although the traditional medallion patterns always remained the favored design of book covers, a predictable outgrowth of designs featuring stamped images of birds and animals was the introduction of pictorial scenes similar to the manuscript illustrations themselves. At first, paint was applied directly to the leather, but workshops soon recognized that the layers of lacquer that fixed the paint could also provide a more stable and lustrous support. The union of lacquer and pictorial designs occurred initially on bindings made entirely of leather, but the flexibility that made leather the logical choice for bookbindings proved to be a less than ideal support for the rigid layers of lacquer. Pasteboard panels subsequently replaced leather-covered boards for the binding's painted area, though sometimes a durable leather border was added along the very edges. This structural change in the binding, in turn, obviated the continuous sheet of leather that was traditionally extended in the form of a leather flap to protect the outer edge of the folios, and this feature ultimately disappeared from lacquer covers.

The binding of the British Library *Khamsa* was refurbished in the manner of the Walters manuscript, but its panels were reversed in the process, probably for reasons of preservation. The result is that the original doublures, which contain large-scale, uncolored scenes of mythical beasts in combat, now appear as the outer covers, and the pictorial scenes are relegated to the inside.[38] Both pictorial panels feature a hunting theme. The front cover depicts hunters presenting an ensnared gazelle, three trussed deer and nilgai, and a pair of rabbits to a figure seated beneath a canopy. Two details make it clear that this scene is no generic treatment of the traditional princely activity of hunting, but a flattering allusion to Akbar's fondness for the sport. First, the artist indulges in a conceit encountered rarely in Mughal illustrations proper, that is, endowing the enthroned figure with Akbar's general features. Second, he grants a place of prominence to the figure of an inspector recording the particulars of the catch in a logbook. This motif, which appears in scenes of gift-giving in many a Mughal manuscript, surely reflects the courtly custom of preparing accurate records of the number and quality of all types of items presented in homage to the sovereign.[39]

The present-day doublure of the rear cover of the British Library *Khamsa* takes up a more commonplace aspect of the hunt, showing a mounted prince and a companion as they unleash arrows at their fleeing prey. The right-to-left movement of the action, and its priority in a putative sequence of events of the hunt, suggest that this panel originally formed the outer front cover. A codicological factor may well have supplied the impetus for this change. When the modern refurbishers added the new surrounds to the pictorial panels, they probably noted the natural convex curvature that the original lacquer panels had acquired over their three centuries of use. This observation led them to switch the position of the two parts of the binding so as to retain their natural cradling tendencies and thereby minimize the physical stress placed on the boards.

The scenes on the binding of the Walters *Khamsa* have less thematic coherence. The front cover depicts the encounter of a worldy prince and a reclusive sage (fig. 69). The theme is a traditional one that forms the subject of the anecdote of the seventh *maqāla* of *Maṭlaʿ al-Anwār*, a popular tale left unillustrated in the Walters manuscript. Here, however, the artist postpones the inevitable exchange of wisdom by presenting the prince at some remove from the sage's rocky lair, still mounted as if in a moment of respite from the hunt. As some of the prince's attendants lash a tiger's carcass to an elephant, four others direct him upward to his human quarry.

The rear cover ventures into the realm of the supernatural, depicting a host of fairies pummeling some outnumbered *dīvs* (fig. 70). The scene has no obvious literary connection to the *Khamsa* itself, and only three contemporary parallels in Mughal painting.[40] It is no less peculiar in composition and detail. The upper reaches of the composition are filled by two *dīvs* and their assailants swirling about in pinwheel fashion. This circular organization is repeated in a bizarre motif in the lower right—a stepped pathway that loops around two fairies before a tent before coming to an abrupt and pointless end. One fairy dribbles something on the lowermost *dīv*, while a human astride a bull playfully spews liquid from a trumpet. Five fairies play no part in the subjugation of these demons, preferring instead to frolic in the broad tank in the foreground. The key to this strange amalgam of imagery lies in the leftmost of these winged creatures, who reaches out toward an object, which, to judge from the two protruding sleeves, can only be a bundle of clothing. The inclusion of the clothing reveals that the artist has transformed one commonly illustrated passage from the story told by the princess of the black pavilion in Niẓāmī's *Haft Paykar*—that is, *hourīs* bathing in the pool of an astonished owner of a luxurious garden—by adding wings to the sprites and covering their bodies with feathers.[41] Likewise, he takes the well-established motif of an amorous couple before a tent and remakes it into a pair of fairies graced once more with wings and feathers. The result of these transformations is fairly nonsensical, as feathered beings bathe and fairies normally sexless indulge in romantic sport. The scene is thus a witty but essentially meaningless compilation of disparate motifs, precisely the type of image that gravitated naturally from the limited fields of border painting to the physically expansive ones of pictorial book covers.

The four scenes on the bindings of the British Library *Khamsa* and the Walters *Khamsa* thus seem to represent different responses to the task of decorating the cover of a book. These range from the straightforward use of generic hunting imagery, on the one hand, to the selection of a popular theme with connections to an anecdote recounted early in the text and the fabrication of an eclectic image from motifs largely stripped of their narrative meaning. These approaches are different more in degree than in kind, however, for each one is only a starting point for the creation of the image, which, whatever its origins, is developed inevitably by the piecemeal addition of extraneous elements from a stock repertoire of motifs. For example, the charging bullock cart in the hunting scene on the cover of the British

Library *Khamsa* is found in many a hunt scene, but is truly appropriate only in ones in which a large entourage is shown on the move; nevertheless, the artist elected to insert the motif below the prince and his sole companion because it could serve the useful formal functions of anchoring the lowermost register and reiterating the right-to-left movement of the chase. Most motifs became highly portable entities because Mughal artists plied them with an eye as much to their formal adaptability as to their thematic specificity. Hence, this same bullock-cart motif could be used just as easily in one border design of the Walters *Khamsa* (fig. 56), where the hunting theme is far more fragmented.

Although the panels are dominated by gold-outlined forms with little or no color on a flat lacquer background, a feature that inherently constrains the exploration of spatial depth, they are consistent enough with the style of the paintings and illuminations in the two *Khamsa* manuscripts, the *Bahāristān*, and the *Ḥadīqat al-Ḥaqīqat* to be attributed to the artists who contributed to these projects in one capacity or another. Of the four pictorial panels, only the battle of fairies and *dīvs* on the Walters *Khamsa* can be attributed with reasonable confidence. The only Mughal artist to render fairies covered with tiny feathers from neck to foot is Manōhara, who does so throughout his Walters *Khamsa* illustration of the youth's adventure in the fairy palace (fig. 32), albeit without the thick, leafy girdle about each fairy's midsection.[42] Manōhara displays a considerable predilection for the Europeanized features and wavy hair found in the fairy in the lower right. The other fairies are modeled less robustly than many of Manōhara's figures, but they bear a strong facial resemblance to the artist's maidens on folio 51a (fig. 11). The ambitious spatial construction of trapezoidal tank and raised platform are typical of Manōhara's interest in architectural space, no matter how unwieldy the result might be. Nothing in Manōhara's own oeuvre predicts the peculiar looping pathway, but it would be entirely in keeping with a habit exhibited throughout Manōhara's career for the artist to have taken the motif of a curving stepped path that his father, Basāvana, used in one of his illustrations in the Walters *Khamsa* (fig. 27) and render it in a harder and somewhat more mannered fashion.

NOTES

1. Following the end of the first and third poems of Niẓāmī's *Khamsa* on the recto side of the folio, *shamsas* occupy folios 31b–32a and folios 168b–169a.

2. These are folio 3b of the Royal Asiatic Society *Gulistān* of Sa'dī (Khwāja Jān Muẕahhib), folio 1b of the Bodleian Library *Bahāristān* (Manṣūr), folios 32b and 169b of the British Library *Khamsa* of Niẓāmī (Khwāja Jān Muẕahhib), and folio 1b and a detached *sarlawḥ* from the British Library *Akbarnāma* (Manṣūr). The name of another illuminator, Yāqūt, appears below a *shamsa* in the slightly later Gulshan Album (no. 261).

3. The former is reproduced in Seyller, *Workshop and Patron in Mughal India*, fig. 214; the latter is published in color in J. Losty, "The 'Bute Hafiz' and the development of border decoration in the manuscript studio of the Mughals," *Burlington Magazine*, 127, no. 993 (December 1985), fig. 14.

4. The latter, a detached page, is reproduced in color in H.-C. Graf von Bothmer, *Die islamischen Miniaturen der Sammlung Preetorius* (Munich, 1982), no. 54.

5. The two *shamsas* also display an identical ring of tiny flame-like forms around their contours; for the latter, see Brend, *The Emperor Akbar's* Khamsa *of Niẓāmī*, fig. 5. The term *sarlawḥ* is used for full-page illuminations at the beginning of a manuscript and for illuminations that mark chapters, as is the case in the *Akbarnāma* manuscript.

6. Folio 1b of the British Library *Khamsa* and folios 1b and 177b of the Chester Beatty Library *Akbarnāma* are surely by his hand. The first of these is reproduced in Brend, *The Emperor Akbar's* Khamsa *of Niẓāmī*, 9.

7. Illuminations signed by Luṯfullāh Muẕahhib appear on nos. 47, 48, 115, 116, 245, and 246. His portrait is indicated by an inscription (*ṣūrat*-i Āqā Luṭfī) on a book before a figure in the upper right margin of no. 247.

8. Khwāja Jān includes the term *muẕahhib* in his signatures on illuminations in the Royal Asiatic Society *Gulistān* and the British Library *Khamsa* of Niẓāmī (folio 169b). Conversely, Manṣūr also enlists the term *naqqāsh* in his signatures on folio 1b of the Walters *Khamsa* (fig. 50) and the detached *sarlawḥ* of the British Library *Akbarnāma*. See also note 27 below.

9. Ḥusayn contributed to the following manuscript illustrations: the *Tārīkh-i Khāndān-i Tīmūriyya*, folio 72a; the V&A *Akbarnāma*, no. 113/117; the Jaipur *Rāmāyaṇa*, nos. A.G. 1856–57; the British Library *Bāburnāma*, folio 386b; the National Museum *Bāburnāma*, folio 191b (Ḥusayn Cela), a detached *Bāburnāma* page (The David Collection 14/1980), and the Royal Library *Dīwān* of Nawā'ī (RCIN 1005033, ca. 1600–5), folio 449a (with Manṣūr). Two independent paintings by Ḥusayn in the Musée Guimet, *The Angel of Tobias* and *Man Offering a Woman a Fish*, are published in A. Okada, *Miniatures de l'Inde impériale* (Paris, 1989), nos. 64–65. Another was sold at Sotheby's, London, 18 October 1995, lot 87. A figure in the lower border of one folio of the Gulshan Album (no. 189) is ascribed to Ustā (Ustād) Ḥusayn.

10. The whole image is reproduced in *An Age of Splendour: Islamic Art in India* (Bombay, 1983), 43.

11. Folios 35b, 110a, 110b, 112a.

12. A representative border of the former manuscript is published in Losty, *The Art of the Book in India*, pl. XX; the latter manuscript is the subject of a comprehensive study by M. S. Simpson, *Sultan Ibrahim Mirza's* Haft Awrang: *A Princely Manuscript from Sixteenth-Century Iran* (London, 1997).

13. For the *Gulistān*, see Losty, *The Art of the Book in India*, no. 87. Losty believes the borders to be later additions, presumably in the 1590s. The borders of a dispersed Safawid copy of the *Gulistān* of ca. 1525, and borders of the 1539–43 British Library *Khamsa* of Niẕāmī (Or. 2265), display the Persian antecedents of these forms. Selections from the two manuscripts respectively are published in S. C. Welch, *Wonders of the Age: Masterpieces of Early Safavid Painting, 1501–1576* (Cambridge, Mass., 1979), nos. 45, 46, 52, 60, and 65.

14. The manuscript is presented in Schimmel and Welch, *Anvari's Divan*.

15. *Bahāristān*, folios 30a, 33b, 45b, 61b; British Library *Khamsa*, folio 169b (published in Losty, "The 'Bute Hafiz'," fig. 22).

16. Examples are reproduced in Losty, "The 'Bute Hafiz'," figs. 12, 16, 25, and 27–34.

17. Figural borders appear on folios 4a, 5b (fig. 56), 6b, 7a, 11a (fig. 55), 12a (fig. 53), 14a, 18b, 19a. Similarly, in *Shīrīn wa Khusraw*, which opens on folio 42b (fig. 48), the figural designs occur on folios 42b, 44b, 45a, 46b, 47a, 48b, 49a, and 50b—all before the first painting in the poem (folio 51a, fig. 11). Thereafter, figures practically vanish from the manuscript's borders, appearing only on folios 71a, 90b (fig. 49), and 112b.

18. See especially Freer Gallery of Art 54.116, published in Beach, *The Imperial Image*, no. 16b.

19. Folio 117a.

20. Individual motifs are inverted in folios 52b and 53a of the *Bahāristān*, and folio 46b of the Walters *Khamsa*.

21. Folios 113a and 160a of a *Kulliyyāt* of Sa'dī dated 1011/1602 in the Government Museum, Alwar, are also inverted.

22. One hundred and ninety of the manuscript's 427 extant borders, or 45 percent, are decorated with medallions.

23. For the former, see Simpson, *Sultan Ibrahim Mirza's* Haft Awrang, figs. 32, 61, and 217. For the latter, see Seyller, *Workshop and Patron in Mughal India*, 293–307; and Leach, *Mughal and Other Indian Paintings*, II, 567–79.

24. A faint ascription to the artist Khiẓr survives below the tiger in the lower margin of folio 25b. The folio is published without mention of the ascription in A. J. Arberry, M. Minovi, and E. Blochet, ed. by J. V. S. Wilkinson, *The Chester Beatty Library. A Catalogue of the Persian Manuscripts and Miniatures*. 2 vols. (Dublin, 1959–60), pl. 37.

25. The names of several border painters are mentioned in *Mughal Miniatures of the Earlier Periods*, 7; and Losty, "The 'Bute Hafiz'," 860. The border decoration of the following folios in the *Bahāristān* are ascribed: Bālacanda, folios 17a, 33b, 44a, 60b (fig. 62); Ḥusayn, folio 21b (fig. 66); Ikhlāṣ, folios 29b, 42b, 43b, 48a (fig. 65), 49b, 64b; Khema (Karana), folio 45b; Khiẓr, folios 60b (fig. 62), 61b (fig. 53); Mādhava, folios 14b, 15a, 15b, 17a; Mukhliṣ, folio 54b; Nanda Cela, folio 23a (fig. 59); Śivadāsa, folios 10a, 12b (fig. 57), 61b (fig. 53); and Sulaymān Kalān, folios 34a, 39a (fig. 63), 52b. On this basis, these folios in the *Bahāristān* can be firmly attributed: Khema Karana, folios 27a, 44b; Śivadāsa, folios 13a, 34b, 35a; Sulaymān Kalān, folios 53a–b, 55a, 56b, 57b, 58a. Indecipherably fragmentary ascriptions appear on folios 8a, 11a, 20a, 30a, 36b, 50a, and 66b.

26. Manṣūr's small paintings of birds in the British Library *Bāburnāma* (Or. 3714, folios 386b, 387a–b, 388a–b) provide the closest comparisons.

27. Gulshan Album, nos. 245 and 258. The signatures are written in gold in cartouches in the lower corners of the folios.

28. Folios 17a, 60b (fig. 62), and 61b (fig. 53). Folios 12b (fig. 57) and 13a are ascribed only to Śivadāsa, but his role was surely limited to the figures, with Mādhava executing the remainder of the border decoration.

29. Chester Beatty Library *Akbarnāma*, folios 152b–153a. One half of this double-page composition is published in E. Smart, "Balchand," *Master Artists of the Imperial Mughal Court* (Bombay, 1991), fig. 4.

30. *Bahāristān*, folio 35b; British Library *Khamsa*, folios 45b, 99b, 298a; Walters *Khamsa*, folio 40a (fig. 9).

31. Ikhlāṣ, for example, signed a lacquer pencase made ca. 1600. The object is published in M. Zebrowski, "Indian lacquerwork and the antecedents of the Qajar style," in ed., W. Watson, *Lacquerwork in Asia and Beyond, Colloquies on Art and Archaeology in Asia*, no. 11 (London, 1982), 335.

32. Mukhliṣ contributed to the *Dārābnāma* (British Library Or. 4615), folios 44a, 52b, 76b, 82a–b, 123a–b; the Khudabakhsh Library *Tārīkh-i Khāndān-i Tīmūriyya*, folios 66a, 138b; and the Jaipur *Razmnāma*, nos. 7, 24, 32. A painter by the name of Khiẓr, son of Niyaz is listed for the 1598–1600 *Razmnāma*; see Seyller, "Model and Copy," Appendix A, no. 160. An artist named Khiẓr Cela collaborated with Mādhava Khūrd on an illustration in the British Library *Bāburnāma* (folio 256b). A painting of a parrot of ca. 1590 sold at Sotheby's, London, 18 October 1995, lot 87, is ascribed to Khiẓr Naqqāsh, as is an unpublished image of two ducks in a private collection. Ikhlāṣ's paintings include nos. 23 and 60 of the V&A *Akbarnāma*, a page from the V&A *Bāburnāma* in the collection of Prince Sadruddin Aga Khan, a scene of an elephant family (Fischer and Goswamy, *Wonders of a Golden Age*, no. 63), four birds (Okada, *Miniatures de l'Inde impériale*, no. 18), and a small pair of birds flanking a golden vessel in the Gulshan Album (no. 220).

33. J. V. S. Wilkinson and B. Gray, "Indian Paintings in a Persian Museum," *Burlington Magazine*, 66 (January–June 1935), 173, state that Basāvana signed folio 84b of the Gulshan Album. Several other major artists, notably Dawlat, Abū al-Ḥasan, Gōvardhana, and Narasimha, also supplied figural border decorations in albums made for Jahāngīr. For Gōvardhana, see Beach, *Grand Mogul*, no. 40, and E. Kühnel and H. Goetz, *Indian Book Painting from Jahangir's Album in the State Library in Berlin* (London, 1926), pl. 38; for Narasimha, see A. Soudavar and M. Beach, *Art of the Persian Courts* (New York, 1992), no. 128a.

34. See S. C. Welch, *Imperial Mughal Painting* (New York, 1978), pl. 8; Losty, *The Art of the Book in India*, pl. XXIV; and Okada, *Indian Miniatures of the Mughal Court*, fig. 78.

35. Part of this garishness is due to the application of a modern varnish, which flouresces, unlike shellac.

36. I have benefitted greatly from my discussions of the technical aspects of the binding with Donna Strahan, formerly of the Division of Conservation and Technical Research at the Walters Art Museum.

37. An identical pattern is found in the outermost band of the lacquer covers of the British Library *Khamsa*, whose restoration seems limited to that area alone.

38. The four panels are reproduced in color in Brend, *The Emperor Akbar's* Khamsa *of Niẓāmī*, figs. 57–60.

39. Similar figures appear, for example, in the V&A *Akbarnāma* nos. 9/117, 91/117, and 114/117, which are published in Sen, *Paintings from the Akbar Nama*, pls. 17, 61, 69. They also figure in folios 147b, 54a, 177a, and 201a of the Chester Beatty *Akbarnāma*, published in Leach, *Mughal and Other Indian Paintings*, color pls. 31, 33, 40, and no. 2.138.

40. Two *Ḥamzanāma* illustrations show a more vigorous and balanced combat between fairies and demons. One, in the Fondation Custodia, Paris, is reproduced in S. Gahlin, *The Courts of India* (Zwolle, 1991), pl. 1; the other, now in the Nour collection, is published in *Treasures of Islam* (London, 1985), no. 119. Three *asūras* do battle with *devatas* and *dīvs* above a tank in an illustration from the dispersed 1598–1600 *Razmnāma* published in A. Farooqi, *Art of India and Persia* (Delhi, 1979), pl. 47.

41. One well-known version of this scene appears in a *Haft Paykar* in The Metropolitan Museum of Art (13.228.13), f. 47a. The painting is published in Lentz and Lowry, *Timur and the Princely Vision*, fig. 94.

42. These same feather-covered creatures are found on folio 208b of the 1599–1600 *Ḥadīqat al-Ḥaqīqat*, published in color on the back cover of the sales catalogue of Bonhams, London, 26 April 1995. Together with the distinctive spongy outcrop in the upper right, the heavy whorls of blue clouds, the three-dimensional rendering of the pavilion, and the fine features of the inquisitive onlookers, these angels support an attribution of this visionary painting to Manōhara.

CHAPTER 7

# Conclusion

The *Khamsa* of Amīr Khusraw was one of the most admired texts in the Islamic world, and it is natural that Akbar would order his active scriptorium to produce a *de luxe* copy even when the library already possessed other copies of the same text. Once this commission was made, the well-developed mechanisms of the library took over. Specially made paper was cut to the appropriate size and assembled into small, regular gatherings for ease of handling, and the area reserved for the text was lightly ruled. In keeping with the intended quality of the manuscript, the most celebrated Mughal calligrapher, Muḥammad Ḥusayn, was called upon to write out the text, a task in which the atelier's usual concerns with efficiency evaporated in the face of an overwhelming desire for perfection.

Before Muḥammad Ḥusayn set pen to paper, however, he must have already conferred with a designer, who remains anonymous. In all likelihood, the designer of the manuscript determined the number of illustrations and their approximate place in the text. It fell to the calligrapher to determine the precise point at which the text would be interrupted as well as the size and shape of text blocks on the folio. The designer of the manuscript seldom strayed from the slender narrative thread of the five poems in his choice of subjects for illustration, giving little heed either to the many auxiliary praises and admonitions or to long passages of allusive description. Beyond this, the text determined the substance of the painters' illustrations in only the most general sense. Through brief oral and written means, the select team of artists was made aware of the particular episode of the poem that had been chosen for illustration. This inevitably was the nominal subject of the painting, so that we find such scenes as Khusraw deceiving Farhād or Alexander discovering Kanīfū's identity at the appropriate place in the manuscript. But as we have seen, from this point on in the process of creation, Mughal artists displayed a strikingly free attitude towards the text and deviated regularly from specific narrative details and even standard iconography.

As I have argued, some of this latitude may be due to the mediating effect of the instructions, which made it unnecessary for artists to refer directly to the text themselves. Still more of it was occasioned by a general tendency to minimize the ostensible subject of the illustration and to give over most of the painting to extraneous features drawn from the Mughal visual repertoire. This repertoire was both large and communal, and it was probably a source of pride in the workshop. Only the most minor motifs—a red swag, a waterwheel, a trio of distant horses—were true hallmarks of individual artists. More generally, one artist's work could be distinguished from another's primarily in subtleties of the handling of familiar elements, such as bearded facial types or soaring rock formations. Although the Mughals took considerable pains to record the name of the artist or artists responsible for the painting—in most cases in the margin below the painting—it is unlikely in this period that paintings were ever commissioned or evaluated on the basis of the reputation of a specific artist. Instead, there is some evidence that Mughal patrons appreciated certain paintings more than others for different reasons.

Foremost among these was a regard for high technical finish, a quality evident in every painting in the Walters *Khamsa* and its companion manuscripts.[1] All forms are precisely drawn, all colors carefully applied, all surfaces meticulously burnished. Only after this pervasive sense of refinement settles in does one notice very minor differences in the rendering of hair, cloth, or rock, or the means by which pictorial space is defined. Any one of these nuances might elicit a particularly positive response from a given viewer; more probably, they passed unnoticed by all but a very few. This brings us to the second level on which these exquisite Mughal paintings seem to have functioned. For those of us with a taste for past cultures but thoroughly modern lives, it is easy to look past the incredibly rich material description embedded in these sixteenth-century paintings. But members of the Mughal court would hardly have been oblivious to the depiction of items they knew and valued in their own lives. Carpets, vessels, musical instruments, and apparel of every fashion and social rank—all these were pointedly included in these paintings, not merely to demonstrate the artist's technical ability to paint such things, but also to strike a chord of recognition among the very people who inhabited that same world. This aspect of painting, which stands well outside the narrative requirements of literary illustrations, is manifested in many periods of world art, but Mughal painting truly distinguishes itself from nearly all its precursors in the Islamic and Indian traditions by the amount of attention it lavishes on visual description.

A third level at which Mughal painting engaged its contemporary audience extends this sense of familiarity to the social and human realm. Few stories are illustrated simply or efficiently; rather, for every king and beloved, there are swarms of retainers who tender wrapped swords, whisk unseen flies, or doze in doorways. In part this was a matter of decorum, for few kings or princesses would ever have been without an attendant at hand. But the omnipresence of ancillary figures even in scenes removed from the courtly environment indicates that their activities were also an excuse to invite different audiences to cast a bemused eye on the daily foibles of their compatriots and to experience the range of emotions—from anxiousness and wonder to mundane preoccupation—that these literary figures feel in our stead.

These human concerns overshadow overtly propagandistic considerations in Mughal painting, a fact that keeps Mughal painting of Akbar's reign free of the burden of political dogma. Mughal manuscript illustrations certainly featured royal themes and virtues, but no more so than ministerial machinations and ordinary vices. Both themes are standard cultural conceits, and their visual expression is ubiquitous in Islamic painting at all levels of patronage. Thus, it seems imprudent to read such illustrations—and particularly those in literary texts—as politically motivated responses to specific historical circumstances.[2] It is possible, of course, that we are still unaware of historical associations that contemporary Mughal viewers might have brought to certain literary figures and actions, but even if these associations did color contemporary perceptions of these images, they did so in an already richly layered set of responses.

The Walters Art Museum *Khamsa* of Amīr Khusraw must have been understood at several different levels at the Mughal court. For some, it was a copy of a stellar work of literature, whose inspiring and amusing pearls were framed by the occasional painting. Others undoubtedly saw the manuscript more as a repository of visual art and were captivated by the sophistication of Muḥammad Ḥusayn's writing and the brilliance of the atelier's best painters. Superseding these viewers in number, if not in sensitivity, were still others who found in this book a bibliographic gem sifted from the capacious imperial library, a precious object to hold and behold. Their delight in the extraordinary splendor of fine lacquer, paint, ink, and gold is an experience that no one can fail to share.

### NOTES

1. For new evidence of the principles of Mughal connoisseurship, see J. Seyller, "A Mughal Code of Connoisseurship," *Muqarnas*, 17 (2000), 178–203.

2. For a politicized interpretation of themes of rulership and conquest in specific illustrations in the British Library *Khamsa*, see Brend, *The Emperor Akbar's* Khamsa *of Niẓāmī*, 70.

APPENDIX A

# Other Copies of the *Khamsa* of Amīr Khusraw

*This appendix lists all known illustrated and unillustrated copies of the* Khamsa *of Amīr Khusraw in chronological order, with illustrated copies preceding unillustrated ones. For each manuscript, the physical details of the manuscript, the place and date of its writing and illustration, the order of the five poems, the subjects of its illustrations, and publication references are listed.*

*Khamsa.* Tashkent, Abu Rayhan Biruni Institute, inv. No. 3317 {C.O.M. II, 1012}. Iran, probably Shiraz, ca. 1370–90. 29.5 x 19.5 cm. Naskhī, 27 lines, 2 cols., text area 24.0 x 12.5 cm. 1 *'unwān,* 37 paintings; spaces for 4 more illustrations have been left blank. Some folios are out of order; many are damaged with water stains.

12a Laylā and Majnūn fall in love at school.
16a Majnūn is visited in the wilderness by his father.
30b Majnūn is visited by his friends.
36a Laylā visits Majnūn in the wilderness.
66a The author discovers a spiritual guide.
69a Moses and the great man.
76b A Muslim pilgrim meets a brahman on the road.
100a Jesus responds kindly to a taunter.
114b Alexander accepts the submission of the Khāqān and reinstates him as a fief.
118b The Khāqān's envoys submit to Alexander by bringing a handful of soil and a sword.
120b Alexander receives the Khāqān's ambassadors.
127a Alexander summons Chinese painters.
130b Alexander defeats the Khāqān in battle.
133a Alexander fortifies his men.
134b Alexander's army attacks the inhabitants of Gōg and Magōg.
143b Khusraw dies after being stabbed by Shīrūya.
144b Alexander's corpse is prepared for burial.
149b Alexander seeks the counsel of sages about his sea voyage.
151b Alexander sets out on his voyage to the Western Isles.
163a Alexander visits Plato.
171a Alexander entertains Kanīfū.
173b Alexander and Kanīfū make love.
198b Muḥammad receives angels and the Burāq.
204b Shāhpūr shows Shīrīn's portrait to Khusraw.
229b Shīrīn summons Farhād to her palace.
235a A letter from Khusraw reaches Shīrīn.
237a Khusraw receives Shīrīn's letter.
238b Khusraw, disguised as a shepherd, visits Farhād.
243b Māh Sāmān poisons Shakar at Shīrīn's request.
257b Khusraw and Shīrīn are reconciled.
273a Khusraw and Shīrīn make love.
302a Bahrām Gūr visits the princess of the Yellow Pavilion.
307b Bahrām Gūr visits the princess of the Green Pavilion.
313b Bahrām Gūr visits the princess of the Red Pavilion.
317a Bahrām Gūr visits the princess of the Blue Pavilion.
325b Bahrām Gūr visits the princess of the Sandalwood Pavilion.
334b Bahrām Gūr visits the princess of the White Pavilion.
344a Bahrām Gūr disappears into a cave while chasing an onager.

Published: G. A. Pugachenkova, "On the Dating and Origin of the *Khamsa* Manuscript of Amir Khusrau Dihlawi in the Collection of the Oriental Institute of the Uzbek SSR Academy of Sciences," *Trudy Tadzhikskoi Arkheologicheskoi Ekspeditsii Instituta Istorii Materialnoi Kultury AN SSR Instituta Istorii Arkheologii i Etnografii AN Tadzhikikskoi SSR,* 7 (1953), 187–96; *Oriental Miniatures of Abu Raihon Beruni Institute of Orientology of the UZSSR Academy of Sciences* (Tashkent, 1980), pls. 3–6; H. Suleiman and F. Suleimanova, *Miniatures Illuminations of Amir Hosrov Dehlevi's Works* (Tashkent, 1983), pls. 1–13; V. Loukonine and A. Ivanov, *Lost Treasures of Persia* (Bournemouth, England, 1996), no. 153.

*Majmū'a-i Ash'ār* (Anthology). Istanbul, Topkapi Saray Museum (TSM) H. 796. Iran, Yazd. Dated by five colophons, the last of which is 19 Rabī' II 810/24 September 1407. ff. 289, 26.0 x 18.0 cm. Nasta'līq, 31 lines, 4 cols., and a single outer one written diagonally. 16 paintings, 7 of which illustrate the *Khamsa* of Amīr Khusraw.

4b *Mi'rāj* of the Prophet.
28a Shāhpūr tells Khusraw of Shīrīn.
34b Khusraw entertains Shakar at his lodging.
58a Nawfal battles Laylā's clan on behalf of Majnūn.
67a Majnūn befriends a dog that lived in Laylā's neighborhood.
75a Dilārām mesmerizes deer with her music.
101b Alexander builds a wall against the creatures of Gōg and Magōg.

Published: I. Stchoukine, "La peinture à Yazd au début du XVème siècle," *Syria,* 43 (1966), 99–104; Lentz and Lowry, *Timur and the Princely Vision,* no. 59, 167, 178; Brend, "Akbar's *Khamsah* of Amīr Khusrau," pl. 14.

*Anthology.* Berlin, Museum für Islamische Kunst I. 4628. Iran, Shiraz, dated 823/1420. Written by Maḥmūd al-Ḥusaynī. 950 pages. 28.2 x 20.2 cm. Nasta'līq, 28 paintings, 2 of which illustrate scenes from *Hasht Bihisht* and *Iskandarnāma.*

p. 866 Bahrām Gūr hunts onagers.
p. 916 Alexander meets the Khāqān of China.

Published: V. Enderlein, *Die Miniaturen der Berliner Baisonqur Handschrift* (Leipzig, 1976), nos. 27–28.

*Anthology.* Dublin, Chester Beatty Library (CBL) P. 124 (vol. 2). Probably India. Written by ʿAlī Pāgīr al-Ashtarjānī, *Hasht Bihisht* dated 23 Ẕīʾl-Qaʿda 839/10 June 1436, *Āʾīnah-i Sikandarī*, 10 Muharram 840/25 July 1436. *Khamsa* section ff. 195, 27.5 x 17.2 cm. Nastaʿlīq, 25 lines, 4 cols. and an oblique marginal script, text area 17.0 x 10.7 cm.

42b–43a Khusraw holds a portrait of Shīrīn.
44b Khusraw and Shīrīn are seated beneath trees.
46b–47a Khusraw battles Bahrām Chūbīna.
49b Khusraw and Shīrīn preside over the wedding of youths.
53b Khusraw listens to music with Shakar.
55b Shīrīn receives Farhād at court.
60b Khusraw visits Farhād disguised as a shepherd.
61b A messenger brings Farhād false news of Shīrīn's death.
63b Shakar is poisoned by Shīrīn's maid.
66a Khusraw grieves on account on Shīrīn's anger towards him.
67a Khusraw reaches Shīrīn's castle.
71a Khusraw and Shīrīn listen to music of Bārbud and Nigīsā.
74b Khusaw and Shīrīn are married.
81a Khusraw is put in chains at the order of Shīrūya.
81b Shīrīn commits suicide on the corpse of the murdered Khusraw.
89b Laylā and Majnūn fall in love at school.
91b Majnūn's father visits him in the wilderness.
93a Majnūn's father asks Laylā's father for his daughter's hand.
94b Nawfal battles Laylā's tribe on behalf of Majnūn.
96b Majnūn is married to Nawfal's daughter against his wishes.
100a Majnūn rests by the bank of a stream.
101a Majnūn befriends a dog that lived in Laylā's neighborhood.
102b Laylā visits Majnūn in the wilderness.
106a Laylā hears false news of Majnūn's death.
108b Majnūn mourns on Laylā's tomb.
118a Bahrām Gūr casts down his favorite, Dilārām, during a hunt.
119a Bahrām Gūr beholds Dilārām mesmerizing onagers with her music.
120b Bahrām Gūr stands before the palace of the seven pavilions.
121b Bahrām Gūr visits the princess of the Black Pavilion.
124a Bahrām Gūr visits the princess of the Yellow Pavilion.
127b Bahrām Gūr visits the princess of the Green Pavilion.
130a Bahrām Gūr visits the princess of the Red Pavilion.
134a Bahrām Gūr visits the princess of the Blue Pavilion.
139a Bahrām Gūr visits the princess of the Sandalwood Pavilion.
143a Bahrām Gūr visits the princess of the White Pavilion.
146b Bahrām Gūr disappears while pursuing an onager into a cave.
157b Alexander meets the Khāqān of China.
162b Alexander receives Kanīfū, whom he had defeated in battle.
164a Alexander kills the Khāqān of China.
168a Alexander observes the manners of the inhabitants of Gōg and Magōg at a feast he gives for them.
169a Alexander has guards posted on the wall erected against Gōg and Magōg.
179b Alexander seeks counsel from Plato.
185b Alexander writes a letter to his son Iskandarūs.
187b Alexander is visited by the angel who guards the sea.
188b Alexander encounters various creatures beneath the sea.
189b Alexander returns to land with the angel of the sea.
190b Alexander receives gifts from various rulers.
193a Alexander is buried.

Published: A. J. Arberry, E. Blochet, M. Minovi, B. W. Robinson, and J. V. S. Wilkinson, *The Chester Beatty Library: A Catalogue of the Persian Manuscripts and Miniatures* (Dublin, 1962), 45–53, pl. 4 (II, f. 61b); B. Brend, "The British Library's *Shahnama* of 1438 as a Sultanate Manuscript," in R. Skelton et al., *Facets of Indian Art* (London, 1986), 90 (f. 223b).

*Khamsa.* London, private collection. Iran, probably Yazd, ca. 1440. ff. 224, 15.8 x 12.6 cm. Naskhī, 21 lines, 4 cols., text area 11.9 x 8.8 cm. 11 paintings. Seals and inspection notes of the Mughal library on f. 1a.

1b Four angels.
15b Shiblī questions the darvish.
27b Four friends die of thirst in the desert when each refuses water from a stranger until the others have drunk.
51a Khusraw examines a painting of Shīrīn.
91b Shīrūya ascends the throne.
107a A crow pecks at Majnūn's eyes.
116a Laylā visits Majnūn in the desert.
140a Alexander defeats Kanīfū in battle.
147b Alexander's soldiers battle the inhabitants of Gōg and Magōg.
186a Bahrām Gūr hunts gazelles with Dilārām.
209b Bahrām Gūr visits the princess of the Sandalwood Pavilion.

Published: *Islamic Manuscripts* (Sam Fogg Rare Books, 2000), no. 27.

*Majnūn wa Laylā* and *Hasht Bihisht.* Chester Beatty Library P. 253. Iran, Shiraz. ff. 158, 24.5 x 14.5 cm. Nastaʿlīq, 23 lines, 2 cols., text area 12.3 x 6.7 cm. 11 paintings in the Shiraz style.

13b Laylā and Majnūn fall in love at school.
22a Laylā hears news of Majnūn.
32a Majnūn is visited in the wilderness by two friends.
34a Bahrām Gūr displays his hunting prowess. (out of order)
42a Nawfal battles Laylā's clan on behalf of Majnūn.
55a Majnūn beholds the dead on the battlefield.
73b Bahrām Gūr visits the princess of the Black Pavilion.
77b Bahrām Gūr visits the princess of the Yellow Pavilion.
82a Bahrām Gūr visits the princess of the Blue Pavilion.
94a A leopard and a gazelle in a landscape.

*Khamsa.* Sotheby's, London, 12 April 1976, lot 181. Iran, Shiraz. ff. 173, 23.2 x 14.5 cm. Nastaʿlīq, 23 lines, 2 cols., text area 12.3 x 6.8 cm. Written by ʿAbdullāh ibn ʿAlī in 843/1439. 8 paintings in the Shiraz style. (The remainder of the manuscript is listed above.)

Farhād and the animals.
The Rūmī champion Parīkaysh defeats the Chinese champion Tangū.
Alexander's men build a wall against the inhabitants of Gōg and Magōg.

*Khamsa.* Istanbul, Topkapi Saray Museum H. 898. Iran, Shiraz, dated Rabīʿ I 950/May 1446. ff. 337, 21.3 x 12.7 cm. Naskhī, 2 cols. of 19 lines, outer col. of 14 lines, both in a text area 15.3 x 8.8 cm. 2 *sarlauḥs*, 7 paintings. (*Maṭlaʿ al-Anwār* 1b, *Shīrīn wa Khusraw* 60b, *Majnūn wa Laylā* 144b, *Hasht Bihisht* 192b, *Āʾīnah-i Sikandarī* 254b).

74b Khusraw and Shīrīn meet by chance on the hunting ground.
107b Khusraw appears before Shīrīn.
123b Khusraw entertains Shakar.
163a Nawfal's clan battles Laylā's clan on behalf of Majnūn.
177b Laylā visits Majnūn in the wilderness.
229b Bahrām Gūr visits the princess of the Blue Pavilion.
281b Alexander defeats the Khāqān in battle.

Published: Titley, "Miniature Paintings," fig. 15; J. M. Rogers, F. Çağman, and Z. Tanindi, *The Topkapi Saray Museum: The Albums and Illustrated Manuscripts* (Boston, 1986), pl. 56.

*Khamsa*. Dispersed. India, possibly Gujarat, Sultanate style, ca. 1450. Folios average 35.0 x 25.0 cm. Naskhī, 17 lines, 4 cols.

*Maṭla' al-Anwār*

Moses and a nobleman discourse on desire and existence. Painting 10.4 x 20.7 cm. Museum of Fine Arts, Boston 62.929.

A learned man burned by a royal lamp reflects upon the safety of scholars before nobles. Folio 35.5 x 26.5 cm., painting 11.9 x 20.9 cm. San Diego Museum of Art 1990.0238. Published: E. Binney, *Indian Miniature Paintings from the Collection of Edwin Binney, 3rd: The Mughal and Deccani Schools* (Portland, 1973), no. 1b; Binney, "Sultanate Painting from the Collection of Edwin Binney, 3rd," in *Chhavi-2* (Varanasi, 1981), fig. 30.

Offered a reward by Khiẓr for years of unswerving worship of God, the pious devotee asks only a vision of God. Folio 31.9 x 24.3 cm.; painting 9.3 x 20.4 cm. The Metropolitan Museum of Art (MMA) 1976.283. Published: R. Ettinghausen and M. L. Swietochowski, "Islamic Painting," *Metropolitan Museum Bulletin* (Fall 1978), 34.

A saint unsuccessfully tries to stay awake until the Night of Power, the twenty-seventh day of Ramaẓān. Folio 34.3 x 25.3 cm., painting 8.0 x 20.1 cm. Collection of Prince Sadruddin Aga Khan. Published: A. Welch and S. C. Welch, *Arts of the Islamic Book* (Ithaca and London, 1982), no. 48; *Treasures of Islam*, no. 117.

A virtuous woman plucks out her eyes to still the advances of the king. Folio 34.3 x 26.2 cm., painting 10.7 x 20.1 cm. Collection of Prince Sadruddin Aga Khan. Published: Fischer and Goswamy, *Wonders of a Golden Age*, no. 2.

*Shīrīn wa Khusraw*

Frontispiece. Folio 33.4 x 24.1 cm., illumination 30.8 x 19.0 cm. Sackler Gallery S1986.125. Published: G. Lowry, M. Beach, R. Marefat, and W. Thackston, *An Annotated and Illustrated Checklist of the Vever Collection* (Washington, D.C., 1988), no. 192.

Khusraw dedicates his poem to Sulṭān 'Alā' al-Dīn Muḥammad Shāh. Folio 35.3 x 24 cm.; painting 12.0 x 22.5 cm. Art Institute of Chicago 62-640. Published: N. Titley, *Persian Miniature Painting and Its Influence on the Art of Turkey and India* (Austin, Texas, 1983), fig. 60.

Khusraw and Shakar consummate their marriage. Folio 32.5 x 24.0 cm., painting 11.0 x 20.3 cm. British Museum 1996 10-5-05. Published: Christie's, London, 17 November 1976, lot 27; *Manuscripts from the Himalayas and the Indian Subcontinent* (London: Sam Fogg Rare Books, 1996), no. 163.

Māh Sāmān poisons Shakar at the order of Shīrīn. Folio 32.2 x 24.0 cm., painting 11.4 x 21.5 cm. Sackler Gallery S1986.124. Published: Lowry, Beach et al., *An Annotated and Illustrated Checklist*, no. 194.

Shīrīn addresses Khusraw from the roof of her palace. Painting 15.1 x 22.7 cm. Private collection. Published: P. Chandra and D. Ehnbom, *The Cleveland Tuti-nama Manuscript and the Origins of Mughal Painting* (Chicago, 1976), no. 19, pl. 6.

A priest settles the marriage portion of Shīrīn with Khusraw. Folio 33.3 to 34.3 x 25.8 cm., painting 11.3 x 21.5 cm. Freer Gallery of Art 59.2. Published: Beach, *The Imperial Image*, fig. 7.

Khusraw questions Buzurg Umīd about the natural sciences. Folio 34.2 x 25.8 cm., painting 11.1 x 20.2 cm. British Library, Oriental and India Office Collections Add. Or. 4686. Published: Christie's, London, 7 July 1976, lot 65; Spink and Sons, *Indian and Islamic Works of Art* 27 April–22 May 1992, no. 52.

Buzurg Umīd tells a story of a haughty king who orders a messenger bearing a request for tribute bound so long as the great tree before his palace stands; within two days, the tree is toppled by a storm. McGill University 1977.47.

Farhād kisses the ground before Shīrīn. Folio 28.6 x 21.6 cm. Location unknown. Published: Sotheby's, New York, 23–26 April 1996, lot 603.

*Majnūn wa Laylā*

Two *dīvs* are ordered by King Solomon to fill the desert with water and the sea with sand. Folio 33.0 x 24.2 cm., painting 12.0 x 20.7 cm. Victoria & Albert Museum I.S. 124-1958.

Majnūn intercedes in the battle of the clans of Laylā and Nawfal. Folio 33.5 x 23.5 cm., painting 12.4 x 20.8 cm. Worcester Art Museum 1935-22. Published: S. Melikian-Chirvani, "L'école de Shiraz et les origines de la miniature moghole," in *Paintings from Islamic Lands*, ed., R. Pinder-Wilson (Oxford, 1969) fig. 85; *Worcester Annual* 1, p. 48; E. Findly, *From the Courts of India: Indian Miniatures in the Collection of the Worcester Art Museum* (Worcester, 1981), 20–21.

Majnūn laments Laylā's death. Folio 34.0 x 26.0 cm., painting 11.3 x 20.9 cm. Freer Gallery of Art 59.3. Published: R. Ettinghausen, *Paintings of the Sultans and Emperors of India in American Collections* (New Delhi, 1961), pl. 1; E. Grube, *The World of Islam* (New York, 1966), fig. 39 (color); Melikian-Chirvani, "L'école de Shiraz et les origines de la miniature moghole," fig. 84; Beach, *The Imperial Image* no. 2b, *Masterpieces of Indian Painting Formerly in the Nasli M. Heeramaneck Collections* (Alice Heeramaneck, 1984), pl. 1 (color).

*Ā'īnah-i Sikandarī*

Frontispiece. Folio 32.4 x 23.3 cm., illumination 27.4 x 19.6 cm. Sackler Gallery S1986.123. Published: Lowry, Beach et al., *An Annotated and Illustrated Checklist*, no. 196.

The boiling of the artificial rice. Folio 32.0 x 23.6 cm., painting 9.3 x 20.7 cm. Freer Gallery of Art 59.4. Published: Beach, *The Imperial Image*, fig. 8.

Alexander's men behold his coffin. Painting 9.3 x 20.7 cm. Collection of Prince Sadruddin Aga Khan.

*Hasht Bihisht*

Khusraw dedicates his work to Sulṭān 'Alā' al-Dīn. 34.5 x 26.0 cm.; painting 12.0 x 22.5 cm. The David Collection, Copenhagen 25/1980. Published: Binney, "Sultanate Painting," fig. 31; *Islamic Art. The David Collection*, no. 39.

Niẓām-al-Dīn Awliyā receives three attendants. Folio 32.7 x 24.2 cm., painting 11.3 x 21.0 cm. Sackler Gallery S1986.122. Published: Lowry, Beach et al., *An Annotated and Illustrated Checklist*, no. 198.

Khusraw receives the encouragement of his friend 'Alī. Folio 30.8 x 22.9 cm., painting 8.5 x 20.5 cm. Seattle Art Museum 63.39.

Dilārām is pulled from her horse after Bahrām Gūr displays his prowess at the hunt. Folio 31.6 x 24.9 cm, painting 12.9 x 23.1 cm. Sackler Gallery S1986.120. Published: *Survey of Persian Art*, pl. 826A; M. Beach, "A Volume of Homage: A Jain Manuscript, 1411," *Asian Art*, 1, no. 3 (1988), 39–56, fig. 15; Lowry, Beach et al., *An Annotated and Illustrated Checklist*, no. 197.

The story of the princess of the Black Pavilion: The three princes of Ceylon demonstrate their cleverness before a foreign king. Folio 30.7 x 22.3 cm., painting 12.6 x 20.8 cm. Cleveland Museum of Art 63.261. Published: L. Leach, *Indian Miniature Paintings and Drawings* (Cleveland, 1986), no. 6.

The baffled king listens to the three perspicacious youths. Folio 33.5 x 24.0 cm., painting 11.3 x 20.8 cm. San Diego Museum of Fine Arts 1990.0237. Published: Binney, *Indian Miniature Paintings*, no. 1a; Binney, "Sultanate Painting," fig. 29.

Bahrām Gūr visits the princess of the Yellow Pavilion. Folio 34.3 x 27.8 cm., painting 11.5 x 21.7 cm. Nelson-Atkins Museum of Art 62-58. Published: *Handbook of the Collection: Nelson/Atkins Gallery* (Kansas City, 1973), 142.

The story of the princess of the Yellow Pavilion: The foolish wife of the dishonest goldsmith is tricked into taking her husband's place imprisoned in a tall tower. Folio 31.2 x 23.2 cm., painting 11.6 x 20.4 cm. Los Angeles County Musem of Art M78.9.3. Published: *The Arts of India and Nepal: The Nasli and Alice Heeramaneck Collection* (Boston, 1966), no. 145; *Masterpieces of Indian Painting*, pl. 2 (backwards); *Arts of Asia* (November–December 1987), no. 69; P. Pal, *Indian Painting* (Los Angeles, 1993), no. 41.

The story of the princess of the Green Pavilion: The queen rejects the advances of the treacherous vizier, who by magic assumed the form of the king. Folio 34.0 x 26.0 cm., painting 11.3 x 20.9 cm. Freer Gallery of Art 59.1. Published: Ettinghausen, *Paintings of the Sultans and Emperors of India*, pl. 1; K. Khandalavala and M. Chandra, *New Documents of Indian Painting—a Reappraisal* (Bombay, 1969), pl. 8 (color); Beach, *The Imperial Image*, no. 2a; *The Arts of India*, fig. 135 (color).

The story of the princess of the Sandalwood Pavilion: Disguised as a woman, Rāma appears before the guards whom he had secretly humiliated the night before by shaving their beards. Folio 33.0 x 23.5 cm., painting 12.7 x 22.5 cm. Virginia Museum of Fine Arts 68-8-45.

The story of the princess of the White Pavilion: The princess of the water tower crosses the river to join a Hindu lover. Whole painting (the left panel of which is repainted) is applied to a leaf of text. Folio 32.5 x 24.0 cm., painting 11.0 x 20.8 cm. British Museum 1996 10-5-06. Published: Christie's, 17 November 1976, lot 28; *Manuscripts from the Himalayas and the Indian Subcontinent* (London: Sam Fogg Rare Books, 1996), no. 163.

## UNIDENTIFIED SCENES

The author discovers a spiritual guide. Folio 32.3 x 25.7 cm., painting 9.6 x 20.6 cm. British Library, Oriental and India Office Collections Add. Or. 4685. Published: *Survey of Persian Art*, pl. 826B; Spink and Sons, *Indian and Islamic Works of Art* 27 April–22 May 1992, no. 51.

A woman embraces a wounded man outdoors. Folio 32.4 x 25.0 cm., painting 14.0 x 20.9 cm. (Text below is unrelated.) Sackler Gallery S1986.126. Published: Lowry, Beach et al., *An Annotated and Illustrated Checklist*, no. 193.

A couple converse outdoors. Folio 33.5 x 25.3 cm., painting 9.3 x 20.1 cm. Painting is attached to an unrelated folio, whose text is also a pastiche. Text below is *Āʾīnah-i Sikandarī* 181:13–183:3. Sackler Gallery S1986.121. Published: Lowry, Beach et al., *An Annotated and Illustrated Checklist*, no. 195.

*Khamsa*. Rampur, Raza Library Persian 4101. Iran, Shiraz school, dated 6 Rajab 855/4 August 1451. Unfoliated. 20.5 x 14.2 cm. Nastaʿlīq, 17 lines, 4 cols., text area 13.2 cm. x 10.2 cm. 1 *shamsa*, double-page *sarlawḥ*, 5 *ʿunwāns*, 9 damaged paintings.

*Miʿrāj* of the Prophet.
A king who accidentally killed a shepherd offers his own life to the youth's mother.
Shīrīn entertains Khusraw.
Khusraw appears before Shīrīn's castle.
Majnūn hears the song of a nightingale.
Parīkaysh, the champion of the forces of Rūm, defeats Tangū, the Chinese champion.
Alexander entertains Kanīfū.
Bahrām Gūr visits the princess of the Black Pavilion.
Bahrām Gūr visits the princess of the Sandalwood Pavilion.

Published: B. Schmitz and Z. A. Desai, *Mughal and Persian Paintings and Illustrated Manuscripts in the Raza Library, Rampur* (forthcoming), Ms. IV.12.

*Khamsa*. Kansas City, Nelson-Atkins Museum of Art 44-22. Iran, Timurid style, first half of the 15th century. ff. 154, 16.3 x 10.4 cm. Nastaʿlīq, 17 lines, 4 cols., text area 5 1/2 x 3 1/2 in. *Maṭlaʿ al-Anwār* 2b, *Shīrīn wa Khusraw* 52b, *Majnūn wa Laylā* 115b, *Hasht Bihisht* (fragment) last.

26b A courtier offers a hermit a position at court.
51a A virtuous woman plucks out her eyes and sends them to the king to still his persistent entreaties.
62b Khusraw and Shīrīn meet by chance during a hunt.
77b Shīrīn meets Farhād.
112a Shīrūya kills Khusraw and ascends his father's throne.
136a Friends visit Majnūn in the desert, where he is surrounded by animals.
145a Laylā weeps in the garden at the rumor of Majnūn's death.

*Khamsa*. Istanbul, Topkapi Saray Museum Revan 1021. Copied by Maḥmūd *al-Kātib* al-Aḥsan in Baghdad in Shawwāl 867/June–July 1463. ff. 190, 36.8 x 22.8 cm. Nastaʿlīq, 25 lines, 4 cols., text area 25.2 x 15.0 cm. 6 *ʿunwāns* (2b, 36b, 80b, 108b, 154b, 185b), 8 paintings.

1b–2a Double-page scene of a feast.
48a Khusraw and Shīrīn together.
86b Laylā and Majnūn fall in love at school.
123a Alexander seizes the Khāqān of China in battle.
147b Alexander is lowered into the sea.
165b Bahrām Gūr visits the princess of the Yellow Pavilion.
185b The story of the princess of the White Pavilion: The king receives the virtuous lady of the wine-cellar tower.

Published: F. Karatay, *Topkapi Sarayi Müzesi Kütüphanesi Farsça Yazmalar Kataloğu* (Istanbul, 1961), no. 592; I. Stchoukine, "La peinture à Baghdād sous Sulṭān Pīr Budāq Qāra-Qoyūnlū," *Ars asiatiques*, 25 (1972), 8, fig. 6; Titley, "Miniature Paintings," fig. 15a; B. Gray, ed., *The Arts of the Book in Central Asia*, color pl. XV (cover); Titley, *Persian Miniature Painting*, fig. 29, 63.

*Khamsa*. State Collection of Manuscripts of the Azerbaijan Academy of Sciences, inv. M-379-33733. Dated 882/1477. 20.5 x 15.0 cm. Nastaʿlīq in 4 cols. 5 illuminations, 25 paintings, bad condition.

103a Bahrām Gūr visits the princess of the White Pavilion.
118a Bahrām Gūr visits the princess of the Blue Pavilion.

Published: Suleiman and Suleimanova, *Miniatures Illuminations*, pls. 14–15.

*Khamsa.* Istanbul, Topkapi Saray Museum H. 795. Iran, Shiraz. Completed Z̲ī'l-Qa'da 882/February–March 1478. ff. 201, 32.7 x 20.6 cm. Nasta'līq, 23 lines, 4 cols., text area 20.4 x 12.5 cm. 4 *'unwāns*, 18 paintings. Seal of Ūzūn Ḥasan 882/1478.

1b A king receives gifts while musicians perform.
2a A woman is shown a portrait of herself.
18a Khiẓr grants a pious devotee a vision of God.
21a A hermit refuses a courtier's offer of a position at court.
28a 'Alī cuts the throat of an infidel who had spat upon him.
39b A virtuous woman resists the king's entreaties.
48a Khusraw hears of Shīrīn from Shāhpūr.
51b Aided by the troops of the Qaiṣar of Rūm, Khusraw defeats Bahrām Chūbīna.
61a Farhād sees Shīrīn.
75b After addressing Khusraw from her castle gate, Shīrīn is reconciled with Khusraw and listens to music with him.
80a Khusraw and Shīrīn are married.
98a Majnūn is visited in the wilderness by his father.
109b Laylā visits Majnūn in the wilderness.
124b The Rūmī champion Parīkaysh lassoes the Chinese champion Tangū.
152a Alexander embarks upon a sea journey to the Western Isles.
168b Bahrām Gūr displays his hunting prowess before Dilārām.
178b Bahrām Gūr visits the princess of the Green Pavilion.
195a Bahrām Gūr visits the princess of the White Pavilion.

Published: Karatay, *Farsça*, no. 593.

*Maṯla' al-Anwār* and *Shīrīn wa Khusraw.* Paris, Bibliothèque Nationale Supp. persan 631. Iran, Shiraz. Completed at Shiraz one Thursday in the month of Z̲ī'l-Qa'da 886/27 December 1481, 3, 10, or 17 January 1482. ff. 89, 23.6 x 16.5 cm. Nasta'līq, 23 lines, 4 cols., text area 16.2 x 9.9 cm. 2 *'unwāns*, 4 paintings.

20a A hermit refuses a courtier's offer of a position at court.
26a Four friends die of thirst in the desert when each refuses water from a stranger until the others have drunk.
60a Shīrīn visits Farhād and sees his rock-cut sculptures.
81a Khusraw and Shīrīn make love.

Published: E. Blochet, *Révue des Bibliothèques*, 1898, 327; B. W. Robinson, "Origin and Date of Three Famous *Shāh-Nāmeh* Illustrations," *Ars Orientalis*, 1 (1954), fig. 6; F. Richard, *Splendeurs persanes. Manuscrits du XIIe au XVIIe siècle* (Paris, 1997), no. 66.

*Khamsa.* Dublin, Chester Beatty Library P. 163. Herat. Written by Muḥammad ibn Aẓhar 1 Rajab 890/14 July 1485. ff. 230, 25.3 x 16.7 cm. Nasta'līq, 21 lines, 4 cols., text area 16.9 x 10.8 cm. Double-page frontispiece (1b–2a), 2 *shamsas* (45a, 97a), 4 *'unwāns* (45b, 97b, 132b, 188b), 13 paintings attributed to Bihzād and his school.

6a Darvishes dance to music before their shaykh and a disciple.
23a A hermit refuses a courtier's offer of a position at court.
28a The king orders an executioner to behead a man who, appalled at the fidelity displayed by two condemned friends who begged to die before the other, confesses to having killed his own brother in order to gain the entire inheritance of his family.
38a An old Sufi man whose amorous overtures toward a beautiful youth in a garden are rejected laments the inevitable passing of youth.
54a Shīrīn receives Khusraw at her palace.
72a Farhād lies dead on Mt. Bīsitūn, having killed himself at the false news of Shīrīn's death brought by Khusraw.
82b Khusraw and Shīrīn listen to music.
104b Majnūn's parents celebrate his birth with a feast.
110b Nawfal leads his tribe in battle against Laylā's clan, who refused to give her in marriage to Majnūn.
120b Laylā visits Majnūn in the desert.
198b Bahrām Gūr visits the princess of the Black Pavilion.
209b The story of the princess of the Green Pavilion: A woman asks a banker for a 1,000 pieces of gold as a price for her favors bestowed upon him in dream; a king, metamorphosed into a parrot, orders the banker to count the sum before a mirror and the woman to content herself with the reflection.
215a The story of the princess of the Red Pavilion: The favorite mistress of the king is abducted by her lover by ship before the king's eyes.

Published: F. R. Martin, *Les miniatures de Behzad dans un manuscript Persan daté en 1485* (Munich, 1912), all illustrations and illuminations; A. J. Arberry, E. Blochet, M. Minovi, B. W. Robinson, and J. V. S. Wilkinson, *The Chester Beatty Library: A Catalogue of the Persian Manuscripts and Miniatures* (Dublin, 1962), II, 19–21; Titley, "Miniature Paintings," figs. 16–26; Gray, ed., *The Arts of the Book in Central Asia*, color pl. LVIII (104b), fig. 108 (120b); Bahari, *Bihzad*, figs. 23–27.

*Khamsa* of Amīr Khusraw and Niẓāmī. Istanbul, Topkapi Saray Museum H. 1008. Iran, Shiraz. Amīr Khusraw section is dated 896/1491, written at Shiraz by Murshīd al-Dīn Muḥammad. ff. 534, 34.7 x 20.9 cm. Nasta'līq, 23 lines, 4 cols., text area 21.2 x 11.2 cm. 2 *sarlawḥs*, 10 *'unwāns*, 43 paintings (*Khamsa* of Amīr Khusraw ff. 330–534).

338a Khiẓr grants a pious devotee a vision of God.
350a A king out hunting accidentally kills a shepherd.
356a An old Sufi laments his lost youth.
359a Two foxes trapped by a hunter lament their imminent separation from their hides and from each other.
380b Khusraw entertains Shakar.
405a Khusraw orders a gathering at which he questions Buzurg Umīd about the natural sciences.
456a The second day of battle.
460b Alexander lifts the Khāqān into the air.
472b A dog loses its food through its greediness.
483b Alexander sets out on his sea voyage to the Western Isles.
502a Bahrām Gūr hunts with Dilārām.
513b The queen puts in a golden cage the parrot whose form the king had assumed by magic.

Published: I. Stchoukine, *La peinture des manuscrits de la "Khamseh" de Nizami au Topkapi Sarayi Müsezi d'Istanbul* (Paris, 1977), 85–87; Gray, ed., *The Arts of the Book in Central Asia*, 86, fig. 51 (cover); Rogers, Çağman, and Tanindi, *The Topkapi Saray Museum*, pls. 66–69.

*Khamsa.* Baku, State Collection of Manuscripts of the Azerbaijan Academy of Sciences, inv. M287-27109. Iran, Yazd, dated 900–1/1494–96. Written by Ḥasan ibn Kamāl al-Dīn al-Hadī al-Ḥusaynī al-Yazdī. 22.0 x 13.5 cm. Nasta'līq, 4 cols., text area 16.0 x 9.5 cm. Frontispieces, illuminations, and 26 paintings. Original black leather binding.

10a Dedication to Sulṭān 'Alā' al-Dīn.
23a A bathhouse worker is consumed by the fire of his love for the king.
26b Two friends about to be executed ask to be killed before the other.

31b	A king who accidentally killed a widow's son offers gold or his own head in recompense.
56a	Khusraw appears before Shīrīn's palace.
61b	Khusraw and Shīrīn preside over the marriage of the ten pairs of youths.
66b	Khusraw entertains Shakar.
70a	Shīrīn visits Farhād on Mt. Bīsitūn.
77a	Farhād kills himself when he hears false news of Shīrīn's death.
94a	Khusraw and Shīrīn make love.
110b	Laylā and Majnūn fall in love at school.
116a	Nawfal battles Laylā's clan on behalf of Majnūn.
122b	Majnūn is visited by his friend in the wilderness.
126b	Laylā visits Majnūn in the wilderness.
132a	Mourners bear Laylā's body in a funeral procession.
156b	Alexander battles the Khāqān of China.
163b	Alexander entertains Kanīfū.
175b	Alexander confers with Plato.
184a	Alexander sets out on a sea voyage to the Western Isles.
189a	Alexander is lowered into the sea.
204b	Bahrām Gūr and Dilārām hunt together.
208a	Bahrām, Dilārām, and Nu'mān view the seven palaces.
212b	The goldsmith Ḥasan brings the golden elephant to the king.
216b	Bahrām Gūr visits the princess of the Green Pavilion.
223a	Having arranged a tryst, the prince and king's favorite make love.
227b	The youth of Rūm is brought before the fay.
237b	The princess of the water tower sees a boat on the lake.

Published: Suleiman and Suleimanova, *Miniatures Illuminations*, pls. 23–37.

*Majnūn wa Laylā*. St. Petersburg, National Library of Russia, inv. Dorn 395. Herat, dated Rajab 900/March–April 1495. ff. 32, 24.6 x 16.0 cm. Nasta'līq, 21 lines, 4 cols., text area 13.1 x 8.8 cm. *'Unwān*, 2 paintings attributed to Bihzād or his school.

16a	Laylā and Majnūn fall in love at school.
20b	Majnūn is visited by friends and his father.

Published: O. Galerkina, "On Some Miniatures Attributed to Bihzād from Leningrad Collections," *Ars Orientalis*, 8 (1970), figs. 13–14; Suleiman and Suleimanova, *Miniatures Illuminations*, pls. 16–17; Loukonine and Ivanov, *Lost Treasures of Persia*, no. 159.

*Khamsa*. Berlin, Staatsbibliothek Ms. 187 (Pertsch 830). Herat, dated 15 Ramaẓān 900/9 June 1495. ff. 176, 34.0 x 22.5 cm. *Shamsa* (1a), 4 *'unwāns* (1b, 63b, 92a, 139b), 34 paintings.

18a	A hermit refuses a courtier's offer of a position at court.
19b	A bathhouse worker is consumed by passion for a young king.
25a	'Alī cuts the throat of an infidel who had spat upon him.
26a	A king out hunting accidentally kills a sleeping shepherd.
26b	The mother of the dead youth asks the sovereign for justice.
32a	An old Sufi laments his lost youth.
34b	Two foxes caught by a hunter's dog lament their imminent separation from their hides and each other.
36a	A virtuous woman plucks out her eyes to still the advances of the love-stricken king.
41a	Khusraw visits Farhād on Mt. Bīsitūn.
47a	Khusraw appears before the palace of Shīrīn.
51a	Khusraw and Shīrīn lie unconscious.
54a	Shīrīn receives a ring from Khusraw.
55a	Wedding of Khusraw and Shīrīn.
56a	Khusraw and Shīrīn make love.
61b	Death of Khusraw.
69b	Laylā and Majnūn fall in love at school.
74a	Nawfal battles Laylā's clan on behalf of Majnūn.
79b	Three friends visit Majnūn in the wilderness.
81b	Majnūn befriends a dog that lives in Laylā's neighborhood.
83a	Laylā visits Majnūn in the wilderness.
86b	Laylā weeps at the gate of the palm grove.
88b	Funeral of Laylā.
103a	Foreigners bring the defeated Nabankuy to Alexander.
105b	Alexander fights the Khāqān of China.
108a	Alexander defeats the ruler of Rūm.
112a	Alexander's soldiers battle the inhabitants of Gōg and Magōg.
145a	Bahrām Gūr hunts gazelles with Dilārām.
148a	Bahrām Gūr visits the princess of the Black Pavilion.
151a	Bahrām Gūr visits the princess of the Yellow Pavilion.
154b	Bahrām Gūr visits the princess of the Green Pavilion.
157b	Bahrām Gūr visits the princess of the Red Pavilion.
162a	Bahrām Gūr visits the princess of the Blue Pavilion.
167a	Bahrām Gūr visits the princess of the Sandalwood Pavilion.
171a	Bahrām Gūr visits the princess of the White Pavilion.

Only a few of the paintings of this manuscript are from the school of Herat at the end of the 15th century, the time of its writing. All the others are partially restored or completely overpainted, probably in India in the 18th century by Mughal artists. Published: P. Schulz, *Die persisch-islamische Miniaturmalerei* (Leipzig, 1914), II, pls. 56a, 57a–b, 58a–b, 59b, 60, 61a–b (ff. 19b, 36a, 41a, 47a, 54a, 81b, 88b, 112a); Titley, "Miniature Paintings," figs. 14–14a; *Islamische Buchkunst aus 1000 Jahren* (Berlin, 1980), 96.

*Khamsa*. National Museum, New Delhi 52.81. Iran, Turkman style. Completed on 10 Ẕī'l-Ḥijja 901/9 August 1496 by Shaykh Muḥammad ibn Niẓāmī al-Dīn 'Alī ibn 'Alī Shaykh Muḥammad al-Fārsī. ff. 246, 26.6 x 16.3 cm., Nasta'līq, 19 lines, 4 cols., text area 18.0 x 10.2 cm. Double-page *sarlawḥ*, 5 *'unwāns*, 12 paintings.

3b–4a	Double-page hunting scene.
38b	The inhabitants of Gōg and Magōg are brought captive before Alexander.
45b	Alexander beholds Chinese painters making marvelous murals.
67a	Alexander returns from the deep and recounts what he has seen.
93a	A hermit refuses a courtier's offer of a position at court.
105b	The milk seller is ruined as a result of years of dishonesty.
146a	Farhād hears false news of Shīrīn's death.
162a	Wedding of Shīrīn and Khusraw.
170b	Death of Khusraw.
181b	Laylā and Majnūn fall in love in school.
244a	Rāma enters the chamber of the sleeping daughter of the lustful vizier.

*Hasht Bihisht*. Istanbul, Topkapi Saray Museum H. 676. Copied by Sulṭān 'Alī al-Mashhadī in Herat for Sulṭān Muḥammad Muḥsin Bahādur Khān in Ṣafar 902/October 1496. ff. 41, 38.0 x 26.0 cm. Nasta'līq, 23 lines, 4 cols., text area 25.3 x 15.5 cm. 2 *'unwāns*. 2 paintings attributed to the school of Bihzād.

1b–2a	Royal hunt. 30.0 x 20.0 cm. Published: Karatay, *Farsça*, no. 602; Z. Akalay, "Amir Khosrow Dehlavi: miniatures," [in Turkish] *Sanat Tarihi Yilligi*, 6 (1974–75), figs. 5, 10 (det.); Gray, ed., *The Arts of the Book in Central Asia*, color pls. LXIII–LXIV; Rogers, Çağman, and Tanindi, *The Topkapi Saray Museum*, pl. 64 (color); Bahari, *Bihzad*, figs. 99–100.

Detached painting from 26b–27a: The favorite maiden of a king is abducted by her lover by ship. Freer Gallery of Art 37.27. 27.0 x 19.3 cm. Published: Gray, ed., *The Arts of the Book in Central Asia*, 205, fig. 114; Bahari, *Bihzad*, fig. 101.

35b–36a Bahrām Gūr in the White Pavilion. Location unknown. Published: Akalay, "Amir Khosrow Dehlavi: miniatures," front and back covers (figs. 1–2), *shamsa* (fig. 3), *'unwān* (fig. 4); Gray, ed., *The Arts of the Book in Central Asia*, pls. XVII–XVIII.

*Khamsa*. Istanbul, Topkapi Saray Museum H. 801. Iran, Yazd. Copied for Sulṭān Maḥmūd by Ḥasan al-Ḥusayn al-Kātib in 902/1497. ff. 332, 20.6 x 12.5 cm. Nasta'līq, 15 lines, 2 cols., text in border in 28 lines; text area 16.4 x 7.9 cm. 5 *'unwāns*, 18 paintings.

- 124a Khusraw and Shīrīn are married.
- 127a Khusraw and Shīrīn make love.
- 149b Laylā and Majnūn fall in love at school.
- 157b Nawfal battles Laylā's clan on behalf of Majnūn.
- 172a Laylā visits Majnūn in the wilderness.
- 197b Bahrām Gūr displays his hunting prowess before Dilārām.
- 204a The camel-driver accuses the three princes of Ceylon of theft before the king.
- 211a The goldsmith's foolish wife takes hold of a rope whose end has been sweetened with sugar and unwittingly helps her husband escape.
- 216b The queen places in a golden cage the parrot whose form the king has assumed by magic.
- 222a The prince and the king's favorite make love.
- 243a The king realizes the accuracy of the talisman that laughs whenever it sees deception or hypocrisy when he spies a princess consorting with a black muleteer.
- 271a Alexander defeats Kanīfū in battle.
- 276a Alexander lifts the Khāqān into the air.
- 282b Alexander's army combats the inhabitants of Gōg and Magōg.
- 287b Alexander engages in amorous dalliance with Kanīfū.
- 303b Alexander confers with Plato.
- 315b Alexander embarks upon a sea voyage to the Western Isles.
- 322a Alexander is lowered into the sea.

Published: Karatay, *Farsça*, no. 594; Gray, ed., *The Arts of the Book in Central Asia*, 235, fig. 138.

*Khamsa*. Istanbul, Topkapi Saray Museum H. 799. Turkey, Edirne studio. Written by Maḥmūd Mīr al- Ḥajj in Ramaẓān 903/April–May 1498. ff. 201, 28.0 x 19.0 cm. Nasta'līq, 24 lines, 4 cols., text area 17.2 x 11.2 cm. *Shamsa*, double-page frontispiece, 4 *'unwāns*, 28 paintings.

- 4a *Mi'rāj* of the Prophet.
- 9b Khusraw discovers a spiritual guide.
- 21a A bathhouse worker is consumed by the heat of his passion for the king.
- 25a Youths dying of thirst in the desert refuse the water of stranger until each of their friends has drunk.
- 26b 'Alī cuts the throat of an infidel who had spat upon him.
- 34a An old Sufi laments his lost youth.
- 48a Khusraw is received by Shīrīn's aunt, Mahīn Bānū.
- 50b Aided by troops of the Qaiṣar of Rūm, Khusraw defeats Bahrām Chūbīna.
- 63a Disguised as a shepherd, Khusraw visits Farhād on Mt. Bīsitūn.
- 73a Khusraw and Shīrīn are reconciled and listen to music.
- 78b Khusraw and Shīrīn make love.
- 84a Shīrīn commits suicide on the corpse of the murdered Khusraw.
- 92b Laylā and Majnūn fall in love at school.
- 97a Nawfal battles Laylā's clan on behalf of Majnūn.
- 104b Majnūn befriends a dog which lived in Laylā's neighborhood.
- 106a Laylā and Majnūn swoon when they see each other in the wilderness.
- 130a Alexander lifts the Khāqān into the air.
- 137b Alexander discusses inventions with Chinese painters.
- 145b Alexander visits Plato.
- 168b Bahrām Gūr displays his hunting prowess before Dilārām.
- 170a Bahrām Gūr witnesses the mesmerizing effect of Dilārām's music.
- 173a Bahrām Gūr visits the princess of the Black Pavilion.
- 175b Bahrām Gūr visits the princess of the Yellow Pavilion.
- 179a Bahrām Gūr visits the princess of the Green Pavilion.
- 182a Bahrām Gūr visits the princess of the Red Pavilion.
- 186b Bahrām Gūr visits the princess of the Blue Pavilion.
- 191b Bahrām Gūr visits the princess of the Sandalwood Pavilion.
- 196a Bahrām Gūr visits the princess of the White Pavilion.

Published: Karatay, *Farsça*, no. 599; Rogers, Çağman, and Tanindi, *The Topkapi Saray Museum*, pls. 129–31; B. Brend, "Elements from Painting of the Eastern Islamic Area in Early Ottoman Manuscripts of the Khamseh of Amir Khusrau Dihlavi," in *Proceedings of the 9th International Congress of Turkish Art*, 1 (Ankara, 1995), figs. 1–3; Z. Tanindi, "Additions to Illustrated Manuscripts in Ottoman Workshops," *Muqarnas*, 17 (2000), figs. 9–10.

*Khamsa*. London, British Library Or. 11327. Probably Transoxiana, dated 903/1497–98. ff. 235, naskhī, 21 lines, 4 cols., 11.7 x 7.3 cm. 1 *shamsa*, 5 *'unwāns*, 24 paintings.

- 3b The Prophet ascends to heaven.
- 26b Young men are overcome by thirst in the desert and perish because each refuses the water offered by a stranger until all of his companions has drunk.
- 28b 'Alī kills the infidel who had spat upon him.
- 51b Khusraw beholds a portrait of Shīrīn brought by Shāhpūr.
- 53b Khusraw is received by Shīrīn and her aunt, Mahīn Bānū.
- 59a Khusraw and Shīrīn quarrel.
- 63b Khusraw and Shakar consummate their marriage.
- 65a Farhād visits Shīrīn at her palace.
- 71a Khusraw visits Farhād on Mt. Bīsitūn while disguised as a shepherd.
- 90a Khusraw and Shīrīn make love.
- 111b Bahrām Gūr visits the princess of the Yellow Pavilion.
- 124a Bahrām Gūr visits the princess of the Red Pavilion.
- 154b Alexander battles the Khāqān of China.
- 164b Alexander's army beholds the inhabitants of the land of Gōg and Magōg.
- 168a Alexander entertains Kanīfū.
- 172a Alexander discusses the invention of scientific instruments with Chinese and other sages.
- 174b Alexander denounces the Zoroastrians and their fire-temples.
- 180b Alexander visits Plato and learns of his imminent death.
- 188a Alexander confers with Khiẓr, Elias, and Aristotle on his sea voyage to the Western Isles.

195b Mourners surround the coffin of Alexander.
197a Alexander's body is borne in a funeral procession.
208b Laylā and Majnūn fall in love at school.
211a Majnūn is stoned by children.
221a Friends visit Majnūn in the wilderness.

Published: N. Titley, *Miniatures from Persian Manuscripts from Persia, India and Turkey* (London, 1977), no. 56.

*Majnūn wa Laylā*. St. Petersburg, National Library of Russia, inv. Dorn 394. Herat style, ca. 1496–98 or early 16th century. Written by Sulṭān Muḥammad Harawī. ff. 34, 25.3 x 18.1 cm. Nasta'līq, 21 lines, 4 cols., text area 15.5 x 9.5 cm. 5 paintings (4 of which are attributed to Bihzād). Original binding.

5b Precepts for Khiẓr, the son of Amīr Khusraw.
9a Majnūn and Laylā fall in love at school.
21b Majnūn befriends a dog that lived near Laylā.
23a Laylā visits Majnūn in the wilderness.
27a Majnūn's envoy tests Laylā's love with false news of Majnūn's death.

Published: E. Kühnel, "Bihzad" in *Miniaturmalerei im islamischen Orient* (Berlin, 1922), pl. 53; Galerkina, "On Some Miniatures Attributed to Bihzād," figs. 16–20; Gray, ed., *The Arts of the Book in Central Asia*, 203, fig. 113 (5b)(cf. 209); Suleiman and Suleimanova, *Miniatures Illuminations*, pls. 18–22.

*Khamsa*. Istanbul, Topkapi Saray Museum H. 798. Khurasan. Written by Maḥmūd *Kātib* in Rabī' II 906/October–November 1500. ff. 266, 24.8 x 17.4 cm. Nasta'līq, 19 lines, 4 cols., text area 17.3 x 11.5 cm. 5 *'unwāns*, 26 paintings.

4b *Mi'rāj* of the Prophet.
26a A hermit refuses a courtier's offer of a position at court.
28b A bathhouse worker is consumed by the heat of his passion for the king.
32b The loyalty of two friends sentenced to death causes a man to confess his crime of fratricide.
38a A king out hunting accidentally kills a young shepherd.
61a Bahrām Gūr hunts with Dilārām.
64b Bahrām Gūr visits the princess of the Black Pavilion.
69a Bahrām Gūr visits the princess of the Yellow Pavilion.
73b Bahrām Gūr visits the princess of the Green Pavilion.
77a Bahrām Gūr visits the princess of the Red Pavilion.
82b Bahrām Gūr visits the princess of the Blue Pavilion.
89a Bahrām Gūr visits the princess of the Sandalwood Pavilion.
94a Bahrām Gūr visits the princess of the White Pavilion.
112b Khusraw and Shīrīn meet by chance on the hunting ground.
113b Khusraw entertains Shīrīn.
126b Shīrīn meets Farhād.
134a Khusraw visits Farhād on Mt. Bīsitūn.
173b Laylā and Majnūn fall in love at school.
180b Appalled by the carnage of the battlefield, Majnūn allows a crow to peck at his eyes.
187a Friends visit Majnūn in the wilderness.
191b Laylā visits Majnūn in the wilderness.
197a Laylā swoons at the false news of Majnūn's death.
216a Alexander receives the defeated Kanīfū in his camp.
221a Alexander defeats the Khāqān.
229b Alexander's army combats the inhabitants of Gōg and Magōg.
233a Alexander engages in an amorous dalliance with Kanīfū.

Published: Karatay, *Farsça*, no. 596; Brend, "Elements from Painting of the Eastern Islamic Area," figs. 4–7, 9.

*Maṭla' al-Anwār*. Paris, Bibliothèque Nationale Ancien fonds 259. Iran, Tabriz (?), ca. 1500. ff. 36, 25.4 x 18.1 cm. Nasta'līq, 4 cols., text area 12.5 x 7.5 cm. Double-page frontispiece 1b–2a. 3 paintings.

9a A hermit refuses a courtier's offer of a position at court.
12a *Mi'rāj* of the Prophet.
27b An old Sufi laments his lost youth.

Published: Blochet, *Révue des Bibliothèques*, 1898, 30; Richard, *Splendeurs persanes*, no. 78.

*Khamsa*. Istanbul, Topkapi Saray Museum H. 800. Khurasan. Completed by Ṭāhir Muḥammad ibn Sulṭān Muḥammad on the last day of Ẕī'l-Qa'da 908/28 May 1503. ff. 233, 24.9 x 16.8 cm. Nasta'līq, 21 lines, 4 cols., text area 15.3 x 10.0 cm. Double-page frontispiece, 4 *'unwāns*, 23 paintings.

4b *Mi'rāj* of the Prophet.
9b Khusraw appears in a visionary garden.
15b An old man reproaches a prattling youth.
21b A hermit refuses a courtier's offer of a position at court.
36a An old Sufi laments his lost youth.
44a Muḥammad receives the Buraq.
51a Khusraw and Shīrīn meet by chance on the hunting ground.
53a Khusraw and Shīrīn feast together.
55a Khusraw entertains Maryam.
86a Khusraw and Shīrīn are married.
103b Laylā and Majnūn fall in love at school.
109b Nawfal battles Laylā's clan on behalf of Majnūn.
116a Friends visit Majnūn in the wilderness.
120a Laylā visits Majnūn in the wilderness.
146a Alexander engages Kanīfū in battle.
153b Alexander's army combats the inhabitants of Gōg and Magōg.
197b Bahrām Gūr visits the princess of the Black Pavilion.
201b Bahrām Gūr visits the princess of the Yellow Pavilion.
206a Bahrām Gūr visits the princess of the Green Pavilion.
209b Bahrām Gūr visits the princess of the Red Pavilion.
215a Bahrām Gūr visits the princess of the Blue Pavilion.
221a Bahrām Gūr visits the princess of the Sandalwood Pavilion.
226b Bahrām Gūr visits the princess of the White Pavilion.

Published: Karatay, *Farsça*, no. 597; Brend, "Elements from Painting of the Eastern Islamic Area," figs. 11–14.

*Hasht Bihisht*. Paris, Bibliothèque Nationale Supp. persan 633. Iran, Shiraz style. Copied by Ibn Mubārak 'Alī al-Fahrajī in Shawwāl 908/April 1503. ff. 45, 22.4 x 15.0 cm. Nasta'līq, 21 lines, 4 cols., text area 15.0 x 11.7 cm. 1 *'unwān*, 8 paintings added ca. 1560.

7b Bahrām Gūr hunts onagers.
11b Bahrām Gūr visits the princess of the Black Pavilion.
15b Bahrām Gūr visits the princess of the Yellow Pavilion.
19b Bahrām Gūr visits the princess of the Green Pavilion.
22b Bahrām Gūr visits the princess of the Red Pavilion.
28a Bahrām Gūr visits the princess of the Blue Pavilion.
34a Bahrām Gūr visits the princess of the Sandalwood Pavilion.
38b Bahrām Gūr visits the princess of the White Pavilion.

Published: Richard, *Splendeurs persanes*, no. 127.

*Shīrīn wa Khusraw*. Hyderabad, Salar Jung Museum A./Nm 623. Iran, early 16th century. Written by Sulṭān 'Alī al-Mashhadī. ff. 127, 30.4 x 20.4 cm. Nasta'līq, 15 lines, text area 18.0 x 10.8 cm. 1 *'unwān*, 2 paintings.

29a Khusraw leads his army in battle.
105b Death of Maḥmūd.

Published: M. Ashraf, *A Concise Descriptive Catalogue of the Persian Manuscripts in the Sālār Jung Museum and Library* (Hyderabad, 1969), no. 1407; Suleiman and Suleimanova, *Miniatures Illuminations*, pl. 40 (29a).

*Majnūn wa Laylā*. London, Keir Collection. Bukhara, first quarter of the 16th century. ff. 29, 23.4 x 16.5 cm. Nasta'līq, 22 lines, 4 cols., text area 16.0 x 11.0 cm. Illumination 1b, 2 paintings.

| | |
|---|---|
| 12a | Nawfal battles Laylā's clan on behalf of Majnūn. |
| 23b | Laylā weeps in the palm grove at the false news of Majnūn's death. |

Published: Robinson, Grube, Meredith-Owens, Skelton, *Islamic Painting and the Arts of the Book*, III.332–33, 196.

*Khamsa*. Istanbul, Topkapi Saray Museum H. 797. Written by Shāh Maḥmūd Nīshāpūrī in Shawwāl 927/September–October 1521. ff. 209, 28.9 x 18.1 cm. Nasta'līq, 21 lines, 4 cols., text area 18.5 x 10.3 cm. 1 *shamsa*, 5 *'unwāns*, 12 paintings.

| | |
|---|---|
| 73a | Khusraw appears before Shīrīn's palace. |
| 84b | Khusraw and Shīrīn make love. |
| 104b | Nawfal battle Laylā's clan on behalf of Majnūn. |
| 112b | Majnūn befriends a dog that lived in Laylā's neighborhood. |
| 133b | Bahrām Gūr visits the princess of the Black Pavilion. |
| 137b | Bahrām Gūr visits the princess of the Yellow Pavilion. |
| 141b | Bahrām Gūr visits the princess of the Green Pavilion. |
| 145a | Bahrām Gūr visits the princess of the Red Pavilion. |
| 150a | Bahrām Gūr visits the princess of the Blue Pavilion. |
| 156a | Bahrām Gūr visits the princess of the Sandalwood Pavilion. |
| 160b | Bahrām Gūr visits the princess of the White Pavilion. |
| 178b | Alexander battles the Khāqān. |

Published: Karatay, *Farsça*, no. 598.

*Khamsa*. Dispersed. Copied by 'Alā' al-Dīn Muḥammad al-Harawī at Balkh in 909/1503–4, painted probably at Herat, ca. 1525. The first and last pages of the text, implausibly called *Ā'īnah-i Sikandarī*, and preserved in the Bibliothèque Nationale (Supp. persan 1954 (1)(legs Marteau, 1916), supply not only the name of the scribe, the date, and provenance, but also the original total of 196 folios and 13 paintings (12 of which have survived).

*Maṯla' al-Anwār*
Amīr Khusraw presents a book of poetry to 'Alā' al-Dīn Khalji. Folio 30.5 x 19.5 cm., painting 12.3 x 12.3 cm. Sackler Gallery S1986.213.

A Muslim pilgrim is so impressed by the piety of a brahman who is crawling toward his idol that he removes his shoes and continues barefoot. Folio 30.0 x 19.8 cm., painting 16.2 x 12.2 cm. The Metropolitan Museum of Art 13.160.4.

Youths die of thirst in the desert. 20.0 x 14.2 cm. British Museum 1920 9-17 0260.

The dishonest milk seller causes a torrent of water to sweep away the herd whose milk he adulterated. Folio 30.5 x 19.7 cm., painting 15.7 x 12.3 cm. Worcester Art Museum 1962.181.

*Khusraw wa Shīrīn*
Khusraw arrives at Shīrīn's palace. 18.2 x 12.5 cm. The Metropolitan Museum of Art 13.160.1.

Shīrīn receives Farhād at her palace. Louvre A.O. 7104.

Khusraw receives the wind-blown treasure of Rūm. Louvre A.O. 7105.

*Majnūn wa Laylā*
Majnūn befriends a dog that lived near Laylā. 15.2 x 12.2 cm. The Metropolitan Museum of Art 13.160.3.

Published: Marteau and Vever, *Miniatures persanes*, fig. 84 (Louvre A.O.7104), fig. 85 (MMA 13.160.4), fig. 88; S. de Ricci, *Catalogue d'une collection des miniatures gothiques et persanes appartenant à Leonce Rosenberg* (Paris, 1913), nos. 144–53; M. Dimand, "Dated Specimens of Mohammedan Art in the Metropolitan Museum of Art—Part II," *Metropolitan Museum of Art Studies*, 1, pt. 2 (1928–29), figs. 5 (MMA 13.160.1) and 6 (MMA 13.160.3); I. Stchoukine, *Les miniatures persanes* (Paris, 1932), 37–39, pl. VI; I. Stchoukine, Les peintures des manuscrits Safavis de 1502 à 1587 (Paris, 1959), no. 7, 56; Grube, *The Classical Style*, nos. 57–59. G. Lowry with S. Nemazee, *A Jeweler's Eye*, pl. 36; Lowry, Beach et al., *An Annotated and Illustrated Checklist*, no. 199 (Sackler Gallery S1986.213); S. Canby, *Persian Painting* (New York, 1993), no. 56 (BM 1920 9-17 0260); Bahari, *Bihzad*, fig. 110 (MMA 13.160.4).

*Khamsa*. Baltimore, Walters Art Museum W. 622. Iran. Written by Pīr Ḥusayn *al-Kātib* Shīrāzī, completed 23 Ẕī'l-Qa'da 935/28 July 1529. ff. 274, 26.7 x 16.7 cm. Nasta'līq, 17 lines, 4 cols., text area 18.6 x 10.1 cm. Double-page illumination 1b–2a, 4 *'unwāns* (55b, 114b, 155b, 224a), 13 paintings.

| | |
|---|---|
| 23a | Khiẓr visits a pious man who asks for only a vision of God as a reward for his devotion. |
| 34b | Four men die of thirst in a desert because each refused the water offered by a stranger until his companions had drunk. |
| 39a | A king out hunting accidentally kills a youth and offers to compensate the boy's mother with his own life or a platter of gold. |
| 66a | Khusraw and Shīrīn meet by chance on the hunting ground. |
| 123a | Laylā and Majnūn fall in love at school. |
| 130b | Nawfal battles Laylā's clan on behalf of Majnūn. |
| 173b | Alexander lassoes a Chinese warrior. |
| 186b | Alexander entertains Kanīfū. |
| 207b | Alexander confers with sages about his decision to descend into the sea to investigate submarine mysteries. |
| 232b | Bahrām Gūr displays his hunting prowess before Dilārām. |
| 244b | Bahrām Gūr visits the princess of the Green Pavilion. |
| 254b | Bahrām Gūr visits the princess of the Blue Pavilion. |
| 267b | Bahrām Gūr visits the princess of the White Pavilion. |

*Khamsa*. St. Petersburg, National Library of Russia, inv. PNS 267. Iran, Tabriz, ca. 1530–40. The date of 12 Muḥarram 1012/22 June 1603 is added in another hand. ff. 254, 33.7 x 21.5 cm. Nasta'līq, 19 lines, 4 cols. Text area 21.4 x 14.5 cm. 5 *'unwāns*, 12 paintings, including one double-page frontispiece. Lacquer covers.

| | |
|---|---|
| 1b–2a | Royal feast and picnic of scholars. |
| 5b | *Mi'rāj* of the Prophet. |
| 27b | A bathhouse worker is consumed by the heat of his passion for the king. |
| 60b | Khusraw and Shīrīn hunt together. |
| 75a | Farhād visits Shīrīn at her palace. |
| 89b | Khusraw comes to Shīrīn's palace. |
| 125a | Nawfal battles Laylā's clan on behalf of Majnūn. |
| 162a | Alexander battles the Khāqān of China in single combat. |
| 184b | Alexander seeks to convert the inhabitants of Rūm by force. |
| 195b | Alexander sets out on a sea journey to the Western Isles and sees sirens. |

223a Bahrām Gūr visits the princess of the Sandalwood Pavilion.
Published: Suleiman and Suleimanova, *Miniatures Illuminations*, pls. 52–60.

*Maṭla ʿal-Anwār*. Patna, Khudabaksh Library HL 414. Written by Mīr ʿAlī in mid-Shaʿbān 947/December 1540 for Sulṭān ʿAbd al-ʿAzīz of Bukhara. ff. 153, 12 x 7 3/4 in. Nastaʿlīq, 12 lines, 2 cols., text area 7 1/2 x 4 1/2 in. 4 paintings unrelated to the text have been placed at the end of the manuscript. Published: V. C. Scott O'Connor, *An Eastern Library* (Glasgow, 1920), 64–65; *Catalogue* vol. 1, no. 129.

*Khamsa*. Paris, Bibliothèque Nationale Supp. persan 1149. Entitled *Panj Ganj*. Iran, Bakharz (Khurasan). Written by Shāh Maḥmūd al-Nīshāpūrī for Bahrām Mīrzā, son of Shāh Ismāʿīl I and brother of Shāh Ṭahmāsp. Dated Ẕīʾl-Ḥijja 959/November–December 1552 at the end of *Majnūn wa Laylā* (125b), and Ṣafar [960 or 961/1553 or 1554] at the end of *Hasht Bihisht* (221). ff. 221, 32.5 x 21.1 cm. Nastaʿlīq, 21 lines, 4 cols., text area 21.6 x 11.9 cm. *Shamsas* 1b, 2a, illuminations 2b, 41b, 42a–b, 94a–b, 125b, 126a–b, 180a–b.

- 22a A hermit refuses a courtier's offer of a position at court.
- 50b Khusraw and Shīrīn meet by chance on the hunting ground.
- 73b Khusraw rests after a hunt during his journey to Shīrīn's castle.
- 79b Khusraw and Shīrīn listen to music and are reconciled.
- 84a Khusraw and Shīrīn marry.
- 112a Friends visit Majnūn in the wilderness.
- 115b Laylā visits Majnūn in the wilderness.
- 138a The Rūmī champion Parīkaysh engages the Chinese champion Tangū.
- 150b Alexander entertains Kanīfū.
- 173a Alexander encourages his men.
- 193b The goldsmith Ḥasan presents the golden elephant to the king.
- 200a Bahrām Gūr visits the princess of the Red Pavilion.
- 207b The youth of Rūm is entertained by the fay.

Published: Blochet, *Révue des Bibliothèques*, 1899, 58–60; Stchoukine, *Les peintures des manuscrits Safavis*, no. 194, pl. LXXVI (73b), who argues that the date 959 was altered from the original 979/April 1572 and questions the dedication to Bahrām Mīrzā. This position is accepted by F. Richard in *Splendeurs persanes*, no. 118, where f. 193b is reproduced in color.

*Khamsa* (only *Maṭlaʿ al-Anwār*, *Shīrīn wa Khusraw*, and *Majnūn wa Laylā*). Dublin, Chester Beatty Library, Persian ms. 226. Iran, probably Khurasan. Written by Muḥammad Ḥusayn between Ramaẓān 963/July–August 1556 and Jumādā I 964/March 1557. ff. 146. Nastaʿlīq, 19 lines, 4 cols., text area 17.6 x 9.9 cm. 8 paintings extracted from another 16th-century manuscript from Shiraz and inserted in this one, so that the miniatures are unrelated to Amīr Khusraw's text. The illuminations on 1b–2a, 50b, and 103b suggest a provenance in Khurasan. Published: Arberry, Blochet, Minovi, Robinson, and Wilkinson, *The Chester Beatty Library. A Catalogue of the Persian Manuscripts and Miniatures* III, no. 226.

*Khamsa*. Jerusalem, Israel Museum 5002.1.79. Iran, Shiraz. Written by Ḥasan al-Sharīf *al-Kātib* in 965/1557 in Shiraz. ff. 238. Nastaʿlīq, 17 lines, 4 cols., text area 18.6 x 10.3 cm. 5 paintings.

- 26b ʿAlī kills an infidel who had spat upon him.
- 50a Khusraw and Shīrīn meet by chance on the hunting ground.
- 71b Farhād digs a channel in Bīsitūn to bring milk to Shīrīn.
- 93b Khusraw and Shīrīn consummate their marriage.
- 130b Laylā weeps in the palm grove at the false news of Majnūn's death.

Published: R. Milstein, *Islamic Painting in the Israel Museum* (Jerusalem, 1984), no. 33, 65 (26b).

*Khamsa*. Washington, D.C., Sackler Gallery of Art S1986.056. Iran, Astarabad. Dated Jumādā I 970/December 1562–January 1563. ff. 238, 20.7 x 13.0 cm. Nastaʿlīq, 19 lines, 4 cols., text area 13.0 x 7.5 cm. Double-page frontispiece (1b-2a), 5 *ʿunwāns* (2b, 44b, 99b, 134b, 180b), 13 paintings.

- 30a A king accidentally kills a youth and offers his own life as compensation to the aggrieved mother.
- 46b *Miʿrāj* of the Prophet.
- 54a Khusraw and Shīrīn meet by chance on the hunting ground.
- 107a Laylā and Majnūn fall in love at school.
- 120b Nawfal battles Laylā's clan on behalf of Majnūn.
- 148a Bahrām Gūr visits the princess of the Red Pavilion.
- 152a Bahrām Gūr visits the princess of the Yellow Pavilion.
- 160b Bahrām Gūr visits the princess of the Blue Pavilion.
- 167a Bahrām Gūr visits the princess of the Sandalwood Pavilion.
- 172a Bahrām Gūr visits the princess of the White Pavilion.
- 197a Alexander vanquishes the Khāqān of China.
- 202b The inhabitants of Gōg are brought as prisoners before Alexander.
- 207a Alexander engages in amorous dalliance with Kanīfū.

Published: Lowry, Beach et al., *An Annotated and Illustrated Checklist*, no. 204.

*Khamsa*. Philadelphia Museum of Art 53-128-4. Iran. Written by Aḥmad ibn ʿAlī al-Shīfakī in 975/1567. ff. 224, 32.9 x 20.7 cm. Nastaʿlīq, 20 lines, 4 columns, text area 17.6 x 10.4 cm. One double-page frontispiece, 5 *ʿunwāns*, and 14 paintings.

- 22a A hermit refuses a courtier's offer of a position at court.
- 43a The virtuous woman rebuffs the king's entreaties by plucking out her eyes.
- 54b Shīrīn entertains Khusraw.
- 76b Khusraw comes to Shīrīn's castle.
- 105a Bahrām Gūr visits the princess of the Black Pavilion.
- 109a Bahrām Gūr visits the princess of the Yellow Pavilion.
- 113a Bahrām Gūr visits the princess of the Green Pavilion.
- 117a Bahrām Gūr visits the princess of the Red Pavilion.
- 122a Bahrām Gūr visits the princess of the Blue Pavilion.
- 128b Bahrām Gūr visits the princess of the Sandalwood Pavilion.
- 133b Bahrām Gūr visits the princess of the White Pavilion.
- 149a Laylā and Majnūn fall in love at school.
- 164a Majnūn swoons at the sight of Laylā in the wilderness.
- 198b Alexander engages in an amorous dalliance with Kanīfū.

*Khamsa*. Location unknown. Iran, Khurasan, dated 976/1568. ff. 221, 23.5 x 16.5 cm. Nastaʿlīq, 19 lines, 4 columns, text area 15.8 x 11.0 cm. One double-page frontispiece, 4 *ʿunwāns*, and 9 miniatures. Published: Sotheby's, New York, 10 December 1981, lot 165.

*Khamsa*. Rampur, Raza Library Persian 4102. Iran. Written by Maḥmūd al-Shāhānī. *Maṭlaʿ al-Anwār* completed 9 Muḥarram 977/24 June 1569, *Shīrīn wa Khusraw* finished Ramaẓān (no year), *Majnūn wa Laylā* completed Ẕīʾl-Ḥijja 975/May–June 1568, *Hasht Bihisht* completed Rabīʿ II 977/September–October 1569, and *Āʾīnah-i Sikandarī* completed Shaʿbān 977/January–February 1570. 441 pages, 31.8 x 22.0 cm. Nastaʿlīq, 21 lines, 4 cols., text area 18.9 x 10.7 cm. 5 *ʿunwāns*,

4 double-page Shiraz-style miniatures added to the manuscript ca. 1600. Published: Schmitz and Desai, *Mughal and Persian Paintings and Illustrated Manuscripts*, Ms. IV.26.

*Khamsa*. Cambridge, King's College, no. Pote 153. Iran, dated 978–79/1570–72. ff. 239, 24.0 x 17.5 cm., 7 paintings (3 double-page), attributed to Farrukh Beg. Published: R. Skelton, "The Mughal Artist Farrokh Beg," *Ars Orientalis*, 2 (1957), fig. 4; B. W. Robinson, *Persian Miniature Paintings from Collections in the British Isles* (London, 1967), no. 170 (unillustrated); Titley, "Miniature Paintings," figs. 38–41; A. Soudavar, "Between the Safavids and the Mughals: Art and Artists in Transition," *Iran*, 37 (1999), pl. 18b.

*Khamsa*. London, British Library Add. 22699. Iran, Shiraz. Written by Muḥsin ibn Luṭfullāh Ma'ād al-Ḥusaynī in 978/1571. ff. 209, 33.5 x 21.5 cm. Nasta'līq, 22 lines, 4 cols., text area 22.4 x 13.5 cm. 5 double-page compositions placed at the beginning of each *maṣnawī*.

1b–2a *Mi'rāj* of the Prophet.
42b–43a Khusraw and Shīrīn are entertained.
89b–90a Bahrām Gūr displays his hunting prowess while Dilārām plays the lute.
128b–129a (precedes *Majnūn wa Laylā*). A prince is entertained by his court poets while a banquet is prepared.
159b–160a (precedes *Ā'īnah-i Sikandarī*). The Khāqān of China is pulled off his horse in battle with Alexander.

Published: C. Rieu, *Catalogue of the Persian Manuscripts in the British Museum* (London, 1879), II, 615–16; Titley, "Miniature Paintings," figs. 42 (43a), 43 (160a); Titley, *Miniatures from Persian Manuscripts*, no. 54.

*Khamsa*. Istanbul, Topkapi Saray Museum Revan 1029. Iran, Shiraz. Written by Muḥammad ibn Isḥāq Canabādī in 979/1571–72. ff. 273, 24.7 x 17.3 cm. Small nasta'līq, 17 lines, 4 cols., text area 15.4 x 10.8 cm. *Sarlawḥ*, 2 paintings. (*Maṭla' al-Anwār* 2b, *Iskandarnāma wa Ā'īnah-i Sikandarī* 53b, *Shīrīn wa Khusraw* 121b, *Majnūn wa Laylā* 172b, *Hasht Bihisht* 209b.

1b A king presides over a feasting scene.
2a A king rides with his entourage to visit prophets.

Published: Karatay, *Farsça*, no. 599.

*Khamsa*. London, British Library Add. 7751. Mashhad, dated 982/1574. ff. 246, 23.5 x 16.5 cm. Nasta'līq, 19 lines, 4 cols., 15.7 x 10.5 cm. 5 *'unwāns*. The 11 paintings were originally contemporary with the manuscript, but were heavily overpainted in the 18th century, while retaining much of their composition.

28b Two friends condemned to death ask to be executed before the other.
46a The virtuous woman plucks out her eyes as a final rejection to the king's advances.
58b Khusraw and Shīrīn meet by chance on the hunting ground.
71b Shīrīn visits Farhād on Mt. Bīsitūn.
94a Khusraw and Shīrīn are married.
96b Khusraw and Shīrīn make love.
121a Majnūn is taken to the bridal chamber.
167a Alexander entertains Kanīfū.
184a Alexander prepares for his sea voyage to the Western Isles.
211b Bahrām Gūr beholds four of the pavilions of the princesses (Black, Yellow, Green, and Red).
240a The king discovers the infidelity of one princess by using a talisman that laughs in the face of hypocrisy.

Published: Titley, *Miniatures from Persian Manuscripts*, no. 53.

*Khamsa*. Washington, D.C., Sackler Gallery of Art S1986.051. Iran, Qazwin. Completed Rabī' II 972/November 1564 (29a), 970/1562–63 (78a), 981/1573–74 (146b). ff. 198, 23.3 x 17.0 cm. Nasta'līq, 22 lines, 4 cols., text area 15.3 x 9.7 cm. 4 *'unwāns* (1b, 30b, 109b, 147b), 7 paintings attributed to Siyawush Beg or his circle.

41b Khusraw defeats Bahrām Chūbīna.
55a Disguised as a shepherd, Khusraw deceives Farhād with false news of Shīrīn's death.
70a Khusraw sends a ring to Shīrīn.
92a Majnūn is reluctantly joined in marriage to Nawfal's daughter.
134a Bahrām Gūr visits the princess of the Blue Pavilion.
161b The captive Kanīfū reveals her identity to Alexander.
187b Alexander crosses the sea.

Published: Lowry, Beach et al., *An Annotated and Illustrated Checklist*, no. 205; Lowry, *A Jeweler's Eye*, pl. 38 (55a).

*Khamsa*. Istanbul, Topkapi Saray Museum H. 866. Iran, ca. 1560–80. ff. 346, 28.9 x 17.4 cm. Nasta'līq, 18 lines, 3 cols., text area 18.6 x 10.6 cm. 5 *'unwāns*, 21 paintings. (The extremely fragile condition of this manuscript precluded a complete examination.)

1b–2a A prince watches the ecstatic dancing of sufis.
97a Khusraw rests on his way to Isfahan to meet Shakar.
102a Shīrīn visits Farhād and sees his sculptures.
127a Shīrīn is reconciled with Khusraw and joins him in listening to music.
134a Khusraw and Shīrīn are married.
160b Laylā and Majnūn fall in love at school.
178b Friends visit Majnūn in the wilderness.
186a Laylā weeps at the false news of Majnūn's death.

Published: Karatay, *Farsça*, no. 600.

*Kulliyyāt* (*Khamsa* and 3 other poems). St. Petersburg, National Library of Russia, inv. PNS 67. Iran, Shiraz, ca. 1570–80. Written by Shāh Muḥammad *al-Kātib*. ff. 421 (with *Khamsa* ff. 1–243), 39.8 x 27.0 cm. Nasta'līq, 18 lines, 4 cols., text area 23.2 x 13.5 cm. Illuminations 1b–2a, 47b, 99b, 133b, 182b, 300b, 364b. 24 paintings. Illuminated black leather binding.

28a Two friends are sentenced to death.
40b An old Sufi laments his lost youth.
62b Shīrīn holds a feast in honor of Khusraw.
69b Shīrīn visits Farhād on Mt. Bisitūn.
91a Khusraw discourses with scholars and poets.
113a Nawfal battles Laylā's tribe on behalf of Majnūn.
120a Friends visit Majnūn in the wilderness.
144a Bahrām Gūr visits the princess of the Black Pavilion.
148a Bahrām Gūr visits the princess of the Yellow Pavilion.
152b Bahrām Gūr visits the princess of the Green Pavilion.
156b Bahrām Gūr visits the princess of the Red Pavilion.
162b Bahrām Gūr visits the princess of the Blue Pavilion.
169b Bahrām Gūr visits the princess of the Sandalwood Pavilion.
174b Bahrām Gūr visits the princess of the White Pavilion.
196a Alexander engages in single combat with the Khāqān.
200b Revelry at Alexander's palace.
210b Alexander entertains Kanīfū.
255b, 272a, 284a (*Qirān al-Sa'dayn*).
320b Khiẓr tries on footwear (*Duwal Rānī Khiẓr Khān*).
332b Khiẓr Khān discusses the marriage contract.
345b Love scene.
394b *Nuh Sipihr*.

Published: Suleiman and Suleimanova, *Miniatures Illuminations*, pls. 61–83.

*Hasht Bihisht.* State Collection of Manuscripts of the Azerbaijan Academy of Sciences, Baku, inv. M161-38088. Iran, Khurasan school, dated Jumādā I 987/June–July 1579. 8 paintings.

Bahrām Gūr displays his hunting prowess before Dilārām.
Bahrām Gūr visits the princess of the Black Pavilion.
Bahrām Gūr visits the princess of the Yellow Pavilion. (24b.)
Bahrām Gūr visits the princess of the Green Pavilion.
Bahrām Gūr visits the princess of the Red Pavilion.
Bahrām Gūr visits the princess of the Blue Pavilion.
Bahrām Gūr visits the princess of the Sandalwood Pavilion.
Bahrām Gūr visits the princess of the White Pavilion.

Published: Suleiman and Suleimanova, *Miniatures Illuminations*, pl. 47.

*Khamsa.* Location unknown. Iran, probably Shiraz, ca. 1580. Copied by Hidayatullāh. ff. 483, 25.5 x 16.0 cm. Nasta'līq, 12 lines, 2 cols., additional column written diagonally. 16 paintings.

26b Bahrām Gūr visits the princess of the Black Pavilion.
39a Bahrām Gūr visits the princess of the Yellow Pavilion.
51b Bahrām Gūr visits the princess of the Green Pavilion.
62b Bahrām Gūr visits the princess of the Red Pavilion.
80a Bahrām Gūr visits the princess of the Blue Pavilion.
100b Bahrām Gūr visits the princess of the Sandalwood Pavilion.
116b Bahrām Gūr visits the princess of the White Pavilion.
160a Laylā and Majnūn fall in love at school.
179b Nawfal battles Laylā's tribe on behalf of Majnūn.
188a Majnūn is taken by his father to the shaykhs.
206b Majnūn befriends a dog that lived in Laylā's neighborhood.
271a Khusraw and Shīrīn meet on the hunting ground.
297a Khusraw and Shīrīn are entertained.
334a Khusraw visits Farhād on Mt. Bīsitūn.
395a Khusraw and Shīrīn make love.
440a Alexander is enthroned.

Published: Sotheby's, London, 22–23 October 1992, lot 598.

*Khamsa.* Keir Collection. Khurasan, probably Herat, dated 1581. ff. 205, 27.4 x 18.0 cm. Nasta'līq, 23 lines in 4 cols., text area 20.0 x 11.0 cm. *Maṯla' al-Anwār* completed on 23 Rabī' I 989/27 April 1581, *Shīrīn wa Khusraw* completed on 19 Rabī' II 989/23 May 1581, *Majnūn wa Laylā* completed on 1 Jumādā I/3 June 1581, *Ā'īnah-i Sikandarī* completed on 2 Ṣafar (year effaced), and *Hasht Bihisht* completed on 1 Ẕī'l Qa'da/27 November 1581. 3 *'unwāns* (1b *Maṯla' al-Anwār*, 40b *Shīrīn wa Khusraw*, and 88b *Majnūn wa Laylā*). 13 paintings, 8 of which are proper text illustrations.

1a A king enthroned in a garden pavilion. (Frontispiece.)
26a 'Alī kills an infidel who had spat upon him.
35b A youth offers a cup of wine to old Sufi in a garden.
39b Khusraw spies Shīrīn bathing. (Between poems.)
84b Shīrīn commits suicide on the corpse on the murdered Khusraw.
86b Sketch of an outdoor feast.
87b–88a A prince and his court are entertained outdoors.
102b Majnūn is forced to marry Nawfal's daughter.
108b Laylā visits Majnūn in the wilderness.
118b A prince and his attendant ride through a landscape.
129a Alexander lifts the Khāqān into the air.
137b The Rūmī champion Parīkaysh defeats the Chinese champion Tangū.
175b Bahrām Gūr demonstrates his hunting prowess.

Published: B. W. Robinson, "An Amīr Khusraw *Khamsa* of 1581," *Iran*, 35 (1997), 35–41.

*Khamsa.* London, British Library Or. 11326. Iran, Qazwin style, ca. 1580–90. ff. 185, 26.6 x 18.1 cm. Nasta'līq, 17 lines in 2 cols., 32 lines in an outer column written diagonally; text area 19.0 x 10.5 cm. 19 paintings. Many folios are out of order.

11b Majnūn befriends a dog that lived in Laylā's neighborhood.
12b Bahrām Gūr visits the princess of the Red Pavilion.
26a Khusraw and Shīrīn meet by chance on the hunting grounds.
33a Khusraw meets Farhād on Mt. Bīsitūn.
36a Shīrīn receives Farhād at her palace.
43a Farhād lies dead on Mt. Bīsitūn.
66a Laylā and Majnūn fall in love at school.
68a Majnūn's friend is horrified to find a crow pecking at Majnūn's eyes after the carnage of the battle of the clans.
74a Friends visit Majnūn in the wilderness.
82b Bahrām Gūr visits the princess of the Sandalwood Pavilion.
103a Alexander sets out for the land of Gōg and Magōg.
107b Alexander engages in an amorous dalliance with Kanīfū.
122a Alexander confers with Plato.
149a Bahrām Gūr slays a wild beast with his bow before Dilārām.
152a Bahrām Gūr sees the herd of deer mesmerized by Dilārām's music.
154a Bahrām Gūr visits the princess of the Black Pavilion.
163a Bahrām Gūr visits the princess of the Green Pavilion.
176b Kanīfū's identity is revealed to Alexander when her helmet is removed.
180a Bahrām Gūr visits the princess of the White Pavilion.

Published: Titley, "Miniature Paintings," figs. 55–58 (ff. 26a, 149a, 11b, 152a); Titley, *Miniatures from Persian Manuscripts*, no. 55.

*Khamsa.* Berlin, Staatsbibliothek Ms. Or. 1615 (Heinz nr. 157). Iran, Shiraz school, ca. 1590–1600. ff. 238, 32.0 x 19.0 cm. 5 *'unwāns* (1b, 46b, 101b, 135b, 191b), 17 paintings, which average 18.3 x 13.0 cm.

15b An old man questions a brash youth about his boastful talk.
32b A king out hunting accidentally kills a sleeping youth.
55b Khusraw and Shīrīn meet by chance on the hunting ground.
73b Khusraw visits Farhād on Mt. Bīsitūn.
80b Khusraw appears before Shīrīn's palace.
93a Khusraw and Shīrīn make love.
109b Laylā and Majnūn fall in love at school.
125a Laylā visits Majnūn in the wilderness.
154a Alexander defeats the King of Rūm.
198b Bahrām Gūr hunts gazelles with Dilārām.
202a Bahrām Gūr visits the princess of the Black Pavilion.
206b Bahrām Gūr visits the princess of the Yellow Pavilion.
210b Bahrām Gūr visits the princess of the Green Pavilion.
214a Bahrām Gūr visits the princess of the Red Pavilion.
219b Bahrām Gūr visits the princess of the Blue Pavilion.
226a Bahrām Gūr visits the princess of the Sandalwood Pavilion.
231a Bahrām Gūr visits the princess of the White Pavilion.

Published: *Deutsche-Iranische Kulturwoche* 1966, pls. V–VI; Stchoukine et al., *Illuminierte Islamischen Handschriften*, no. 27, 77–80, pl. 30 (32b, 55b); *Islamische Buchkunst aus 1000 Jahren*, 67 (15b, color).

*Khamsa.* Location unknown. Iran, dated Ẕī'l-Qa'da 1007/May 1599, and Ẕī'l-Qa'da,Ẕī'l-Ḥijja and Ṣafar 1008/1600. ff. 278 plus 7 flyleaves, 27.8 x 17.2 cm. Nasta'līq, 17 lines, 2 cols., text area 18.0 x 11.5 cm. Written by Mu'izz al-Dīn Ḥusayn Langarī. 5 illuminations (1b, 55b, 121b, 162b, 215b), 20 paintings on ff. 29a, 35a, 47b, 66b, 72a, 80a, 82a, 89b, 98a, 136a, 144a, 149b, 172b, 175a, 179a, 183a, 188a, 194b, 201a, 206b. Published: Christie's, London, 25 April 1995, lot 59. The catalogue reproduces only the following scene: Khusraw entertains Shakar.

*Khamsa* (only *Majnūn wa Laylā, Āʾīnah-i Sikandarī,* and *Hasht Bihisht*). Location unknown. India, Mughal, 1600. Written by Ḥusayn ibn Ḥaydar ibn Muḥammad Kashmīrī and dated Rajab 1008/ January–February 1600. ff. 146, 28.0 x 18.0 cm. Nastaʿlīq, 19 lines, 4 cols., text area 18.0 x 10.8 cm. 3 *ʿunwāns* (1b, 38b, 99b), 6 paintings.

| | |
|---|---|
| 15b | Nawfal battles Laylā's tribe on behalf of Majnūn. |
| 28a | Majnūn swoons at the sight of Laylā in the wilderness. |
| 88a | Alexander engages in an amorous dalliance with Kanīfū. |
| 107a | Bahrām Gūr hunts gazelles while Dilārām plays the lute. |
| 119a | Bahrām Gūr visits the princess of the Green Pavilion. |
| 127b | Bahrām Gūr visits the princess of the Blue Pavilion. |

Published: Bonhams, London, 24 April 1996, lot 481.

*Kulliyyāt* (including *Khamsa*). Baltimore, Walters Art Museum W. 623. Iran, early 17th century. (Dated the last day of Ramaẓān 1017/January 1609 on f. 64a; 22 Ẕīʾl-Ḥijja 1017/1609 on f. 111b.) ff. 269, 34.6 x 21.7 cm. Nastaʿlīq, 25 lines, 4 cols., text area 22.5 x 12 cm. Some folios are out of order. 5 *ʿunwāns*: 2b (*Maṭlaʿ al-Anwār*), 40b (*Majnūn wa Laylā*), 64b (*Āʾīnah-i Sikandarī*), 111b (*Hasht Bihisht*), 147b (*Shīrīn wa Khusraw*).

| | |
|---|---|
| 1b | Hunting scene. |
| 2a | Court scene. |
| 26a | ʿAlī kills an infidel who had spat in his face. |
| 28a | A king out hunting accidentally kills a youth and offers his own life or a platter of gold in recompense to the boy's mother. |
| 49a | Majnūn's father brings him to his family again. |
| 72a | The Khāqān of China receives a letter from Alexander demanding that he surrender. |
| 81b | Alexander searches for the Fountain of Life, which is made invisible by Khiẓr and Elias. |
| 89b | Alexander invents a mirror that, when mounted on a tower, shows everything within a radius of 60 *farsangs* and thus enables Alexander's men to attack marauding pirates. |
| 95b | While visiting Plato in his cave, Alexander asks the sage to come to court. |
| 108b | Alexander's army carries his casket back to Greece. |
| 118b | Bahrām Gūr recognizes Dilārām by the music with which she enchants the animals. |
| 129b | The story of the princess of the Red Pavilion: A prince enamored of the king's favorite and his companions befriend an old woman, who allows the prince to gain entry to the tower and ultimately abduct his beloved. |
| 139a | Bahrām Gūr visits the princess of the Sandalwood Pavilion. |
| 160b | Khusraw makes love to Shīrīn. |
| 169b | Khusraw discusses his dream with Buzurg Umīd. |
| 179b | Khusraw and Shīrīn are entertained at their wedding. |
| 188b | Buzurg Umīd tells Khusraw the story of a king's punishment of a rude messenger. |
| 193b–223a | *Qirān al-Saʿdayn.* |
| 212b | Sulṭān Muʿizz al-Dīn is reconciled with his father Nāṣir al-Dīn Bughrā Khān. |
| 223b–269a | *Nuh Sipihr.* |
| 237b | Shāh Jahān returns to his court in India. |
| 250b | Scenes from the wintry month of Day (December–January). |
| 259b | A school scene. |
| 263b | A court scene. |
| 268a | A court scene. |

*Khamsa.* Staatsbibliothek, Berlin Ms. Or. 1278. India, subimperial Mughal, ca. 1610–17.ff. 225, 29.4 x 18.5 cm. Nastaʿlīq, 21 lines, 4 cols., text area 16.2 x 10.8 cm. Allegedly written by Sulṭān ʿAlī at the end of the 15th century, and probably once contained paintings by the circle of Bihzād. Refurbished between 1610 and 1617, when it entered ʿAbd al-Raḥīm's library. The manuscript retains 7 of its original 21 paintings. Illuminations and decorated borders throughout. (A gap in the manuscript is indicated by consecutive folios separated by a slash.)

| | |
|---|---|
| 5b/6a | Illustration to the preface, probably a scene of dancing dervishes. Location unknown. |
| 36b/37a | An old Sufi approaches a youth in a garden. British Museum 1920-9-17 0259. |
| 43a | Amīr Khusraw presents the *Khamsa* to ʿAlāʾ al-Dīn Khaljī. |
| 65b/66a | The disguised Khusraw comes to Farhād on Mt. Bīsitūn. British Museum 1920-9-17 0267. |
| 70b/71a | Farhād dies out of love for Shīrīn. Location unknown. |
| 73b/74a | An old woman comes to Shīrīn as Khusraw and Shīrīn lie unconscious. Location unknown. |
| 95b | Presentation scene. |
| 100b/101a | Two *dīvs* are ordered to fill the sea with sand and the desert with water. Location unknown. |
| 116b/117a | Majnūn befriends a dog that lived near Laylā. Location unknown. |
| 127a | A hunter watches a jackal chase two rabbits. |
| 134b/135a | Bahrām Gūr displays his hunting prowess before Dilārām. British Museum 1920-9-17 0258. |
| 137b/138a | The story of the princess of the Black Pavilion: The three princes of Ceylon. Location uncertain, probably Islamic Museum, Teheran. |
| 147b | The story of the princess of the Yellow Pavilion: The foolish wife of the dishonest goldsmith is tricked into changing places with her imprisoned husband. (The folio is original folio no. 157, and properly belongs between ff. 142 and 143, but is now out of order.) |
| 146b/147a | The story of the princess of the Green Pavilion: The king whose body was occupied by his evil vizier during a demonstration of transmigration reoccupies his body and orders the execution of the vizier, who was tricked into assuming the body of a bird. Islamic Museum, Teheran. Published: L. Hájek, *Indian Miniatures of the Mogul School* (London, 1960), pl. 1. |
| 152b/153a | The story of the princess of the Red Pavilion: The king's favorite mistress is abducted by sea. Freer Gallery of Art 45.28. |
| 157a | The story of the princess of the Blue Pavilion: A youth from Rūm learns from a recluse that the beings who had enchanted him the previous night were fairies. |
| 165b/166a | The story of the princess of the White Pavilion. Exact subject unknown. Location unknown. |
| 166b | A shepherd fluting. (The folio is original folio no. 187, and belongs after modern folio 170, but is now out of order.) |
| 182b/183a | Alexander battles the Khāqān of China. Location unknown. |
| 193b/194a | Alexander orders his men to build a wall against the inhabitants of Gōg and Magōg. Dated 1019/1610–11. Private collection. Published: T. McInerney, *Indian Painting 1525–1825* (London, 1982), no. 9. |
| 225b | Three gazelles in a landscape. |

Published: T. Arnold and A. Grohmann, *The Islamic Book* (Paris, 1929), pls. 84–87; Stchoukine et al., *Illuminierte Islamischen Handschriften*, 163–64, Beach, *The Imperial Image*, no. 14, and figs. 25–26; J. Seyller, *Workshop and Patron in Mughal India. The Freer Rāmāyaṇa and Other Illustrated Manuscripts of ʿAbd al-Raḥīm* (Zürich, 1999), figs. 191–204, 218–19.

*Majnūn wa Laylā*. Hyderabad, Salar Jung Museum A./Nm 838. Completed Ṣafar 1030/December 1620. (Original foliation 115–146). ff. 31, 23.4 x 15.4 cm. Nasta'līq, 18 lines, 4 cols., text area 14.0 x 11.0 cm. 1 *'unwān*, 3 paintings. Published: Ashraf, *A Concise Descriptive Catalogue*, no. 1406.

| | |
|---|---|
| 16a | Three youths are seated in a garden. |
| 18b | A group of men and women in a garden. |
| 19b | Laylā holds the head of Majnūn, who is surrounded by animals. |

*Khamsa*. Location unknown. Iran, Isfahan, ca. 1620. ff. 220, 25.2 x 15.2 cm. Nasta'līq, 21 lines, 4 cols. 5 *'unwāns*, 13 paintings. Published: Christie's, London, 13 October 1998, lot 61.

*Khamsa*. Oxford, Bodleian Library Ms. Elliott 185. ff. 243, Nasta'līq, 19 lines, 4 cols. 5 *'unwāns*, 2 paintings. (1b–2a). Khusraw wa Shīrīn 2b, *Majnūn wa Laylā* 57b (Muḥarram 987/March 1579), *Ā'īnah-i Sikandarī* (Ẕī'l-Qa'da, no year), *Hasht Bihisht* 149b (5 Rabī' I 1043/9 September 1633), *Maṭla' al-Anwār* 197b (end Rabī' I 1063/end February 1653).

*Khamsa*. New York, Metropolitan Museum of Art 13.228.34. Bukhara, ca. 1660–70. ff. 246, 19.6 x 12.5 cm. Nasta'līq, 19 lines, 4 cols., text area 16.2 x 9.2 cm. 6 illuminations (1b–2a, 46b, 103b, 139b, 186b). 17 paintings, 7 of which are signed by Muḥammad Salīm, 1 by 'Awaz Muḥammad, and 2 by Lāchin.

| | |
|---|---|
| 4b | *Mi'rāj* of the Prophet. |
| 54a | Khusraw beholds a portrait of Shīrīn brought by Shāhpūr. |
| 68a | Shīrīn visits Farhād and sees his rock-cut sculptures. |
| 81a | Khusraw displays his skill at the hunt. |
| 94a | Khusraw and Shīrīn entertain each other at the palace. |
| 111a | Laylā and Majnūn fall in love at school. |
| 120a | Majnūn suffers from love before the elders. |
| 128a | Laylā visits Majnūn in the wilderness. |
| 134b | Laylā dies of the pain of separation from Majnūn. |
| 156a | Bahrām Gūr visits the princess of the Green Pavilion. |
| 159a | Bahrām Gūr visits the princess of the Red Pavilion. |
| 165a | Bahrām Gūr visits the princess of the Blue Pavilion. |
| 172a | Bahrām Gūr visits the princess of the Sandalwood Pavilion. |
| 177b | Bahrām Gūr visits the princess of the White Pavilion. |
| 200a | Alexander lassoes a Chinese warrior. |
| 206b | Alexander breaks the arm of the Khāqān of China. |
| 233b | Alexander confers with Khiẓr and Elias before undertaking a voyage to the Western Isles. |

Published: A. Jackson and A. Yohannan, *Catalogue of Persian Manuscripts in the Cochran Collection* (New York, 1914), no. 15.

*Khamsa*. Location unknown. Iran, Isfahan, dated 1085/1674–75. ff. 208, 31.0 x 18.5 cm. Nasta'līq, 23 lines, 4 cols., text area 22.8 x 12.5 cm. 5 *'unwāns*, 41 paintings, 6 of which are signed by Ṭālib. Published: Christie's, London, 10 October 2000, lot 75.

*Khamsa*. Paris, Bibliothèque Nationale Supp. persan 629. End of 17th/early 18th century. ff. 135, 37.0 x 25.0 cm. Nasta'līq. Text written both in text area and in the margins. 13 paintings.

| | |
|---|---|
| 10b | A Muslim pilgrim meets a brahman on the road. |
| 32a | Khusraw and Shīrīn meet by chance on the hunting ground. |
| 42a | Khusraw visits Farhād on Mt. Bīsitūn. |
| 49a | Khusraw is entertained by Bārbud outside Shīrīn's castle. |
| 60a | Solomon commands two *dīvs* in his presence. |
| 70b | Laylā visits Majnūn in the wilderness. |
| 85b | The goldsmith asan brings the golden elephant before the king. |
| 87b | The queen rejects the advances of the vizier who had assumed the form of the king. |
| 99b | A king sees a princess in a secret tryst with a black muleteer. |
| 110b | Alexander battles the Khāqān of China. |
| 117a | Alexander builds a wall against the inhabitants of Gōg and Magōg. |
| 124b | Alexander confers with Plato. |
| 129b | Alexander embarks upon a sea voyage to the Western Isles. |

*Majnūn wa Laylā*. Location unknown. India, dated 1099/1687–88. ff. 89, 15.8 x 10.2 cm. Nasta'līq, 13 lines, 2 cols., text area 10.8 x 5.1 cm. 39 paintings, a few of which are later additions. Published: Christie's, London, 10 October 1989, lot 260.

*Khamsa*. Princeton, Princeton University Library Hitti 14. Written 930/1524 at Herat. Eight paintings (four double-page compositions) attributed or ascribed to Turābī Bey Khurasānī inserted ca. 1920. The illustrations are pastiches of Safawid paintings and are unrelated to the text.

## UNILLUSTRATED COPIES

*Khamsa*. Tashkent, Abu Rayhan Biruni Institute of Oriental Studies of the Uzbek Academy of Sciences, inv. No. 2179. Dated 756/1355. Written by Ḥāfiz Shīrāzī and Aḥmad ibn Walī ibn 'Abdullāh Maḥmūd (the latter only *Maṭla' al-Anwār* and *Majnūn wa Laylā*). 29.5 x 19.8 cm. Published: Suleiman and Suleimanova, *Miniatures Illuminations*, pls. 87–88 (*shamsa* and colophon).

*Khamsa*. Madras, Kutub Khana Madarassa Mohammadi. Dated 830/1426. Published: *Amir Khusrau Memorial Volume*, 11 (reproduces only the 'unwān of Shīrīn wa Khusrau).

*Khamsa*. State Collection of Manuscripts of the Azerbaijan Academy of Sciences, inv. no. 2. Dated 1421. Written by Dā'ūdī.

*Khamsa*. Oxford, Bodleian Library Ms. Elliott 191. Dated 840/1436–37. ff. 240, 7 3/4 x 5 in. Small nasta'līq, 20 lines in 2 center-columns, and 38 lines in one margin-column. 3 illuminated frontispieces (2b, 83b, 177b), illuminated headings on the margin of 88b, 203b, 226b. Center cols. *Maṭla' al-Anwār* 2b, *Shīrīn wa Khusraw* 83b, *Majnūn wa Laylā* 177b; margin-column *Hasht Bihisht* 2b, *Ā'īnah-i Sikandarī*, and two smaller *maṣnawīs* 88b.

*Khamsa*. Oxford, Bodleian Library Ms. Elliott 188. Dated the end of Ṣafar 848/June 1444. ff. 240, 9 1/4 x 6 in. Nasta'līq, 19 lines, 4 cols. Written by Faẕlullāh bin Luṭfullāh al-Ḥāfiz *athdar* of Sabzwar. 5 *'unwāns*.

*Khamsa*. Oxford, Bodleian Library Ms. Elliott 189. Iran, Shiraz. Written by Maḥmūd Muḥammad Jama... at Shiraz. ff. 192, 9 5/8 x 6 7/8 in. Small Nasta'līq, 25 lines, 4 columns. Illuminated headings at the beginning of each *maṣnawī*. *Maṭla' al-Anwār* 2b, *Shīrīn wa Khusraw* 38b, *Majnūn wa Laylā* 82b (copied 866), *Kitāb-i Sikandarnāma* 110b (27 Jumādā I 867), *Hasht Bihisht* 156b (beginning of Rajab 867/March 1463). 4 paintings (1b–2a, 191b–192a). Listed: E. Sachau and E. Ethé, *Catalogue of the Persian, Turkish, Hindustani, and Pushtu Manuscripts in the Bodleian Library* (Oxford, 1889), I, no. 768.

*Khamsa.* Location unknown. Probably Herat, second half of 15th century. Approximately ff. 200, 23.4 x 16.0 cm. Nasta'līq, 21 lines, 4 cols. 1 *shamsa*, 4 *'unwāns*. Published: Sotheby's, London, 18 April 1983, lot 76.

*Khamsa.* London, British Library Or. 2949. Written by Aḥmad Masīḥī. One book was completed at the beginning of Sha'bān 895/June 1490; another was finished at the beginning of Ramaẓān 896/July 1491. *Ā'īnah-i Sikandarī* is not included in this volume. ff. 338, 19.8 x 10.7 cm. Naskhī, 19 lines, 2 cols., text area 15.0 x 6.5 cm. 4 *'unwāns* (1b, 73b, 183b, 250b), one of which is modern.

*Khamsa.* Tashkent, Abu Rayhan Biruni Institute, serial 1013/actual 191. Written by Maḥmūd, dated 905/1499–1500.

*Maṯla 'al-Anwār* and *Shīrīn wa Khusraw.* Istanbul, Topkapi Saray Museum Revan 1030. Written in 905/1499–1500. ff. 75, 28.5 x 20.5 cm. Nasta'līq, 19 lines, 4 cols. Published: Karatay, *Farsça*, no. 603.

*Khamsa.* London, British Library Add. 24983. Herat. Written by Muḥammad 'Alī ibn Darwish in 917/1511–12. ff. 136, 26.5 x 17.7 cm. Nasta'līq, 22 lines in 4 cols., 48 lines in an outer column written diagonally, total text area 17.6 x 11.3 cm. 5 *'unwāns*. Listed: *The Arts of Islam* (London, 1976), no. 586.

*Khamsa.* Iran, dated 925/1519. ff. 162, 31.7 x 19.0 cm., naskhī, 23 lines, 4 cols. 3 headpieces, and 5 *'unwāns*. Published: Sotheby's, London, 22 October 1993, lot 161.

*Khamsa.* Tashkent Akad., serial 1014/actual 2218. Written by Ḥusayn Pīr Ḥasan Shīrāzī in 940/1533–34.

*Khamsa.* Istanbul, Suleimaniya Esad Ef. 2574. Completed by Luṯfullāh ibn Ḥasan in 943/1536–37. ff. 234, 26.0 x 17.5 cm. Nasta'līq, 20 lines, 4 cols., text area 15.8 x 11.4 cm. 1 *sarlawḥ*, 4 *'unwāns*.

*Khamsa.* St. Petersburg, National Library of Russia PNS 249. Written by Muḥammad ibn 'Alā' al-Dīn Raẓā'ī between Rabī' II–Sha'bān 966/January–June 1559. ff. 241, 24.6 x 16.2 cm. 2 *shamsas*, 5 *'unwāns*.

*Khamsa.* Istanbul, Türk ve Islam Eserleri Müzesi 2060. Written by Khalīl ibn Darwish in Rajab 972/February–March 1565. ff. 230, 24.5 x 17.3 cm. Nasta'līq, 19 lines, 4 cols., text area 15.8 x 10.1 cm. Double-page frontispiece, 4 *'unwāns*.

*Khamsa* and *Qirān al-Sa'dayn.* St. Petersburg, National Library of Russia, Dorn 388. Written by Sulaymān ibn Rūḥāran al...20 Shawwāl 974/30 April 1567. ff. 317, 25.0 x 18.7 cm. Nasta'līq, 18 lines, 4 cols., text area 15.0 x 10.3 cm. (*Khamsa* text ff. 1–260). 5 *'unwāns*, original black leather binding with tooled medallion.

*Khamsa.* Patna, Khudabakhsh Library HL no. 297. Written by Muḥammad 'Alā' al-Dīn. *Maṯla' al-Anwār* dated the middle of Shawwāl 974/10–20 April 1567, 46b *Shīrīn wa Khusraw*, dated Ẕī'l-Ḥijja 974/June–July 1567, 98b *Majnūn wa Laylā*, dated Jumādā II 975/December 1567, 133b *Ā'īnah-i Sikandarī*, dated Ẕī'l-Qa'da 974/May–June 1567, 191b *Hasht Bihisht*, dated Ẕī'l-Ḥijja 974/June–July 1567. The last two books were written by Kamāl al-Dīn Ḥūsayn ibn Jalāl al-Dīn Maḥmūd. ff. 235, 25.1 x 15.7 cm. Nasta'līq, 21 lines. 1 double-page illumination (1b-2a), 4 *'unwāns*.

*Khamsa.* State Collection of Manuscripts of the Azerbaijan Academy of Sciences, inv. M 248-11543. Dated 1577.

*Khamsa.* Paris, Bibliothèque Nationale Supp. persan 1910. Second half of the 16th century. ff. 219, 16.3 x 11.0 cm. Naskhī, 20 lines, 4 cols., text area 12.1 x 8.2 cm. 5 *'unwāns*.

*Samaniya* (Collection) of Amīr Khusraw. Paris, Bibliothèque Nationale Supp. persan 627. Iran, Shiraz or Isfahan, ca. 1560. The manuscript bears an inspection note of Muḥammad Qulī Quṯb Shāh of Golkonda dated 28 Shawwāl 994/12 October 1585, a verse of Amīr Khusraw that he inscribed on 20 Ramaẓān 1023/24 October 1614, and three impressions of his seal. ff. 411, 28.6 x 18.0 cm. Nasta'līq, 19 lines, 4 cols., text area 17.7 x 10.2 cm. Double-page *sarlawḥ*, 6 *'unwāns*. The volume contains *Maṯla' al-Anwār* (2b), *Shīrīn wa Khusraw* (47b), *Majnūn wa Laylā* (102b), *Sikandarnāma* (137b), *Hasht Bihisht* (196b), *Duwal Rānī Khiẕr Khān* (241b), *Qirān al-Sa'dayn* (302b), and *Nuh Sipihr* (354b).

*Khamsa.* Calcutta, Asiatic Society, no. 44. 16th century. Slightly defective copy. 24.0 x 15.0 cm. Nasta'līq, 25 lines, 4 cols., text area 19.0 x 11.0 cm. 1 *shamsa* and 1 *sarlawḥ* remain in the manuscript. Listed: W. Ivanow, *Concise Descriptive Catalogue of the Persian Manuscripts in the Collection of the Asiatic Society of Bengal* (Calcutta, 1926), no. 558.

*Khamsa.* Location unknown. Iran, 16th century. ff. 177, 21.6 x 14.3 cm. Nasta'līq, 21 lines, 4 cols. 4 illuminations. Published: Sotheby's, London, 22 October 1993, lot 169.

*Khamsa* of Niẓāmī and Amīr Khusraw. London, Keir Collection. Iran, Mashhad, 1577. ff. 317, 28.3 x 17.5 cm. Nasta'līq, 20 lines, 4 cols. (Nizami), 48 lines in a diagonally written marginal column (Amīr Khusraw), text area 22.0 x 13.5 cm. Written by Khalīl ibn Darwish Muḥammad al-Jāmī between Ẕī'l-Qa'da 984/February 1577 and Rabī' I 985/July 1577. Four double-page paintings are unrelated to the text. Amīr Khusraw poems begin *Maṯla' al-Anwār* 3b, *Shīrīn wa Khusraw* 75a, *Majnūn wa Laylā* 161b, *Hasht Bihisht* 215b, *Ā'īnah-i Sikandarī* 269b.

*Khamsa.* St. Petersburg, National Library of Russia, Dorn 389. 16th century. ff. 211, 30.0 x 19.0 cm. 5 *'unwāns*.

*Khamsa.* Hyderabad, Salar Jung Museum A.Nm. 210. Late 16th century. ff. 226, 22.0 x 14.6 cm. Nasta'līq, 21 lines, 4 cols., text area 16.2 x 10.4 cm. 5 *'unwāns* (*Maṯla' al-Anwār* 1b, *Shīrīn wa Khusraw* 43b, *Majnūn wa Laylā* 96b, *Iskandarnāma* 129b, *Hasht Bihisht* 185b). Published: Ashraf, *A Concise Descriptive Catalogue*, no. 1399.

*Khamsa.* St. Petersburg, National Library of Russia, Dorn 390. Written by Khalīl ibn Darwish Muḥammad al-Jāmī in Muḥarram 991/January–February 1583. ff. 240, 29.1 x 17.5 cm. Nasta'līq, 19 lines, 4 cols., text area 18.7 x 10.5 cm. Double-page illumination, and 4 *'unwāns*.

*Khamsa.* Hyderabad, Salar Jung Museum A.Nm. 854. Muḥarram 1013/May 1604. ff. 100, 32.6 x 19.6 cm. Nasta'līq, 25 lines, 4 cols., text area 22.0 x 11.6 cm. 3 *'unwāns*. *Majnūn wa Laylā* 1b, *Shīrīn wa Khusraw* 29b, *Ā'īnah-i Sikandarī* 73b (defective at end), *Hasht Bihisht* 100b. Published: Ashraf, *A Concise Descriptive Catalogue*, no. 1401.

*Khamsa.* Paris, Bibliothèque Nationale Supp. persan 1329. Written by Ismā'īl al-Tūnī in Ẕī'l-Ḥijja 1016/March–April 1608. ff. 248, 26.5 x 16.3 cm. Nasta'līq, 19 lines, 4 cols., text area 18.5 x 11.6 cm. 5 *'unwāns*.

*Khamsa*. Paris, Bibliothèque Nationale Supp. persan 630. Written by Muḥammad, son of Mullā Mīr al-Ḥusaynī or Mīr *al-Kātib* 1607–10. ff. 231, 29.9 x 18.0 cm. Nasta'līq, 20 lines, 4 cols., text area 19.3 x 10.8 cm. *Maṭla' al-Anwār* is dated the middle 10 days of Ramaẓān 1015/10–19 January 1607; *Shīrīn wa Khusraw*, Rabī' II 1016/August 1607; *Majnūn wa Laylā*, 1017/1608–9; *Iskandarnāma*, 2 Rabī' I 1018/5 June 1609; and *Hasht Bihisht* 1018/1609–10. Incomplete decoration.

*Khamsa*. Hyderabad, Salar Jung Museum A.Nm. 561. Early 17th century. ff. 123, 24.2 x 17.7 cm. Nasta'līq, 21 lines, 4 cols., text area 17.0 x 11.0 cm. 2 *'unwāns*. *Ā'īnah-i Sikandarī* 1b, *Hasht Bihisht* 56a, *Maṭla' al-Anwār* 82a (defective at beginning). Published: Ashraf, *A Concise Descriptive Catalogue*, no. 1402.

*Khamsa*. New Delhi, National Museum inv. 6750. 17th century. Frontispiece 1b–2a. Published: Suleiman and Suleimanova, *Miniatures Illuminations*, pls. 28–29.

*Khamsa*. Location unknown. Iran, written by Shamsa al-Dīn Dihlawī (?) in 1045/1635–36. ff. 231, 29 x 18.5 cm. Nasta'līq, 19 lines, 4 cols., text area 19.1 x 12.4 cm. Double-page illumination, 4 *'unwāns*. Published: Christie's, London, 18 October 1994, lot 80.

*Khamsa*. Istanbul, Topkapi Saray Museum Revan 601. Written by Muḥammad in Ẕī'l-Qa'da 1061/October–November 1651. ff. 262, 28.5 x 16.5 cm. Nasta'līq, 17 lines, 4 cols. *Maṭla' al-Anwār* 1b, *Shīrīn wa Khusraw* 52b, *Majnūn wa Laylā* 113b, *Hasht Bihisht* 151b, *Ā'īnah-i Sikandarī* 199b. Published: Karatay, *Farsça*, no. 601.

Collected Works. Location unknown. Comprised of *Majnūn wa Laylā*, *Hasht Bihisht*, *Ā'īnah-i Sikandarī* , *Duwal Rānī Khiẓr Khān*, *Shīrīn wa Khusraw*, *Qirān al-Sa'dayn*. Written by ibn Muḥammad Mīrak *al-Kātib*, slightly defective. ff. 315, 21.4 x 13.5 cm. Nasta'līq, 20 lines, 4 cols. 6 *'unwāns*. Published: Sotheby's, London, 18 April 1983, lot 100.

*Khamsa*. Hyderabad, Salar Jung Museum A./Nm. 209. Late 17th century. ff. 288, 24.6 x 17.8 cm. Nasta'līq, 16 lines, 4 cols., text area 15.2 x 11.2 cm. 5 *'unwāns*. *Maṭla' al-Anwār* 1b, *Majnūn wa Laylā* 55b, *Shīrīn wa Khusraw* 96b, *Ā'īnah-i Sikandarī* 161b, *Hasht Bihisht* 234b. Published: Ashraf, *A Concise Descriptive Catalogue*, no. 1398.

*Khamsa*. Hyderabad, Salar Jung Museum A./Nm 839. Early 18th century. ff. 76, 25.4 x 15.4 cm. 21 lines, 4 cols., text area 18.6 x 10.2 cm. 1 *'unwān*. *Majnūn wa Laylā* 1b, *Maṭla' al-Anwār* 35a. Published: Ashraf, *A Concise Descriptive Catalogue*, no. 1403.

*Maṭla' al-Anwār*. Hyderabad, Salar Jung Museum A./Nm 860. Early 18th century. ff. 43, 28.2 x 17.4 cm. Nasta'līq, 21 lines, 4 cols., text area 20.6 x 11.0 cm. 1 *'unwān*. Published: Ashraf, *A Concise Descriptive Catalogue*, no. 1404.

*Khamsa*. Hyderabad, Salar Jung Museum A./Nm. 211. Late 18th century. Written by Ḥusayn ibn Ḥaydar in Shawwāl, with the year cut off. ff. 247, 24.8 x 16.4 cm. Nasta'līq, 19 lines, 4 cols., text area 18.2 x 11.0 cm. 5 *'unwāns*, spaces for paintings left blank. Published: Ashraf, *A Concise Descriptive Catalogue*, no. 1400.

*Maṭla 'al-Anwār*. Paris, Bibliothèque Nationale Supp. persan 632. Copied by Malik Hayat Beg ibn Shāh Malik, completed one Tuesday of Rabī' II 1097/26 February, 5, 12, 19, or 26 March 1686. ff. 116, 24.1 x 12.8 cm. Nasta'līq, 15 lines, 2 cols., unruled.

*Ā'īnah-i Sikandarī*. Hyderabad, Salar Jung Museum A./Nm 94/1. India. Written by Pīr Muḥammad ibn Maḥbūb on 16 Ẕī'l–Ḥijja, *julūs-i wala*, probably Bahādur Shāh I, i.e., 1118/10 March 1707. ff. 46, 26.4 x 18.2 cm. Nasta'līq, 24 lines, 4 cols. Published: Ashraf, *A Concise Descriptive Catalogue*, no. 1408.

*Khamsa*. St. Petersburg, National Library of Russia PNS 180. Completed in 1280–81/1863–65. ff. 287, 25.5 x 17.5 cm. 5 *'unwāns*.

*Maṭla 'al-Anwār*. Hyderabad, Salar Jung Museum A./Nm 961. Late 19th century. ff. 118, 20.2 x 13.6 cm. Nasta'līq, 15 lines, text area 14.4 x 7.8 cm. Published: Ashraf, *A Concise Descriptive Catalogue*, no. 1405.

*Khamsa*. Oxford, Bodleian Library Ms. Elliott 190. ff. 241, 9 3/4 x 6 1/4 in. Nasta'līq, 19 lines, 4 cols. Illuminated headpiece at the beginning of each *maṣnawī*, first two pages richly adorned, all headings in gold. *Maṭla' al-Anwār* 1b, *Shīrīn wa Khusraw* 49b, *Majnūn wa Laylā* 105b, *Hasht Bihisht* 141b, *Ā'īnah-i Sikandarī* 187b.

## DETACHED PAGES FROM UNIDENTIFIED MANUSCRIPTS

Majnūn is visited in the wilderness by two members of his family. Bibliothèque Nationale, Réserve du dép. des Estampes, Od. 41 In.-4, no. 39. Iran, Shiraz, ca. 1490. Published: Richard, *Splendeurs persanes*, no. 70.

Alexander returns home after his long journey. Bibliothèque Nationale, Réserve du dép. des Estampes, Od. 41 In.-4, no. 38. Iran, Shiraz, ca. 1490. Published: Richard, *Splendeurs persanes*, no. 70.

The story of the princess of the White Pavilion: The king who refrained from marrying from dread of being cuckolded receives four prospective queens. Bibliothèque Nationale, Réserve du dép. des Estampes, Od. 41 In.-4, no. 41. Iran, Shiraz, ca. 1490. Published: Richard, *Splendeurs persanes*, no. 70.

Laylā and Majnūn fall in love at school. Iran, Shiraz, ca. 1560. 19.7 x 13.9 cm. Israel Museum 572.69. (unillustrated)

Double-page frontispiece to a *Khamsa* manuscript. Iran, Shiraz, second half of 16th century. Folio 2.6 x 18.8 cm., text area 18.3 x 11.0 cm. Published: *Die islamischen miniaturen der Sammlung Preetorius* (Munich, 1982).

APPENDIX B

# The Tradition of Illustration of the *Khamsa* of Amīr Khusraw

*This appendix is a subject index to the illustrations of the* Khamsa *of Amīr Khusraw. It lists all the scenes ever illustrated in the* Khamsa *and documents their appearance in various illustrated copies of the text. The manuscripts are designated by an abbreviated form of their institutions and accession numbers and are listed in chronological order. The numbers in the far right column are those of the text point, which I have designated as the last line immediately preceding the break in the text column. The numbers are those of the page and line numbers of the critical edition of the five books of the* Khamsa, *which were published separately in Moscow from 1964 to 1978. For particulars of these books, see the publications listed under Amīr Khusraw Dihlavi in the bibliography.*

### ABBREVIATIONS

| | |
|---|---|
| BL | British Library, London |
| BN | Bibliothèque Nationale, Paris |
| Baku | State Collection of Manuscripts of the Azerbaijan Academy of Sciences, Baku |
| Berlin | Museum für Islamische Kunst, Berlin<br>Staatsbibliothek, Berlin |
| CBL | Chester Beatty Library, Dublin |
| Kansas City | Nelson-Atkins Museum of Art, Kansas City |
| Keir Collection | Keir Collection, London |
| MMA | Metropolitan Museum of Art, New York |
| National Museum | National Museum, New Delhi |
| Philadelphia | Philadelphia Museum of Art |
| Sackler | Arthur M. Sackler Gallery, Washington, D.C. |
| St. Petersburg | National Library of Russia, St. Petersburg |
| TSM | Topkapi Saray Museum, Istanbul |
| Tashkent | Abu Rayhan Biruni Institute, Tashkent |
| WAM | Walters Art Museum, Baltimore |

### FRONTISPIECE

| | |
|---|---|
| TSM R. 1021 | |
| TSM R. 1029 | |
| WAM W. 623 | |

### *MAṬLAʿ AL-ANWĀR*

#### *MIʿRĀJ*

| | |
|---|---|
| TSM H. 796 | |
| TSM H. 799 | 22:7 |
| BL Or. 11327 | 22:1 |
| BN anciens fonds 259 | 5:7 |
| TSM H. 798 | 25:11 |
| TSM H. 800 | 23:5 |
| St. Petersburg PNS 267 | 23:3 |
| BL Add. 22699 | frontis |
| MMA 13.228.34 | 21:7 |

#### DANCING DARVISHES

| | |
|---|---|
| CBL P. 163 | 36:4 |
| Berlin Or. 1278 (missing) | 36 |

#### COURT OF ʿALĀʾ AL-DĪN

| | |
|---|---|
| Baku M287-27109 | |
| Balkh (Sackler S1986.213) | 43:10 |

#### AUTHOR IN A GARDEN

| | |
|---|---|
| TSM H. 800 | 68:10 |

#### *MAQĀLA*

1. Moses describes the lesson of his vision of God

| | |
|---|---|
| Tashkent 3317 | |
| Sultanate (Boston) | 94:1 |

2. Learned man and the danger of the royal lamp

| | |
|---|---|
| Sultanate (San Diego) | 109:3 |

3. Old man reproaches a prattling youth

| | |
|---|---|
| TSM H. 800 | 124:6 |
| Berlin Or. 1615 | |

4. Muslim pilgrim sees a brahman's piety

| | |
|---|---|
| Tashkent 3317 | |
| Balkh (MMA 13.160.4) | 137:9 |
| **WAM W.624 (MMA.29) (fig. 4)** | **137:7** |
| BN supp. pers. 629 | 137:4 |

5. Khiẓr grants devotee a vision of God

| | |
|---|---|
| Sultanate (MMA) | 151:1 |
| TSM H. 795 | 150:4 |
| TSM H. 1008 | 150:4 |
| WAM W. 622 | 150:4 |

6. Shiblī questions the darvish

| | |
|---|---|
| Private collection | 163:4 |

7. Hermit refuses a position at court

| | |
|---|---|
| Kansas City 44-22 | 175:6 |
| TSM H. 795 | 175:3 |
| BN supp. pers. 631 | 176:2 |
| CBL P. 163 | 176:6 |
| Berlin Or. 187 | 175:5 |
| National Museum 52.81 | 175:6 |
| TSM H. 798 | 175:7 |
| BN anciens fonds 259 | 176:9 |
| TSM H. 800 | 176:4 |
| BN supp. pers. 1149 | 175:3 |
| Philadelphia | 175:4 |

8. Bathhouse worker is consumed with love for the king

| | |
|---|---|
| Baku M287-27109 | 188:2 |
| Berlin Or. 187 | 188:2 |
| TSM H. 799 | 188:4 |
| TSM H. 798 | 188:2 |
| St. Petersburg PNS 267 | 187:3 |
| **WAM W.624 (MMA.31) (fig. 5)** | **188:5** |

9. Traveler reproaches a thorn for its insincerity

| | |
|---|---|
| Unillustrated | |

10. Fratricide witnesses the loyalty of two friends

| | |
|---|---|
| CBL P. 163 | 213:9 |
| Baku M287-27109 | 212:8 |
| TSM H. 798 | 213:6 |
| BL Add. 7751 | 213:4 |
| St. Petersburg PNS 67 | 213:1 |
| **WAM W.624 (fig. 6)** | **213:9** |

11. Youths die of thirst in the desert

| | |
|---|---|
| Private collection | 224:3 |
| BN supp. pers. 631 | 225:2 |
| TSM H. 799 | 225:4 |
| BL Or. 11327 | 225:2 |
| Balkh (BM) | |
| WAM W.622 | 224:4 |

12. ʿAlī slays an infidel

| | |
|---|---|
| TSM H. 795 | 239:9 |
| Berlin Or. 187 | 239:3 |
| TSM H. 799 | 239:9 |
| BL Or. 11327 | 239:9 |
| Israel Museum | 239:9 |
| Keir Collection | 239:5 |
| WAM W.623 | 239:2 |

13. King accidentally kills a youth

| | |
|---|---|
| TSM H. 1008 | 253:5 |
| Baku M287-27109 | 252:2 |
| Berlin Or. 187 (26a) | 252:2 |
| Berlin Or. 187 (26b) | 252:11 |
| TSM H. 798 | 252:2 |
| WAM W.622 | 252:9 |
| Sackler S1986.056 | 251:7 |
| Berlin Or. 1615 | 252:1 |
| **WAM W.624(MMA.26) (fig. 7)** | **252:12** |
| WAM W.623 | 251:7 |

14. Dishonest milk seller

| | |
|---|---|
| National Museum 52.81 | 266:7 |
| Balkh (Worcester) | 266:4 |

15. Crow reveals an eye remedy

| | |
|---|---|
| Unillustrated | |

16. Jesus responds kindly to a taunter

| | |
|---|---|
| Tashkent 3317 | |

17. Old Sufi laments his lost youth

| | |
|---|---|
| Rampur 4101 | |
| CBL P. 163 | 303:8 |
| TSM H. 1008 | 303:9 |
| Berlin Or. 187 | 304:2 |
| TSM H. 799 | 304:10 |
| BN anciens fonds 259 | 303:9 |
| TSM H. 800 | 303:9 |
| St. Petersburg PNS 67 | 303:9 |
| Keir Collection | 303:8 |
| **WAM W.624 (fig. 8)** | **304:8** |
| Berlin Or. 1278 (BM) | 303:9 |

18. Saint who tried to stay awake during the Night of Power

| | |
|---|---|
| Sultanate (Aga Khan) | 316:6 |

19. Hunter traps two foxes

| | |
|---|---|
| TSM H. 1008 | 327:6 |
| Berlin Or. 187 | 327:6 |

20. Virtuous woman placates the king by plucking out her eyes

| | |
|---|---|
| Sultanate (Aga Khan) | 343:9 |
| Kansas City 44-22 | 343:4 |
| TSM H. 795 | 342:1 |
| Berlin Or. 187 | 343:3 |
| Philadelphia | 343:1 |
| BL Add. 7751 | 342:2 |
| **WAM W.624 (fig. 9)** | **343:9** |

## PRESENTATION TO SULṬĀN ʿALĀʾ AL-DĪN

Berlin Or. 1278

## *SHĪRĪN WA KHUSRAW*

## *MIʿRĀJ*

| | |
|---|---|
| TSM H. 800 | 9:1 |
| Sackler S1986.056 | |

## COURT OF ʿALĀʾ AL-DĪN

| | |
|---|---|
| Sultanate (Chicago) | 17:12 |

### KHUSRAW SEES A PAINTING OF SHĪRĪN

| | |
|---|---|
| Tashkent 3317 | |
| TSM H. 796 | |
| CBL P. 124 | 53:1 |
| CBL P. 124 | 55:11 |
| Private collection | 56:1 |
| TSM H. 795 | 57:1 |
| BL Or. 11327 | 55:11 |
| MMA 13.228.34 | 55:10 |

### KHUSRAW'S LETTER TO SHĪRĪN

| | |
|---|---|
| Tashkent 3317 | |

### KHUSRAW AND SHĪRĪN MEET ON HUNTING GROUNDS

| | |
|---|---|
| CBL P. 124 | 66:4 |
| TSM H. 898 | 63:10 |
| Kansas City 44-22 | 60:5 |
| TSM H. 799 | 64:4 |
| TSM H. 798 | 63:12 |
| TSM H. 800 | 60:8 |
| WAM W.622 | 60:5 |
| BN supp. pers. 1149 | 60:4 |
| Israel Museum | 60:5 |
| Sackler S1986.056 | 60:5 |
| BL Add. 7751 | 64:7 |
| Sotheby's 23 Oct. 1992 | 60:2 |
| BL Or. 11326 | 63:12 |
| Berlin Or. 1615 | 65:7 |
| BN supp. pers. 629 | 60:3 |

### KHUSRAW WITH SHĪRĪN AND MAHĪN BĀNŪ

| | |
|---|---|
| CBL P. 163 | 66:9 |
| BL Or. 11327 | 67:2 |

### SHĪRĪN ENTERTAINS KHUSRAW

| | |
|---|---|
| TSM H. 798 | 68:4 |
| TSM H. 800 | 70:9 |
| Philadelphia | 70:6 |
| **WAM W.624 (fig. 11)** | **67:3** |

### KHUSRAW DEFEATS BAHRĀM CHŪBĪNA

| | |
|---|---|
| CBL P. 124 | 82:1 |
| CBL P. 124 | 83:6 |
| TSM H. 795 | 82:9 |
| TSM H. 799 | 83:7 |
| Sackler S1986.051 | 81:9 |

### KHUSRAW AND MARYAM

| | |
|---|---|
| TSM H. 800 | 83:2 |

### KHUSRAW RECOVERS A WINDBLOWN TREASURE

| | |
|---|---|
| Balkh (Louvre) | 89:8 |

### KHUSRAW AT SHĪRĪN'S PALACE

| | |
|---|---|
| Baku M287-27109 | |

### KHUSRAW AND SHĪRĪN MEET OUTSIDE THE CITY

| | |
|---|---|
| TSM R. 1021 | 98:7 |
| St. Petersburg PNS 67 | 101:2 |

### KHUSRAW AND SHĪRĪN PRESIDE OVER THE WEDDING OF YOUTHS

| | |
|---|---|
| CBL P. 124 | 101:8 |
| Baku M287-27109 | 101:2 |
| BL Or. 11327 | 101:3 |
| **WAM W.624 (fig. 12)** | **113:10** |

### KHUSRAW ENTERTAINS SHAKAR

| | |
|---|---|
| TSM H. 796 | 132:12 |
| CBL P. 124 | 133:7 |
| CBL P. 253-Sotheby | |
| TSM H. 898 | 133:2 |
| TSM H. 1008 | 133:7 |
| Baku M287-27109 | 133:2 |
| TSM H. 866 | 134:5 |
| Christie's 25 April 1995 | 139:6 |

### KHUSRAW AND SHAKAR MAKE LOVE

| | |
|---|---|
| Sultanate (BM) | 142:1 |
| BL Or. 11327 | 142:5 |

### FARHĀD VISITS SHĪRĪN AT COURT

| | |
|---|---|
| CBL P. 124 | 146:9 |
| Sultanate (Christie's 23 April 1996) | 146:9 |
| BL Or. 11327 | 148:5 |
| Balkh (Louvre AO 7104) | 147:12 |
| St. Petersburg PNS 67 | 148:3 |
| BL Or. 11326 | 148:7 |

### SHĪRĪN SEES FARHĀD'S SCULPTURES

| | |
|---|---|
| Kansas City 44-22 | 147:5 |
| TSM H. 795 | 153:6 |
| BN supp. pers. 631 | 153:8 |
| Baku M287-27109 | 153:9 |
| TSM H. 798 | 144:6 |
| BL Add. 7751 | 144:3 |
| TSM H. 866 | 154:3 |
| **WAM W.624 (fig. 13)** | **147:4** |
| MMA 13.228.34 | 144:8 |

### FARHĀD AND ANIMALS

| | |
|---|---|
| CBL P. 253-Sotheby | 156 |

### BUZURG UMĪD EXPLAINS KHUSRAW'S DREAM

| | |
|---|---|
| WAM W.623 | 173:10 |

### FARHĀD RECEIVES SHĪRĪN'S LETTER

| | |
|---|---|
| Tashkent 3317 | 180 |

### KHUSRAW VISITS FARHĀD ON MT. BĪSITŪN

| | |
|---|---|
| Tashkent 3317 | 185:9 |
| CBL P. 124 | 187:8 |
| Berlin Or. 187 | 185:11 |
| TSM H. 799 | 185:6 |
| BL Or. 11327 | 186:2 |
| TSM H. 798 | 185:7 |
| Israel Museum | 185:5 |
| Sackler S1986.051 | 185:9 |
| BL Or. 11326 | 185:8 |
| Berlin Or. 1615 | 187:5 |
| Berlin Or. 1278 (BM) | 153:9 |
| BN supp. pers. 629 | 187:1 |

### FARHĀD HEARS FALSE NEWS OF SHĪRĪN'SDEATH

| | |
|---|---|
| CBL P. 124 | 196:3 |
| National Museum 52.81 | 196:3 |
| **WAM W.624 (fig. 14)** | **198:1** |

### FARHĀD DIES ON MT. BĪSITŪN

| | |
|---|---|
| CBL P. 163 | 196:10 |
| Baku M287-27109 | 197:12 |
| BL Or. 11326 | 196:8 |
| Berlin Or. 1278 (missing) | 197:1 |

### MĀH SĀMĀN POISONS SHAKAR

| | |
|---|---|
| Tashent 3317 | 208:11 |
| CBL P. 124 | 209:12 |
| Sultanate (Sackler S1986.124) | 207:8 |

### MĀH SĀMĀN FINDS KHUSRAW AND SHĪRĪN UNCONSCIOUS

| | |
|---|---|
| Berlin Or. 1278 (missing) | 210-213 |

### KHUSRAW DISPLAYS HIS HUNTING SKILL

| | |
|---|---|
| MMA 13.228.34 | 226:11 |

### KHUSRAW RESTS AFTER HUNT ON VOYAGE TO SHĪRĪN'S CASTLE

| | |
|---|---|
| BN supp. pers. 1149 | 227:8 |

### KHUSRAW LAMENTS HIS LONELINESS

| | |
|---|---|
| CBL P. 124 | 229:3 |

### KHUSRAW APPEARS BEFORE SHĪRĪN'S CASTLE

| | |
|---|---|
| CBL P. 124 | 235:11 |
| Sultanate (Priv. coll.) | 232:8 |
| Rampur 4101 | 232:7 |
| Berlin Or. 187 | 233:4 |
| TSM H. 797 | 226:10 |
| Balkh (MMA) | 264:10 |
| St. Petersburg PNS 267 | 232:9 |
| Philadelphia | 232:6 |
| Berlin Or. 1615 | 230:5 |

### KHUSRAW AND SHĪRĪN LISTEN TO MUSIC

| | |
|---|---|
| Tashkent 3317 | |
| CBL P. 124 | 270:12 |
| TSM H. 795 | 265:1 |
| CBL P. 163 | 265:11 |
| Berlin Or. 187 | 264:10 |
| TSM H. 799 | 265:11 |
| BN supp. pers. 1149 | 264:11 |
| BL Add. 22699 | frontis |
| TSM H. 866 | 264:13 |
| WAM W.623 | 265:2 |
| BN supp. pers. 629 | 265:9 |

### SHĪRĪN RECEIVES A RING FROM KHUSRAW

| | |
|---|---|
| Berlin Or. 187 | 289:11 |
| **WAM W.624 (fig. 15)** | **289:10** |

### PRIEST SETS THE MARRIAGE PORTION

| | |
|---|---|
| Sultanate (FGA 59.2) | 293:5 |

### WEDDING OF KHUSRAW AND SHĪRĪN

| | |
|---|---|
| CBL P. 124 | 294:7 |
| TSM H. 795 | 295:10 |
| Berlin Or. 187 | 294:11 |
| National Museum 52.81 | 294:9 |
| TSM H. 801 | 295:10 |
| TSM H. 800 | 295:6 |
| BN supp. pers. 1149 | 294:3 |
| BL Add. 7751 | 293:11 |
| Sackler S1986.051 | 295:5 |
| TSM H. 866 | 295:12 |

### KHUSRAW AND SHĪRĪN MAKE LOVE

| | |
|---|---|
| Tashkent 3317 | |
| BN supp. pers. 631 | 306:11 |
| Baku M287-27109 | |
| Berlin Or. 187 | 306:8 |
| TSM H. 801 | 307:7 |
| TSM H. 799 | 306:11 |
| BL Or. 11327 | 306:7 |
| TSM H. 797 | 307:7 |
| Israel Museum | 307:4 |
| BL Add. 7751 | 306:12 |
| St. Petersburg PNS 67 | 307:1 |
| Berlin Or. 1615 | 307:9 |
| WAM W.623 | |

### KHUSRAW AND SHĪRĪN ENTERTAIN EACH OTHER

| | |
|---|---|
| MMA 13.228.34 | 308:10 |

### KHUSRAW AND BUZURG UMĪD

| | |
|---|---|
| Sultanate (Christie's 7 July 1976) | 310:11 |
| TSM H. 1008 | 310:3 |

### BUZURG UMĪD RELATES STORY OF A MESSENGER BOUND TO A TREE FELLED BY THE WIND

| | |
|---|---|
| Sultanate (McGill) | 334:8 |
| WAM W.623 | 337:1 |

### KHUSRAW IS FETTERED AT SHĪRŪYA'S ORDER

| | |
|---|---|
| CBL P. 124 | 347:3 |

### SHĪRŪYA ASCENDS THE THRONE

| | |
|---|---|
| Private collection | 347:2 |
| Kansas City 44-22 | 347:1 |

### DEATH OF KHUSRAW

| | |
|---|---|
| Tashkent 3317 | 349:2 |
| Berlin Or. 187 | 349:6 |
| National Museum 52.81 | 349:6 |

### SHĪRĪN COMMITS SUICIDE ON KHUSRAW'S CORPSE

| | |
|---|---|
| CBL P. 124 | 350:4 |
| TSM H. 799 | 350:3 |
| Keir Collection | 350:4 |

## *MAJNŪN WA LAYLĀ*

### BANQUETING PRINCE

| | |
|---|---|
| BL Add. 22699 | frontis |

### SOLOMON AND TWO *DĪVS*

| | |
|---|---|
| Sultanate (Virginia) | 44:2 |
| **WAM W.624 (fig. 16)** | **44:2** |
| Berlin Or. 1278 (missing) | 45-48 |
| BN supp. pers. 629 | 43:1 |

### KHUSRAW'S ADVICE TO HIS SON KHIẒR

| | |
|---|---|
| St. Petersburg Dorn 394 | 48:3 |

### CELEBRATION AT THE BIRTH OF MAJNŪN

| | |
|---|---|
| CBL P. 163 | 71:8 |

### LAYLĀ AND MAJNŪN FALL IN LOVE AT SCHOOL

| | |
|---|---|
| Tashkent 3317 | |
| CBL P. 124 | 77:3 |
| CBL P. 253-Sotheby | 73:8 |
| TSM R. 1021 | 75:1 |
| Baku M287-27109 | 74:2 |
| St. Petersburg Dorn 395 | 79:10 |
| Berlin Or. 187 | 75:10 |
| National Museum 52.81 | 77:5 |
| TSM H. 801 | 75:9 |
| TSM H. 799 | 73:8 |
| BL Or. 11327 | 73:10 |
| St. Petersburg Dorn 394 | 76:3 |
| TSM H. 798 | 74:1 |
| TSM H. 800 | 73:10 |
| WAM W.622 | 73:4 |
| Sackler S1986.056 | 73:8 |
| Philadelphia | 77:5 |
| TSM H. 866 | 75:10 |
| BL Or. 11326 | 73:10 |
| Berlin Or. 1615 | 79:1 |
| **WAM W.624 (fig. 17)** | **76:5** |
| MMA 13.228.34 | 73:4 |

### MAJNŪN IS STONED BY CHILDREN

| | |
|---|---|
| BL Or. 11327 | 91:3 |

### MAJNŪN IS VISITED BY HIS FATHER

| | |
|---|---|
| Tashkent 3317 | |
| CBL P. 124 | 95:4 |
| TSM H. 795 | 94:3 |
| **WAM W.624 (fig. 18)** | **94:3** |
| WAM W.623 | 98:9 |

### MAJNŪN'S FATHER ASKS FOR LAYLĀ'S HAND

| | |
|---|---|
| CBL P. 124 | 110:1 |

### BATTLE OF THE CLANS

| | |
|---|---|
| TSM H. 796 | |
| CBL P. 124 | 123:4 |
| CBL P. 253-Sotheby | 119:1 |
| TSM H. 898 | 119:6 |
| Sultanate (Worcester) | 120:4 |
| CBL P. 163 | 118:6 |
| Baku M287-27109 | |
| Berlin Or. 187 | 118:5 |
| TSM H. 801 | 118:10 |
| TSM H. 799 | 118:2 |
| TSM H. 800 | 118:9 |
| Keir Collection (ML) | 118:2 |
| TSM H. 797 | 117:9 |
| WAM W.622 | 117:9 |
| St. Petersburg PNS 267 | 118:1 |
| Sackler S1986.056 | 119:7 |
| St. Petersburg PNS 67 | 118:2 |
| Bonhams 24 April 1996 | 119:3 |

### A CROW PECKS AT MAJNŪN'S EYES

| | |
|---|---|
| CBL P. 253-Sotheby | 123:5 |
| Private collection | 123:7 |
| TSM H. 798 | 123:4 |
| BL Or. 11326 | 123:5 |

### LAYLĀ HEARS NEWS OF MAJNŪN

| | |
|---|---|
| CBL P. 253-Sotheby | 126:8 |

### MAJNŪN BROUGHT BY HIS FATHER TO HIS FAMILY

| | |
|---|---|
| MMA 13.228.34 | 138:7 |

### MAJNŪN IS FORCED TO MARRY NAWFAL'S DAUGHTER

| | |
|---|---|
| CBL P. 124 | 139:4 |
| BL Add. 7751 | 138:10 |
| Sackler S1986.051 | 138:9 |
| Keir Collection | 140:10 |

### MAJNŪN IS VISITED BY FRIENDS IN DESERT

| | |
|---|---|
| Tashkent 3317 | |
| CBL P. 253-Sotheby | 169:3 |
| Kansas City 44-22 | 169:2 |
| Baku M287-27109 | |
| St. Petersburg Dorn 395 | 172:11 |
| Berlin Or. 187 | 169:1 |
| BL Or. 11327 | 169:3 |
| TSM H. 798 | 167:8 |
| TSM H. 800 | 169:3 |
| BN supp. per. 1149 | 169:1 |
| TSM H. 866 | 169:10 |
| St. Petersburg PNS 67 | 169:3 |
| BL Or. 11326 | 169:1 |

### MAJNŪN HEARS A NIGHTINGALE

| | |
|---|---|
| CBL P. 124 | 174:11 |
| Rampur 4101 | 168:3 |

### MAJNŪN BEFRIENDS A DOG

| | |
|---|---|
| TSM H. 796 | 183:6 |
| CBL P. 124 | 182:10 |
| Berlin Or. 187 | 183:1 |
| TSM H. 799 | 183:2 |
| St. Petersburg Dorn 394 | 182:8 |
| TSM H. 797 | 182:6 |
| Balkh (MMA 13.160.3) | 182:3 |
| BL Or. 11326 | 182:6 |
| **WAM W.624 (fig. 20)** | **191:8** |
| Berlin Or. 1278 (missing) | 182:10 |

### LAYLĀ VISITS MAJNŪN IN THE WILDERNESS

| | |
|---|---|
| Tashkent 3317 | |
| CBL P. 124 | 198:6 |
| CBL P. 253-Sotheby | 198:7 |
| Private collection | 198:7 |
| TSM H. 898 | 198:1 |
| TSM H. 795 | 198:6 |
| CBL P. 163 | 201:2 |
| Baku M287-27109 | 198:5 |
| Berlin Or. 187 | 200:5 |
| TSM H. 801 | 198:6 |
| TSM H. 799 | 199:2 |
| St. Petersburg Dorn 394 | 198:7 |
| TSM H. 798 | 198:6 |
| TSM H. 800 | 199:1 |
| BN supp. pers. 1149 | 198:1 · |
| Philadelphia | 198:5 |
| Keir Collection | 201:5 |
| **WAM W.624 (fig. 21)** | **204:4** |
| Berlin Or. 1615 | 198:6 |
| Bonhams 24 April 1996 | |
| MMA 13.228.34 | 203:11 |
| BN supp. per. 629 | 198:2 |

### MAJNŪN'S FRIEND BRINGS FALSE NEWS OF MAJNŪN'S DEATH TO LAYLĀ

| | |
|---|---|
| CBL P. 124 | 234:6 |
| Kansas City 44-22 | 232:7 |
| Berlin Or. 187 | 234:2 |
| St. Petersburg Dorn 394 | 231:7 |
| TSM H. 798 | 236:1 |
| Keir Collection (ML) | 231:11 |
| Israel Museum | 232:1 |
| TSM H. 866 | 232:1 |

### MAJNŪN WITNESS THE FUNERAL OF LAYLĀ

| | |
|---|---|
| Baku M287-27109 | |
| Berlin Or. 187 | 251:8 |
| MMA 13.228.34 | 256:2 |

### MAJNŪN EMBRACES LAYLĀ'S TOMB

| | |
|---|---|
| CBL P. 124 | 257:1 |
| Sultanate (FGA 59.3) | 256:1 |

## *Ā'ĪNAH-I SIKANDARĪ*

### ALEXANDER LASSOES AN OPPONENT

| | |
|---|---|
| **WAM W.624 (fig.22)** | **45:17** |

### THE KHĀQĀN RECEIVES ALEXANDER'S LETTER DEMANDING SURRENDER

| | |
|---|---|
| WAM W.623 | 49:11 |

### ALEXANDER RECEIVES THE KHĀQĀN'S AMBASSADORS

| | |
|---|---|
| CBL P. 124 | 54:15 |
| TSM H. 798 | 55:7 |

### RŪMĪ CHAMPION PARĪKAYSH DEFEATS THE CHINESE CHAMPION TANGŪ

| | |
|---|---|
| CBL P. 253-Sotheby | 66:9 |
| Rampur 4101 | |
| TSM H. 795 | 67:5 |
| Berlin Or. 187 | 67:4 |
| BN supp. pers. 1149 | 65:4 |
| Keir Collection | 64:13 |

### ALEXANDER BATTLES THE KHĀQĀN

| | |
|---|---|
| Tashkent 3317 | |
| Berlin I. 4628 | 70:13 |
| TSM R. 1021 | 68:4(?) |
| BL Or. 11327 | 65:3 |
| TSM H. 797 | 62:10 |
| BL Add. 22699 | frontis |
| St. Petersburg PNS 67 | 68:5 |
| TSM H. 1008 | 71:6 |
| Berlin Or. 1278 (missing) | 63:11 |
| MMA 13.228.34 | 68:2 |
| BN supp. pers. 629 | 66:3 |

**ALEXANDER DEFEATS KANĪFŪ**

| | |
|---|---|
| CBL P. 253-Sotheby | |
| Private collection | 79:10 |
| Berlin Or. 187 | 82:4 |
| TSM H. 798 | 78:8 |
| TSM H. 800 | 80:7 |
| TSM H. 801 | 79:9 |
| WAM W.622 | 79:10 |

**ALEXANDER DISCOVERS KANĪFŪ'S IDENTITY**

| | |
|---|---|
| Sackler S1986.051 | 84:5 |
| BL Or. 11326 | 83:10 |
| **WAM W.624 (fig. 23)** | **83:7** |

**ALEXANDER ENTERTAINS KANĪFŪ**

| | |
|---|---|
| Tashkent 3317 | |
| CBL P. 124 | 88:8 |
| CBL P. 253-Sotheby | |
| Rampur 4101 | |
| St. Petersburg PNS 67 | 88:3 |

**ALEXANDER LIFTS THE KHĀQĀN INTO THE AIR**

| | |
|---|---|
| CBL P. 124 | 97:7 |
| CBL P. 253-Sotheby | |
| TSM H. 898 | 97:7 |
| TSM R. 1021 | 97:6 |
| TSM H. 1008 | 97:5 |
| Baku M287-27109 | 97:5 |
| Berlin Or. 187 | 97:6 |
| TSM H. 801 | 97:5 |
| TSM H. 799 | 97:6 |
| Sackler S1986.056 | 97:2 |
| Keir Collection | 97:12 |
| Berlin Or. 1615 | 97:5 |
| MMA 13.228.34 | 97:6 |

**THE KHĀQĀN SUBMITS TO ALEXANDER**

| | |
|---|---|
| Tashkent 3317 | 103 |
| **WAM W.624 (fig. 24)** | **104:2** |

**ALEXANDER SEARCHES FOR FOUNTAIN OF LIFE**

| | |
|---|---|
| WAM W.623 | 112:11 |

**ALEXANDER ENCOURAGES HIS MEN**

| | |
|---|---|
| Tashkent 3317 | 116:8 |

**ALEXANDER SETS OUT FOR THE LAND OF GŌG AND MAGŌG**

| | |
|---|---|
| BL Or. 11326 | 116:14 |

**BATTLE AGAINST BARBARIANS OF GŌG AND MAGŌG**

| | |
|---|---|
| Tashkent 3317 | |
| Private collection | 121:16 |
| Berlin Or. 187 | 122:14 |
| TSM H. 801 | 121:14 |
| TSM H. 798 | 121:10 |
| TSM H. 800 | 121:15 |

**INHABITANTS OF GŌG ARE BROUGHT CAPTIVE BEFORE ALEXANDER**

| | |
|---|---|
| CBL P. 124 | 124:9 |
| National Museum 52.81 | 125:11 |
| BL Or. 11327 | 121:9 |
| Sackler S1986.056 | 124:7 |

**ALEXANDER ERECTS A WALL AGAINST THE INHABITANTS OF GŌG AND MAGŌG**

| | |
|---|---|
| TSM H. 796 | |
| CBL P. 253-Sotheby | 127:9 |
| Berlin Or. 1278 | 129:4 |
| BN supp. pers. 629 | 128:14 |

**GUARDS ARE POSTED ON THE WALL**

| | |
|---|---|
| CBL P. 124 | 130:2 |

**ALEXANDER IN DALLIANCE WITH KANĪFŪ**

| | |
|---|---|
| Tashkent 3317 | |
| Rampur 4101 | 139:10 |
| Baku M287-27109 | 139 |
| TSM H. 801 | 139:12 |
| TSM H. 799 | 147:5 |
| BL Or. 11327 | 139:2 |
| TSM H. 798 | 137:13 |
| WAM W.622 | 139:12 |
| BN supp. pers. 1149 | 138:6 |
| Sackler S1986.056 | 146:7 |
| Philadelphia | 138:13 |
| BL Add. 7751 | 139:12 |
| St. Petersburg PNS 67 | 138:7 |
| BL Or. 11326 | |
| Bonhams 24 April 1996 | 137:12 |

**BOILING OF ARTIFICIAL RICE**

| | |
|---|---|
| Sultanate (FGA 59.4) | 153:4 |

**ALEXANDER DISCUSSES THE INVENTION OF SCIENTIFIC INSTRUMENTS WITH THE CHINESE**

| | |
|---|---|
| Tashkent 3317 | 159 |
| BL Or. 11327 | 159:15 |

**ALEXANDER BEHOLDS CHINESE PAINTERS**

| | |
|---|---|
| National Museum 52.81 | 161:1 |

**ALEXANDER MOUNTS HIS MIRROR**

| | |
|---|---|
| WAM W.623 | 166:8 |
| **WAM W.624 (MMA.32) (fig. 25)** | **169:1** |

**A DOG LOSES ITS PREY**

| | |
|---|---|
| TSM H. 1008 | 171:4 |

**ALEXANDER DENOUNCES THE ZOROASTRIANS**

| | |
|---|---|
| BL Or. 11327 | 172:11 |

ALEXANDER DROWNS THE GREEKS

**WAM W.624 (fig. 26)** **191:9**

ALEXANDER VISITS PLATO

| | |
|---|---|
| Tashkent 3317 | |
| CBL P. 124 | 206:2 |
| CBL P. 253-Sotheby | |
| Baku M287-27109 | |
| TSM H. 801 | 204:5 |
| TSM H. 799 | 205:4 |
| BL Or. 11327 | 205:11 |
| BL Or. 11326 | 206:5 |
| **WAM W.624 (MMA.30) (fig. 27)** | **214:6** |
| WAM W.623 | 206:2 |
| BN supp. pers. 629 | 203:14 |

ALEXANDER DISCUSSES HIS SEA JOURNEY

| | |
|---|---|
| Tashkent 3317 | 238 |
| WAM W.622 | 238:8 |
| MMA 13.228.34 | 247:5 |

ALEXANDER'S SEA JOURNEY WITH ARISTOTLE AND OTHERS

| | |
|---|---|
| Tashkent 3317 | |
| TSM H. 795 | 247:5 |
| TSM H. 1008 | 245:9 |
| Baku M287-27109 | 247:13 |
| TSM H. 801 | 248:1 |
| BL Or. 11327 | 248:1 |
| St. Petersburg PNS 267 | 247:4 |
| BL Add. 7751 | 247:6 |
| Sackler S1986.051 | 248:4 |
| BN supp. pers. 629 | 253:12 |

ALEXANDER SENDS A LETTER TO ISKANDARŪS

| | |
|---|---|
| CBL P. 124 | 249:6 |

ALEXANDER IS VISITED BY THE ANGEL WHO GUARDS THE SEA

| | |
|---|---|
| CBL P. 124 | 262:5 |

ALEXANDER IS LOWERED INTO THE SEA

| | |
|---|---|
| CBL P. 124 | 267:6 |
| TSM R. 1021 | 268:11 |
| Baku M287-27109 | 272:13 |
| TSM H. 801 | 272:13 |
| **WAM W.624 (MMA.27) (fig. 28)** | **264:9** |

ALEXANDER IS BROUGHT UP FROM THE SEA AND RECOUNTS WHAT HE HAS SEEN

| | |
|---|---|
| CBL P. 124 | 273:2 |
| National Museum 52.81 | 276:3 |
| BN supp. pers. 1149 | 273:5 |

ALEXANDER RECEIVES GIFTS FROM KINGS

| | |
|---|---|
| CBL P. 124 | 277:8 |

ALEXANDER LIES IN HIS COFFIN

| | |
|---|---|
| Tashkent 3317 | |
| BL Or. 11327 | 288:9 |

ALEXANDER'S FUNERAL PROCESSION

| | |
|---|---|
| CBL P. 124 | 293:10 |
| Sultanate (Aga Khan) | 295:6 |
| BL Or. 11327 | 294:16 |
| WAM W.623 | 293:3 |

*HASHT BIHISHT*
FRONTISPIECE

| | |
|---|---|
| TSM H. 676 | |

*MI'RĀJ*

| | |
|---|---|
| Tashkent 3317 | |

NIẒĀM AL-DĪN AWLIYĀ AND ATTENDANTS

| | |
|---|---|
| Sultanate (Sackler S1986.122) | 16:6 |

KHUSRAW DEDICATES POEM TO 'ALĀ' AL-DĪN

| | |
|---|---|
| Sultanate (David Collection) | 22:1 |

KHUSRAW BEFORE HIS FRIEND 'ALĪ

| | |
|---|---|
| Sultanate (Seattle) | 31:2 |

BAHRĀM GŪR HUNTS WITH DILĀRĀM

| | |
|---|---|
| Berlin I. 4628 | 57:2 |
| CBL P. 124 | 58:8 |
| CBL P. 253-Sotheby | 57:5 |
| Private collection | 57:5 |
| TSM H. 795 | 50:5 |
| TSM H. 1008 | 57:2 |
| Baku M287-27109 | 57:2 |
| Berlin Or. 187 | 56:7 |
| TSM H. 801 | 57:3 |
| TSM H. 799 | 56:7 |
| TSM H. 798 | 56:9 |
| BN supp. pers. 633 | 50:2 |
| WAM W.622 | 57:7 |
| BL Add. 22699 | frontis |
| Baku M161-38088 | |
| Keir Collection | 57:3 |
| BL Or. 11326 | 49:8 |
| Berlin Or. 1615 | 56:7 |
| **WAM W.624 (missing)** | |
| Bonhams 24 April 1996 | 57:9 |
| Berlin Or. 1278 (missing) | 56-57 |

DILĀRĀM IS PULLED FROM HER HORSE

| | |
|---|---|
| Sultanate (Sackler S1986.120) | 58:8 |

BAHRĀM GŪR SEES THE EFFECT OF DILĀRĀM'S MUSIC

| | |
|---|---|
| TSM H. 796 | 71:1 |
| CBL P. 124 | 68:8 |
| TSM H. 799 | 68:8 |
| BL Or. 11326 | 69:1 |
| **WAM W.624 (MMA.28) (fig. 29)** | **71:2** |
| WAM W.623 | 69:6 |

### BAHRĀM GŪR, NU‘MĀN, AND DILĀRĀM VIEW THE SEVEN PALACES

| | |
|---|---|
| Baku M287-27109 | 80:7 |

### PRINCESSES OF THE SEVEN PAVILIONS

| | |
|---|---|
| CBL P. 124 | 80:1 |
| BL Add. 7751 | 79:2 |
| **WAM W.624 (fig. 30)** | **81:1** |

### BAHRĀM GŪR VISITS THE BLACK PAVILION

| | |
|---|---|
| Tashkent 3317 | |
| CBL P. 124 | 87:9 |
| CBL P. 253-Sotheby | 82:2 |
| Rampur 4101 | |
| CBL P. 163 | |
| Berlin Or. 187 | 83:6 |
| TSM H. 799 | 83:5 |
| TSM H. 798 | 82:3 |
| TSM H. 800 | 82:7 |
| BN supp. pers. 633 | 83:3 |
| TSM H. 797 | 82:4 |
| Philadelphia | 83:1 |
| St. Petersburg PNS 67 | 82:3 |
| BL Or. 11326 | 82:4 |
| Baku M161-38088 | 82:2 |
| Berlin Or. 1615 | 82:2 |

### THREE PRINCES OF CEYLON

| | |
|---|---|
| Sultanate (Cleveland) | 88:10 |
| TSM H. 801 | 92:1 |
| **WAM W.624 (missing)** | |
| Berlin Or. 1278 (missing) | 85:7 |

### KING LISTENS TO THE THREE PRINCES EXPLAIN THEIR PERSPICACITY

| | |
|---|---|
| Sultanate (San Diego) | 99:3 |

### BAHRĀM GŪR VISITS THE YELLOW PAVILION

| | |
|---|---|
| Tashkent 3317 | |
| CBL P. 124 | 110:4 |
| CBL P. 253-Sotheby | 111:3 |
| Sultanate (Kansas City) | 111:3 |
| TSM R. 1021 | 110:3 |
| Berlin Or. 187 | 110:9 |
| TSM H. 799 | 111:5 |
| BL Or. 11327 | 110:1 |
| TSM H. 798 | 111:3 |
| TSM H. 800 | 110:5 |
| BN supp. pers. 633 | 111:2 |
| TSM H. 797 | 110:3 |
| St. Petersburg PNS 267 | 110:7 |
| Sackler S1986.056 | 110:2 |
| Philadephia | 111:1 |
| St. Petersburg PNS 67 | 110:3 |
| Berlin Or. 1615 | 111:6 |

### GOLDSMITH PRESENTS THE ELEPHANT TO THE KING

| | |
|---|---|
| BN supp. pers. 1149 | 113:3 |
| Baku M161-38088 | 111:8 |

### FOOLISH WIFE OF THE GOLDSMITH IS TRAPPED IN THE TOWER

| | |
|---|---|
| Sultanate (Los Angeles) | 134:3 |
| Baku M287-27109 | |
| TSM H. 801 | 128:4 |
| **WAM W.624 (fig. 31)** | **132:5** |
| Berlin Or. 1278 | 128:1 |

### BAHRĀM GŪR VISITS THE GREEN PAVILION

| | |
|---|---|
| Tashkent 3317 | |
| CBL P. 124 | 142:3 |
| TSM H. 795 | 140:5 |
| Baku M287-27109 | |
| Berlin Or. 187 | 141:6 |
| TSM H. 799 | 141:5 |
| TSM H. 798 | 141:4 |
| TSM H. 800 | 140:7 |
| BN supp. pers. 633 | 141:5 |
| TSM H. 797 | 140:7 |
| WAM W.622 | 140:7 |
| Philadelphia | 140:4 |
| St. Petersburg PNS 67 | 140:4 |
| Baku M161-38088 | 140:4 |
| BL Or. 11326 | 141:2 |
| Berlin Or. 1615 | 140:1 |
| Bonhams 24 April 1996 | 143:2 |
| MMA 13.228.34 | 140:3 |

### QUEEN RECOILS FROM THE VIZIER

| | |
|---|---|
| Sultanate (FGA 59.1) | 148:7 |

### COURTESAN DEMANDS PAYMENT FROM A BANKER

| | |
|---|---|
| CBL P. 163 | 155:9 |

### QUEEN CAGES THE PARROT

| | |
|---|---|
| TSM H. 1008 | 157:5 |
| TSM H. 801 | 158:1 |

### KING KILLS THE PARROT

| | |
|---|---|
| Berlin Or. 1278 (Teheran) | 162:9 |

### BAHRĀM GŪR VISITS THE RED PAVILION

| | |
|---|---|
| Tashkent 3317 | |
| CBL P. 124 | 165:1 |
| Berlin Or. 187 | 165:7 |
| TSM H. 799 | 166:2 |
| TSM H. 798 | 165:9 |
| TSM H. 800 | 164:8 |
| BN supp. pers. 633 | 165:1 |
| TSM H. 797 | 164:7 |
| BN supp. pers. 1149 | 164:6 |
| Sackler S1986.056 | 164:6 |
| Philadelphia | 164:7 |
| St. Petersburg PNS 67 | 164:6 |
| Baku M161-38088 | 164:5 |
| BL Or. 11326 | 164:4 |
| Berlin Or. 1615 | 164:3 |
| MMA 13.228.34 | 164:4 |

PRINCE AND HIS COMPANIONS BEFRIEND AN OLD FEMALE SERVANT TO GAIN ACCESS TO THE KING'S MISTRESS

WAM W.623 174:8

PRINCE AND THE KING'S MISTRESS MAKE LOVE

TSM H. 801 188:7

PRINCE AND HIS FRIENDS ABDUCT THE KING'S MISTRESS

CBL P. 163 201:5
Baku M287-27109
TSM H. 676 (FGA 37.27) 201:4

BAHRĀM GŪR VISITS THE BLUE PAVILION

Tashkent 3317 203
CBL P. 124 204:2
CBL P. 253-Sotheby 204:3
TSM H. 898 204:6
Baku M379-33733
Berlin Or. 187 205:1
TSM H. 799 205:4
BL Or. 11327 204:4
TSM H. 798 205:3
TSM H. 800 204:7
BN supp. pers. 633 205:1
TSM H. 797 204:4
WAM W.622 204:7
Sackler S1986.056 204:2
Philadelphia 203:7
Sackler S1986.051 215:10
St. Petersburg PNS 67 204:3
Baku M161-38088 204:2
Berlin Or. 1615 204:1
Bonhams 24 April 1996 206:5
MMA 13.228.34 204:1

YOUTH OF RŪM IS BEWITCHED BY THE FAIRY

CBL P. 253-Sotheby (?)
Baku M287-27109
BN supp. pers. 1149 222:7
**WAM W.624 (fig. 32) 218:11**

HERMIT TAKES PITY ON THE BEWILDERED YOUTH

Berlin Or. 1278 233:7

BAHRĀM GŪR VISITS THE SANDALWOOD PAVILION

Tashkent 3317
CBL P. 124 247:6
Private collection 248:1
Rampur 4101
Berlin Or. 187 248:5
TSM H. 799 247:5
TSM H. 798 248:4
TSM H. 800 247:4
BN supp. pers. 633 248:2
TSM H. 797 247:5
Sackler S1986.056 247:5
Philadelphia 247:4
St. Petersburg PNS 67 247:4
Berlin Or. 1615 247:2
MMA 13.228.34 248:5

DISGUISED AS AN OLD WOMAN, RĀMA TRICKS THE VIZIER

WAM W.623 260:5

RĀMA LEARNS MAGIC SPELLS

**WAM W.624 (fig. 33) 254:8**

RĀMA APPEARS BEFORE GUARDS WHOSE BEARDS HE HAD SHAVED SURREPTITIOUSLY

Sultanate (Virginia) 266:3
TSM H. 676 (missing) 276

RĀMA ENTERS THE CHAMBER OF THE SLEEPING DAUGHTER OF THE LUSTFUL VIZIER

National Museum 52.81 268:6

BAHRĀM GŪR VISITS THE WHITE PAVILION

Tashkent 3317 280
CBL P. 124 282:3
Baku M379-33733
TSM H. 795 281:4
Berlin Or. 187 281:5
TSM H. 799 281:2
TSM H. 798 280:5
TSM H. 800 280:7
BN supp. pers. 633 281:8
TSM H. 797 280:4
WAM W.622 280:4
Sackler S1986.056 280:4
Philadelphia 280:3
St. Petersburg PNS 67 280:3
Baku M161-38088 280:4
BL Or. 11326 280:4
Berlin Or. 1615 280:1
MMA 13.228.34 281:3

TALISMAN LAUGHS AT HYPOCRISY

TSM R. 1021 (missing) 294
Baku M287-27109 292:4
**WAM W.624 (fig. 34) 289:3**

KING SEES ONE QUEEN WITH A MULETEER

TSM H. 801 297:7
BL Add. 7751 289:6
Berlin Or. 1278 (missing) 293:10

BAHRĀM GŪR DISAPPEARS INTO A CAVE

Tashkent 3317 310:11
CBL P. 124 311:6

# Bibliography


Abū'l Fazl (Abū al-Fazl). *Ā'īn-i Akbarī.* Trans. H. Blochmann. 3 vols. Reprint, New Delhi: Oriental Books Reprint Corporation, 1977.

Adamova, Adel. "Repetition of Compositions in Manuscripts: The Khamsa of Nizami in Leningrad." In *Timurid Art and Culture. Iran and Central Asia in the Fifteenth Century,* 67–75, eds. Lisa Golombek and Maria Subtelny. Leiden, New York, and Koln: Brill, 1992.

Ahmad, Nazir. "An Accomplished Critic." In *Amir Khusraw: Memorial Volume,* 103–18. New Delhi: Ministry of Information and Broadcasting, 1975.

Akalay, Z. "Amīr Khosrow Dehlavi: miniatures" [in Turkish]. *Sanat Tarihi Yilligi,* 6 (1974–75), 347–73.

Alexander, Jonathan J. G. *Medieval Illuminators and Their Methods of Work.* New Haven and London: Yale University Press, 1992.

Amīr Khusraw Dihlawī. *Ā'īnah-i Sikandarī.* ed. J. Mirsayyidov. Moscow, 1977.

*Hasht Bihisht.* ed. J. Iftikhar. Moscow, 1972.

*Majnūn wa Laylā.* ed. T. A. Muharramov. Moscow, 1964.

*Maṭla' al-Anwār.* ed. T. A. Muharramov. Moscow, 1975.

*Shīrīn wa Khusraw.* ed. Gh. 'Aliev. Moscow, 1978.

Ansari, Noorul Hasan. "Amir Khusrau, the Poet and Patriot." *Indo-Iranica,* 39 (1986), 88–99.

Arnold, Thomas W., and Adolf Grohmann. *The Islamic Book.* Paris: Pegasus Press, 1929.

Arnold, Thomas W., and James V. S. Wilkinson. *The Library of A. Chester Beatty: A Catalogue of the Indian Miniatures.* 3 vols. London: Oxford University Press, 1936.

Arberry, Arthur John, Edgar Blochet, M. Minovi, Basil Robinson, and James V. S. Wilkinson. *The Chester Beatty Library: A Catalogue of the Persian Manuscripts and Miniatures.* 3 vols. Dublin, 1959–62.

Ashraf, Muhammad. *A Concise Descriptive Catalogue of the Persian Manuscripts in the Sālār Jung Museum and Library.* 5 vols. Hyderbad: Shri Masood Ahmed Razvi, 1969.

Bābur, Ẓahīr al-Dīn Muḥammad. *The Baburnama. Memoirs of Babur, Prince and Emperor.* Translated, edited, and annotated by Wheeler M. Thackston. New York and Oxford: Oxford University Press, 1996.

Bahari, Ebadollah. *Bihzad. Master of Persian Painting.* London: IB Tauris and Co., 1996.

Bailey, Gauvin. *The Jesuits and the Grand Mogul: Renaissance Art at the Imperial Court of India, 1580–1630.* Washington, D.C.: Freer Gallery of Art and Arthur M. Sackler Gallery, 1998.

Bayani, Mahdi. *Aḥwāl wa Āṣār Khūshnawīsān.* 3 vols. Teheran: Dānishgāh-i Tihrān, 1966.

Beach, Milo. *Early Mughal Painting.* Cambridge, Massachusetts, and London: Harvard University Press, 1987.

——. *The Grand Mogul: Imperial Painting in India 1600–1660.* Williamstown: Francine and Sterling Clark Museum, 1978.

——. *The Imperial Image: Paintings for the Mughal Court.* Washington, D.C.: Smithsonian Institution, 1981.

——. "Jahāngīr's *Jahāngīr-Nāma.*" In *The Powers of Art,* 224–34, ed. Barbara Stoler Miller. Delhi: Oxford University Press, 1992.

——. *Mughal and Rajput Painting.* Cambridge: Cambridge University Press, 1992.

Berthels, E. "Niẓāmī Gandjawī." *Encyclopaedia of Islam,* new ed., VIII, fasc. 131–32, 76–81. Leiden: Brill, 1993.

Brand, Michael, and Glenn Lowry. *Akbar's India: Art from the Mughal City of Joy.* New York: Asia Society Galleries, 1985.

Brend, Barbara. "Akbar's *Khamsah* of Amīr Khusraw Dihlavī—A Reconstruction of the Cycle of Illustration." *Artibus Asiae,* 49, nos. 3/4 (1988/89), 281–315.

——. "Elements from Painting of the Eastern Islamic Area in Early Ottoman Manuscripts of the Khamseh of Amir Khusrau Dihlavi." In *Proceedings of the 9th International Congress of Turkish Art*, 1, (Istanbul, 1991), 423–38. Ankara, 1995.

——. *The Emperor Akbar's* Khamsa *of Niẓāmī.* London: The British Library, 1995.

——. *Illustrations to the* Khamsah *of Amīr Khusrau Dihlavī in the Tīmūrid Period.* Ph.D. thesis, School of Oriental and African Studies, University of London, 1986.

Bürgel, J. C. "The Romance." In *Persian Literature*, ed. Ehsan Yarshater. Albany: State University of New York Press, 1988.

Canby, Sheila. *Princes, Poets & Paladins.* London: British Museum, 1998.

Chandra, Pramod. *The Ṭūṭī-Nāma of the Cleveland Museum of Art and the Origins of Mughal Painting.* 2 vols. Graz: Akademische Druck-u. Verlagsanstalt, 1976.

Chelkowski, Peter. *Mirror of the Invisible World: Tales from the Khamseh of Nizami.* New York: Metropolitan Museum of Art, 1975.

Dickson, Martin, and Stuart Cary Welch. *The Houghton Shahnameh.* 2 vols. Cambridge, Massachusetts: Harvard University Press, 1981.

Dimand, Maurice. "Mughal Painting under Akbar the Great." *Bulletin of the Metropolitan Museum of Art*, 12 (1953), 46–51.

Elliott, Sir Henry Miers and John Dowson. *The History of India as Told by Its Own Historians: The Mohammedan Period.* London: Trubner, 1867–77; reprint New York: AMS Press, 1966.

Elwell-Sutton, Laurence P. *The Persian Metres.* Cambridge: Cambridge University Press, 1976.

Ettinghausen, Richard. "Near Eastern Bookcovers and Their Influence on European Bindings." *Ars Orientalis*, 3 (1959), 113–31.

——, and Marie Swietochowski. "Islamic Art." *Metropolitan Museum of Art Bulletin* (Fall 1978).

Galerkina, Olympiade. "On Some Miniatures Attributed to Bihzād from Leningrad Collections." *Ars Orientalis*, 8 (1970), 121–38.

Glynn, Catherine. "An Early Mughal Landscape Painting and Related Works." *Los Angeles County Museum of Art Bulletin*, 20, 2 (1974), 64–72.

Grabar, Oleg. *The Illustrations of the Maqamat.* Chicago: University of Chicago Press, 1984.

——. *The Mediation of Ornament.* Princeton: Princeton University Press, 1992.

——. "Toward an Aesthetic of Persian Painting." In *The Art of Interpreting: Papers in Art History*, 129–39. University Park: Pennsylvania State University, 1995.

Griffiths, Robert J. and Alexander Rogers. *In Persia's Golden Days.* Translation of *Khusrau wa Shirin.* London: Griffiths and Son, 1889.

Grube, Ernst. *The Classical Style in Islamic Painting: The Early School of Herat and Its Impact on Islamic Painting of the Later 15th, the 16th and the 17th Century.* New York, 1968.

Habib, Mohammad. *Hazrat Amir Khusrau of Delhi.* Bombay: D. B. Taraporevala Sons and Co., 1927.

Hájek, Lubor. *Indian Miniatures of the Mogul School.* London: Spring Books, 1960.

*The History of Bookbinding 525–1950 A.D.* Baltimore: Walters Art Gallery, 1957.

Husain, Mumtaz. *Amir Khusrau Dehlavi.* Karachi: Saad Publications, 1986.

Jackson, Abraham, William Valentine, and Abraham Yohannan. *A Catalogue of the Collection of Persian Manuscripts Including Also Some Turkish and Arabic Manuscripts Presented to the Metropolitan Museum of Art, New York, by Alexander Smith Cochran.* New York: Columbia University Press, 1914.

Karatay, Fehmi Edhem. *Topkapi Sarayi Müzesi Kütüphanesi Farsça Yazmalar Kataloğu.* [A Catalogue of the Persian Manuscripts in the Topkapi Sarayi Museum.] Istanbul: Topkapi Sarayi Müzesi, 1961.

Koch, Ebba. "Netherlandish Naturalism in Imperial Mughal Painting." *Apollo*, 152, no. 465 (November 2000), 29–37.

Krishna, Anand. "A Study of the Akbari Artist: Farrukh Chela." In *Chhavi-Golden Jubilee Volume*, 353–73, ed. Anand Krishna. Banaras: Bharat Kala Bhavan, 1971.

Leach, Linda. *Mughal and Other Indian Paintings from the Chester Beatty Library.* 2 vols. London: Scorpion Cavendish Ltd, 1995.

——. *Paintings from India.* London: The Nour Foundation, 1998.

Lentz, Thomas and Glenn Lowry. *Timur and the Princely Vision.* Washington, D.C.: Sackler Gallery of Art and Smithsonian Press, 1989.

Losty, Jeremiah. *The Art of the Book in India.* London: British Library Board, 1982.

——. "The 'Bute Hafiz' and the development of border decoration in the manuscript studio of the Mughals." *Burlington Magazine*, 127 (December 1985), 855–71.

——. *Indian Book Painting.* London: British Library Board, 1986.

Loukonin, Vladimir, and Anatoli Ivanov. *Lost Treasures of Persia.* Bournemouth, England: Parkstone Press, 1996.
Lowden, John. *The Octateuchs.* University Park, Pennsylvania: Pennsylvana State University Press, 1992.
Lowry, Glenn, Milo Beach, Roya Marefat, and Wheeler Thackston. *An Illustrated and Annotated Checklist of the Vever Collection.* Washington, D.C.: Smithsonian Institution, 1988.
Marek, Jan. "Persian Literature in India." In *History of Iranian Literature,* 711–30, Jan Rypka, written in collaboration with Otakar Klima and others. Dordrecht: Reidel, 1968.
Martin, Fredrik Robert. *The Miniature Paintings and Painters of Persia, India, and Turkey.* 2 vols. London: B. Quaritch, 1912.
——. *Les miniatures de Behzad dans un manuscript persan daté en 1485.* Munich: F. Bruckmann, 1912.
Masani, Rustom Pestinji. *Court Poets of Iran and India, an anthology of verse and wit.* Bombay: New Book Company, 1938.
Meisami, Julie. *Medieval Persian Court Poetry.* Princeton: Princeton University Press, 1987.
Meredith-Owens, G. M., et al. "Manuscripts from the Dyson Perrins Collection." *British Museum Quarterly,* 23, no. 2 (1961), 27–38.
Milstein, Rachel. *Islamic Painting in the Israel Museum.* Jerusalem: The Museum, 1984.
Mirza, Mohammad Wahid. *Life and Works of Amir Khusrau.* Lahore: Panjab University Press, 1962.
Morris, Rekha. "Some Additions to the Known Corpus of Paintings by the Mughal Artist Farrukh Chela." *Ars Orientalis,* 13 (1982), 135–51.
*Mughal Miniatures of the Earlier Periods.* Oxford: Bodleian Library, 1953.
Nizami Ganjavi. *The Haft Paikar* (The Seven Beauties). Translated by C. E. Wilson. 2 vols. London: A. Probsthain, 1924.
——. *Lailī and Majnun, A Poem from the Original Persian of Nazāmi.* Translated by James Atkinson. London: Oriental Translation Fund, 1836. Second ed. 1894; Indian reprint 1915.
——. *The Story of Layla and Majnun.* Translated by Rudolph Gelpke. Oxford: Cassirer, 1966.
——. *Sikandar Nama-e Bara, or the Book of Alexander the Great.* Translated by H. Wilberforce Clarke. London: W. H. Allen, 1881.
——. *Makhzanol Asrār, The Treasury of Mysteries by Nezami of Ganjeh.* Translated by Gholam Hosein Dārāb. London: A. Probsthain, 1945.
*Nizami Ganjavi.* Edition of Wahid Dastgirdi, Teheran.
*Makhzan al-Asrār.* 1343/1924.
*Khusraw wa Shīrīn.* 1333/1915.
*Laylā wa Majnūn.* 1333/1915.
*Haft Paikar.* 1334/1916.
*Sharaf-nāmeh.* 1335/1917.
*Iqbāl-nāmeh.* 1317/1899.
Pinder-Wilson, Ralph, Ellen Smart, and Douglas Barrett. *Paintings from the Muslim Courts of India.* London: World of Islam Festival Publishing Co., 1976.
Richard, Francis. *Splendeurs persanes. Manuscrits du XIIe au XVIIe siècle.* Paris: Bibliothèque Nationale, 1997.
——. "An Unpublished Manuscript from the Atelier of the Emperor Humāyūn, the Khamsa Smith-Lesouëf 216 of the Bibliothèque Nationale." In *Confluence of Cultures. French Contributions to Indo-Persian Studies,* 37–53, ed. Françoise Delvoye. New Delhi: Manohar, 1994.
Robinson, Basil W. "An Amīr Khusraw *Khamsa* of 1581." *Iran,* 35 (1997), 35–41.
Robinson, Basil, Ernst Grube, G. M. Meredith-Owens, and Robert Skelton. *Islamic Painting and the Arts of the Book.* London: Faber and Faber Limited, 1976.
Rogers, J. Michael, Filiz Çağman, and Zeren Tanindi. *The Topkapi Saray Museum: The Albums and Illustrated Manuscripts.* Boston: Little, Brown and Company, 1986.
Schimmel, Annemarie. "Islamic Literatures of India." In *History of Indian Literature,* vol. VII, part 4, ed. Jan Gonda. Wiesbaden: Harrassowitz, 1973.
——. "Persian Poetry in the Indo-Pakistani Subcontinent." In *Persian Literature,* 405–21, ed., Ehsan Yarshater. Albany: State University of New York Press, 1988).
——. *A Two-Colored Brocade. The Imagery of Persian Poetry.* Chapel Hill and London: University of North Carolina Press, 1992.
——. "Turk and Hindu: A Poetical Image and Its Application to Historical Fact." In *Islam and Cultural Change in the Middle Ages,* 107–26, ed., Speros Vryonis. Wiesbaden: Harrassowitz, 1973.
——, and Stuart Cary Welch. *Anvari's Divan: A Pocket Book for Akbar.* New York: Metropolitan Museum of Art, 1983.
Schmitz, Barbara, and Ziyaud-din Desai. *Mughal and Persian Paintings and Illustrated Manuscripts in the Raza Library, Rampur.* New Delhi, 2000.
Schulz, Philipp. *Die persisch-islamische Miniaturmalerei.* 2 vols. Leipzig: K. W. Hiersemann, 1914.
Sen, Geeti. *Paintings from the Akbar Nama: A Visual Chronicle of Mughal India.* Varanasi: Lustre Press, 1984.

Seyller, John. "Codicological Aspects of the Victoria and Albert Museum *Akbarnāma* and Their Historical Implications." *Art Journal*, 49 (1990), 379–87.
——. "The Inspection and Valuation of Manuscripts in the Imperial Mughal Library." *Artibus Asiae*, 57, nos. 3/4 (1997), 243–349.
——. "Model and Copy: The Illustration of Three *Razmnāma* Manuscripts." *Archives of Asian Art*, 38 (1985), 37–66.
——. "A Mughal Code of Connoisseurship." *Muqarnas*, 17 (2000), 178–203.
——. "Painter's Directions in Early Indian Painting." *Artibus Asiae*, 59, nos. 3/4 (2000), 303–18.
——. "The School of Oriental and African Studies *Anvār-i Suhaylī*: The Illustration of a *De Luxe* Mughal Manuscript." *Ars Orientalis*, 16 (1986), 119–51.
——. "Scribal Notes on Mughal Manuscript Illustrations." *Artibus Asiae*, 48, nos. 3/4 (1987), 247–77.
——. *Workshop and Patron in Mughal India. The Freer* Rāmāyaṇa *and Other Illustrated Manuscripts of 'Abd al-Raḥīm.* Zürich: Artibus Asiae, 1999.
Simpson, Marianna Shreve. *Sultan Ibrahim Mirza's* Haft Awrang: *A Princely Manuscript from Sixteenth-Century Iran.* London: Yale University Press, 1997.
Smart, Ellen. "Akbar, Illiterate Genius." In *Kalādarśana*, 99–107, ed., Joanna Williams. New Delhi: Oxford and IBH Publishing Co., 1981.
——, and Daniel Walker. *Pride of the Princes: Indian Art of the Mughal Era in the Cincinnati Art Museum.* Cincinnati: Cincinnati Art Museum, 1985.
Soucek, Priscilla. *Illustrated Manuscripts of Nizami's Khamseh 1386–1482.* Ph.D. thesis, New York University, 1971.
Srivastava, R. P. "Mohammad Hussain Kashmiri Zarin Qalam." *Lahore Museum Bulletin*, 3, no. 2 (July–December 1990), 65–75.
Stchoukine, Ivan. "La peinture à Yazd au début du XVème siècle." *Syria*, 43, nos. 1–2 (1966), 99–104.
——. *Les peintures des manuscrits de la "Khamseh" de Nizami au Topkapi Sarayi Müsezi d'Istanbul.* Paris: Paul Geuthner, 1977.
Stchoukine, Ivan, B. Flemming, P. Luft, and H. Sohrweide. *Illuminierte islamische Handschriften.* Wiesbaden: F. Steiner, 1971.
Storey, Charles Ambrose. *Persian Literature: A Bio-Bibliographical Survey.* 2 vols. London: Luzac and co., 1927–39.
Suleiman, Hamid, and Fazila Suleimanova. *Miniatures Illuminations of Amir Hosroe Dehlevi's Works.* Tashkent: Fan Publishers, 1983.
Titley, Norah. *Miniatures from Persian Manuscripts from Persia, India and Turkey.* London: British Library Board, 1977.
——. *Persian Miniature Painting and Its Influence on the Art of Turkey and India.* Austin: University of Texas, 1983.
——. "Miniature Paintings Illustrating the Works of Amir Khusrau: 15th, 16th, 17th Centuries." *Marg*, 28, no. 3 (June 1975), 19–52.
Wade, Bonnie. *Imaging Sound: An Ethnomusicological Study of Music, Art, and Culture in Mughal India.* Chicago: University of Chicago Press, 1998.
Warner, Sir George. *Descriptive Catalogue of Illuminated Manuscripts in the Library of C. W. Dyson Perrins.* Oxford: Oxford University Press, 1920.
Welch, Anthony, and Stuart Cary Welch. *Arts of the Islamic Book.* Ithaca and London: Cornell University Press, 1982.
Welch, Stuart Cary. *The Art of Mughal India.* New York: Asia Society, 1963.
——. *India: Art and Culture 1300–1900.* New York: Metropolitan Museum of Art, 1985.
——. "Miniatures from a Diwan of Hafiz." *Marg*, 11, no. 3 (1958), 56–62.
——. "The Paintings of Basawan." *Lalit Kalā*, 10 (1961), 7–17.
Yarshater, Ehsan. "Some Common Characteristics between Persian Poetry and Art." *Studia Islamica*, 16 (1962), 61–72.

# Glossary

ʻAMAL(-I) Work (of); term used in ascriptions to individual artists

AMĪR, MĪR Prince, lord, military officer, often forming part of a name

CATCHWORD First word or two of the text on the left page of an opening in a manuscript written in the lower margin of the right page; this device ensures the continuity of the text

COLOPHON Inscription at the end of manuscript providing information about its scribe, date, and place of production

DĀM Unit of currency, one hundreth of a rupee

DHOTI Man's garment wrapped about the waist and between the legs

DĪV Demon

DĪWĀN Collection of a poet's works

GHAZAL Short Persian monorhyme, normally five to twelve verses long

HOURĪS Virgins of Paradise

JAMA Knee-length tunic or overgarment

KĀTIB Scribe

KHAMSA Arabic word for five, used in Persian as a title for a quintet of books

MAQĀLA, PL. MAQĀLAT Discourse, one of twenty didactic units in the first book of the *Khamsa*

MAṢNAWĪ Persian verse form with rhyming couplets

MIʻRĀJ Muḥammad's mystical journey through the heavens

MUHR Unit of currency equivalent to ten rupees

MUẔAHHIB Literally "gilder," more generally designating the role of illuminator

NAQQĀSH Painter or craftsman

NASTAʻLĪQ "Hanging" cursive script

ONAGER Wild ass, known in Persian as *gūr*

QAṢĪDA Persian monorhyme verse form often used for a panegyric or praise of God

SARLAWḤ Large decorative illumination at the beginning of the manuscript

SHAMSA Starburst decorative feature used to mark the beginning of a major section of a text

SĪMURGH Mythical phoenix-like bird

SUFI Islamic mystic

SULTAN King

TEXT POINT Point at which the text of a manuscript is interrupted to accommodate an illustration

ʻUNWĀN Decorative headpiece, often used interchangeably with *sarlawḥ*, found at the beginning of a poem

VIZIER Minister

ZARRĪN QALAM Literally "golden pen," an honorific title given to the calligrapher Muḥammad Ḥusayn

# Index


A

'Abd al-Ṣamad 26, 30–32, 38n. 49, 117n. 50
'Abd al-Raḥīm (calligrapher) 38nn. 70–71, 39
Abū al-Fazl 28–30, 34–35, 37–39
  account of painting in the *Ā'īn-i Akbarī* 28, 30–32, 34, 37n. 29, 38
Agra 25–27
*Ā'īnah-i Sikandarī* 15, 19, 23, 41–42, 78–91
*Ā'īn-i Akbarī* 28, 30–31, 37
Akbar
  as art patron 5, 26, 29–34, 36n. 4, 37, 142
  illiteracy 29, 37nn. 23–24
  interest in Hindu culture 26, 28–29, 33, 100
  portraits of 34–35, 38n. 58, nn. 61–62, 137
*Akbarnāma* of Abū al-Fazl
  Victoria and Albert Museum manuscript 35, 38, 138n. 9, 139n. 32, 140n. 39
    1596–97 manuscript 36, 39, 40, 43n. 5, 44n. 12
    British Library volume (Or. 12988) 43n. 5, 70, 84, 86, 92, 94, 119–20, 123, 131, 138n. 2
    Chester Beatty Library volume (Ms. 3) 120, 132, 138n. 4, n. 6, 140n. 39
'Alā' al-Dīn Khaljī 9, 11, 14–15, 18–19
'Alī Qulī 42, 68
Amīr Khusraw Dihlawī
  life 7–12
  *Khamsa* 6, 9, 14–15, 18, 20, 23, 29
  other literary works by 7, 9–11, 13
  rivalry with Niẓāmī 13–15, 18–19
*Anwār-i Suhaylī*
  1570 manuscript in the School of Oriental and African Studies, University of London 36, 38n. 69, 114, 117n. 45
  1596–97 manuscript in the Bharat Kala Bhavan 72, 110–11, 114
*'Ashīqa* of Amīr Khusraw 10
  National Museum manuscript 36, 123, 139n. 12

B

Bābur 25, 35, 36nn. 5–6
*Bāburnāma*
  illustrated manuscripts 113
    ca. 1590 British Library manuscript (Or. 3714) 113–14, 138n. 9, 139n. 26, n. 32
    1597–99 National Museum manuscript 68, 86, 138n. 9
*Bahāristān* of Jāmī 36
  1595 Bodleian Library manuscript 39
    borders 41,119, 123–24, 127, 129–32, 136, 138n. 2, 139n. 15, n. 20, n. 25
    paintings 42, 50, 56, 72, 107–8, 119, 133, 136, 139n. 30
Bālacanda 130, 132, 139n. 25, n. 29
Balban (see Ghiyāṣ al-Dīn Balban)
Basāvana 31, 46, 58, 88, 126, 133, 136, 139n. 33
Bayram Khān 26
Berlin Album 124, 129
Bhīma Gujarātī 31
Bihzād 25, 52
bookbinding 31, 35, 136
Brend, Barbara 6, 74, 105–6, 116nn. 7–10, 142n. 2
Bughrā Khān 8

D

Delhi 7–11, 25–27
*de luxe* illustrated manuscripts 36, 131–33, 141
Dharmadāsa 31, 42, 44, 64, 70, 74, 84, 110–11, 116n. 32, 117n. 33
*Dīn-i Ilāhī* 28, 34, 37n. 14
*Dīwān* of Anwarī 36
  1588 Sackler Museum manuscript 36, 123
*Dīwān* of Ḥāfiẓ
  1605 British Library manuscript 124, 138n. 3, 139n. 16
  Chester Beatty Library manuscript 124, 127, 128, 129

F

Farrukh Cela 31, 42, 44n. 21, 66, 94
Fīrūz Shāh 9

G

Ghiyāṣ al-Dīn Balban 8
Ghiyāṣ al-Dīn Tughluq Shāh 10–11
*Ghurrat al-Kamāl* 11n. 1, 12n. 21, 13, 23n. 1
Grabar, Oleg 105, 115, 118nn. 51–53
Grube, Ernst 105
*Gulistān* of Sa'dī 33, 35–36
  1582–83 manuscript in the Royal Asiatic Society 39–40, 123, 138n. 2, n. 8, 139n. 13
  dispersed 1596 manuscript 36, 38n. 70, 48, 117n. 50
Gulshan Album 43n. 8, 68, 120, 131, 138n. 2, n. 9, 139n. 27, nn. 32–33

H

*Ḥadīqat al-Ḥaqīqat* of Sanā'ī 13, 36
  1599–1600 manuscript 36, 38n. 71, 138, 140n. 42
*Haft Awrang* 6
  Freer Gallery of Art manuscript 123, 128, 138n. 12, 139n. 23
*Haft Paykar* 13, 15, 19–20, 24, 137, 140n. 41
Ḥātim Khān 8–9
*Hasht Bihisht* 15, 19–20, 33, 41–42, 92–103
Humāyūn 26, 32, 34–35, 37, 94
Ḥusayn 120, 122–23, 132, 138n. 9, 139n. 25

I

Ikhlāṣ 130, 132, 138n. 25, 139nn. 31–32
imperial library 29, 32–33, 37nn. 17–19, n. 22, 114, 117n. 44
*Iskandarnāma* 14

J

Jagannātha 31, 44, 78
Jahāngīr 5, 29, 32, 36n. 5, 38n. 46, 39, 43n. 5, 123, 132–33, 139n. 33
*Jāmi' al-Tawārīkh*
  1596 manuscript 37n. 36, 68, 82, 117n. 43

K

Kabul 25–27, 31
Kaiqubād, Mu'izz al-Dīn 8–9
*Khamsa* of Amīr Khusraw
  composition 14–24
  date 1–15, 18–20
  Walters Art Museum manuscript (W. 624) 6, 27, 31, 33, 36, 39–42, 141–42
    binding 136–38
    borders 39, 41, 119, 123–36, 137, 139n. 17, n. 20, n. 22
      use of stencils 127–29
    calligraphy 39–41, 141, 142
    date 39–40, 43n. 6
    illumination 41, 119–23
    missing folios 40–41, 44nn. 14–15, 92, 116n. 11
    paintings 31, 33, 41–42, 44nn. 15–16, 45–103, 106–7, 109–11, 114, 132–33, 139n. 30, 141
*Khamsa* of Niẓāmī 6, 9, 13–14, 23n. 9, 33, 76, 78, 84, 110–11
  Bibliothèque Nationale manuscript 26, 34, 37nn. 8–10, 38n. 60
  British Library manuscript (Or. 12208) 36, 39–40, 114, 119–20
    binding 35, 137, 139n. 37, 140n. 38
    border decoration 124, 129, 139n. 15
    illumination 44n. 12, 119–20, 138nn. 1–2, nn. 5–6, n. 8
    paintings 38, 42, 44, 50, 56, 62, 64, 66, 70, 74, 80, 84, 86, 90, 94, 100, 110–12, 133, 137, 139n. 30, 142
    production time 39, 44nn. 10–11
    Walters Art Museum portion (W. 613) 64, 84, 119, 132
  date of composition 13–14, 23
  dispersed manuscript of ca. 1595 44n. 20, 110, 113–15, 117n. 33, n. 46
  Keir Collection manuscript 32, 35, 38n. 62, 114, 117n. 46
Khāqānī 13–14, 29
Khiẓr (Mughal painter) 124, 129–30, 136, 139nn. 24–25, 32
Khiẓr Khān 10, 12
Khwāja Jān Shīrāzī 120, 123, 138n. 2, n. 8
Khusraw (see Amīr Khusraw)
*Khusraw wa Shīrīn* 13

L

Lahore 26–27, 31, 37, 39, 43n. 8
Lāla 31, 35, 54, 72, 76
*Laylā wa Majnūn* 13
Luṭfullāh 120, 123, 138n. 7

M

Mādhava 31, 35, 56, 125–27, 130–33, 139n. 25, n. 30, n. 32
*Majnūn wa Laylā* 14, 18–19, 23, 41–42, 68–77, 109
*Makhzan al-Asrār* 9, 13–15, 24n. 26
Manōhara 31, 39–40, 58, 96, 98, 138, 140n. 42
Mansur 119, 121, 123, 131–32, 136, 138n. 2, nn. 8–9, 139n. 26
*Maṭla' al-Anwār* 11n. 5, 14–17, 27, 41, 46–57, 106–8, 133
*Miftāh al-Futuḥ* 9
Mīr 'Alī 39
Mīr Sayyid 'Alī 26, 30–31
Miskīn 31, 35, 42, 52, 76, 92, 94
Mubārak Shāh 10
Mughal painting
  adaptation of effects of European art 33, 38, 46, 52, 56, 62, 72, 76, 78, 80, 90, 98, 136
  imperial atelier 26, 31
    salaries 31–32, 37nn. 41–42, 38n. 44, n. 46, 39
    specialized functions within 31, 35, 37, 46, 94, 119, 123, 129, 131–33, 141
  portraits 34–35, 38nn. 47–48, 39–40
  stylistic developments during Akbar's reign 33, 35–36, 96, 123–24, 128
Muḥammad Ḥakīm 27
Muḥammad Ḥusayn (Zarrīn Qalam)
    career 39, 43n. 9
    manuscripts written by 39–41, 43n. 5, n. 9, 141–42
    other specimens of writing by 39, 43nn. 8–9
Muḥammad Khān 8
Muḥammad Sharīf 32–35, 38nn. 51–54
Mukhliṣ 129, 136, 139n. 25, n. 32
Mukunda 31, 50, 60, 90, 100, 107–8

N

Nanda Cela 129, 139n. 25
Narasimha (Narsingh) 31, 48, 76, 117n. 50, 139n. 33
Niẓām al-Dīn Awliyā 10–11, 15, 18–19, 33
Niẓāmī 6, 9, 13–15, 18–20, 23n. 8, 29, 36, 40, 84, 88, 92, 110–11, 137
*Nuh Sipihr* 10, 11n. 1

P

painter's directions 112–15, 117nn. 37–40, 141
painting cycles 42, 105–15

Q

*Qirān al-Sa'dayn* 9, 11n. 13, 14, 23

R

*Rāmāyaṇa* 29, 33
  1588–91 Jaipur manuscript 32, 37n. 36, 114, 117n. 47, 138n. 9
*Razmnāma* 29, 33
  1598–1600 manuscript 37n. 37, 139n. 32, 140n. 40
  Jaipur manuscript 32, 139n. 32

S

Sa'dī 8, 11n. 12, 33
Salīm (see also Jahāngīr) 28
Sānvala 31, 42, 60, 62, 80, 82, 112
*Shāhnāma* 6, 29, 33, 36, 105, 114, 118n. 51
Shams al-Dīn Iltutmish 7
*Shīrīn wa Khusraw* 14, 18, 41–42, 58–67, 108
Simpson, Marianna Shreve 105
Śivadāsa 124, 127, 132–33, 138n. 25, 139n. 25, n. 28
Sulaymān Kalān 120, 127, 130–32, 139n. 25
Sultān 'Alī 39
Sūradāsa Gujarātī 31, 86, 102

T

*Tārīkh-i Khāndān-i Tīmūriyya* 64, 123, 138n. 9, 139n. 32
*Tuḥfat al-Ṣighar* 7, 11n. 11, 13, 23n. 3

W

Weitzmann, Kurt 105, 116n. 1